A Celebration of Young Poets

Pennsylvania – Spring 2006

Creative Communication, Inc.

A Celebration of Young Poets
Pennsylvania – Spring 2006

An anthology compiled by Creative Communication, Inc.

Published by:

CREATIVE COMMUNICATION, INC.
1488 NORTH 200 WEST
LOGAN, UT 84341

Copyright © 2006 by Creative Communication, Inc.
Printed in the United States of America

ISBN 10: 1-60050-030-7
ISBN 13: 978-1-60050-030-5

Foreword

Welcome! Thank you for letting us share these poems with you.

This last school year we surveyed thousands of teachers asking what we could do better. We constantly strive to be the best at what we do and to listen to our teachers and poets. We strongly believe that this is your contest. Several changes were made to this anthology as we adapt to what was requested.

In this and future editions of the anthology, the Top Ten winners will be featured on their own page in the book. Each poet that is included in this book is to be congratulated, however, the Top Ten Poets should receive special recognition for having been chosen as writing one of the best poems. The Top Ten Poems were selected through an online voting system that includes thousands of teachers and students. In a day and age where television programs use viewer voting to determine which contestant is the winner, it is appropriate that our poetry winners are chosen by their peers.

Over the years we have had many parents contact us concerning the privacy of their children. The comments focus on the fact that publishing a poet's name, grade, school name, city and state with each poem is too much information. We want to address these concerns. In the Fall 2005 edition of the anthology, we made the decision to only list the poet's name and grade after each poem. Whereas we received many calls and letters concerning the issue that we were publishing too much information, we received thousands of calls and letters requesting that we again publish more information to include a student's school name and state with each poem. Therefore, for this and future editions we will publish each student's name, grade, school name and state unless specifically instructed not to include this information. Just as this information is included in a school yearbook, we provide this information in this literary yearbook of poetry. This decision hopefully makes it easier to find classmates in the book and brings appropriate recognition to the schools.

We are proud to provide this anthology. In speaking to the poets in our anthologies we have found that our anthologies are not stuffy old books that are forgotten on a shelf. The poems in our books are read, loved and cherished. We hope you enjoy reading the thoughts and feelings of our youth.

Sincerely,
Gaylen Worthen, President
Creative Communication

WRITING CONTESTS!

Enter our next POETRY contest!

Enter our next ESSAY contest!

Why should I enter?

Win prizes and get published! Each year thousands of dollars in prizes are awarded in each region and tens of thousands of dollars in prizes are awarded throughout North America. The top writers in each division receive a monetary award and a free book that includes their published poem or essay. Entries of merit are also selected to be published in our anthology.

Who may enter?

There are five divisions in the poetry contest. The poetry divisions are grades K-3, 4-6, 7-9, 10-12, and adult. There are three divisions in the essay contest. The essay division are grades 4-6, 7-9, and 10-12.

What is needed to enter the contest?

To enter the poetry contest send in one original poem, 21 lines or less. To enter the essay contest send in one non-fiction, original essay, 250 words or less, on any topic. Each entry must include the writer's name, address, city, state and zip code. Student entries need to include the student's grade, school name and school address. Students who include their teacher's name may help the teacher qualify for a free copy of the anthology.

How do I enter?

Enter a poem online at:
www.poeticpower.com
or
Mail your poem to:
    Poetry Contest
    1488 North 200 West
    Logan, UT 84341

Enter an essay online at:
www.studentessaycontest.com
or
Mail your essay to:
    Essay Contest
    1488 North 200 West
    Logan, UT 84341

If you are mailing your poetry entry, please write "Student Contest" at the top of your poem if you are in grades K-12. Please write "Adult Contest" at the top of your poem if you are entering the adult division.

When is the deadline?

Poetry contest deadlines are December 5th, April 5th, and August 15th. Essay contest deadlines are October 17th, February 15th, and July 17th. You can enter each contest, however, send only one poem or essay for each contest deadline.

Are there benefits for my school?

Yes. We award $15,000 each year in grants to help with Language Arts programs. Schools qualify to apply for a grant by having a large number of entries of which over fifty percent are accepted for publication. This typically tends to be about 15 accepted entries.

Are there benefits for my teacher?

Yes. Teachers with five or more students accepted to be published receive a free anthology that includes their students' writing.

For more information please go to our website at **www.poeticpower.com**, email us at editor@poeticpower.com or call 435-713-4411.

Table of Contents

Spring 2006
Poetic Achievement
Honor Schools

* Teachers who had fifteen or more poets accepted to be published

The following schools are recognized as receiving a "Poetic Achievement Award." This award is given to schools who have a large number of entries of which over fifty percent are accepted for publication. With hundreds of schools entering our contest, only a small percent of these schools are honored with this award. The purpose of this award is to recognize schools with excellent Language Arts programs. This award qualifies these schools to receive a complimentary copy of this anthology. In addition, these schools are eligible to apply for a Creative Communication Language Arts Grant. Grants of two hundred and fifty dollars each are awarded to further develop writing in our schools.

Allison Park Elementary School
Houston
Cammy Feriozzi*

Avonworth Elementary School
Pittsburgh
Jennifer Friedman*
Cheryl Scannelli*

Bedford Middle School
Bedford
Lisa Cessna*
Lori Dunkle
Dawn Ickes

Bellmar Middle School
Belle Vernon
Carol Aten Frow*

Bermudian Springs Middle School
York Springs
Anne Swick*
D.R. Waltemyer

Brecknock Elementary School
Denver
Karen Huber
Kerry Kuipers
Beverly Libell

Bridle Path Elementary School
Lansdale
Anita Walker
Ruth Anne Wells

Bushkill Elementary School
Nazareth
Dennis Hahn
Kathy Roth
Mr. Uliana

California K-8 School
Coal Center
Debbie Carnello*

Chambersburg Area Middle School
Chambersburg
Nancy Deardorff*
Mrs. Evans
Sharon Kuhns
Jacqueline K. Perdas

Claysville Elementary School
Claysville
Monica Held
Miss Maglietta
Tammy Yukon

Concord Elementary School
Pittsburgh
Marcy Grollman
Joan Schuerle*

Conemaugh Township Area Intermediate
School
Johnstown
Meribeth DeBarto*

Daniel J Flood Elementary School
Wilkes Barre
Marie Lishnak*
Carol McNulty
Sheryl Sealock
Kathleen Segar
Suzanne Swithers

Deibler Elementary School
Perkasie
Petit Ritchie
Melissa D. Young*

East Stroudsburg Elementary School
East Stroudsburg
Lauren Baughman
Mr. Cole
Mrs. Digregorio
Stephanie Hymes
Mrs. Thurber

Easterly Parkway Elementary School
State College
Katie Fonash
Lisa Malloy*
Judy Weaver

Edgeworth Elementary School
Sewickley
Shirley Benedict*

Elizabeth Seton Elementary School
Pittsburgh
Bernadine Skraba*

Ephrata Middle School
Ephrata
Roberta Bear*
Ms. Chastain
Jean Good*
Michael C. Miller*
Diane Pavlek

Fishing Creek Elementary School
Lewisberry
Clair E. Richcrick*

Freedom Area Middle School
Freedom
Mrs. Moore*

Grasse Elementary School
Sellersville
Mr. Jameson
K. Singley*
Mrs. Svanson

H Austin Snyder Elementary School
Sayre
Jane E. Jewell*

Hamilton Elementary School
Lancaster
Mrs. Aulisio
Mrs. Barbusca*

Hillcrest Elementary School
Holland
Laura Shanley
Jim Vacca
Kelly Weiss

Holy Spirit School
Allentown
Vita Young*

Immaculate Conception School
Levittown
Mrs. Benoit
Sr. Rita Charles*
Mary Katz

Independence Charter School
Philadelphia
Scott Craig
Krista Pfeiffer*

Indian Lane Elementary School
Media
Mrs. Hendrixson
Ms. Peifer
Ms. Valentine

Jenkintown Elementary School
Jenkintown
Mrs. Abdollahi
Doris Heise*

Lincoln Elementary School
Pittsburgh
Cynthia Biery*
Linda McElhinny

Locust Grove Mennonite School
Lancaster
Pat Shelly*

Lower Salford Elementary School
Harleysville
Susan Mandia*

Manoa Elementary School
Havertown
Debbie Blume*

McMurray Elementary School
McMurray
Nancy S. McKenna*
Don Shipman

Mount Jewett Elementary School
Mount Jewett
Patricia Driscoll
Linda Hearst
Robynn Kowatch

Mount Nittany Middle School
State College
Scott W. Given*
Natalie Tiracorda

Neil Armstrong Middle School
Bethel Park
Leanne Cupp*

Newberry Elementary School
Etters
Jill Boreman
Mrs. Marshall

Newtown Elementary School
Newtown
Suzanne Antonelli
Wanda Harrison*
Jill Sharp*
Betsey Urban

Northern Cambria Catholic School
Nicktown
Ellen L. Hoover*

Our Lady of Grace Elementary School
Pittsburgh
Kirstina Popey*

Our Lady of Mount Carmel School
Doylestown
Paula Kin*

Our Mother of Perpetual Help School
Ephrata
Veida Wissler*

Panther Valley Elementary School
Nesquehoning
C. Diekman
Ms. Enama

Penn-Kidder Campus
  Albrightsville
    Howard Gregory*
    Mrs. A. O'Rourke*
    Diane Reese

Pine-Richland Middle School
  Gibsonia
    Dr. Susan Frantz*
    Jennifer Hartle Fink
    Aleta Lardin
    Jennifer Latronica
    Carolyn Pettit
    Gregg Somerhalder

Portersville Christian School
  Portersville
    Sally Moya-Mendez*
    Sheila Powers

Rhawnhurst School
  Philadelphia
    Brenda Kaufman*

Rolling Hills Elementary School
  Holland
    Nancy Peyser*

Sacred Heart Elementary School
  Pittsburgh
    Patricia Faub*

Sacred Heart of Jesus School
  Dupont
    James Renfer*

Sacred Heart School
  Oxford
    Cara Grebner*

Shafer Elementary School
  Nazareth
    Lynn Ann Post*

South Park Elementary Center
  South Park
    Kristen Golia
    Carol Nester*

St Alexis School
  Wexford
    Sandra Ross*

St Ambrose School
  Schuylkill Haven
    Mary Anne Rohrer*

St Cyril of Alexandria School
  East Lansdowne
    Rosemary Goodwin*

St Genevieve School
  Flourtown
    Sr. Marie Leahy*

St Hilary of Poitiers School
  Rydal
    Mary Ann Powell*
    Patricia Sermarini*

St Maria Goretti School
  Hatfield
    Mrs. Garner
    Linda Love
    Joanne Ryan

St Rosalia Academy School
  Pittsburgh
    Gloria Sciulli*

St Sebastian Elementary School
  Pittsburgh
    Shannon Poleto
    Susan L. Slifkin*

St Valentine Elementary School
  Bethel Park
    Katherine Menees*

Stackpole Elementary School
Southampton
Stephanie Badulak*

State Street Elementary School
Baden
Stacey Brock*

Strodes Mills Middle School
Mc Veytown
Lani Reese*
Heidi Welham*

United Hebrew Institute
Kingston
Barbara Welch*

Urban League of Pittsburgh Charter School
Pittsburgh
Ella Macklin*

Villa Maria Academy Lower School
Immaculata
Mrs. Gephart
Maureen Wible*

Watsontown Elementary School
Watsontown
Becky Geiger
Jenn Harer
Don Hodge
Alison Newman
Dana Pick
Marcia Saam
Jan Schreck

West Allegheny Middle School
Imperial
Deana Mack*

West Bradford Elementary School
Downingtown
Susan Shafer*

West Branch Area Elementary School
Morrisdale
Cheri Carr
Christina Onuskanich
Stacy Ricciotti
W. Timblin*

Wexford Elementary School
Wexford
Mrs. Prentice*

Wharton Elementary School
Farmington
Miss Patek*

Language Arts Grant Recipients 2005-2006

After receiving a "Poetic Achievement Award" schools are encouraged to apply for a Creative Communication Language Arts Grant. The following is a list of schools who received a two hundred and fifty dollar grant for the 2005-2006 school year.

Acushnet Elementary School – Acushnet, MA
Admiral Thomas H. Moorer Middle School – Eufaula, AL
Alta High School – Sandy, UT
Alton R-IV Elementary School – Alton, MO
Archbishop McNicholas High School – Cincinnati, OH
Barbara Bush Elementary School – Mesa, AZ
Bellmar Middle School – Belle Vernon, PA
Bonham High School – Bonham, TX
Cool Spring Elementary School – Cleveland, NC
Douglas Elementary School – Liberty, KY
Dumbarton Middle School – Baltimore, MD
Edward Bleeker Jr High School – Flushing, NY
Emmanuel/St. Michael Lutheran School – Fort Wayne, IN
Floyds Knobs Elementary School – Floyds Knobs, IN
Fox Creek High School – North Augusta, SC
Friendship Jr High School – Des Plaines, IL
Gibson City-Melvin-Sibley High School – Gibson City, IL
Hamilton Jr High School – Hamilton, TX
John F. Kennedy Middle School – Cupertino, CA
John Ross Elementary School – Edmond, OK
MacLeod Public School – Sudbury, ON
McKinley Elementary School – Livonia, MI
Monte Cassino School – Tulsa, OK
New Germany Elementary School – New Germany, NS
North Beach Elementary School – Miami Beach, FL
Paradise Valley High School – Phoenix, AZ
Parkview Christian School – Lincoln, NE
Picayune Jr High School – Picayune, MS
Red Bank Charter School – Red Bank, NJ
Sebastian River Middle School – Sebastian, FL
Siegrist Elementary School – Platte City, MO

Language Arts Grant Winners cont.

Southwest Academy – Baltimore, MD
St. Anthony School – Winsted, CT
St. John Vianney Catholic School – Flint, MI
St. Paul the Apostle School – Davenport, IA
St. Rose School – Roseville, CA
St. Sebastian School – Pittsburgh, PA
Sundance Elementary School – Sundance, WY
Thorp Middle School – Thorp, WI
Townsend Harris High School – Flushing, NY
Warren Elementary School – Warren, OR
Washington High School – Washington Court House, OH
Wasilla Lake Christian School – Wasilla, AK
Woodland Elementary School – Radcliff, KY
Worthington High School – Worthington, MN

Young Poets
Grades 4-5-6

Note: The Top Ten poems were finalized through an online voting system. Creative Communication's judges first picked out the top poems. These poems were then posted online. The final step involved thousands of students and teachers who registered as online judges and voted for the Top Ten poems. We hope you enjoy these selections.

Top Poem Grades 4-5-6

The Pencil

I'm so yellow and bare,
With not even one hair.
All alone from 3:00 to 10:00,
Until the next morning I sit with a pen.
Dropped in the hallway rolling down ramps,
Been to 1,300,002 camps.
Picked up again by a lucky new child,
Oh man! I can tell this one is wild.
Sharpened two inches in only one day,
Back in the desk where each evening I lay.
My life is so hectic can't you see?
Not one bit of eraser is left on me!
The day is soon over but fun is not met,
I warn you don't pass that. Oh please, just not yet.
You're gonna get caught anyone would agree,
At least do it quick before the teacher sees.
Today was not good, too evil to mention,
This night I spend my time in detention.

Emily Bittner, Grade 6
Freedom Area Middle School

Top Poem Grades 4-5-6

The Price of Freedom

Waiting, waiting, this is her occupation, waiting for her son to come home
War, war, this is the son's occupation, trying not to come home in a box.
Both very tired and alone, fear gripped them like an owl on its prey.
The son was literally running for his life.
The son gave his life for the freedom of others,
And the mother gave her son for the freedom of others.
The mother can never see her beloved son again;
No friends could reassure her — not now, not ever.
Not 'til that size seventeen shoe crosses the threshold.
Like a house divided cannot stand, a house without her son cannot stand.
The suspense was unbearable, like a nagging splinter in your palm
Suddenly loud bullets buzzed like bees over their heads.
The boy ran, he ran for his life lunging lowly, lightheaded, and tried to find cover.
The mother tried to find cover for her feelings, but couldn't.
BAM!
They fell.
The mother felt something, as if that same, sour gunsmoke filled her lungs.
It was as if that same bullet had pierced her heart.

Jon Cox, Grade 6
Mount Nittany Middle School

Top Poem Grades 4-5-6

Amusement Parks

Do you like to get real wild?
Scream so loud, act like a child?
Well then this place is for you
At amusement parks, that's all you do!

Lots of people, loads of fun
Yummy food and room to run
Roller coasters, water slides
Slow or fast, there's many rides!

Some shake, some slide, some go real high
At times you feel you're in the sky
Exciting they are from finish to stop
Some take you away and let you drop!

The amusement park is where I'll be
With my twin sister and my family
Hopefully you will see me there,
But look up high — I'll be in the air!

Louisa Gibson, Grade 5
Vandergrift Elementary School

Top Poem Grades 4-5-6

Me

What did you say, what do I think about me?
Well if you look on, then maybe you'll see,
That I find myself artistic, caring, and odd,
And when I'm with friends, we're peas in a pod.

There are many things that I like to do,
But I'll narrow them down to only a few.
Knitting and stitching were some skills that came,
But I think that drawing will bring me to fame.

When I get older I plan to have a job
As a zookeeper that feeds animals corn on the cob.
Or maybe I'll be an artist, a sculptor, a painter
But there's a dream that I have that is oh so much fainter.

I love my family as if they were treasures,
And helping people makes me feel light as feathers.
Maybe this love will open my heart,
And allow me to make decisions that are always smart.

Well, what do you think of me now?
Can I step back and take a bow?
Now you've learned a thing or two,
About me and the things that I like to do.

Olivia Migliori, Grade 5
Bushkill Elementary School

Top Poem Grades 4-5-6

The Fall Day

Wind howling
against my face
butterfly bush
jerking and struggling in the wind
goose bumps exploding
down my spine
pebbles sprinting and booming
down the path
bark on the honey locust
crinkling apart
leaves the color of pumpkin pie
birds soar into their homes for shelter
small drops of rain
shooting slightly out of the sky
leaves crackling, spinning
and turning all over
the bird bath
drowning with leaves
fall is here and I know it

Ian Miller, Grade 5
Lower Salford Elementary School

Top Poem Grades 4-5-6

America

America is very special to me,
From north to south and from sea to sea.
With stars and stripes hanging from above,
Our flag represents freedom and love.
From New York to California, America is full of pride,
With firefighters, police officers, and soldiers always by our side.
When terrorists attacked us we stood strong,
With good leaders defending us, nothing can go wrong.
Great Olympic athletes always trying their best,
To win a medal, they let their hearts take care of the rest.
I love this country, it really is quite true,
I will always honor the flag, our red, white, and blue.

Jacey Mrozowski, Grade 6
St John Holy Rosary Eastside Catholic School

Top Poem Grades 4-5-6

The Moon Fairy

She wisps around in moonlight when the fireflies glow,
her hair is bright like fire and her tiny face glints like snow,
her shiny green eyes upon her face sparkle like champagne,
her lips are soft as rose petals covered in droplets from the rain,
she feeds alone on moonshine in the midst of the dark and sacred night,
and the tiny little cloak she wears is made of soft moonlight,
yet she fears the coming of the golden glow of day,
for this is when her delicate soul will shrink and wither away.

Sophie Najjar, Grade 5
Easterly Parkway Elementary School

Top Poem Grades 4-5-6

My Hero

He was just a little boy, but brave as he could be.
He could ride his bike real fast, and climb most any tree.
He talked of driving big trucks and fighting battles big and small.
He wanted to be a hero more than anything at all.
Time went fast and he became a very fine young man.
And now he's fighting far away to protect our home land.
He truly is a hero, as all the world can see.
I'm thankful for this little boy, protecting you and me.

Haley Redshaw, Grade 5
Wharton Elementary School

Top Poem Grades 4-5-6

Snow Fall

As I sit at my window side
the snow whips across the
glass with fear.
A sea of venturous snowflakes
each one a different design
when they drift off into the sky
their crystal clear color is
moaning to me.
In the moonlight they seem
like a wonderful memory swirling
in the night singing a beautiful song
as I shiver drifting off to sleep.

Julia Staltari, Grade 4
Lincoln Elementary School

Top Poem Grades 4-5-6

My Sister

I go into the hospital room, my heart starts to pound;
I never knew that my little sister would be so small and round!
I carefully go to hold her, her eyes are tightly closed.
I trace my finger lightly over her eyes, her mouth, and nose.
They all remind me slightly of my own features on my face,
And they all seem to be put in just the right place.
Finally her eyes open, her angelic face shines.
I hug her tight and firm, knowing happily that she is mine!
Mine to love and play with, and mine to teach and show
All of the things my parents taught me, all of the things I know.
We might have some arguments, some silly little fights,
But only for a while, we won't get into that plight.
I come back in reality, and I put her gently down.
Wow, I can't believe it! She's asleep, safe and sound.
Goodbye, little sister, I'm out for the night.
I knew we were meant to be together, that's why it feels so right!

Lillian Xu, Grade 6
Park Forest Middle School

You Can Make a Difference
We are different in many ways
We are different like the days
Whether you are brown, white, or tan
You really can
Make a difference
Or an inference
No matter if you're tall
Or even if you're small
You can make a difference in the world
It doesn't matter if you're a boy or a girl
Hair straight or having a curl
Shy, outgoing, smart, or slow
You can help our world to grow.

Scout Young, Grade 5
Vandergrift Elementary School

Liar
There once was a man from Crete,
Who said he will never eat.
He stepped on a scale,
To prove his tale.
He finally admitted defeat.

Crysta Clear, Grade 6
Freedom Area Middle School

By Myself*
When I am by myself
And I close my eyes
I am a good figure skater
I am a chocolate maker
I am a Bulgarian translator
I am a lifeguard saving the people
I am a famous singer
I am a good dancer
I am a very good swimmer
I am an athletic person
I am the person who found America
I am a very good artist
I am whatever I want to be
An anything I want to be
And when I open my eyes
What I care to be
Is me!

Borislava Chobanova, Grade 5
East Stroudsburg Elementary School
*Inspired by Eloise Greenfield.

Jealousy
Jealousy is blush red
Tastes like warm ice tea
Smells like a hot tamale
Feels like cold air
Sounds like a wolf howling
Jealousy is a windy night.

Taylor Carlin, Grade 4
Fairview Elementary School

I Want to Be a Monkey
I want to be a monkey
One who swings on vines
And dance really funky
In trees all the time

At home I was kept in jail
I wanted to be wild
So I started to grow a tail
I was no longer a child

When I climb the tallest tree
I say to the birds
"I'm free, I finally live in a tree"
That's why I want to be a monkey

Katelyn Shinavski, Grade 5
Central Elementary School

Homework
Hard, complicated
Working, marking, boring
Homework can be hard or easy

Matthew Nawrocki, Grade 4
Moscow Elementary Center

American Flag
American flag
patriotic
blowing in the breeze
like leaves twisting
and turning
outside my classroom
red
white
blue
with stars

Megan Miller, Grade 4
South Park Elementary Center

Horses
Horses are pretty,
Horses eat a lot of grass.
Horses are so cool,
Horses have manes on their backs.
Horses stay in the stables.

Ashley Nuss, Grade 4
Manoa Elementary School

Blue Sue
There once was a girl named Sue.
She was sick in bed with the flu.
She got a letter,
Saying she wouldn't get better.
Then she was terribly blue.

Spencer Scott, Grade 4
Avonworth Elementary School

Poems
P oems are so fun and
O n occasions
E ach one
M ay
S ilently put you asleep!

Jacob Hudock, Grade 6
H Austin Snyder Elementary School

Tissue Friend
Linda was my bestest friend
The world would ever know
We did everything together
From jumping rope to tying bows
But then I left her in my jeans
Boy my mom was very mean
And washed her to a smithereen
Linda was my bestest friend
The world would ever know

Katie Heininger, Grade 5
Easterly Parkway Elementary School

Williamsport
W orld Series of little league
I mpossible to win (almost)
L osers go home
L ittle teams make it
I ndescribable excitement
A mazing fields to look at
M illions striving to win
S uper competitive
P ennsylvania is its location
O riginal little league tournament
R ecognized around the world
T ournament for the best of the best

Jimmy Clarke, Grade 4
West Bradford Elementary School

Hockey
H aving fun
O n the ice all the time
C ome play hockey
K ey is to get a goal.
E veryone can play
Y et when it's over we're still having fun.

Taran Beckett, Grade 6
West Allegheny Middle School

Spring Is
Spring is green grass
Along with flowers blooming.
Robins are fluttering around
When the sun is shinning bright.
Kites are flying.
While seeds are sprouting.

Sara Clauto, Grade 4
All Saints Catholic School

Harriet Tubman

Freed the black slaves and lived long ago.
Showed a lot of bravery and that we all know.
Fought for the bravery to set things right,
No matter what the danger, she kept up the fight.

Got hit on the head at a very young age,
To save the poor people who worked for no wage.
Had to keep going and never could rest,
In all of the world, her courage was the best.

The Underground Railroad was her main road,
The lives of many people must have been a heavy load.
She traveled on through in the dark of night,
But slunk very carefully not to be in sight.

Harriet Tubman was determined 'till death,
And she spoke fair words 'till her very last breath.
She's a hero to all and that's a true fact,
And all should remember her kind admirable act.

Molly Davis, Grade 5
Villa Maria Academy Lower School

Fall

Fall, the best time of the year,
Ah, everything full of cheer.
The swirl of yellow, orange, and brown,
There is no way you can possibly frown.

Wonderful holidays, such as Thanksgiving,
Just carry on your life and keep on living.
Blessed times, happiness, and glad,
In this season nobody can get sad!

I like to play in the leaves and jump,
I sometimes hit with a bump! Thump! Crump!
Wrestling in the leaves I like to do,
I even get little parts in my shoe.

Now my poem is coming to an end,
I may see you again.
Now my poem is time to end,
Good-bye to all and 'bye again!

Lucas Garman, Grade 6
Conemaugh Township Area Intermediate School

What Is Blue?

Blue is the color of a never-ending sky
Blue is the color of my grandmother's twinkling eyes
Blue is the color of the always moving ocean
Blue is how your heart feels when it has a sad notion
Blue is the color of flowers so rare
Where blue flowers bloom people stare.
Blue is the soft blanket that keeps me safe and warm
When I am wrapped in blue I am safe from harm.

Kelsey Zaremba, Grade 5
Claysville Elementary School

The Roller Coaster of Friendship

Friendship is a roller coaster
It's up
It's down
It's all around
It's the best time of your life
But you may also want to stay away from it
You'll laugh about it until you get old
But it also makes you sick
It can seem short
It can seem forever
But most of the time
You love it
And want to keep riding the journey called
Friendship

Alexandra Agasar, Grade 6
Hillcrest Elementary School

Christmas Eve

Now I see we are done Christmas Eve
The next day we get to believe.
My brothers and my sister and I see who's here
We see who is coming and we cheer for the rest of the year.

Patrick Coyne, Grade 4
West Bradford Elementary School

Useless Things

a pencil without lead a bedroom without a bed
a star without a twinkle a Shar Pei without a wrinkle

a car without space a racetrack without a race
a tire without grip a face without a lip

a notebook without lines a road without signs
a song without a beat a fire without heat

clothes in a store without a tag school without Miss Mag
candy without its taste a glue bottle without paste

a hot-dog without a bun a hunter without his gun
a marker without a lid a mother without a kid

a title without a story a gem without its glory
three without two me without you

Cydney Comfort, Grade 5
Claysville Elementary School

Artificial and Real

Artificial
fake, synthetic
imitating, generating, pretending
programmed, computer, genuine, human
thinking, trying, hoping
imperfect, true
Real

Jane Hughes, Grade 6
St Genevieve School

The Tropical Rain Forest

The tropical rain forest is
Mist over water
Palm trees and grass
The tops of wet trees
A dark green sky
A clear green lake
Alex Rae, Grade 5
Jenkintown Elementary School

Which One Are You?

Hero
Strong, undefeatable
Willing, adventuring
Brave, bold, scared, weakling
Crying, whimpering
Wimp, gutless
Coward
Ricardo Diaz, Grade 6
St Genevieve School

Turkey Breast

Turkey breast from KFC.
It's so good just can't you see.
Turkey breast, turkey breast
It is better than the rest.
If only I could I'd eat it for
Breakfast, brunch and lunch galore.
How I wish it sold for a dime
Then I'd eat it all the time.
Gavin Fogelman, Grade 4
Watsontown Elementary School

Wind

The wind blows the grass
And the grass will move.

The wind whistles
Like a very nice person singing.

The wind is strong and powerful.
I like when the wind blows!
Brooke Semelsberger, Grade 4
Northern Cambria Catholic School

Love Is Like a Flower...

Love is like a flower,
you need to give it time to grow.
By giving it time it will get stronger,
that you may never know.
You need to give it warmth,
with all the hugs you share.
Because it will die,
if you don't seem like you care.
Kayla Geray, Grade 6
Allison Park Elementary School

The Kite

The kite is flying in the sky
Over, under, way up high

With many colors does it glide
Up, down, and on its side

The kite is the sky's love
Flying, flying up above
Katelyn Clark, Grade 4
All Saints Catholic School

Friends

Friends
funny, playful
caring, comforting, exciting
help me when times are hard
amigo
Megan Moffett, Grade 6
St Hilary of Poitiers School

Spring

The sun
warm
a light mist
in the air
little baby birds
are born
and start to peep
for their mother
flowers bud
everything is quiet
and peaceful
Jessica Thomas, Grade 4
South Park Elementary Center

Spring Opposites

Spring
fun, hard
hunting, challenging, looking
Easter, eggs, leaves, trees
raking, jumping, falling
orange, yellow
Fall
Jimmy Shaw, Grade 4
West Branch Area Elementary School

Big Green Bear

Once I saw a big green bear.
It was big and scary.
It had tons of hair and
Didn't look much like a normal bear.
And, if you see the big green bear
With tons of hair.
It will give you a great big scare.
John Hornick, Grade 4
Northern Cambria Catholic School

NASCAR

Ig **N** ition
G **A** soline
S tart
Ra **C** e
P **A** ss
Checke **R** ed
Michael Maloy, Grade 6
Our Lady of Grace Elementary School

Red

Red
Blue is pool water
Yellow is the sun's hot beam
Red is the strawberries
I put on my ice cream

Purple is for Kings
Black is ink
Red is Cherry Coke
That I like to drink

Green is for grass
Silver is the shopping cart
Red is a color
The color of your heart
Pawel Jelski, Grade 6
Guth Elementary School

Peter

There once was a boy named Peter
Though his clothes could've been neater
He played a card game
He played it quite lame
And now that makes him a cheater
Kyle Chiavetta, Grade 4
West Bradford Elementary School

Monkey

Monkey
Adorable small
Running, climbing, swinging
What a cute animal
Primate
Caleb Schweter, Grade 4
East End Elementary School

Spring

S ummer's almost here
P retty blooming flowers and trees
R ainy and chilly
I nsects come out from their burrows
N ests being built for baby birds
G rowing flowers and trees
Madalyn Lutz, Grade 6
West Allegheny Middle School

Ode to Dad
My dad is my role model.
I look up to him like he is Superman,
running, passing, playing basketball.
I love my dad, so much.
He loves me back.
We love hanging out together.
Fun, funny, fantastic that is my dad.
Like Rocky and Bullwinkle
we know each other so well.
Our relationship is very unique.
He takes time to hang with me,
sometimes it is hard due to our busy lives.
But when we get the chance we have a blast!!
When I want to talk he will listen,
because he is always there if I need him.
When I grow up I hope to be like my father,
the greatest dad in the world.
My dad is my best friend.

Colton Leonard, Grade 6
Hershey Middle School

Super Steelers
Jeff Reed has just done the kickoff,
The crowd is as crazy as in the play-offs.
Roethlisberger has just thrown a touchdown,
And it's even in Pittsburgh's hometown.

It is now the championship game,
Pittsburgh can feel the Super Bowl fame.
Parker is so fast, he is a bullet,
Super Bowl XL is where they'll get it.

The Steelers are now at the top,
Big Ben is impossible to stop.
This is the game that will be a quest,
'Cause Pittsburgh's coming, and they're the best.

Polamalu is a great big scare,
But it's not just his very long hair.
The Steelers are coming into town,
And they're bringing the steel curtain down.

Super Bowl XL is on my birthday,
Everyone knows Seattle will pay.
Fans look at the scoreboard and see,
Pittsburgh 100, Seattle 3.

Dustin Grogan, Grade 5
Bermudian Springs Middle School

Joe
There once was a frog named Joe
Who ate a ginormous Ho Ho
He swelled up so big he looked like a pig
All his friends said "he's gonna blow!"

Jessica Johnson, Grade 5
McMurray Elementary School

They Have Yarns
Of the runners of the track team
are faster than a cheetah.

Of my dog who is so smart
she could be a school teacher.

Of a jack-o-lantern who is scarier
than a mummy jumping out in front of you.

Of the swimming pool that was so little
not even a gnat could fit in it.

Of a shopping mall that was so huge
you could fit the city of Pittsburgh in it.

Of a dancer that could dance so quick
she went faster than a tornado.

Sarah Kosela, Grade 6
Freedom Area Middle School

Summer
When I feel the summer's air
I cannot wait to fix my hair
The schools are out; it's time to party
Now teachers don't yell, for being tardy
We just can't wait to hit the pools
And we don't have to worry about any more rules
Can't wait to go on a vacation
Because it's going to be a sensation
So let's get started on the planning
While I get started on my tanning
Sleepovers are the best
But you don't want to know the rest
I love feeling sand in between my toes
Just as much as wearing bows
No more homework, none at all
Soon school will come in fall
I love to kick the ball around
Even if it hits the ground
When playing sports I love to win
But school is just about to begin

Ashley Hurey, Grade 6
West Allegheny Middle School

Christmas Wonderland
C hristmas is a joyful time of year —
H ang ornaments on the Christmas tree,
R ide sleds down the hill so much my whole body is numb!
I cicles form on houses like a glacier,
S eeing white snow on the ground,
T asting red and white candy canes,
M any presents fill my living room like a toy store!
A s I fall asleep I think of all the good food coming the next day.
S eeing hot cocoa on the table on Christmas morning.

Alexandra Mease, Grade 4
Bushkill Elementary School

Autumn Days

Golden leaves swirling
Away from the honey locust trees
Shadows dancing
On the brick walls
Sun shining bright
Little birds call for their mothers
Wind whispers
Kids happily yelling at recess
Clouds
Feathery and light
Golden sun rays
Feel warm
I see autumn leaves
Crisp and worn
The sun sparkles
Like the ocean
Autumn's here to stay

Megan Furey, Grade 5
Lower Salford Elementary School

Spring

Spring

Flowers are blooming,
Bunnies are hopping,
Easter is coming!
Baskets are full,
Eggs are colored.
Birds are chirping,
Grass is growing!

Spring

Kayla McGoran, Grade 6
West Allegheny Middle School

Day/Night

Day
Hot, sunny
Playing, running, jumping
Sun, rainbow, pillow, TV
Sleeping, snoring, calling
Soft, warm
Night

Taylor Allison, Grade 4
West Branch Area Elementary School

The Kite

The kite is always fun,
If you think you're done.
All kites fly in the sky,
Above all the houses, oh so high.
They're like a diamond in the sky.
My kite fell from the sky,
Due to a tree, oh so high.

Brody Shuty, Grade 4
All Saints Catholic School

Green

Green tastes like a juicy apple on a sunny day,
green beans freshly cut from the stalk,
and Sprite sprinkling down my throat.

Green smells like freshly cut grass in the afternoon,
lime scented markers from my coloring box,
and seaweed floating on the ocean.

Green sounds like a bug flying by my ear at the zoo,
trees swaying back and forth in the wind,
and the waves of the ocean swishing when I swim.

Green feels like a bumpy and hard Jolly Rancher in my mouth,
prickly grass touching my face when I lay down,
and the happy and sad feeling I got when I brought my cat home for the first time.

Green looks like an army suit on a man just about to go to war,
leaves blowing in front of me,
and money that I found on the ground.

Erin Robert, Grade 4
Indian Lane Elementary School

The Beginning

The dawning of winter is over, but the dawning of spring has begun.
It may not last forever but you should enjoy it while it lasts.
The lady bug lays on your foot; the joy of it won't last forever.
From afar you can hear the trees howling, as if they are talking to you.
And as soon as it starts — it's finished,
So, enjoy, while you can.

Thomas Horvath, Grade 5
St Ambrose School

I Wish...

I wish...
That I had a unicorn as a pet, and my brother was nice;
That my neighbor's house was made of candy;
Sharks only ate seaweed and lived really far down in the ocean;
No one would die, they would live forever until they wanted to die;
That I was so popular around the world and a really good ice skater;
I wish...
There was no smoking allowed;
No bad grades and bad things in the world at all times;
My family has a great year in our new home;
That every wish of mine comes true;
I have more wishes to wish for.

Christine Seitzinger, Grade 5
Schnecksville School

Candy

I see people with buckets of brightly colored candy ready to be eaten
I hear the wrappers unwrapping and being tossed into the bag
I taste the sweet, chocolaty, juicy candy on my taste buds
I smell the tangy fresh smell of it melting in my mouth
It is always smooth as glass

David Haizlip, Grade 5
Southside Elementary School

Best Friends

Best friends are the most important thing to me
I can trust her and tell her important secrets
Her name is Miranda Kessler
She and I will be friends forever we say
That is the truth
She always makes me laugh when I hurt
I tell her we will be best friends forever
And we both know that that is the truth

Brena McMahon, Grade 6
Strodes Mills Middle School

Friends

My two best friends are in a fight
And I'm trying to make everything all right.
But they're pulling me two separate ways.
I just wish I could rewind time a few days
And keep them from getting mad at each other.
Wish me luck I'm stepping in.
Just like a game. But who will win?

Gabriella Puteri, Grade 4
Our Lady of Peace School

Rockne

My little puppy Rockne, he is my old pal.
I love him and praise him, but when he is naughty, I don't.
He is even my best friend.

My mom loves him my dad loves him too,
But I love him most of all my family, it's true!

Kelsey Micklas, Grade 4
Christ the King School

Stars

One dark night there were stars
They were shining from afar
I went out that cold night
And what I saw was such a beautiful sight
It was my grandpa looking down
Watching me go all around town
I knew it was him all along
I was so happy because I missed him
He said I can't wait to see you all grown up
In Heaven one day at those pearly gates
So now I know it was him that bright beautiful shining light
My grandfather

Desirae Detweiler, Grade 6
Strodes Mills Middle School

Christmas

Hear the sound of sleighs sliding over snow
Shopping carts going through stores
The sound of gift-wrap crunching
People filling glasses with eggnog
The sound of sleigh bells ringing

Benjamin Hall, Grade 4
West Bradford Elementary School

Song of the Trees*

Trees trees, their smooth soft voices as they sing their song

we are the trees of the forest we sing our song with this chorus
we sing all night and we sing all day and this is what we say
we sing we sing as the wind blows by to the great blue sky
we sing so proud and high
we sing with each other and together
so please don't cut us down
because we are the trees

Matt Beiswenger, Grade 6
Park Forest Middle School
*Inspired by Mildred Taylor's "Song of the Trees"

Good Friends Bad Friends

Good friends are always with you
Bad friends are never there
Good friends always know if you're hurt
Bad friends never care
Good friends always share secrets with you
Bad friends never tell you anything
Good friends always cheer you up
Bad friends are never comforting
Good friends are always going to like you
Bad friends are never going to turn to you

Cara Petrofes, Grade 6
Ss Peter and Paul Elementary School

Daisy Low

My famous person is Juliette Gordon Low
Her nickname is "Daisy" you may all know.
She always went with the flow
Until fifty, she never said no.

To the U.S.A. she would go
With the girl scout program in tow.
She taught the girls how to knit and sew
On a journey where all girls could grow.

Camping by the fire aglow
Singing Do-Re-Me-Fa-So-La-Ti-Do.
Selling cookies made out of dough
Strong skills of leadership all Girl Scouts show.

Bronze, silver, and gold awards stand in a row
Just as Juliette dreamed it so.
The Girl Scouts continue to grow
Because of Juliette Gordon Low.

Laura Hall, Grade 5
Villa Maria Academy Lower School

Night Owl

As the moon rises upon thee,
Look to the Forest and up in a tree,
Where an Owl is sitting lonely and free...

Hannah Volkman, Grade 4
Avonworth Elementary School

Wonderful Spring

Springtime air is everywhere,
Bringing lots of love and care.
Many times there are many showers,
Showers bring lots of flowers.

Children in the park having fun,
Playing as they please, as they run.
Kids all around,
Tired, laying on the ground.

The sun is about to set,
Everybody putting away their nets.
Now the sky is red,
When the children are in bed.
Gabby Sliwinski, Grade 4
Avonworth Elementary School

Softball and Basketball

Softball
Dirty, fun
Hitting, catching, throwing
Bats, helmets, net, backboard
Passing, running, shooting
Exciting, aggressive
Basketball
Audree Kunsman, Grade 6
Allison Park Elementary School

Stars

Twinkling up high
Just waiting for their next chance
To shine down on us.
Joshua McMaster, Grade 4
Colonial Elementary School

Laptop

I am a laptop
I can be carried around
You can take me anywhere
Even on campground

You can look up information
You can pick a different font
You can search the World Wide Web
I can type anything you want.
Sarah Smart, Grade 5
McMurray Elementary School

Nothing

Nothing
Question, help
Empty, white, lost
Hard, alone, thoughtless, sad
Blank
Crystal Wolf, Grade 4
Hereford Elementary School

Bunnies

Smart, cute
Running very fast
Making me feel happy
Cute
Christopher Trovato, Grade 5
Penn-Kidder Campus

The Storm

The storm was over
The storm was gone
Our worst fears
Down the drain
But still
There is trouble
Lurking around
As we do our best
To put our foot down
Now the work begins
To clean up
The wind
That took away
Our hopes and dreams
For a new
And better
Life
Tom Sternberg, Grade 6
Hillcrest Elementary School

Rain

Rain
watery, drippy
dripping, wetting, misting
watery, drippy, sunny, bright
burning, brightening, lighting
sunny, brightly
Sun
Gunnar Geyer, Grade 4
St Sebastian Elementary School

Betty

There once was a lady named Betty
Who liked to eat spaghetti.
She put it in a bowl
With a Tootsie Roll
Too bad she had no confetti.
Christine Gaab, Grade 5
McMurray Elementary School

My Dog

My dog is really funny.
He looks like a little bunny.
He is small and cute.
And also sweet as honey.
Jennifer Ellis, Grade 5
Rhawnhurst School

Stars

They twinkle, they shine,
They are all around the sky.

They make wishes come true.
They just love to stay around the moon

They love to dance.
Megan Jackson, Grade 4
Northern Cambria Catholic School

Hot Chocolate

Warm, brown
Soothing, satisfying, comforting
Chocolaty, sweet, hot, tasty
Blowing, slurping, steaming,
Splendid, delicious
Heaven in a mug
Henry Gillespie-Hill, Grade 4
Memorial Elementary School

Dad's Description

D ependable, determined, daring
A ffectionate, astonishing, adventurous
D elightful, dedicated, directing
James Francis Magurno III, Grade 6
H Austin Snyder Elementary School

Where I Am From

I am from Havertown, PA,
Richard and Tina.
I am from Avalon, NJ,
A fun-filled summer.

I'm from energetic cheerleading.
From round-off back hand springs,
To simple preps.
From loud cheers to sharp motions.

I am from Blue,
My beautiful Quarter horse.
I am from his bouncing lope,
That brings a fun laughter to me.
Nicole Erickson, Grade 6
Haverford Middle School

The Box

In a box
You will see
Not a crumb
Nor a tree
In a box
You will find
A dog, a dog
That's what's inside!
Abigale G. Bailey, Grade 4
Eshleman Elementary School

The Grand Canyon

The Grand Canyon hot and dry
And watching little woodpeckers fly by,
Tons of feet below sea level it may be,
But alas it's all me,
Climbing, climbing, climbing up to the top,
Be careful or you'll have a big drop,
Up and up to the highest peak,
And below the lowest creek.

John Tereskun, Grade 5
Immaculate Conception School

Summer

Hurray, woo hoo, it's summer at last
The cold and the snow is in the past
The best thing is that there's no school
Just relaxing and swimming in the pool

Squirt guns, jump ropes, and bikes.
Running, jogging, and going on hikes
Don't forget tanning in the sun
Without a doubt, summer is the most fun.

Instead of being at school getting an education
People are having family vacations.
Like water parks with pools and slides
And amusement parks with wicked rides.

It's not spring, winter, or fall
Summer is my favorite of all
Eventually it will come to an end
And I'll wait for it to come again.

Tijana Henry, Grade 6
Conemaugh Township Area Intermediate School

Luge

Rushing, rushing, down the course
Adrenaline going down my spine
Maneuvering twists in the course
Trying to get perfect time.

Almost finished, but I hit the course's side.
I finally pass the finish line, waiting for my score.
"Neil McGuire 4th place," my mouth goes agape
Thinking I would get something better than 4th place.

Once again rushing, rushing, down the course
Adrenaline going down my spine
And after some time
I finally reach the finish line.

Now, it's the moment I've been waiting for
Gold, silver, or bronze.
Once I heard the words I jumped out of my seat
"Hoo-rah" the medal I had won was gold.

Neil McGuire, Grade 4
Greenock Elementary School

School

School,
sometimes cool
And sometimes cruel.
Makes you do work at home and at school.
Teachers mean
And lunches green.
Some days boring
Teachers keep kids snoring.
Sometimes fun
When we can run.
The things we learn make us smart,
But if you don't study it will all fall apart.
All us kids really want to know
"Why is the clock going so slow?"
School…sometimes cool
Or very, very, very cruel!!!

A'zani Carpenter, Grade 5
Independence Charter School

Fighting

There were two boys who knew how to fight
It was mostly happening at night
There was pain everywhere
But they just couldn't bear
I just hope they didn't bite.

Greg Graf, Grade 4
South Park Elementary Center

Broken

I don't feel good, not at all.
All because of a great big fall.
It broke my leg and my arm.
I guess that fall had an evil charm.
I also have a great big bruise.
My fall should have been on the news.
I'm not going to tell what it was like.
But it was because of my brand new bike!

Megan Werner, Grade 4
Our Lady of Peace School

Gymnastics

Gymnastics can be dangerous
   If you don't know what to do
Cartwheels, splits, there's so much you can do.
   You should always try your best
But make sure to take a rest!

Rylie Krapf, Grade 4
Panther Valley Elementary School

Why Did This Happen?

Separated families,
Departing their loved ones,
Scared and devastated from what they see,
Why did this happen how could this be?

Alex Jade Crotty, Grade 6
Chambersburg Area Middle School

Winter Weather
Cold, snowy
Freezing, blistering, and chilling
Slush, flurries, bad roads, icy
Blowing, sleeting, covering
Wet, beautiful
Winter
Jonah Chamberlain, Grade 4
Memorial Elementary School

Spring Is Here
Spring is finally here,
Where children laugh and cheer.
Flowers are popping out of the ground,
In the river fish splash around.

The blue sky is so outrageous,
No more sickness that is contagious.
It is such a beautiful spring day.
Come on, let's go out and play.

Trees are growing back their leaves,
As the wind gives a wonderful breeze.
Birds like to sing lots of tunes,
This never ends, not even through June.
Isaac Wimer, Grade 4
Avonworth Elementary School

Dogs
Dogs
Cute creatures
Barking, running, playing
Loving small gentle amazing
K-9
Natosha Smathers, Grade 4
East End Elementary School

Pittsburgh
Pittsburgh
The Steel City
Making steel all the time
Go there to see the Steelers win
Blitzburgh
Steven Maker, Grade 4
South Park Elementary Center

Spring
Spring is fun,
Spring is great.
Warm weather,
and Easter break.
Play some games,
and be with friends.
Spring is a time to celebrate.
Nina Vecchi, Grade 6
West Allegheny Middle School

Books
Books can have hooks,
Books can see,
Books can read,
Books can sit,
Books can climb,
Books can swim,
Books can eat,
Books can do anything!

Wait!
Books can't have hooks,
Books can't see,
Books can't read,
Books can't sit,
Books can't climb,
Books can't swim,
Books can't eat,
Books can't do anything!
But if you use your imagination,
A book can do everything!
Julia Kivlin, Grade 4
Lionville Elementary School

Frogs
Frogs are the color green.
Frogs feel like a silky cloth.
Frogs taste like chicken.
Frogs smell like rotten eggs.
Frogs look like a rocky road.
Frogs sound like a cricket.
Michael Huang, Grade 5
Rhawnhurst School

Sun
Sam says
she loves
the shining
sun on her skin.
Cassie Anderson, Grade 6
Allison Park Elementary School

Sibling
Sibling
Short, awkward
Likes to annoy people
Loves to be wild and crazy
Brother
Nicholas Pellechia, Grade 5
Newtown Elementary School

Caribbean
Hawaiian music
Waves wash up on sandy shore
Relaxing and calm
Christina Cole, Grade 5
Penn-Kidder Campus

Pope John Paul
He loved us all
Each one the same
Loved all the children
His time had came
Living with God
And his angels and saints
Pope John Paul is really great
He died in peace
And loved and cared
And even shared
Pope John Paul
Had loved us all
So now he rests
In peace
In love
Up above
Lea Christopher, Grade 6
St Boniface School

Shining Sun
Shines bright in the sky
Sunbeams stream down to my face
Shines for all to see
Shea Metzgar, Grade 4
Center Elementary School

The Moon Is a Marble
The moon is a marble
Smooth and white
See it sparkle
Flawless and bright
Dangling in the open midnight sky
Adam Thomas, Grade 6
Freedom Area Middle School

My Dog
My dog barks, my dog howls,
Sometimes he even growls.
Bees like to sting me
But he likes to lick me
When I take him outside,
He will hide.
Terry Orris, Grade 5
Cheswick Christian Academy

Baseball and Basketball
Baseball
White, hard,
Pitching, hitting, running
Bat, glove, ball, lay-up
Passing, running, shooting
Laced, orange
Basketball
Anthony Zelensky, Grade 4
West Branch Area Elementary School

Jake's Horrible Day

I once knew a boy named Jake
he had trouble getting awake,
he would stay in his bed
to rest his big head
until mom yelled, "Get up for goodness sake."

Now once Jake got up out of bed
he was punched by his big brother Fred,
Jake yelled to his mother he got punched by his brother
and now Jake wants to go back to bed!

Jake's mom wouldn't let him do that
she said, "Go to school, you little brat"
so Jake ran out, without a doubt
that his mother was very, very mad!

At school Jake failed an English Test
he was tired and couldn't do his best
he was ordered to go to the principal's lair
so he sighed and slowly got up from his chair

Oh the things Jake was thinking inside of his head
and now all Jake wanted was to go back to bed!

Alex Johnson, Grade 6
Manheim Township Middle School

4 a Friend

When it seems like storms come your way strong
Know good is there to make you carry on
If you feel like you can no longer carry on
I'm always here through right or wrong
Needing praise from all who you know
The prayers of your friend grow and grow
Sometimes for you at night I cry
We need not wonder why
But when my life is made right and straight
For us both our joy I'll make great.

Kristen Risko, Grade 6
Moss Side Middle School

Hockey

I skate down the ice carrying the puck,
I look at my opponent who looks as strong as a buck.
I stickhandle to the side,
I glide towards the goal.
Aiming to shoot,
I look for a hole.
I pass the puck to the defense,
The play grows tense.
He shoots the puck across the ice,
It slicks into the net.
The buzzer is sounding,
With my heart still pounding.
We win!

Paul Cornely, Grade 6
Carson Middle School

Hot Chocolate

The warm summer breeze is hot chocolate steam.
It blows and makes the day warm.
Until it steams away.
And the summer days turn to winter.

As ice cubes cool the day.
Summer's gone away.
And we sled ride and play.
In the cold winter day.

Nathan Summerville, Grade 6
Freedom Area Middle School

My Uncle in Iraq

I pray for my uncle before my dreams,
He's a brave soldier in the Marines.

He works hard to investigate;
Examines the evidence before it's too late.

He's patriotic and wanted to do his part,
Lucky for him he's very smart.

He's a brave uncle, husband, soldier, and son,
He will be home once his job is done.

He works all day long in the hot desert heat,
He never knows who he might meet.

His wife is at home waiting for him to get back,
When he's done serving his country in the war in Iraq.

Lindsay Whipple, Grade 6
H Austin Snyder Elementary School

The Lonely Road

Have you ever seen that lonely, lonely road.
"I have a dream," he said as he trod.
And, oh, how that message would grow,
for him, and him only the words would come,
yes, they would flow,
they soon defeated the foe.
Many would stop to take a break,
to not continue would be their fate.
Some started off at too late an age,
they never reached the end, it was too late.
I'll tell you,
his words saved more than a few.
The end was reached,
the traffic had been breached,
with glee some screeched.
Equality came in quantity that marvelous day.
The road is now gone
so sing a song.
Segregation is gone,
it left with that lonely, lonely, road.

Kaitlin Rizzo, Grade 6
St John Holy Rosary Eastside Catholic School

Volcano
Fiery, scary,
Erupting, burning, destroying
Lava bursts everywhere.
Monster
Bobby Potts, Grade 5
Immaculate Conception School

Puppy
Puppy
Small, barks
Licking, fun, energetic
Puppies have small barks
Puppy

Dog
Loud, barks
Plays, fun, catches
Dogs are very playful
Dog

Mutts
Mixed, energetic
Playful, fast, fun
Mutts are very furry
Mutts
Rachel Cotton, Grade 4
Indian Lane Elementary School

Rain Dance
Like diamonds slipping from Heaven,
the rain falls from the sky.
I stare out of my windowpane,
Nothing in sight is dry.

The trees are umbrellas for the birds,
The sun is hidden away.
Flowers drink up the dripping drops,
As butterflies do ballet.

One lonely ladybug climbs the glass,
I watch it flutter by.
A beautiful day, I tell myself,
Pure nature's lullaby.
Haley Myers, Grade 5
Bermudian Springs Middle School

Summer/Winter
Summer
sunny, hot
running, jogging, jumping
fans, t-shirts, snowflakes, snowman
sleeting sledding, sliding
cold, icy
Winter
Nathaniel Holmes, Grade 5
East Union Intermediate Center

Sparrow Secrets
In the sky is a sparrow flying high high high
Full of pride is the sparrow no one ever knew quite why
Then one day said the sparrow, "I've a secret I can't tell!"
"Tell us please!" cried the sparrows as they wondered what it was
"Not at all!" said the sparrow secret keeper that he was
Suddenly flew the sparrow far from all the questioning
And today still the sparrow flies high in the sky
Like a cloud is the sparrow flying unpredictably
And though lonesome the sparrow does not think of misery
Yet instead does the sparrow sing a song of being free?
Like a prisoner set loose does he fly the skies with glee?
No one ever knows the sparrow's thoughts as he soars the skies
Going whoosh! And swoosh! And up and away
Only pausing at the end of the day
In the quiet, he sleeps and dreams of things unimaginably happy and kind
He misses his friends but cannot return to all their questioning
He does not remember that this whole thing started with one sparrow secret
Teresa Donnellan, Grade 6
Mount Nittany Middle School

Bad
I'm talking mean!
I'm talking evil!
I'm talking lousy, rotten, careless!
I'm talking poor, miserable, wretched, unacceptable!
I'm talking horrible, not good, naughty, sinful, spoiled!
I'm talking disobedient, unpleasant, disagreeable, unfavorable, yucky, hurtful!
I'm talking misbehaved, rude, terrible, shame, unfortunate, wrong, unspeakable!
I'm talking bad!
Chelsea Mielke, Grade 6
Grasse Elementary School

Winter
Winter
Best season of all
Adults keep warm inside the house
Children frolic in the snow
Throwing snowballs…SMACK!
On the cheek and then the ground
One more is thrown…BAM!
On the back, into the fort
Winter, fun and harsh too
Some days snow will fall 'til the sun goes down
Making you shovel 'til dark
As if you were its slave and picking up what it had dropped
Though when you sit to enjoy it
The snow looks like a field of sparkling diamonds
Winter is a wonderful season
Between shoveling driveways and throwing snowballs in your sibling's face
Winter doesn't last forever
Soon leads to the warm blazing sun,
The first dandelion popping from the ground
Goodbye winter
Hello spring
Rachel Woll, Grade 6
Mount Nittany Middle School

Dogs

Like fuzzy pillows
Lovable, playful, cute
Always by your side when you're lonely
Munch, munch, munching everything in sight
Bow wow woof woof grrrrr
Faster than a shooting star in space
Running in circles catching its tail
Licking my face
Chasing cats and rabbits
Sniffing, snooping, snoozing all day
Hate the sound of thunder
Friendly to everyone
Rolling around in the grass
Caring, loving, trustworthy
Dogs

Amelia Cawley, Grade 6
Mount Nittany Middle School

A Cold and Icy Night

Ice
Shiny blocks
Shining on the ground
A bright block of ice outside
Cold

Zoe Frey, Grade 4
Cathedral School of St Catharine of Siena

Friendship Sandwich

Friendship is like a sandwich
The golden bread is your parents
that encourage you to make friends,
The cheese is
you and your friends having fun for years
And the juicy meat is
the memories
that you have your friends make and will never
ever
ever
forget

Taylor Farese, Grade 6
Hillcrest Elementary School

Spring

The aroma of daffodils in the air
a gentle breeze
like a rabbit's soft fur
life blooming all around
children laughing
birds chirping
the sweetness of honey
vivid colors everywhere
purple violets, pink tulips, yellow dandelions
a wonderful time of year
when the world awakens

Joseph Dayrit, Grade 4
Benchmark School

I Like Lots of Things

I like swimming and puppies.
I like snakes and tarantulas.
But I do not like tomatoes.
I like pickles and mushroom pizza.
I like Pasta! Pasta! Pasta! And frogs and flamingos.
But I looooove my family.

Bryanna Ford, Grade 4
Maureen M Welch Elementary School

Changing Seasons

In fall I hate to see,
the once-so-green leaves fall off every tree.
Because then winter will come
and the trees will be so leafless, dull, and dumb.
Snow will cover the ground
and the birds who once sang won't ever make a sound.
Then I'll strive
for the day spring will arrive.
When the animals come out
and wander about,
then warm weather will be here
and I can tell summer is near.
Sometimes the seasons change so fast,
That I forget the fun that has passed!

Michelle Fernando, Grade 6
Sacred Heart of Jesus School

Doggy

Dogs are really sweet.
They love to have a treat.
When they're puppies they like to snuggle
And play in puddles.

Amanda Smith, Grade 5
State Street Elementary School

Sunny Day

A flower smiles at the bee,
A butterfly blinks at you and me.
A cloud casts a shadow on the ground,
As the bright sun shines all around.

The breeze whispers a lullaby,
A bird sings along up in the sky.
The cloud has floated far away,
Now it's a peaceful, sunny day!

Alexis Tate, Grade 5
Bermudian Springs Middle School

The River's Current

The river's current was running fast!
Swift like pouring milk in a glass!

As fast as a fish can swim downstream!
Fast as the wind blows leaves from a tree!

Noah Noel, Grade 4
Northern Cambria Catholic School

Fear

Fear is pitch black
It tastes like a sour grape
It smells like a garbage dump
It's hard as a rock
It sounds like, BOO!
Fear is as scary as a ghost.
Stephen Doutt, Grade 4
Fairview Elementary School

A Baby in a Manger

Oh precious little, pure, baby boy,
The night You were born was full of joy,
On that holy day You had no toy,
A song was played by a drummer boy,
There is no evil You can't destroy.
Kelsey Brown, Grade 5
Verna Montessori School

Friendship

Great
Fun
Trust
Faith

Laughter
Gladness
Secrets
Sharing

Sleep overs
Movie nights
Funny jokes
That's friendship
Julia Bamburg, Grade 4
Fishing Creek Elementary School

Puddle

There was a puddle on the ground.
I jumped in the puddle.
Splash! Splish! Squash!
My books got all dirty
like a baby eating ice cream and cake.
Cameron Goins, Grade 4
Easterly Parkway Elementary School

Springtime

Springtime is almost here
Her beauty makes people come near
She gives life to the trees and the flowers
She has wonderful powers
She sprinkles rain upon the ground
She makes you want to look all around
Spring is like fresh air on my face
Springtime is almost here
Kimberly Knepp, Grade 5
Easterly Parkway Elementary School

Ocean Waves

Astonishing glare.
Refreshing ocean breezes.
Peaceful, ocean splash.
Amanda Filipovits, Grade 5
Bushkill Elementary School

Earth

Clean
Sun
Hard
Fun

Lousy
Depressing
Tricky
Fair

Dangerous
Opportunities
Exciting
Living
Taylor Thompson, Grade 4
Fishing Creek Elementary School

Trees

Trees are green and brown,
They have roots stuck in the ground.
That's why they don't move.
Hannah Baggott, Grade 4
Sacred Heart School

A Slice of Cheese

For a Valentine I got a slice of cheese
It smelled so very bad
It made me want to sneeze
This made me very mad
Brandon Pash, Grade 4
West Branch Area Elementary School

Summer

Summer is my favorite season
Maybe you can guess the reason.
Summer is the time for swimming.
Summer is the time for winning.

Summer has a lot of surprises.
Summer is when the sun rises.
The sun is many different sizes.

Summertime is the time to run
Summer is loads of fun!
Summertime you get no rest
Summertime is the best.
Paige Gasiorowski, Grade 5
Concord Elementary School

Peaceful Storm

Welcome, welcome clouds.
With your rain, to sprinkle me.
Soft drops within me.
Kyle Schmitt, Grade 4
Center Elementary School

West Chester Pike

On West Chester Pike,
A kid was riding his bike,
He said "Hey, I'm wild"
But I just looked at him and smiled,
His so-called bike was a trike.
Julian DeGideo, Grade 6
Haverford Middle School

Spring

When spring comes around
Flowers are often found
While weather becomes warm
Nature starts to form
Animals run wild
A bunch of people smiled
When a garden is grown
The leaves do not need to be blown
I like spring very much
I also like that the leaves don't crunch
Ian Olewine, Grade 6
Moravian Academy Middle School

I Wasn't Lucky

I woke up one morning
And I looked at the clock
Screaming and Yelling
It was nine o'clock!

I forgot to shower
And to brush my hair
My socks were two different colors
But I didn't care

My daddy was laughing at me
So was my sister
Holding a cup of hot tea
My mommy let out a slight laughter

I ran at full speed to school
But no one was there
I looked like an angry bull
All I could do was stare

It was warm and sunny
Everything was delightful and gay
But I guess I wasn't lucky
Because I realized it was Saturday
Kue Eun Park, Grade 6
Sacred Heart Elementary School

Broadway

In the world today you have to have smarts
Especially if you're into performing arts
Acting is so hard to do,
You have to be good at singing too
Dancing is also a building block
There are some musicals that have rock
My favorite musicals are rock ballets,
but who knows, it could be a phase
I love going to see the shows,
Maybe I'll be in them someday, who knows?
From Annie to the Phantom
to Sweet Charity in Scranton
I love them all the same,
hopefully those Broadway lights will say my name.

Laura Victorelli, Grade 6
West Allegheny Middle School

Reading

R eading is fun for everyone.
E veryone is welcome to jump in and read.
A t the library when you walk in you're lost in books.
D arn fun to read don't you think.
I n you go, into the book.
N othing can help you when you are gone.
G oing, going, going, gone never coming back.

Paige Smith, Grade 6
H Austin Snyder Elementary School

Life Goes On...

Bleeding in my sorrow.
Drowning in my pain.
Looking for the answers is just
causing me more pain.
Anger getting stronger,
Envy growing big,
love just isn't there no more.
My heart needs no sewing
there isn't any hope.
Life just isn't good for me or I'm no good for life.
Burning now it can't be stopped.
I'm gone but the world hasn't stopped.
Life goes on and I keep bleeding
on this cold hard ground.

Julianna Rattenni, Grade 6
West Allegheny Middle School

John Elway

John Elway
Amazing, athletic
Passing, running, winning
Super Bowl ring, MVP trophy, nickname, company
Shooting, dunking, scoring
Skillful, legendary
Michael Jordan

Alex Aharonian, Grade 4
Brecknock Elementary School

Ode to My Dog

My dog Ali's fur is white like fizz on coffee.
She is small like a lion cub.
She's shaggy like a porcupine
And scrappy like a mobster.
Ali loves dog bones, she chews them to the core.
She's the world's barking champ.
She can wag her tail at supersonic speeds.
When you pet her she will trap you with her eyes.
Ali riffles through snow as easily as a plow.
She creates a tornado when she chases her tail.
She jumps with grace like a rich kangaroo.
She cuddles up for hours like a sleeping bear.
Ali always attacks the bows in her hair.
She can be fooled into fetching a bone that isn't there.
In her sleep she kicks like a karate master.
She opens her mouth and it looks like a smile.

Luke Masa, Grade 6
St Sebastian Elementary School

What Would the World Be...?

What would the world be with you still here with me?
Happier and better and like it used to be?
All of those memories we shared,
All of the things we bared,
All I want to be is with you,
All I want to see is your bright smiling face gleaming at me,
Why you are gone I don't understand,
I guess it wasn't part of your plan,
Now I have to let go of someone who I love,
And someone I used to know...
But when I wake up in the morning,
What do I see?
I see the dark world,
That you left behind for me,
I wish you could be here to brighten up my heart,
And make my worries come free,
What would the world be with you still here with me?

Emilee Brought, Grade 6
Strodes Mills Middle School

Love Song

I'll say I love you when you do the simplest things.
Like hug me or kiss me or smile when I sing.
But I want to be saying it all day long.
Singing it out like a short little song.
Then we'll smile and laugh
And you'll sing it too,
For saying I love you
Is a song that goes through.
Through the mind,
Through the soul,
Three words that pierce the heart.
Three powerful words.
In which a strong bond can start.

Hannah McGrath, Grade 6
Groveland Elementary School

General to Hippie
General
loud, strict
demanding, yelling, marching
stoic, serious, wild, colorful
dancing, loving, protesting
joyous, long hair
Hippie
Tyler Levers, Grade 5
Claysville Elementary School

Fire to Ice
Fire
Hot, flames
Burning, searing, scorching
Blaze, inferno, arctic, frigid
Freezing, chilling, nipping
Polar, icy
Ice
Jessica Bahr, Grade 5
Claysville Elementary School

Winter
Speeding sleds
Greens and reds

Colorful lights
Lots of sights

Fire blazing
Children dazing

Snowy weathers
Get togethers

Snow is falling
Winter is calling

Christmas trees
Furnace fees

Winter!
Alexandra Wheeler, Grade 4
McQuistion Elementary School

Breeze
The cool breeze runs through my hair
as I walk across the beach.
Also, I find sea shells on the shore,
which looks so rare.
I lay down on the warm white sand
as I hear people sounding like a band.
Spring has come
this time no one is to blame.
Ashley Niznik, Grade 6
West Allegheny Middle School

Freedom
Freedom to me means,
To not be ruled by another country,
Or be ruled by a king,
This is what it means, to not be free.

Freedom to me means,
Able to say what you think,
Able to do what you want
Or go to the roller rink.

Freedom to me means,
Being able to leave the state or city,
Maybe have your own pet like a dog,
Or even a cute kitty.

Freedom to me means,
Having a capital and even a flag,
Able to write what you want,
Having a king can be such a drag.

Freedom to me means,
Making your own choices,
Having your own religion,
At mass rejoice with your voices!
Riley Dillon, Grade 4
St Alexis School

Pilgrims/Indians
Pilgrims
Hunting, sailing, sharing
Ships, guns, nature, justice
Defending, repopulating, creating
Kind, sharing
Indian
Nic Carmello, Grade 5
East Stroudsburg Elementary School

Afraid
A lone in the dark
F rightening
R eady to scream
A scary night
I hope to see a light
D oomed
Victoria McClellan, Grade 6
St Maria Goretti School

Ocean
Ocean
Enormous, choppy
Waving, splashing, glistening
Deep, sandy, rocky, shallow
Fast, calm
Stream
Kurt Barthel, Grade 5
Penn-Kidder Campus

Butterfinger
Crunchy
Butterfinger
Smells like having a dream
When I am done, I always feel
Real good.
Reece McGovern, Grade 4
Stackpole Elementary School

Colors of My World
Green is cool grass in the spring
Yellow makes you want to sing.

White like a perfect rose
Red like a stuffy nose.

Orange like an autumn leaf
Brown like hot roast beef.

Black like a starless night
Blue like the birds in flight.

Pink as the sun goes down
Gray makes me want to frown.

What colors are in your world?
Nina DelPrato, Grade 6
Moss Side Middle School

Steelers
S teal the ball
T eam
E xtraordinary
E xcitement
L osing is not an option
E xtra good
R eady to go
S uper football team
Seth Beerbower, Grade 4
East End Elementary School

My Soul
In the day my soul is inside of me
In the night it breaks free
It soars in the night sky
Through the open trees
It gathers with the magic
Deep within the wood
And as I wake with the morning dawn
It flies back to me
My soul is so important
My soul helps me to see
The world of imagination
My soul inside of me.
Alexandra Fay Dunn, Grade 6
Chambersburg Area Middle School

Angel/Devil
Angel
peaceful, bright
charming, helping, praying
compassionate, friendly, vile, inconsiderate
killing, threatening, intimidating
bold, selfish
Devil

Nicholas Roberts, Grade 5
Claysville Elementary School

Cool Colors
Orange is like big round pumpkins in a patch.
Orange is like the bright fire on a match.
Orange is like my old skateboard rolling down the hill.
Orange is like big fat clown fish gills.

White is like doves in the sky.
White is like my friend's dog trying to bite my eye.
White is like paper made from a tree.
White is like clouds putting shade on me.

Black is like a spooky night sky.
Black is like my sunglasses protecting my eyes.
Black is like my big round bow tie.
Black is like my sweater hanging to dry.

Zach May, Grade 6
Immaculate Conception School

Sisters
Some people say we look the same
One thing is for sure we both want fortune and fame

Since we are sisters it is normal for us to fight
But trust me neither of us bite

We both like animals especially monkeys
But one of our least favorite animals is the donkey

My sister and I are a team
When we are together we shine like sunbeams

Anastasia Weckerly, Grade 6
St Hilary of Poitiers School

Watermelon
Watermelon smells like sweet summer.
You can only eat it in the summer what a bummer.
Watermelon is so crunchy.
It goes so well with your lunchy.
If you bite it the juice will squirt out.
It will make you run about.
Watermelon is so yummy.
It tastes good in your tummy.
I wish it was only a dime.
So I could eat it all the time.

Courtney Kitchen, Grade 4
Watsontown Elementary School

Orange
Orange tastes like a juicy, plump orange,
a sweet, sugary tangerine,
and a crunchy, fresh, wet carrot.

Orange smells like a sweet rose,
the cool, autumn air,
and a crunchy pile of leaves in the fall.

Orange sounds like a stream by a tropical island,
the crackling of a fire,
and the "boing" of a basketball.

Orange feels like a soft piece of cheese,
the little bumps on a basketball,
and a hot, crunchy taco.

Orange looks like the sun on a cool autumn day,
a jack-o'-lantern with glowing eyes,
and the sunset at the end of a brisk day.

Brett Biscoll, Grade 4
Indian Lane Elementary School

Winter Solstice
The sky glows through
the early morning
A black bird sits
at the very top of a weak branch
Stillness travels into the distance of the sky
The pale skies glow over trees
making dark shadows
on the cold concrete
Dead, crinkled leaves roll around,
tumbling over each other
on the ground of the deserted parking lot
Birds fly west across the gray sky
into the distance
until they are lost in the sea of clouds
and no one can see them anymore

Alexa Wall, Grade 4
Lincoln Elementary School

The Sneaky Sea Critter
In the seaweed I hide
Where I patiently stand
Waiting to use my claws just like hands
I may strike unexpectedly
Which will make you try to flee
But you can't escape me
You may become my breakfast, lunch, or dinner
Or even a little late night snack
Due to my sneaky attack
Oh yes, I am a sneaky crab
And that is what I do
Until I am hunted by you!

Tyler Ivey, Grade 4
General Nash Elementary School

Talking to the Flag

The flag is a person,
waving so high.
It talks but we just don't hear.
It is very proud of itself.
It is important to all people.
It stands for our country.
It is that great.

Kayla Hickey, Grade 6
Freedom Area Middle School

No Gifts for Christmas

There once was a little boy
Who really loved his special toys,
And every single Christmas night
He would dream with all his might
Of toys, presents, and Christmas trees
And how he never ate his peas.
But when he woke up Christmas morn,
He cried with tears and shameful scorn,
For there were no Christmas gifts
Because of his selfishness.
Then he sat down in his chair
With anger and an evil glare.
His parents said, "Eat your peas!"
Then the boy got on his knees
And begged them, "Take the peas away!"
But the boy ate peas that day.
Discipline had served him right
Because the next Christmas night
The boy was changed without a doubt
For he would never scream or pout.

Molly Duffy, Grade 6
Portersville Christian School

Love

Love is so special.
When it is here, you will know.
It can't be beaten.

Nicole Hancher, Grade 6
Allison Park Elementary School

Season's Stories

The leaves
On the trees
Tell me things I didn't know.
The rain
Will explain
Things that made no sense to me.
The sun
Is the one
To ask about history.
The snow
Has to know
The things that the seasons say to me.

Yelena Gulkewicz, Grade 5
Schnecksville School

The Day My Heart Was Torn

Every day I think about the day my heart was torn
Every night I sit and cry myself asleep
But in my dreams I see myself laughing and smiling with him
Then I wake up with a smile because I know he is happy at the place he is in
He is standing at the pearly gates waiting for the family and I
Waiting with the others in my family who have died
And when we are all together again we will laugh, smile, and cry
When we are all together again, in that great place above the sky

Erica Peters, Grade 6
Strodes Mills Middle School

Life

Life is like a roller coaster
going up and down, side to side,
and sometimes just straight like an arrow.
With these motions come emotions,
in someone's life they will feel every emotion known to man.
Lives are defined by the people who are living them!
People's lives change every day because of the smallest things.
A life can be taken in a heartbeat,
what will define you when you die?
What will define you is how you lived,
what kind of impact you made.
Many people are able to make an impact
those people are the great men and women you read about in books.
Every day you should try to live your life to the fullest
because you don't know if it could be your last.
Is there life after death for all who lay to never get up?

Sinfree V. Makoni, Grade 6
Mount Nittany Middle School

The Steelers

S is for the Steelers who won the Super bowl!
T hanks to the Steelers, Pittsburgh is #1!
E very winter the Steelers try to be the best that they can be with team work!
E specially when Bill Cowher coaches the team.
L is for liking the Steelers.
E ach Steeler plays hard.
R oethlisberger is a good quarterback
S is for all the screaming and cheering when the Steelers won the "big" game.

Chelsea Kowalski, Grade 4
Immaculate Conception School

Anger

It rages like a forest fire about to destroy.
It erupts like a volcano on an island.
People say it's like a lion about to pounce.
To feel it is like a clock ticking loudly in your head.
It's like smoke suffocating head to toe.
To know it's there is like you're carrying the world on your shoulders.
It's like a bomb detonated in the back of your head.
It's like lightning about to strike.
It's like a fire siren about to sound.
Anger is like you can never be found.

Casey Provident, Grade 6
Neil Armstrong Middle School

April!

A pril showers is a poem
P retty flowers blossom and bloom
R ain helps grow them
I nstead of you
L oving and caring for the flowers in bloom.

Jon Sabec, Grade 5
Wharton Elementary School

Coasters

Millennium Force, Top Thrill Dragster, Demon Drop
I want to ride them all day long and never stop.

Upside down, round and round
My feet will never touch the ground.

Coasters are so much fun
I'll ride them until the day is done!

Rachel Peffer, Grade 5
Cheswick Christian Academy

Soccer

S stands for how sensational your team played
    when you had a shutout
O stands for how outstanding you did
    when you made the winning goal
C stands for the crowd
    that watches you and cheers you on
C stands for the cheerfulness
    when your team mate scores a goal
    and gives them a hi-five
E stands for the excitement inside you
    when you score plenty of goals
R stands for the referee
    that controls the game
    and sometimes makes stinky calls

Marissa Dykta, Grade 6
West Allegheny Middle School

Water

Glistens in the sun like a shiny silver dollar,
Cools me on a hot summer day,
Reflects anything in its path.

A perfect place for a picnic for relaxation,
A nesting ground for children in search of swimming,
A perfect place for ice-skating in the wintertime.

Quenches my thirst after a long day of hard work,
Used in many cooking recipes.

The water in the waves flew in on airplane jets,
It feels like tiny needles poking me,
Gives me chills down the spine when I touch it,
Relaxes me after a hard day of thinking at school.

Riley Weber, Grade 6
Our Lady of Mount Carmel School

Sister

My sister is a hissing cat,
Whose hands are paws grabbing out to hit.
Nails are claws stretching out to cut.
Her eyes may see for miles,
Or through the darkness of the sky.
For every hiss there's a word,
That she has to tell,
In a loud screaming yell.

Danielle Lindsay, Grade 6
Freedom Area Middle School

Independence

The spirit of independence is deeply planted,
But should not be taken for granted.
Independence is a feeling so free,
It's the feeling that's inside you and me.

Independence is what made our nation,
It turned our country into a wonderful creation.
Independence makes us want to shout,
We are happy and there is no doubt.

It gives us the freedom to do and to say,
And helps us appreciate every day.
The freedom to write ideas without fear,
And practice our faiths that we hold so dear.

The freedom to vote if we choose,
So we never fail to lose.
Independence lets us live as we please,
And lets us feel at ease.

Our independence, we should always protect,
Against the people who will object.
I love my independence and our great nation,
May God always bless America until the end of creation.

Kelly O'Keeffe, Grade 4
St Alexis School

A Holiday

I love wintertime,
Because I hear the bells chime,
That mark the day that He was born alive,
That day number is twenty-five.

The season of caring,
Is too much to be bearing,
You think you'd want to miss it all,
The season that is after fall.

It happens only once each season,
If you disagree
I want a reason,
After you drink your cup of coffee.

Matthew Krachanko, Grade 5
Allegheny-Hyde Park Elementary School

Ode to Gymnastics
There is this cool sport called Gymnastics.
There are all these cool things that you do.

The Balance Beam is as long as a row of 8 decks. The Floor is as bouncy as a Trampoline.
The Bars are as high as the Eiffel Tower. The Vault can be as high as a door or lower. I have been doing it since I was 4 years old. I have never wanted to quit. I have had a couple of injuries.

My coaches are as nice as teachers at school. I have made it to Nationals twice in Colorado. I have so much fun when I'm doing it. My friends and family support me and they understand if I have a bad meet.

Arianna Gesford, Grade 6
Hershey Middle School

Freedom Rocks
I once thought that freedom was not important,
Until I realized what the world would be like without it.
I began to remember why we fought for freedom,
If we would have lost, you and I could be slaves right now.

If it wasn't for old Abe Lincoln,
We would be the ones having the slaves.
I salute all the people who stood up for what they thought was right,
Because in my mind, they are the greatest patriots ever.

Our country's history includes many freedom fighters,
They are the people I admire most of all.
Like Martin Luther King Jr., he was a believer,
And if I were alive when he was, I would have been with him.

George Washington, why he led us to victory in the war,
I think we should give him the respect he needs and deserves.
Thomas Jefferson played a huge role in our freedom
He wrote the Declaration of Independence and made a strong point.

I especially give thanks to all the soldiers that went through that cold winter at Valley Forge
And fought the bloodiest battle ever in Gettysburg.
All of these patriots played a big part in this fight for freedom,
And they are all brave men and women.

Patrick Fuscaldo, Grade 4
St Alexis School

Headache
It was coming again, the pain in my head going down again. I want it somewhere else it stays there in my head, burning in my head, pounding driving me crazy. I say to myself, "When will it end. I cannot bear the pain." I shout in my head awaiting an answer because I cannot speak aloud what is going through my head again. It burns it burns why is it here again.

Jesse Buck, Grade 6
H Austin Snyder Elementary School

The Kite
The reddish kite, blowing in the wind, will catch your eyes for the first time,
Only waiting for you to open the door and let it out to rise and fly.

It will be looking down on your smiling face, glad to be in the air and even sometimes looking up at the daylight sky.

At that moment, you hear a snap and your kite wanders off never to be seen again.

Matthew Jacobson, Grade 4
Lower Gwynedd Elementary School

Frederick Douglass

Frederick Douglass was born a slave
He was probably very brave
He was an abolitionist and believed in equality
He gave speeches about freedom and morality
Douglass continued to give awesome speech
And he got to where he wanted to reach
He was only 23 years old
But he accomplished his goal
He was very nervous and stressed
But in the end he got a lot of rest

Reginald Marchaman, Grade 6
Christopher Columbus Charter School - South

Freedom

Be free like an eagle and fly to the sky
Fly without care of gravity's pull
Spin, loop, roll, dive, and race passing planes
You have wings more beautiful than a sunset in July
Wings made of over one hundred feathers
King of all other birds — a respected emperor
Walking down a red carpet, ahhhhhh goes the crowd
Flying freestyle farther into the forest
To other birds you're like a million dollars to a man in need
Do not forget that you're the symbol of the USA
The USA, the greatest country in the world
Taking off two hundred to three hundred feet
Zoooom, whoooosh you go
Now you are unstoppable — you are untouchable
United States of America — the land of the free.

Steven Seitz, Grade 6
Mount Nittany Middle School

Nature Walk

If you take a walk in the woods,
you will probably see a gigantic hive of bees
and, many, many trees.

You may see squirrels at play,
but after the day,
the raccoons are out,
walking about,
the dry leaves crinkling and the owls singing.

When another day starts,
the birds are chirping in the most beautiful way,
and the night animals start fading away.
All of the animals are starting a new day.

Now you see little ants scavenging,
and if two colonies meet,
they will start battling,
So the cycle repeats
again and again,
until the day the repeating will end.

Nick Albright, Grade 4
Washington Heights Elementary School

The Color Red

Red is the laces on a baseball,
The color you feel when you hear a bad call.

The color of a bright juicy apple,
The delicious red of Raspberry Snapple.

The color of the octagon that says stop,
The color of blood that goes drop, drop, drop.

Red is the tower made of bricks,
Your throat when you put on the medicine Vicks.®

The color of Clifford, the big red dog,
The color of your face when you take a jog.

Red is the color of a great big fire,
Red is a color, but also a desire.

Ryan Walter, Grade 5
Maureen M Welch Elementary School

Evil Cat

There was an evil cat
who then sat on my lap
She dug her claws right into my thigh
so I let out a big cry.

I think her horns stick out of her fading halo
as she pounces on you while you're sleeping
She also pushes your head up
it gets really annoying.

This cat is as devilish as the devil
this cat is so rude and not gentle
She loves to bite and bite
this evil cat of mine.

Megan Gochenauer, Grade 5
Lincoln Elementary School

Summertime

Summer is a time where flowers smell nice.
People get married and guests throw rice.
Swimming is an activity that I like to do
The days are so warm and the sky is blue.

Jenna Metzger, Grade 6
West Allegheny Middle School

Angel/Devil

Angel
bringing peace, compassion
spreading the word, caring, blessing, watching over us
nonviolent, flying, horns, red and black
cursing, stealing people's hearts, lying
encased in darkness
Devil

Mikayla Lunardini, Grade 5
Claysville Elementary School

Math Time
Math
Learning, fun
Teaching, reading, answering
Math is fun to me.
Arithmetic.
John Cantolina, Grade 4
West Branch Area Elementary School

Corey
There once was a boy named Corey.
All he wanted was a girl named Lorrie.
He asked her on a date.
But Lorrie was late.
She like a new boy named Morey.
Lorrie Middleton, Grade 5
Rhawnhurst School

Ancient Sequoia Tree
I am an ancient Sequoia Tree,
Though very old I still stand,
I can see beyond the forest,
I have lots of friends too,
I hear the life in the forest,
And feel the soil against my roots,
I talk to the woodpecker,
And listen to the squirrel.
Madeline Kubica, Grade 6
Freedom Area Middle School

Sadness
Sadness seems blue
I see sad pictures in my mind
I hear small whispers in my ear
I smell the thick air
I touch the picture of the one that's gone
I taste tears falling from my eyes
Brenna Haney, Grade 4
West Bradford Elementary School

Time
Time is timeless
Time never ends
Time just keeps going
And going
And going
And going
Time can be soft
Or
Time can be hard
Time can be fastidious as a grass
Sometimes time is fast
Sometimes time moves as fast as a snail
When you think it is over
It isn't
Naomi Rockefeller, Grade 6
Hillcrest Elementary School

Christmastime
Every year we put up a tree
Which we decorate with much glee.
On Christmas day our Savior was born
To heal our hearts, sinful or torn.
Children caroling merrily,
Parents wrapping presents lovingly.
Christmas is a gift of love from above
To share with everyone you love.
Megan Hoover, Grade 6
Portersville Christian School

Taylor
T rustful
A stonishing
Y outhful
L oyal
O riginal
R are
Taylor Cavalovitch, Grade 6
West Allegheny Middle School

Music
M ythical when heard.
U ps your anty.
S ings to your soul.
I t has many varieties.
C omes in sequence.
Jacob Ciaccia, Grade 5
Wharton Elementary School

Gina the Mouse
Gina the mouse
Lived in a house.

She ate cheese
But never squeaked please.

The owner Jean
Was very mean.

He captured the mouse
In a smaller house.
Bianca Leonard, Grade 4
South Park Elementary Center

Basketball and Football
Basketball
Round, orange
Dribbling, shooting, dunking
Court, backyard, field, street
Throwing, catching, running
Brown, lemon-shaped
Football
Jordan Joseph, Grade 5
Our Lady of Grace Elementary School

Kentucky Lady
There was a young lady from Kentucky,
Who was happy and very lucky,
When she ran out of luck,
She fell in love with a guy named Chuck,
She had to go back to Kentucky unlucky.
Christina Beagle, Grade 6
Freedom Area Middle School

Trying My Best!
A m good at football and
T ry to do my best.
H yperactive doing sports and
L istening to my teammates.
E ating before the game, not good
T ruly scoring.
I nteracting with my coach and
C ompeting to win.
Garrett Mohrbacher, Grade 6
Freedom Area Middle School

Hot Fries
Crunchy, munchy, burning hot
So good, so hot, so be ready
Yummy and tasty
All you'll hear your taste buds say is
"Yum, yum, tasty tasty
WE WANT MORE!"
Devon Shaw, Grade 4
Manoa Elementary School

I'm Thankful For
Pie, pudding, cupcake, and cake
Steering wheel, pedal, radio, and brake

Shade, switch, light bulb, and lamp
Tent, flashlight, sleeping bag, and camp

Bathtub, soap, conditioner, and shower
House, building, skyscraper, and tower
Amanda Forte, Grade 6
Locust Grove Mennonite School

Joy
Joy is sweet
It is even good enough to eat
Joy is good
It is even in your neighborhood
Joy is in everyone
Even mom, dad, daughter and son
Joy is something that cannot be bought
It is something that can't be taught
Joy is something that comes from inside
It is something to share
I know because I have tried.
Jessica Wittig, Grade 5
Brecknock Elementary School

Spring Planting
Spring planting is sprouting and blooming.
People growing plants.
Spring plants that smell good.
Pretty petals, colorful and smooth.
Spring planting needs water and sun to grow.
Spring planting.

Kaitlyn O'Doherty, Grade 4
Avon Grove Intermediate School

State Things
Our state animal is the White-tailed Deer
What's that in the woods I hear?
Our state insect is the firefly
That's what glows in the night sky
The Hemlock is our state tree
An evergreen with short dark leaves
Our state fossil (Phacops rana) means frog eyes
It's in a museum where other fossils lie
The Great Dane is our state's 'best friend'
It comes from England like our founder, William Penn
If you happen to fish in a stream with brook trout
You'll most likely pull our state fish out
The Ruffled Grouse is our state bird
It makes a drumming sound, have you heard?
As you drive and see pink and white floral
You will see our state's Mountain Laurel
Our state's locomotive is called 4859
It was made in Pennsylvania, just fine
Pennsylvania is called the Keystone State
Come and visit us; our state's great!

Gabrielle Kosobucki, Grade 4
St Alexis School

A Bright Season
Christ
Messiah
Caring for others
Sent us the Holy Spirit
Peace

Christopher Jakob Santos, Grade 4
Cathedral School of St Catharine of Siena

Nature
Nature helps things to grow,
Just like when we plant a flower.

It grows and grows
Just like people building the Twin Towers.

But sometimes when nature comes,
our plants don't last for long.

People destroy our nature,
like they destroyed the Twin Towers.

Paige Weiland, Grade 4
Northern Cambria Catholic School

Dance
Everybody knows I love to dance.
When I come on stage, I take a chance.
A chance in getting a bronze, silver, or gold.
But my heart for dance will always be bold.

Emily Burton, Grade 5
State Street Elementary School

My Brother
My brother's name is Matthew, he likes to be called Matt.
I think it's kind of weird, so I never call him that.

When he was born, I wasn't there,
Because I was not alive. He will be an heir.

When he was two, I was born.
He was very mad, you'd think he was forlorn.

When he was five, he went to school.
All he did was cry, no one thought he was cool.

Now he's fourteen, he goes to high school now,
I used to think he was weird, but he's kind of cool now.

When he's sixteen, he'll drive me to places like the mall.
If he says no I'll ask my mom, the greatest mom of all.

Andrea Cary, Grade 6
Freedom Area Middle School

The Test on Friday
The capital of South America is Argentina
Right?
The capital of the USA is North America
No
A test is on Friday
I think I'm prepared
Geography is easy with only
38 continents and 17 oceans
How could I go wrong?
No need to study, no need to sweat
Because I just happen to be a teacher's pet.

Leanna Goldman, Grade 5
Falk Laboratory School

Summer Break
At summer break, I always have fun,
There are lots of things to do in the sun.
Vacation time is down the shore,
The beach, the waves, we always want more.
School is over, now I'm fine,
"Hey" that hot-dog it's mine!
Running, skating, and jumping is cool,
I also like to play in the pool.
Summer is almost over, now I'm sad,
Until summer comes next year, then I'll be glad.

Tyler Jones, Grade 5
Hatfield Elementary School

Puppies

Puppies
devilish, curious
running, rolling, sitting
Puppies are nice.
Dogs
Travis Fenush, Grade 4
West Branch Area Elementary School

A Shoe in My Locker

I don't know what to do
Because in my locker is a shoe.
To whom it belongs I have no clue.
Does it belong to you?
Jenessa Young, Grade 6
Freedom Area Middle School

Ducks

Baby yellow ducks,
Splashing in the clear water
The mother close by.
Kari Evans, Grade 6
Locust Grove Mennonite School

Blue

Cherries are red,
Yellow is the sun,
Blue is the ocean,
Filled with lots of fun!

Basketballs are orange,
The grass is green,
Blue Jays are blue,
But none can be seen.

Flowers are pink,
The snow is white,
The sky is blue,
Until it turns night.
Brittany Rebuck, Grade 6
Guth Elementary School

Yellow Fever

Y oung and old with discolored skin,
E veryone is sick, weak, and thin.
L iving in a condemned city,
L ulling everywhere is pity.
O n every door rail is a rag,
W aving through the night like a flag.

F evers are breaking out once more,
E xcept this time it's at every door.
V ast amounts of empty road,
E rily saying, "Leave your home."
R eally, it happened. Yellow Fever.
Asher Jablon, Grade 5
Thomas Fitzwater Elementary School

Happy feet are my feet,

Happy feet are my feet,

Only running,

Wishing I could always be,

Never falling,

Happy feet are my feet,

Happy feet are my feet,

September

Who was there on 9-11 of 2001?
When the first airplane came down on the first tower
Everyone in the building was trying to run.
Everyone lost their power
Who was there on 9-11 of 2001?
How the building came down
Everyone left in tears
But we all know that without a doubt they all left with fear and frowns.
Adam Errett, Grade 6
Freedom Area Middle School

What to Do in Washington, PA

Jump on the trampolines to see who can go the highest
Ride your bikes down the hill to see who can go the fastest
Go hiking in the woods to see new places every time
Ride the quads to see who will get the dizziest doing donuts
Visit the neighbor's house to go swimming
See the new puppy that lives right down the street
Climb the trees to see who can go the highest
When you're in the neighbor's pool, see who can stay under the longest
Wade in the creek behind the woods
Run away from yelling neighbor because of trespassing.
Jessica Lindsay, Grade 5
Claysville Elementary School

Spectacular Lime Green

Lime green is flower petals and apple Jolly Ranchers and feels soft.
Spectacular lime green is the taste of juicy apples.
Watermelons, kiwi, and freshly cut grass smell like lime green.
Spectacular lime green makes me feel wonderful.
Lime Green is the sound of an alarm clock and firecrackers.
Spectacular lime green is an orchard, and amusement park,
and when I go on vacation.
Lime green is going to the mall.
When I have a good dream it is always lime green.
Lime green is a freshly painted room.
Nicole Wolowski, Grade 5
McMurray Elementary School

Happy Feet

Racing down the track.

Never holding back.

Wild and free,

The person hidden deep within me.

Ever free.

Flying through the air,

When I see you there.
Elena Connelly, Grade 6
Southern Lehigh Middle School

The Pennsylvania Sea

Pennsylvania is the place to be,
It is so nice you will feel free.
Museums, forests, and history,
Much more than the deep blue sea.
Places to visit and sights to see,
Pittsburgh's the place where you'll find me.
Erie is a city that's next to a beach,
A short drive there is well within reach.
Pittsburgh is a city that sits on three rivers,
Many of the people are generous givers.
The ride through Altoona takes a lot of nerve,
It's a city that sits on a great big curve.
Along the Delaware River Philadelphia sits above,
It is known as the City of Brotherly Love.
There's much to see, don't sit and wait.
Come and visit this wonderful state.
If you really need to feel alive and free,
Explore the depths of the Pennsylvania Sea.

Kelly O'Keeffe, Grade 4
St Alexis School

Trees

It's a beautiful day out in the woods
Where all the trees are still and tall.
All pretty and colorful in the fall
Until it's time for the leaves to fall.
And when they do the trees will stand, cold and small.
With the snow on top of the trees
Until the beginning begins again.

Denym Winkle, Grade 6
Freedom Area Middle School

My Sister

My sister, Jennifer, is annoying sometimes
Like she trips me, kicks me
And even frames me.

Despite all of that she has many redeeming sides.
One great thing about her is that she can help me
On my homework and ride bikes with me.
In fact, if it weren't for her I wouldn't be here.
She whined and cried because she wanted a brother.
So even if she is annoying I still love her.

George Edward Stoffa Searfoss, Grade 5
East Stroudsburg Elementary School

Niagara Falls

I am in Canada
Millions of people come to me every year.
I have a lot of water flowing out of me.

I am located in Quebec.
I am one of the seven natural wonders of the world.
I am Niagara Falls.

Andrew Verbonitz, Grade 6
Our Mother of Perpetual Help School

Family

Family is the ones you love.
The people you can count on when you need to talk.
Your sisters and brothers.
Your fathers and mothers.
The ones you hate to let go.
The center of your heart.
True happiness throughout your home.
Super-heroes in your time of need.
Funny people to make you laugh.
A dose of love and care.
Family is a special gift from above.

Allyson DiRenzi, Grade 5
Rolling Hills Elementary School

Nontoxic

This bottle of detergent is sure to be safe,
So, I'll pack it up into my suitcase
And drink it on the way.
On the way to where you say?

To a poisonous snake farm to spend the day.
The cobra says nontoxic, so I'll pack the snake up too.
I'll bring it home as a special gift and give the snake to you!
This skull and crossbones bottle, its contents are unknown
So I'll bring it with me also to my very own home.

So there's no invisible toxins creeping up into my head,
None that will badly poison me, or make me drop dead.
Indeed these nontoxic things pose no actual major threat,
No horrible poisons that will make me fuss or even fret

Although I have made quite an unusual discovery
These "nontoxic" things have badly poisoned me.
So next time I see something labeled "Nontoxic,"
I won't take it home because they make me sick!

Liam McInerney, Grade 5
Edgeworth Elementary School

Clouds

Clouds are as soft as the snow.
A meadow is as colorful as a box of crayons.
Winter is a peaceful baby sleeping.
Cereal is a box full of surprises.

Becky Harper, Grade 6
Moss Side Middle School

Emotion

Happiness seems yellow
I see kids singing bon fire songs
I hear the laughter of kids playing
I smell the smoke of the fire
I touch the warm seat near the swing set
I taste the hot steaming marshmallows that were cooked
Over the fire

Anna Curdo, Grade 4
West Bradford Elementary School

Erin

Erin is as helpful as a doctor
Erin is as funny as a comedian
Erin is as smart as a genius
Erin is as fast as a cheetah
Erin is as sweet as a chocolate cake

Lindsey Myers, Grade 5
Newtown Elementary School

Pizza

A triangular head with 6 red eyes
Or is it 8
I don't know
But maybe some are noses
Maybe some are mouths
No one knows
Probably never will
But I call them eyes
The eyes have no pupils
They look like round red circles
It's face is yellow
With some orange spots
The top feels soft
While the bottom is a little harder
It has no bones
And it isn't an animal
It tastes really good too

Sarah Owens, Grade 5
Jenkintown Elementary School

My Car

My car refused to start,
In nineteen sixty-three.
I found an old part,
That contained part of a tree.

So I took it to the shop,
Where they fixed my Chevrolet.
But then they heard a pop,
And said there would be a delay.

So they fixed up my Corvette,
And on that exact same day,
I wrecked and I got upset,
Then I really had to pay.

Brock Flemmens, Grade 5
Bermudian Springs Middle School

Boys

Boys
Nerd, freaky
Running, jumping, hopping
Always sports and TV
Kids.

Amanda D'Ottavio, Grade 4
Avonworth Elementary School

Bees

Bees
Loud buzzing
Flying, stinging, gathering
Black and yellow threat
Summer

Rebecca Fike, Grade 5
Wharton Elementary School

Summer and Spring

summer
warm, sunny
swimming, diving, tossing
rabbits, birds, Easter, fawns
growing, cleaning, gardening
beautiful, cute
spring

Jade Williams, Grade 4
West Branch Area Elementary School

Imagination

If you are fanciful
You have imagination
If you are imaginative
You have creativity
If you wish you were one of these
Think again
Because you already are

Jillian Holmes, Grade 6
Fairfield Private Academic School

Mind

As light as a feather, as strong as a bull.
Strength varies with age and sight.
Controls the bosom in unseen ways.
Cannot smell it, hear it, see it, only
Know it.

Comes from its own kind,
One soft and pure,
But still is so different than any of yore.

Commander of the body,
Leader of the soul,
But still follows another,
Who is great and old.

Sean Palmer, Grade 6
Our Lady of Mount Carmel School

Outer Space

S olar system
P lanets
A liens
C rop circles
E xtreme

McKenna Shockley, Grade 5
Wharton Elementary School

My Vacation

As I lay on the sand,
Watching the sizzling sun.
I feel I am getting a tan,
I can have so much fun.

On this wonderful land,
The sun in the sky burns a ton.
I wish I had a fan,
My vacations is now done.

Katelyn Milhimes, Grade 5
Bermudian Springs Middle School

Christmas

What is Christmas?
A time of joy!
You spend time with your family,
And rip open every toy.

The real meaning of Christmas;
Is the birth of our Savior,
He saved us from sin
Believe me he did us a favor.

The weather is cool,
The presents are nice.
Snow is fun for everyone,
I don't know about the ice.

We get out of school for a while,
It is great to get a break,
But we have to go back,
For our teacher's sake.

Gianna Iaconelli, Grade 6
Holy Spirit School

Loser

Loser
Terrible, unfair
Down, dying, falling
Not fair for losers
Loser

Winner
Awesome, super
Flying, gloating, killing
In your face losers
Winner

Tie
Obnoxious, annoying
Trying, hard, close
No winner or loser
Tie

John George, Grade 4
Indian Lane Elementary School

Freedom

We wanted freedom. A king, no more.
Also free religion but there's more.

We went through war and punishment
to get where we are today.

Many, many problems met along the way:
equality, rights, slaves, and more.

Important speeches, battles, war
helped shape this country year after year.

Some were for freedom, equality,
rights, and many other reasons.

Many things have happened
presidents, laws, discussion all led up to this.

Some of these I mention happened many times,
but we have fixed them almost every time.

Luke Stegeman, Grade 4
St Alexis School

Remembering the Children*

A land of rugged mountains and farmlands,
where homes are made of plaster and mud,
and people play soccer, tennis and volleyball.

You may have been an artist
who would have been famous for your work,
a professional tennis player who got the most important medal,
a farmer who came up with a new crop.

I will be thankful for my life,
as I remember you.

Gina Thomas, Grade 6
Deibler Elementary School
*In remembrance of the children in Ethiopia.

New Schools

When you're at a new school
You get this feeling like you don't know what to do
But let me tell you something
You have to choose what you do

Create a new feeling that's in front of you
If you go to a new school do what you think is best for you
Because what's best for you is always the solution of what to do
This might seem like a lame poem, but it's true

Believe in yourself and only you
Remember that you are always going to be
The new kid but that's okay
Just do what I say, and everything will be okay

Hope Spencer, Grade 6
Sacred Heart Elementary School

Spring's Call

The sky is bright and blue,
Do you get the clue?
Spring is on it's merry way.
I can see the buds of flowers,
It must be the April showers.
The wind is still here,
The sky is clear, and the temperature is rising.
There are still dead leaves, from fall,
I can hear spring's call.
Winter is at its end,
But spring will you be my friend?

Alexa Sangregorio, Grade 5
St Ambrose School

Alone and Forgotten

As I walk down the road I hear many sounds.
But one sound I hear very well!
I hear a baby cry
I look around finally there is the baby
Alone and forgotten

My mind races and my heart thumps
I scoop up the baby and then I realize something
Isn't it true that this baby has parents
So it can't be forgotten, only alone
But wait! I'm here and no one knows what I'm doing.
So aren't we all...
Alone and forgotten

But then I know, I am with this baby
The baby is with me, so neither of us are...
Alone and forgotten

Alison Packard, Grade 5
Mount Jewett Elementary School

Summertime

The joyful thought of no more school for a while,
The thought of heat,
The wonderful thought of summertime,
Students come racing out of school,
Screaming and yelling like a stampede of smiling faces,
At the time it was great,
But now, one far away dream,
No one can believe it passed that fast,
Now it's back to the mind trap,
Though now many smiling faces have faded,
Still some remain,
The reuniting of friends from last school year,
The teachers can't believe it either,
Vacation ends so soon,
Now the rotten kids are back to pester me all day,
Still the teachers smile at all the new kids from fifth grade,
No one can quite figure out how summer passed so fast.

Kelan Albertson, Grade 6
Southern Lehigh Middle School

Life

Life is like a river
It just keeps flowing.
You never know
Where it is going.

You could be doing well in school
Or you're on the wrong path.
If I were you
I'd stick to math.

So play some sports
And have fun with friends.
Because great friendship
Will never end.

Love your family
And mistakes will be few.
You'll be glad
When life is good to you.

Aubrey Lubin, Grade 6
St Valentine Elementary School

Sunrise

Creatures waking up
Peeking over mountain tops
Majestic, soothing

Amanda Petrin, Grade 5
Penn-Kidder Campus

The Seasons

Summertime is cool,
It is the hottest season.
I love summertime!

Spring is hot and cold,
It is fun to play outside.
Spring is very fun!

Fall is beautiful,
The leaves have different colors.
Fall is colorful!

Snow is very fun,
That is why I like winter.
It is very cold.

Melanie Werbos, Grade 4
Sacred Heart School

Ant

Ant
Incredible precious
Crawling eating chasing
A smart little creature
Insect

Alicia DeMuro, Grade 5
Penn-Kidder Campus

Cars

C ool cars
A wesome
R acing
S ome awesome cars

Matt Steelman, Grade 4
Manoa Elementary School

Brothers

Brothers,
Brothers,
Brothers.
Nice brothers,
Nasty brothers.
Poopy, cranky, jumpy brothers.
Christian, helpful, thoughtful brothers.
Those are just a few.
Wet pants brothers,
Super smart brothers.
Running, cunning, sunning brothers.
Testing, playing, sleeping brothers.
Crying brothers too.
Dumb brothers,
Bossy brothers,
Happy brothers.
Don't forget your friends' brothers.
Last of all — best of all —
I like my brothers.

Kelly McCosby, Grade 5
Claysville Elementary School

Colors

As red as an apple
As blue as the sky
As white as a goat
As black as the cat
As yellow as the sun
As green as the grass
As gray as the fog
As purple as the plum
As orange as the orange
As pink as the rose

Sierra Mary Castro, Grade 4
Maureen M Welch Elementary School

No Name

I have no name
And the Nazis are to blame
I was only three
When they deleted my family tree
They took me and beat me
How can this be
I have no name
And the Nazis are to blame

Hannah Curfman, Grade 6
Chambersburg Area Middle School

October's Ocean

Leaves hypnotize me
As they dive bomb
Into the cold pebbles
Wind so cold I can't move
Sounds of screaming and laughing
From the playground
Rings in my ears with fright
Pine leaves the color of teal
Look like the ocean
Look there!
Dead branches cling together
Forming an underwater cave
Ouch!
The sun burning like spilled coffee
Shadows climbing higher
Than the brick walls provide
Clouds move like
Gleaming pirate ships
Across a cold, blue ocean
October must have skipped fall

Jessica Kraus, Grade 5
Lower Salford Elementary School

Sisters

As supportive as your mom or dad,
As frustrating as your division problem,
As loving as a newborn puppy,
Are my three sisters who are the best!

Gabriella Schneider, Grade 4
St Francis of Assisi School

Summer and Fall

Summer
hot, pretty
swimming, tanning, body boarding
wedding, driven, photograph, camp
carving, horseback riding, camping
colorful, red
Fall

Lauren Ashley Godissart, Grade 4
West Branch Area Elementary School

The Meet

Step up, take your mark — beeeep!
Swimmers dive into the pool so deep.

Parents' hearts skip a beat;
Their kid's team may win the meet!

Swimmers kick as fast as they can;
Timers time, a lady and a man.

Swimmers hit the board.
Our team won! Thanks Lord.

Kaylee Faull, Grade 6
Portersville Christian School

Magnificent Magenta

Magenta is butterflies and roses and is hilarious.
Magnificent magenta is the taste of red cabbage.
Watermelon, grapes, and grape juice smell like Magenta.
Magnificent magenta makes me feel like shopping.
Magenta is the sound of Easter and birds.
Magnificent magenta is Spain, Mexico, and Florida.
Magenta is something I won or something I did right.
Magnificent Magenta is spring rain.
Magenta is beautiful and is light from the sun
and is the summer breeze and the sound of the breeze.

Carla Buzzatto, Grade 5
McMurray Elementary School

The Book of Life

I found a rusty old book on the shelf.
Some pages were torn.
But that didn't matter.

I read a few pages and found out a soldier had died.
I read some more and read another story.
And found out a baby was born.

It was wonderful and it had many wonders.
This book felt like it was going on forever.
Some parts were sad.
But I still kept going and going and going.

Sasha Aronzon, Grade 6
United Hebrew Institute

Tasty Visitors

I awoke in the middle of the night.
There was a loud crash I heard,
And I was gripping my pillow tight.

I ran out of the house
To see what had happened.
There was a spacecraft 10 times bigger than a mouse.

From the craft emerged 2 jellybeans
One lemon, the other lime,
At least from what I had seen.

The little beans pleaded,
"Take us home! Please!
Before we get eated!"

They claimed their fuel was crackers,
So I ran to the kitchen,
And I gave them some generic "Uncle Smackers."

So off they flew,
And my close encounter ended.
"Oh no!" I said. "What if the media knew?!"

Greg Perciavalle, Grade 6
State Street Elementary School

Jaguars and Hippos and Rabbits, Oh My

Hurry!
They're getting away!
Roger Rabbit is running rapidly in his ravishing,
red, rubber-soled Reeboks!
At the same time,
Helga Hippo has her high tops
helping her to hide
with her parents Hidi and Harold Hippo!
Finally,
Jamie Jaguar is jumping to Japan
for a jumbo
jaguar jamboree!

Camille Boufford, Grade 5
Wexford Elementary School

Spring Fever

Nature is a beautiful thing. You can taste spring fever
Mother Nature is great,
you could even faint,
'cause it's so beautiful.
You can feel the wind
it's been,
a wonderful surprise.
You can hear the birds,
leaves, and even though it's nature,
there's still things like airplanes,
and trucks going by, and ordinary things
that you can hear.
The azure sky is a beautiful sight,
it just might
be the best thing.
The onion grass, the leaves being whipped around;
it feels like you're less than a pound.
The hair in your face,
is something you can taste.
You can smell the start of spring;
Yes, it's a beautiful thing!

Tierney Adams, Grade 5
St Ambrose School

The Ocean

When I look at the ocean,
I see many things.
Hope is gleaming in the swells,
Cheerfulness is seen in the fish.
And I hear the ocean sing to me.
Even though this cannot be,
I still hear the way it hums to me.
Faith is a virtue in life,
that everyone needs to have for the hardships you'll face.
Even in the darkest place of this world,
I will still remember the ocean's tune.
And I'll never forget,
when I met you last June.

Meghan Blose, Grade 6
Mount Nittany Middle School

My Lab

He wags his tail and winks his eyes,
He gave a yell to my surprise.
He sits and waits outside my door,
And sometimes drools upon my floor.

He has thick and yellow fur,
He is a Lab and not a cur.
He always knows when I am sad,
He makes me happy; he makes me glad.

Chloe Pohlman, Grade 5
Bermudian Springs Middle School

Flowers

Flowers
Beautiful, different
Blooming, prospering, delighting
Brightens up the day
Plants

Allison McCallister, Grade 6
St Hilary of Poitiers School

Wolves

Wolves howl at the moon
Wolves prowl around at nighttime
Wolves sleep through the day.

Zac Ryan, Grade 5
McMurray Elementary School

Winter

Cold, blustery
Freezing, blowing, sleeting
Slippery, windy, icy, snowy
Skiing, snowboarding, iceskating
White, wet
Winter

Logan Yartz, Grade 4
Memorial Elementary School

The Four Seasons

First of the seasons,
When the flowers start to bloom,
This season's called spring.

This season is next,
When the land is so hot,
It is called summer.

The third, not the last,
Is when the leaves start to fall,
This season's called fall.

The final, the last,
Is the wonderful winter,
When Jesus is born!

Eve Hamilton, Grade 4
Sacred Heart School

Stranger

Standing on the corner like a stranger in a small town.
Looking around and seeing thousands of pairs staring down.
Want to cry but would create a flood.
People yelling. People screaming. Saying mean words.
Hope is lost.
Until…Someone walks by.
With a glare in his eye.
Ready to join those around.
But instead walks up and stares at me.
Beneath those deep blue eyes I see a kitty meow in the morning sun.
He shows no fear.
He speaks and I taste the dew on the ground below.
Then it STOPS. The wind is still. The taste is lost.
I speak for myself.
People stop yelling. People stop screaming.
People stop saying mean words.
The man speaks these words of wisdom.
"Don't let others put you down.
Stand tall and fight for what you believe.
And be proud of what makes you, you."

Geneva Russell, Grade 6
Our Lady of Mount Carmel School

Sisters

Sisters make me crabby, we yell and fight and scream.
Slamming doors, calling cruel names, some would say it's mean.
But sometimes sisters are the best of the best.
Like the times you stare into each other's eyes and burst out into laughs.
Or stay up all night long talking about the new boy in your class.
One minute I wish she'd get eaten by a dragon,
the next I want her there to comfort me.
My sisters are great. They're mean. No! They're nice.
I really can't make up my mind.
One day in the future some say I'll love her as my best friend.
But for today she'll just be my sister.
At times a little more, at others a little less.

Olivia Mast, Grade 6
Locust Grove Mennonite School

This Tree

This tree of mine is so beautiful like the end of the first rain in spring.
This tree of mine looks so bare, lonely, and in despair.
But the way its branches are set so perfectly make this tree so wonderfully beautiful.
This tree of mine, it's all alone, swaying in the wind.
Yet at the night, when the stars are bright, it glows within.
This tree of mine, its bark is white, whiter than snow itself.
This tree will always be standing there tall with confidence and pride.
Because of this, it gives me great hope and will always stand by my side.
This tree of mine shadows me with its cooling shade.
Your perfection could never ever be man made.
Now I thank you for the light you set off in my heart.
For so many things can dim it every day.
This tree of mine, its natural beauty, shines through its ugly yet comforting self.
It makes other trees look dull and boring, this tree I call my help.

Rachel Bily, Grade 6
Our Lady of Mount Carmel School

Spring

I see a colorful rainbow in the delightful blue sky from the rain.
I smell the delicious aroma of the spring barbeque.
I feel the radiant warmth of the sun's rays shining down on me.
I hear the beautiful, luxurious sound of the blue birds singing.
I taste the sweet, delectable, yellow lemonade.

Bridgette Devlin, Grade 4
Colonial Elementary School

Sky

Sky.
Beautiful blue pools with marshmallows.
Soft and fluffy they are.
It looks like you could just float away in a state of happiness.
Sky.

Adam Rok, Grade 6
Foot of Ten Elementary School

Baseball Is Fun

I was playing it one day in my backyard
I hit it far
It felt like I hit it as far as Barry Bonds
We were so tired after we were done, we fell down
we weren't done, yet we were running
It was nice the next day, it was shining!
We played baseball
I hit it far
On my team they were cheering for me
Hit, Hit, Hit, Hit the baseball
I smacked it out of the ball park
It was their turn to bat
Their first person struck out! Second person struck out!
Last person hit a homerun and it was tied.
The next person came up to bat and hit a homerun!
It was over — they won!

Paul Yoder, Grade 6
Mount Nittany Middle School

These Tears

These tears that I cry I cry, I wonder why I cry them,
as I sit by my window wondering why daddy never drives by
I wipe my tears from my eye
I smile because I know that mama is by my side
she holds me tight and tells not to cry
'cause these tears I don't have to cry
because mama is by my side.

Jada Williams, Grade 4
South Park Elementary Center

Ruining Earth

E ndless meadows,
A nd rising mountaintops.
R ushing streams curve around exotic
T rees of every kind, but that changed when
H umans set foot upon this land.

Caroline Keener, Grade 6
H Austin Snyder Elementary School

Glasses

A portal to a new world,
The opening to great possibilities
Without them some people would not be as important
The inventor must be a powerful man,
Like the sunflower that towers above all the others

Hatcher Ballard, Grade 5
Jenkintown Elementary School

The Ocean

As the sun rises along the ocean's horizon,
The water washes up along the shore,
Splish, splash, splish, splash,
Pebbles and seashells rolling on the sand
In the water, round and round,
Splish, splash, splish, splash,
Little birds run up and down,
Up and down, up and down,
As the water comes in and goes out,
Sand crabs' holes open and close
Open and close, open and close,
Sea gulls diving to get fish,
Or just sitting there peacefully,
The splish, splash of the waves,
The constant hum of the ocean,
The dolphins jumping out of the ocean,
For a breath of air, breathe in, breathe out,
The foam of the ocean leads the water up onto the beach,
As if it was watering a sprouting seed,
As the sun rises on the horizon of the ocean.

Katherine Carroll, Grade 5
Annunciation B V M School

Freedom

Martin Luther King helped create freedom
Rosa Parks would not give up her seat on the bus
Whipping, beating, it was not fair
Things were not fair
Crying, dying
Things were not right
People were not right
White and black
Both the same
Trading and taking away
All the hurt, all the pain
Bad people did this
Sick people did this
Hoping, praying
Abolish slavery
Freedom now rings across our land
New memories are made firsthand
God bless the people everywhere
God bless our leaders past and here
Freedom is a gift

Daniel Wethli, Grade 4
St Alexis School

A Sister

A sister is like a rose,
Always loving and always caring,
They're sweet and kind,
A great feeling,
To have their heart,
They're loyal and smart
So as long as there are sisters,
There will be love everywhere.
Jamie Gilpin, Grade 6
West Allegheny Middle School

Football

Football
Touchdowns
Running, shaving, scoring
Awesome, fun, goals, scores
Scoring, kicking, tripping
Good job
Soccer
Sierra Shoemaker, Grade 5
Southside Elementary School

Nature

Nature is wonderful,
    If you like to explore.

Nature is wonderful,
    If you like to climb trees.

Nature is wonderful,
    Because God created it all.
Abigail Clarke, Grade 4
Northern Cambria Catholic School

Winter

It's cold.
It's fun.
It melts in the sun.
It's white.
It's bright
And it falls from a great height.
It's frozen.
It's wet.
When I play in it, I sweat.
It's slippery.
It's fine.
I wish it was all mine.
I shovel.
I sled.
I can build a bed.

I make angels in the
SNOW!!!
Jordan Gebhardt, Grade 6
Mount Nittany Middle School

Hurricanes

I'm a hurricane big and strong
I can even destroy your town
Better board up your house
Or I'll blow it down

I'm always ready
You never know when I'll come
So grab all your stuff
And then take a run

My name is always different
From A to Z
You just never know
How big I may be

I'm a hurricane big and strong
I can even destroy your town
Daniel Bunker, Grade 4
General Nash Elementary School

My Lord

My Lord is my Savior,
My Lord is my Messiah,
My Lord
Can never stop being
My True God!
Yvette Ramos, Grade 5
Our Mother of Perpetual Help School

Spring

Spring is when the flowers bloom,
    the grass grows green with glee.

The flowers grow with beauty,
    as the leaves blow free.

The sun goes down from a day of shining
    and the moonlight is so bright.

This light will help me through the night,
    'till the sun comes up in the morning.
Alyssa Panzer, Grade 4
McDonald Elementary School

The Blue Sea

The blue sea
Where I see fish swimming,
Some big, some small,
Looking like tiny little peas.

I see big sea turtles
The sea is like a shining jewel.
Sometimes the sea looks green
But, that's my big blue sea.
Rachel Kwisnek, Grade 4
Northern Cambria Catholic School

Darla and Victoria

Darla
Cuddly, energetic
Playing, sleeping, slobbering
Cute, friendly, groovy, superior
Exciting, caring, charming,
Funny, weird
Victoria
Victoria Brucker, Grade 6
Bridle Path Elementary School

Best Friend

Best friends are there until the end,
They help, care and share.
That is why you are my best friend,
We make such a good pair!
Gretchen Kedrowitsch, Grade 6
H Austin Snyder Elementary School

Having a Sister

Having a sister is so much fun
Like sun bathing under the sun.

Sisters love to go to the mall;
Shop 'till they drop, they have a ball.

About little things sisters fight,
But in big things they find delight.

Having a sister is so awesome,
Like a flower, friendships just blossom.
Ashley Grooms, Grade 6
Portersville Christian School

Food

Food food glorious food
Loot the fridge for the potpie
Don't get food on your tie
What about apple pie
Stay away from my pancake
Or your tong I will take
Eat the pizza while it's hot
Eat the broccoli I will not
Steal the chicken eat the steak
Clean the food off your plate
Ryan Myers, Grade 6
H Austin Snyder Elementary School

Dragon

Dragon
Scary scaly
Frightening destroying fire-breathing
They aren't really playful
Reptile
Christopher Thomas O'Rourke, Grade 5
Penn-Kidder Campus

Life

Life is short.
Make sure you do not waste it.
Life is sweet,
so take time to taste it.
Life is right there for you.
There are so many wonderful things to do.
Live it well and live it good.
Do the right things as you should.

Marjorie Washkalavitch, Grade 4
Sacred Heart School

Christmas

Christmas is a day of joyful fun.
It's celebrated by everyone.
Jesus our Lord was born on this day,
And He slept in a bed of soft hay.
Christmas is a time when white snow falls,
And we get to make big round snowballs.
I like to have funny snowball fights
And look at the pretty Christmas lights.
But sometimes during those snowball fights,
I tend to break those beautiful lights.
When Santa comes into my quiet house
He does not even disturb a mouse.
Santa comes down my chimney at night,
Knowing that he will be out of sight.
He leaves us nice gifts under the tree,
Hopefully some of them are for me.
If they aren't, I will not make much fuss.
After all, our Father gave Jesus to us!

Cameron Shaffer, Grade 4
Verna Montessori School

Christmastime

Christmas is the best time of year,
The children have no fear, 'cause Santa is here.
They get what they ask for, if they have been good,
Even toy trains, made out of wood.

Jesus was born in a stable with hay,
We celebrate this magical moment all day.
With His mother as Mary and Joseph His dad,
The three wise men traveled and gave what they had.

The lights are lit, the houses are glowing,
What a beautiful day, it has begun snowing.
The children are sledding and having a race,
The parents are gathered by the fireplace.

Christmas is a magical day,
To celebrate in a special way.
The children are tired, they're falling asleep,
They're finally quiet, SHH! Don't make a peep.

Ronnie Vespasiani, Grade 6
Holy Spirit School

Love Without You

Love without you is like life without a dream,
Love without you is like a robber without a scheme,
Love without you is like a song sung out of key,
Love without you is like being stung by a bee.

How can I live one more day,
Knowing that my love has been taken away?

Love without you is like a diamond with no shine,
Love without you is lonely all the time,
Love without you is like a joke that's not funny,
Love without you is like a bear with no honey.

How can I live one more day,
Knowing that my love has been taken away?

Love without you is like being hit by a car,
Love without you is like being stuck in some tar,
Love without you is like a sunless day,
Love without you is watching my dreams drift far, far away.

Love without you wouldn't be love at all.

Geoff Ciecierski, Grade 6
Strodes Mills Middle School

Panther

As it slips through the darkness
    A shadow.

It jumps up,
    High as an air pumped ball.

Up a tree, unseen
    A whispering willow,

And down it comes
    A slithering snake

On the forest floor
    Continuing its journey.

Oksana Kuznetsova, Grade 5
East Stroudsburg Elementary School

Fuzzy Creatures

Fuzzy creatures who lay in bed.
As father and children lay at mother's head.
Still, flat leaves lay on ground.
The leaves make a bed nice and round.
Sticks built up over their heads.
To make them a nice little shed.
In the wood as the wind blows.
There are sleeping bucks and does.
Squirrels and chipmunks looking for acorns.
As a baby buck is starting to grow his horns.

Lacy Clites, Grade 5
Southside Elementary School

Snowball Fights
Fun, cool
Throwing, dodging, hitting
Hurts, intense, wet, sneaky
Missing, hiding, exciting
Compact, messy
Snowball fights
Kelly Knorr, Grade 4
Memorial Elementary School

First Things First
First the rain and then the flood
First the devastation and the mud
First things first
First the lightning and then thunder
First the storm and then the plunder
First things first
First the tornado and then the debris
That's the way it had to be
First things first
Coy Scott, Grade 5
Claysville Elementary School

Ten
One wide woman wobbles weirdly;
Two toothless tigers trot towards town;
Three thirsty thugs thinking thoughtfully;
Four freaky fellows frolic freely;
Five famous fathers fish on Friday;
Six slithering snakes sneak some snacks;
Seven sea serpents swim sideways;
Eight electric elephants eating eggs;
Nine nutty nerds kneeling nicely;
Ten terrible toenails touching tile.
Erik Capra, Grade 5
Claysville Elementary School

School
School starts at eight o'clock
Kids are there and all ready to rock

Books and pencils at the ready
Take it slow nice and steady

The morning's gone before we know
Full of highs and full of lows

Lunch time comes and there's a riot
Not the time to be on a diet

On the menu lots of food
Pizza, burgers and that's good

The afternoon goes by in a flash
For the school bus we must dash
Lewis Bain, Grade 6
Neil Armstrong Middle School

My Cat
I have a cat grayish-black,
When he is feisty he will smack.
He sits on his chair all day long,
Sleeps and switches positions.
Sometimes he gets woken up,
And he is in a bad condition.
My sister loves him and gives him food,
Whenever they are together,
They are both in a good mood.
Courtney Busse, Grade 6
Freedom Area Middle School

Skiing Is Fun
Skiing is rather fun,
Whether on the slopes in the Alps
Or in Aspen till the day is done.

Gliding, sliding, tumbling down the hill,
Skiing is fun because of the thrills.

Warming up by the fire,
Drinking hot cocoa, too.
Skiing is fun for me and YOU!
Kyle Poorman, Grade 5
Easterly Parkway Elementary School

The Teacup Yorkie
There was a teacup Yorkie.
She lived at Aunt Susie's house.
She drank Starbuck's coffee.
She chewed on her toy mouse.

She barked at a mailman.
She barked at a snowflake.
She barked at the windchime.
And she barked at a snake.

She ran after the ball.
She ran after the bee.
She ran after the bird.
But she hit the oak tree.
Justin Juliano, Grade 6
Haverford Middle School

The Moon Is a Guardian
The moon is a guardian,
Floating high above us each night.
It watches over our Earth and sky
At such an amazing height.
As time goes by and day comes,
It's lunch break time for our moon.
It hands the job over to the sun
Until night comes again too soon.
Melanie Socash, Grade 6
Freedom Area Middle School

I Wish for Sports
I wish I could play some ball,
Up and down the fifth grade hall.
I would give it such a kick,
And it would always go so quick.

I wish I could play some soccer,
Inside the very biggest locker.
I would give it such a bash,
And it would make a big crash.

I wish I could play some hockey,
With the most famous jockey.
As I'm riding a horse,
While I'm on a track, of course.

I wish I could play tennis,
If I ever went to Venice.
When I didn't hit it hard,
It would only go a yard.

I wish I could do all these things,
But all these things are meant for kings.
But some day later, oh, who knows?
I could become one of those.
Josh Wright, Grade 5
Bermudian Springs Middle School

Ed's Dead Brother
There once was a person named Ed
His brother was once claimed dead
He became sad
Then became glad
His brother was alive instead.
Jordan Carr, Grade 4
South Park Elementary Center

Daddy and Me
Long bunny ears
Gently gliding against my face

The feeling of soft flower petals
And a sweet lullaby

In my crib bundled in a blanket
About to fall asleep

Reaching up to get him
trying to touch the sky

The soft feeling of his hands
Holding mine

The best feeling of happiness
When I am with him
Victoria DiGiacobbe, Grade 4
Benchmark School

Little Red Bucket

You look like a little hat
And you are as red as a robin.
After a while, your metal sides become as rough as sand paper.
Please will you bring me a picnic!
I wish I was always as nice as you are.

Joseph Miele, Grade 6
Sacred Heart of Jesus School

A Mother's Love

A mother's love is very very sweet,
She's someone anyone would want to meet.
A mother's love is very true,
You'll be stuck to her like glue.
Her love is softer than the softest teddy bear,
She will always be there.
You should know about your mother's love,
It's more beautiful than the finest dove.
A mother's love is something to behold,
It's more precious than a pot of gold!

TyLeah Williams, Grade 5
Christ Christian Academy

Spring

Spring is the season that everybody loves,
Spring is the season when you can see some doves,
In April we have Easter Day,
And after that it will be May.

You plant your seeds in the ground,
While you listen to the rain making a drip, drop sound,
When you play baseball America's past-time,
And when it is over it is not going to be the last time.

Michael Stephenson, Grade 4
Concord Elementary School

Faulty Clothes

Small purple and white dress
    that's ribbons fell off.
Oversized red, white, and black sweater
    that got ripped on the shoulder.
Plain blue jeans
    that had a hole in the knee when I fell down.
Ugly pink and white sweater
    that I purposely don't wear.
Red sunflower jacket
    that was stolen when I forgot it at the park
Pretty long white skirt
    that shrunk in the wash.
Orange and red flower socks
    that had a hole in the toe.
Striped red, blue, and green pajamas
    that I lost at Monterey Bay.
Big purple Gap sweater
    that I still wear today.

Sana Ali, Grade 5
Newtown Elementary School

Someday I Will

Someday I will have a big house
    with a red and black bedroom
I will keep it clean all of the time
I will live out in the country
Someday I will be a teacher
I will do fun things
    but also take care of the children
Someday I will travel around the world
    learning many different languages and cultures
Someday I will have a life of my own, but right now…
    I have to live with just being a kid

Anna Leigh Newton, Grade 5
Claysville Elementary School

Waterpark

'Splash' is what you hear at the water park.
Not an oink, meow, or even a bark,
Dripping and splashing, the party's begun!
The water park is so much fun!
Children scream, "Yay!"
But it's almost the end of the day.
I don't want to go home, I'll fight and I'll roar!
I'll beg my mom, "Five minutes more?"

Madison Rumpf, Grade 4
West Bradford Elementary School

I Forgot My Homework

I forgot my homework I'm very sad to say
I forgot my homework so this isn't much my day
I left my homework back at school
And let me tell you that isn't very cool
I wish I would have paid attention
Now I'm going to get in trouble not to mention
A big fat F and a detention
When my mom finds out she will have a heart attack
Not to mention an aching back
So I'll run away to where homework is forbidden to mention
And escape from homework and a detention

Sarah Stenske, Grade 4
St Joseph the Worker School

A Day in Spring

The wandering sky propels with the wind,
as the trees stir in the air.

The withered leaves blast around,
as the birds replenish the sky with sound.

The sprouting buds complete the scene,
as the onion grass beats in the wind.

The taste of spring is on my tongue,
as the smell of enchanting flowers fill my lungs.

Joseph Anthony DeLeon, Grade 5
St Ambrose School

Cheetah
Black and yellow spots
Running dancing and growling
Fast at hunting prey
Michael Harleston, Grade 5
Penn-Kidder Campus

Fishing
Fishing
Fun, neat
Casting, reeling, catching
Fishing is fun.
Hobby
Robbie Pearce, Grade 4
West Branch Area Elementary School

Puppies
They chew
They cry
They dig
They make messes

Cry, cry, cry
Dig, dig, dig
Chew, chew, chew
Messes, messes, messes
Sleep, sleep, sleep

They are here
They are there
They are everywhere

Let me have a treat
Let me play in the mud
Let me chew on the couch
Leave me alone
I'm going to sleep
Katie Jones, Grade 6
Westmont Hilltop Middle School

Super Bowl XL
All football fans gather 'round,
The Super Bowl's come into town.
Get ready for the big game,
Super Bowl 40 is the name.

Sunday, February 5th is the date,
So buy tickets and don't be late.
Seahawks, Steelers, they're the two best,
One's from the east and one the west.

They're real good, and they can push,
Just like ol' Reggie Bush.
They are the last two fish in the pond,
They will go above and beyond.
Ryan Nesselrodt, Grade 5
Bermudian Springs Middle School

Abuse
Abuse is when a man beats his wife,
Abuse is when someone has no respect for others life.

Abuse is when someone starts to shoot,
Abuse is when you gamble all of your loot.

Abuse is when you lose your education,
Abuse is when you go through incarceration.

Abuse is when you are a drug dealer,
Abuse is when you are a serial killer.

Abuse is when you are in the streets thugging,
Abuse is when a man has more than one woman he's loving.

Abuse is crazy, because it makes you dumb, ignorant and even lazy.
Laurence Jones, Grade 6
Theodore Roosevelt Middle School

About a Story Called a Wednesday Night
Over at my boyfriend Joe Turner's house. On a Wednesday night.
I'll go over to his house at night.
When the stars shine bright as right.
When the moon goes around at night
I am feeling sad in moody blue.
When it's time to leave I was shutting the door behind me
In a kiss good bye from him
The winds blew the bad roads away from me.
Inside now good bye everyone.
I hope you enjoy.

Shauncia McCall, Grade 5
Kanner Learning Center

Yellow
Yellow is fall leaves and the sun and being generous.
Yellow is the taste of tender chicken and yellow rice.
Hummer cologne and tall evergreens smell yellow.
Yellow is the sound of robins chirping and severe thunder clapping.
Yellow is Seven Springs Ski Resort, Rolling Hills C.C., and the tropical island of Hawaii.
Coming in first place at a national golf tournament is yellow.
Winning the PAHL hockey tournament is also yellow.
Yellow is the sandy beach.
Tommy Nettles, Grade 5
McMurray Elementary School

The Majestic Clouds
Majestic clouds riding on the wind
Cotton, free-floating…yet dominating the sky with an iron fist.
Clouds are puffs of steam from God's own tea kettle.
Strong to captivate water and release it as it pleases.
They are sewn cotton to God's ever-so-immense blanket of space.
Enrages, they conjure up lightning and bellow the roar of a lion.
Tamed, they are the angels recliners, and Apollo's lookout towers.
Always versatile in moods, they stay true wonders of God.
Ezra Guzman, Grade 6
Chalutzim Academy

Max, My Puppy

My puppy, Max is his name,
He loves to run and play a game.

Fluffy, soft and furry,
He does everything in a hurry.

He is my best friend since Christmas last year,
And every time I call him he turns an ear.

Max will lick you and jump and play,
And doesn't get tired all day.

Max was the best present I got
And I can say I love him a lot.

Geno Brady, Grade 5
Holy Family Academy

Exciting

Exciting seems red
I see the view from the sky ride
I hear the seagulls screeching
I smell the fresh air
I touch the cold drink on a hot summer day
I taste the Dippen Dots ice cream

Nina DiNunzio, Grade 4
West Bradford Elementary School

An Ode to Soccer

A fun game that can't be beat
When you run down the field with the ball at your feet

When you are running you think,
Wow! how this is amazing,
Amazing how it feels
to play on the fields!

Now I go to shoot the ball,
Oops, I accidentally fall!

I stand up with a pout and a frown,
How embarrassing it is to fall down!!

Alexander McIlvried, Grade 6
Carson Middle School

Snowball

Snow is falling down, down here it comes!
When the first snow has fallen we love its beautiful white gleam
And how it shimmers all night and day
Snowballs are falling everywhere
Tomorrow kids will fill the fields with their sleds and play
Snowballs, snowballs, how fun they can be
They are cold for you and they are cold for me
Snow is falling down, down here it comes!

Selina Vinski, Grade 6
Pine-Richland Middle School

The Leprechaun Named Pat

There once was a leprechaun named Pat.
Who always wore a green hat.
Went out to find a pot of gold.
And got tricked and fooled.
And now he is old and has no cat.

Sierra Wagner, Grade 4
West Branch Area Elementary School

My Poem I Made Today

Today I sit
and ponder words,
To write a poem
about some birds.
They flew over my head you see,
But they landed
on water not a tree.
I watch them swim in the sun,
To be one of them would be so much fun
Then I see my tiny dog,
Standing there barking at a frog.
I am at peace
To sit and watch
These silly and playful geese.

Tyler Sepcoski, Grade 5
Sacred Heart of Jesus School

Cookies

Cookies
from the oven
smell fresh after baking,
so delicious for a late snack
with milk.

Tyler Earley, Grade 6
Bedford Middle School

Wishbone: A Great Dog

A dog named Wishbone
Awesome detective
A great dog who I can count on every day
A great storyteller
He's cute and cuddly
Incredible sniffer
Friend to all the people
Reader

Nicole Fell, Grade 5
Schuylkill Valley Elementary School

Dancing

Dancing is my passion
It's like a flame in my heart that never goes out
Dancing is definitely not about fashion
It's all about the counts
1, 2, 3, 4, 5, 6, 7, 8,
Dancing to me is like fate

Hannah Diday, Grade 6
West Allegheny Middle School

Wetlands

I am the wetlands big and green
Tall grass and waters mean
All sorts of animals that I see
Some of them swim in me
Otters, ducks, and raccoons too
These animals will not harm you
Alligators, snakes, and mosquitoes too
These animals might harm you
You always have to watch your back
In case of a carnivore attack
Cedar, red maple, and birch too
You can see far and through
Lots of plants within and through
Here are some I'll recite to you
Orchids, cattails, and arrowheads too
I am the wetlands big and green
Tall grass and waters mean
Frederick Vanderburg, Grade 4
General Nash Elementary School

In Your Way

A fence is a brick wall
It never moves out of your way
You can try, try, try again
But it's trying to keep you away.
Andrew Trivino, Grade 6
Guth Elementary School

Friends

F ull of fun
R eading notes
I . M.
E xciting movies
N o fights
D ance-offs
S leep-overs
Alyx Mance, Grade 6
West Allegheny Middle School

Posters

There are too many posters on my walls,
You can't see the purple paint at all.
Drake Bell and Hilary Duff,
To take them down would be too tough.
They fill up all the empty space,
My room is decorated my way.

Sometimes people are surprised,
Because of all the staring eyes.
Big and small, I have them all,
Green or blue, I have them too.
I could never take my posters down,
I love having celebrities all around!
Lauryn Luchaco, Grade 6
H Austin Snyder Elementary School

On Thanksgiving I Will See…

Turkey
feathered, delicious
gobbling, baking, sizzling
dinner, stuffing, gravy, cranberry sauce
running, fluttering, satisfying
brown, tasty
Turkey

Family
fun, silly
loving, caring, eating
grandparent, baby, aunt, uncle
adoring, grinning, gleeful
Relatives
Katherine Boufford, Grade 6
Pine-Richland Middle School

All About Me

I am funny,
I jump like a bunny
I am cool,
some say I rule
I am nice,
with sugar and spice
I like to give hugs,
I love ladybugs
if you love me
and I love you,
we once were one
but now are two,
I am the one,
who's o-so fun
and rocks this world,
like I'm a famous one
oh, life's the best you would admit,
but did you have the best of it
I am the girl,
that shines like a pearl
that is all about me!
Audrey Hulsizer, Grade 5
Warrior Run Middle School

World!

The sun in the sky is yellow
When he is up he says hello.

The sky is so blue
It's like the ocean to you.

The grass is so green
At night it cannot be seen.

And the clouds are so swirled
OH! What a wonderful world!
Troy Lattimer, Grade 6
H Austin Snyder Elementary School

My Dog

My dog is fun.
He may be small, but he can still run.
He is a puppy,
Not a yuppie.
That is my dog.

My dog is cool,
Though he may drool.
He is tough,
But not really rough.
That is my dog.

My dog eats. He eats a lot!
Sometimes it takes him a while to stop!
That is my dog.

He is black and brown.
He is not happy when people frown.
He may be short, long, and stubby,
But he can still be my very best buddy.
Leah Bailey, Grade 6
State Street Elementary School

Tigers

Tigers love to roam the forest,
When they jump their legs are sore.
Tigers are eating machines,
After a big meal they roar.

Tigers move as cautiously as a snake,
They are black and white striped.
Tigers blend into their surroundings,
Tigers come in many types.
Ceara Laughman, Grade 5
Bermudian Springs Middle School

Balloon

I bought a new balloon today.
It's yellow like a daisy.
The sky, it seems so far away
with clouds so soft and lazy.
Around my wrist is one loose knot,
so simple to just untie.
I say, "No! I really should not!"
but I want to see it fly!
I pull gently on the string
and release it to the skies.
To see this makes me want to sing!
The air has claimed its prize.
It will journey every sea,
visit Europe, Timbuktu.
And, once it comes back home to me,
I'll send it off to you.
Maureen McGrath, Grade 6
Academy-Notre Dame De Namur

A Friend

I'm going to tell you about a friend of mine
She likes me when I'm mad
and helps me when I'm sad
When she comes around everything seems fine!

My friend likes to play with toys
Her days are full of fun
and when outside she likes to run
She always finds something that she enjoys!

So now do you know who my friend might be
Now remember the things I have said
and all the clues that you read
My cat Twinkie is a good friend to me!

Hailey Haney, Grade 6
St Gregory Elementary School

Dana

Polite, peaceful, timid.
Wishes to be a dog so I can run faster.
Dreams of being a hip hop dancer.
Wants to be a famous tennis pro.
Who wonders if angels are real.
Who fears having a broken bone.
Who likes eating dark chocolate.
Who believes in God and Jesus.
Who loves my family.
Who plans to go to Virginia Beach.
I cannot wait for my eighteenth birthday so I can go to college.

Dana Snyder, Grade 4
Bushkill Elementary School

Ode to Clara

As the first building shatters to the ground
like a dropped glass vase,
people screaming and crying
yelling and running
pushing and shoving
to get out of the way.
As the second building goes down,
dust in the air
filling the city
with silence and tears.
Seeing the fear in her eyes
trying to escape
there's no way out.
Heroes coming from the mist of the rubble
but too late,
everything's over. People staring
in a mournful, miserable, manner.
Cuando Dios susurra tu nombre
(When God whispers her name)
it gives me a touch of spirit.
Clara, woman of Bravery and Strength.

Sarah Cruz, Grade 6
Hershey Middle School

A Spider Building a Web

Outside on my porch, I am building my web.
Down from the top to the bottom and back up again.
Over to the right and then back to the left.
Up, down, left, right, over and over.
It is very boring building a web,
But this is how I catch my dinner.
Oh look, there is a fly, I hope he comes over…
Yes! Dinner has arrived. Now I must go and prepare my catch.

Heath Nye, Grade 6
Freedom Area Middle School

Ode to My Neighbor's Dog

My neighbor's dog's eyes shimmer like a pearl.
It has as much fur as a bear.
It runs almost as fast as a cheetah.
Its nose is as black as the dark.
It's as energetic as someone who just had too much sugar.
Its fur is as gold as a 14 carat necklace.
It plays fetch really well.
It follows its owners like a hound.
It loves to bark as loud as a coyote.
It loves to be outside on a warm day as me.
It's as happy as a koala when dogs pass by.
It loves food as much as a hungry wolf.
It barks at people then smiles happily.
It loves to run around the house energetically.
It loves to bark at other dogs amusingly.
It follows its owners trying not to be seen, like a sly fox.
It's as big as three backpacks put together.

Myriam Bejjani, Grade 6
St Sebastian Elementary School

Pappy Lauterbach

My Pappy was a special man,
He was always lending others a loving hand.
Pappy was so filled with glee,
Pappy had 8 kids and 24 grand kids you see.
His heart was so big and filled with love for anyone,
No matter who you be!

Julia Rodaitis, Grade 5
St Valentine Elementary School

Skateboard

S kateboarding is my favorite thing to do
K ickflips are a really hard trick
A lot of practice to learn something new
T ony Hawk knows how it feels to fall like bricks
E veryone should try it
B oards can be customized by you
O h, make sure your helmet is the right fit
A lways wear your pads too
R adical time can be had by all
D on't forget try not to fall

Josh Walker, Grade 6
West Allegheny Middle School

Freedom

Is is just a word? Many have died for it we have heard.
In our schools we have been taught, that through the years wars have been fought.

So that everyone will have the right, to follow their dreams and be what they might.
From Boston's Harbor to Gettysburg's fields, our heroes stood firm and did not yield.

They fought with words and guns and knives. They risked everything including their lives.
Our forefathers gathered together and took a stand. Freedom would be the foundation of this land.

Did they take into consideration, when they met to form this great nation,
That treason was what they planned to do when they wrote the Declaration and the Bill of Rights too?

Of our liberty and freedoms we do sing, we quote speeches by Lincoln and Dr. King.
We must remember the sacrifices of those that came before. They created a haven for the hopeless, the tortured and the poor.

We are so lucky to live in the "Land of the Free," within the light of the torch of Lady Liberty.
So do not take your freedom for granted, each one of us must protect the seeds of freedom they planted.

Danielle Schneider, Grade 4
St Alexis School

Wonders of Space

As I wander in the endless realm of space
I see many mind-grasping things that I have dreamed of seeing up close
The first thing I see is the mighty, luminous sun
It shines as bright as an exploding bomb although I am very far away from it
Too bright for my eyes to withstand and my hands reach up to shield my face
From the blinding light and scorching blaze
I slowly move away from the sun
The light soon fades away and I am once again in solitude and darkness
I waited for my eyes to adjust to the sudden darkness and as my vision clears
It is almost like I am being swept into a whirlwind of stars
I stare in awe at all the different stars where each one is unique in its own way
A smile passes over my face
I look around me and one star twinkles much more than the other
It is Polaris, the king of the stars
It seems so different from on Earth, almost like an illusion
Slowly, a figure forms around Polaris
I let out an amazed sigh and I realize that it is the Big Dipper that I am seeing
Time passes, imaginary lines connect the stars, I see endless constellations covering the sky
And I stare at the countless number of stars
I know I have dreamed of coming here and now my dream has come true

Elaine Kang, Grade 6
Park Forest Middle School

Crash

Heading out of the house, into the car. Going to dad's. Everything perfectly normal. Driving. Talking with my mom, getting along. Turning, red light, crash, ears popping, scared to death, a sudden impact, hit by another car. Hugging. Loving, embracing being all right. Shaking, airbags. I will never forget. I remember the sound, I remember the impact. The sudden rush of blinking one time, crashing the next. Mom was ok, I was ok, the other driver was, but his passenger injured. A woman comes to us, are you ok? Yes. Lets us use her cell phone, and then I call my dad, too afraid to speak my mom takes over. Dad is here, saved. Going home. Safe.
For tonight, I just thought how lucky I was that my little sister wasn't in the car as well. For I was scared, and she would even more. And now I realize how lucky I can be, for at any sudden moment, your life can flash before you. And so make the best of life, I warn you all, and cherish goods and bads.

Tresier Mihalik, Grade 6
Hillcrest Elementary School

Love

Me, him,
The world is spinning around us,
My hands in his hands,
His eyes in my eyes,
Our feet are apart,
But our hearts stay together.
And everything is so perfect,
As perfect as it can be.

But then her,
Her looks, her talents, her body and mind,
Are more than mine.
He breaks away to her,
I look back and weep asking…why, why

Him, her
The world is spinning around them,
They look so happy.

Me, alone

Christina Harman, Grade 6
Maple Point Middle School

Best Friend by Your Side

A best friend is like a pillow,
You can always fall on them and trust them.
Everyone has a best friend,
They can be tall, small, happy, or sad,
But they can always help you out when you are mad.
Where would I be without my best friend?
What would I do?
If I didn't have you and you didn't have me,
Who would I cry with,
And laugh with,
Who would I talk to,
And share memories with?
A best friend is a building block,
You get stronger and stronger when they are by your side.
Best Friend

Nicole Duca, Grade 6
Our Lady of Mount Carmel School

Thomas Jefferson's Fountain Pen

Hi, I am a fountain pen,
I love to talk to people,
I write on paper a lot.
I hate making mistakes.
Because I don't have an eraser,
I wish I was a pencil.
They have erasers.
If he wouldn't write so fast,
He would not make so many mistakes.
If I had one wish it would be to become a pencil.

Cate Huddy, Grade 6
Freedom Area Middle School

This Cat I Know!

This cat I know, well, he's a treat, he loves to pounce and play.
I once discovered him outside, he must have been a stray.
That little guy's quite cute, I really have to say!
Now this dog I know, well, she chases him away.
But luckily he knows to come back and stay someday.

Rachel Strongowski, Grade 4
Christ the King School

Crash

Make a right down Hartman Road
Take a glance in their direction
See the crash that happened there
Look at the faces, sense the tension

Grandmom saw it on the news
And mom mom on the radio
But the fact it was my dad
We definitely didn't know

And then that dreaded moment came
Two policemen knocked at our door
They whispered in my mother's ear
She told us we had to go next door

Woke up in my bed the next morning
Mom told me what happened to dad
He was hit head on by a truck
He might die, and I was sad

Day after day, week after week
Slowly his face became less and less pained
And after a long five years
My dad is able to walk with a cane

Marlee Milkis, Grade 6
Bridle Path Elementary School

Good-bye

When it is time to say good-bye,
You think you have no more tears to cry.
Then they come right back to you,
Just when you thought you made it through.
With all the memories I touch,
I am missing you so much.
Please come back to me.
I want to see
Your smiling, pretty face.
You left without a trace.
It is so hard for me to say,
I want us to be together and gay.
Forever in Heaven you lay.
I will stay here crying and pray.
I want you to know,
I loved you so.
Good-bye.

Hayley Stettner, Grade 6
Ross Elementary School

Sunrise, Sunset

Sunrise, sunset,
Total beauty and pride,
Love and peace,
Over hills and mountains,
Of Colorado,
Mixed colors of,
Purple, pink, red,
Orange, and of course yellow,
Beauty and love,
Birds fly by,
Sunrise, sunset,
Oh, here it comes,
Shhh!
Be quiet.

Lauren Matthews, Grade 5
Honey Brook Elementary Center

Butterflies

As delicate as a snowflake,
As untamed as a wild animal,
As bashful as a little girl,
Are butterflies that fly so high.

Alexandra Knaub, Grade 4
St Francis of Assisi School

Holy Night

Such a beautiful night,
Such a holy night.
Only one big star,
Shining so bright.

Such a loving night.
God's people rejoice.
We celebrate this day,
Because of Mary's trusting choice.

Such a beautiful night,
Such a holy night.
Because of our Savior,
God's love is in sight.

Allie Nigro, Grade 6
Holy Spirit School

Storm

The storm is lovely
Just look at it glow
The rain refreshing

Dimitrios E. Menas, Grade 4
Center Elementary School

Love

Love is a great thing.
I will forever love you.
Please always know that.

Kayla Senkinc, Grade 6
Allison Park Elementary School

Victorious

One, only one will proceed.
The final circle, the final cut.
The tension, the nerve, you can't take it.
The trophy smiling back at you.
You would give your arm for it.
Your hair stands on end, your fingers curl.
You try to brace for the future, but some of you wants to stay in the past.
Ding! Ding! Ding! The end of the match.
You won! You won! Your victory, your happiness,
Your satisfaction is too good to be true.
Or, sadness, tragedy.
Did it really happen?
Did all of my work go to waste?
You wonder.
Is life better, wondering or knowing?
Knowing or about to know?
The feelings all compare, the good and bad.
The anticipation can rip you apart,
but the outcome could do even worse.

Ginger Woolridge, Grade 6
Mount Nittany Middle School

It's Not Fair

It's not fair to be judged by color
It's not fair to be treated differently
It's not fair when others are allowed to do something and you're not
It's not fair to be kept out of places because of prejudice
It's not fair to be locked up for what you believe in
It's not fair to be judged because of what you look like or believe in
It's not fair to be laughed at, talked about, tortured or killed
IT'S JUST NOT FAIR

Liam Dague, Grade 5
Shafer Elementary School

Blue

Blue tastes like a fresh picked blueberry on a warm summer day,
cotton candy so puffy and sweet,
and lollipops that you could lick all day.

Blue smells like the salty smell of the deep blue sea,
a blueberry pie fresh out of the oven,
and a delicious slushy, so icy and refreshing.

Blue sounds like soft footsteps crunching on the snow,
waves crashing on the sea,
and the loud cry from a blue jay.

Blue feels like new jeans that fit just right,
sometimes my mood that is melancholy and sad,
and the stars that I touch twinkling in the night.

Blue looks like the gorgeous blue sky on a cool spring day,
a beautiful portrait hanging on the wall,
and a flock of bluebirds flying high in the sky.

Casey Miller, Grade 4
Indian Lane Elementary School

My Dog

I have a dog named Lita that is black and white
She doesn't know the difference between wrong and right
My little doggy likes to play with her toys
She goes crazy when she hears a thunderclap noise

This Boston Terrier sleeps with me every night
When the sun is out, she likes to lie in the light
She is sometimes peaceful and sometimes mean
Sometimes she acts like she is a beauty queen!

When she goes to the bathroom we give her a treat
At the dinner table we give her some meat
My dog Lita is sometimes wild and sometimes bad
But Lita is the best doggy I have ever had

Tom Easterly, Grade 5
Edgeworth Elementary School

Swimming

Water rushing past my face
Getting ready for my next big race
Stepping up to the block
I cannot be stopped
For when the buzzer goes off
I will swim so fast that I cannot be passed
Coming up to the wall I know I will not mess up at all
Flipping myself over and pushing off the wall
With all my might I will swim to the end
When I get to the wall I was helped out by a friend

Kayla Causer, Grade 6
Westmont Hilltop Middle School

The Nashua's Beauty

The rapid flowing river,
From this high mountain, it is a silver sliver.

I see the brown moose and colorful ducks as they drink,
Watching closely from this high mountain peak.

Examining the animals eat and drink rapidly all day,
In a very cute kind of way.

And through the Nashua's crystal clear river,

I observe the pebbled bottom and say,
"I hope this river stays this way."

Ethan Wilson, Grade 4
Washington Heights Elementary School

Brother

Brother
Kind, compassionate
Helping, caring, understanding
There when I need him
Friend

Kurtis C. Saar, Grade 4
West Branch School

Cell Phones

Cell phones are awesome
You can download music
You can call people on them
Like bowling or trying not to hit a bird
You change the color of the background
But mostly everybody loves cell phones
Sure one day cell phones might wear out from use

Nicole Hunt, Grade 6
Strodes Mills Middle School

At a Picnic

March! March!
I see some cake on a plate,
as I stand on my feet I reach up high,
Got it! Got it! I put it down on the ground,
but then I see some bread,
YUM! I thought that's good too!
I run back to the plate,
but it's too late!
I'm smooshed in a blink of an eye!

Zoe Shingler, Grade 6
Freedom Area Middle School

Friendship

Friendship is like a bucket and a shovel,
Always sticking together,
Never leaving each other's side.

Sometimes great,
And sometimes bad.
No matter what,
You'll always have a best friend.

Friendship may fly away,
Like a paper caught by the wind.
Friendship may stay with you for years and years,
Like glue on paper.

Either way, friendship is always by your side.

Taylor Hunt, Grade 6
Hillcrest Elementary School

Spring

The birds are chirping, they are always lurking,
as spring begins.
I hear the crash from the waterfall's splash
from the ice that has been melting away.
The grass is now green and we are in between
the bridging of winter and spring.
The flowers are blooming,
can you not see them growing each day?
All of the beautiful colors of spring and summer,
return more and more each day.

Melissa Ayoob, Grade 6
West Allegheny Middle School

New York

Amazing skylines
An outrageous place to live
I used to live there
Shannon Solano, Grade 5
Penn-Kidder Campus

Summertime

S pring is over
U niversal studios is very popular
M ost heat in the year
M ore people are at beaches
E veryone has fun
R ains a lot in some places
T ime to run in the sun
I t is very exciting to have family fun
M ost people swim in pools
E veryone loves summertime
Bradley McKitish, Grade 6
Sacred Heart of Jesus School

Dance

Dance through the night
Dance through the day
Dance in the light
Dance in the dark
Dance with style
Dance with grace
Tie your lace
Strap your buckle
Tap your tap shoe
Point your pointe shoe
Spin on your foot
Spin on your knee
Whatever you do
Dance
Melissa Kropf, Grade 6
St Ann Elementary School

My Dad

Works on cars
Junkyard cars
Demolition derby
Fixes them all year

Takes out metal
Paints outside
Pads inside

Helmet safety first
Dad races
I'll race soon
Love dad
Maybe next time
It was fun
Jimmy Graf, Grade 5
Benchmark School

Family

They're people
You love for
They're people
You care for
The chaos
You long for
And couldn't live without
The shoulder you cry on
When you fall
On your bike
Or on your luck
The everlasting memories
You make when they are there
The loud
Obnoxious
Crazy
Elephant herd
You cradle
Very
Very
Dear
Kelsey Hannah, Grade 6
Hillcrest Elementary School

Night

when night starts to creep
I don't make a peep
I might start to weep
I count my sheep
and fall into a deep
peaceful sleep
Taylor Shea, Grade 5
Southside Elementary School

Mall/School

Mall
free, decorated
shopping, bustling, closing
exciting, enjoyable, horrible, strict
boring, torturing, educating
crowd, loud
school
Harley Justice, Grade 5
Claysville Elementary School

Christmas Snow

Snow is great for Christmas.
It sprinkles down gently,
It glitters peacefully.

If you look from far away,
Nature won't even look real
Snow on the fields is beauty.
Josie Bender, Grade 4
Verna Montessori School

Pizza

Pizza

Covered in cheese

Pizza

Covered in pepperoni

Pizza

Has a lot of anchovies

Pizza

Has a lot of sauce

Pizza

Can easily fall apart

Pizza

Time to sit down and enjoy.
Mark Stewart, Grade 4
Avon Grove Intermediate School

Love

Dazzled and speechless
Thinking about each other
Caring and thoughtful
Giavanna Gomez, Grade 5
Penn-Kidder Campus

Ode to My Brother's Adoption

I had a great life
When I was an only child,
I got all the attention
And everything was fantastic!
Then my parents decided to adopt a
Little girl from Ukraine!
I didn't know what to think
When they left it was
Snowing golf balls and
I missed them a lot.
When they called they said they got a
Little boy named Genya
Instead of a girl.
Then they came home
And there was just a
Little boy sitting there not talking
For the next couple of days
It felt like he got all the attention
But now he can talk and
I think he's cute, cuddly, and cunning
I love him very much!!!
Alexandra Schaller, Grade 6
Hershey Middle School

My Dog Abby

Abby is as fast as a car
Abby is as crazy as a roller coaster
Abby is as noisy as a bird
Abby is as cute as a sleeping baby
Abby is as kind as a teacher
Abby is as soft as a feather
Geoffrey Matz, Grade 5
Newtown Elementary School

Our Soldiers

Boom, bang, rata-tata
The sound of war.
Our soldiers out there for us
We get to stay home,
They get to see victory or defeat.
Waiting like the anxious fishermen,
Then suddenly striking on cue.
They know they might die.
Each soldier out there for us
All of them hearing the echoing.
Each shot echoing, echoing, echoing.
Shooting until all is quiet.
Their dreams of seeing their families —
Hoping one day they will —
Could be broken.
The wind, sun, and rain furiously hitting,
Hitting down at the soldiers.
This is their life, their hopes and dreams,
That they put on the line,
The line that protects their country.

Sean May, Grade 6
Mount Nittany Middle School

George Washington

George Washington
First president of the U.S.

Looks like a man with cotton on his head.
Father of our country.
Skin is white as snow.

James Thomas, Grade 5
Jenkintown Elementary School

Autumn

Autumn is the season when
Leaves fall in color blends
The breeze is cool but just right
To sit on the porch and relax all night

In different colors the leaves do shed
From orange, to brown, to yellow, and red
But it is a wonderful sight
To watch leaves fall in dimming light

Shovel them is what we do
Then jump in both me and you
The leaves will go most everywhere
And even some will be in your hair

These are some reasons
Why it is my favorite season
Over winter, summer, and spring
So now you know that autumn is my favorite thing.

Madison Stahr, Grade 6
Conemaugh Township Area Intermediate School

A Man Named Aesop

Once in Africa long, long ago
there was a boy called Aesop as we know.
As a boy he became a slave
he probably did not behave.
When he grew up he was taken out
of slavery without a doubt.
He went to Athens and began to write
mostly fables that taught wrong and right.
Some fables were written in his name
that is how he grew in fame.
His stories are filled of animals galore
everyone wanted more and more.
One of his writings is The Lion and the Mouse
In the beginning the lion was a louse
The Lion said the Mouse would be no help
but the Mouse came running when she heard the Lion's yelp.
Aesop lived for 60 years.
When the Delphians killed him people shed many tears.
His fables are still read today,
from Brooklyn to Bombay.

Christina Witmer, Grade 6
Cathedral School of St Catharine of Siena

Spring Days

On spring days,
I would take a hike on my bike.
I would look around,
even on the ground.
When I look, I would see flowers
and pick them for hours.
Sometimes, in the day,
I would go out and play.
Sometimes, I would see lovely bunnies,
and bees with honey.
Every day, I would go down to the pond and look at fish
and make a wish.
I would wish that everything would be fine today,
because now it's a spring day.

Hannah Zondlo, Grade 5
Sacred Heart of Jesus School

The Sun

The Sun is like a bright symbol for all.
Making rainy days bright.
Graceful dawn, when the sun arises,
Brings unto the world a heavenly peace.
Brings new life to our lives.
At day it is found without being sought.
At night it is lost without being stolen.
Its wonders we will admire for centuries to come.
It is a golden dollar.
It is like a spirit.
It is whatever you want it to be,
Anything at all.

Charlie O'Connor, Grade 6
Our Lady of Mount Carmel School

Mountains
They are fantastic
There is so much wildlife
It is amazing
Anjelica Poalillo, Grade 5
Penn-Kidder Campus

Winter
Hyper kids playing
White snowflakes falling down fast
Indeed it's winter.
Nick Malinaric, Grade 5
Schnecksville School

Winter
Winter is here.
I inhale the fresh, crisp air.
As the snow falls slowly.
Anna Wiesike, Grade 4
Marlborough Elementary School

Cheer
C heer up the crowd
H appy to be the leader of my team
E nthusiastic all the time
E ncouraging the squad to keep going
R owdy and ready to cheer
Cheerleading is life
Chelsy Lalama, Grade 6
West Allegheny Middle School

Soccer
I
Love to play soccer
At Washington Crossing Park
In the cool, sunny afternoon
Because I can be the best I am
Alyssa Mangano, Grade 5
Newtown Elementary School

Night
Night.
The darkened version of day.
Swallowing up everything
All the light, all the joy.
Night.
The blackened version of sun.
Cold and heartless.
It eats up everything in its path.
Night.
The evil version of light.
Pouring over the world.
Just when we think it's going to get us,
It's day.
Gina Lupica, Grade 5
The Pen Ryn School

Dogs and Cats
Dog
Intelligent, crazy
Salivates, cuddles, hunts
Flexible, cunning
Cat
Elizabeth Coyle, Grade 5
Bushkill Elementary School

Winter!
The winter the winter how cold it is
The winter the winter how fun it is
The winter the winter how white it is
The winter the winter
Oh how I love winter!!!
Emily Roxberry, Grade 5
Schnecksville School

Mad Scientist
A scientist going quite mad,
made a mixture that went bad.
Test tubes exploded,
which made him bloated,
and destroyed the lab he had.
Branden Zembower, Grade 6
Bedford Middle School

Dogs and Cats
Dogs
furry, and cute
barking, cuddling, whining
happy, loving, cute, hairy
scratching, meowing, hiding
small, striped
cats
Lauren Brungo, Grade 4
St Sebastian Elementary School

Mark
R&B **M** usic
c **A** ke
R eading
K ind to friends
Mark Roman, Grade 5
East Stroudsburg Elementary School

War
It is amazing how our soldiers fight,
But we are not right,
We should not go to war,
It will just bring more.
Even though they bombed us,
Their terror, is what made us lose trust,
All though we know, it is a quest,
Is it really just a test?
Hope Kuchinski, Grade 5
East Stroudsburg Elementary School

Little Butterfly
Flutter, flutter to the sky
Flutter, flutter high and high

Flutter, flutter to the sea
Flutter, flutter all the way to me

When we meet we'll have some fun
Soar all the way to the sun

If you want to fly away
You have to come back another day

When you leave I'll try not to cry
Goodbye, goodbye little butterfly!
Christine Bruno, Grade 5
Central Elementary School

Animals
As shiny as the moon
As careless as a baboon
Some things are tall
Others are small
No matter how they are I like them all
Austin Stuckley, Grade 4
Panther Valley Elementary School

Why I Love Winter
Rooftops smoking in the sky,
Children playing staying dry.
Ice, wind scratching at your face,
Like a snow storm at the race.
Now it's time for bed,
Snuggle up and rest your head.
Snow is almost gone,
Now the snow day's done.
Shannon Troy, Grade 4
McDonald Elementary School

Writing a Poem
It's hard to write a poem.
The words I just can't write.
I sit down and think awhile
Until I've said it right.

The words I can never think of
But as I write them now
I've always wondered how
I found the words I've found.

It's hard to write the words
As you can see
I've wrote this poem now
And it reflects me.
Bailey Bennett, Grade 6
St Gregory Elementary School

Spring

Spring is the best time of the year.
Sunflowers, grass, and daisies are growing.
All the trees are getting their leaves.
Winter is cold but spring is warm.
The bees are buzzing;
The squirrels are munching on acorns.
The birds are migrating north and are nesting in trees.

Eric Montgomery, Grade 6
Elizabeth Seton Elementary School

Nature's Rebirth

As nature dies it is also reborn.
As something living dies
It becomes the earth.
As the beauty of a flower fades
It gives way to new life.
As the wind changes,
Everything changes.
The plants, the animals,
Anything, everything…changes.
As the sun reflects off the water
It sheds colors…
Beautiful, shining,
Powerful colors that command reflection.
The wind changes again
But this time it is different.
Spring is coming.
Spring is a time when the dove flies
And the eagle soars.
Thank God for beginnings.
Thank God for peaceful endings.
Thank God for life.

Polly Macchiarola Macharola, Grade 6
St Rose of Lima School

Clouds Above

On a bight blue-skied November day.
The birds soar above.
The sky is filled with the soft figured clouds.
The sky is so high, I wish I could fly.
The birds are flying high too.
I think they can sit in the sky.
If I were so high I would sit on the clouds.
I think birds have places to be.
What wonderful lives they must lead.

Derek Hiester, Grade 5
St Ambrose School

All the Saints

Saints
God's prophets
Spreading God's teachings
Always praying to Jesus
Christ

Nicholas Roma, Grade 4
Cathedral School of St Catharine of Siena

Benny

There once was an inventor with a key
He had more ideas than I'll ever see
He met with the Philly locals
And when he could no longer see, invented the bifocals
Where would we be without his electricity

The Pennsylvania Gazette told it all
Poor Richards Almanac gave good advice that was tall
Every house with a stove and a lightning rod
He greeted his fellow man with a smile and a nod
For you Mr. Franklin, nothing was too small

Louis Di Bonaventura Jr., Grade 6
St Hilary of Poitiers School

Rainforest

I am the rainforest
Green and old
And inside of me I'm barely cold.
Inside of me there is a ton of trees
And they're really easy, easy to see.
Every morning the tigers take a jog
And right behind them comes the Poison Dart Frogs.
And then guess what slithers up on my old rainforest rug?
Guess, just guess, it's a banana slug!
Then it appears out of a big old log —
It's a, it's a, it's a tailed frog!
Here it comes on my big old trail —
What is it, what is it, it's a Western Tiger Swallowtail!
My most hated animal
Knowing my luck —
Here it comes, it's a Harlequin duck.
Look who's visiting, it's Kinkajou.
He visits, why don't you?
I am the rainforest
Green and old
And inside of me I'm barely cold.

Kaylee Butler, Grade 4
General Nash Elementary School

The Rainbow Filled Sky

Once upon a time there was a rainbow filled sky,
It was so beautiful I thought I was going to cry.

The colors were as wonderful as can be,
They flowed as if they were the sea.

The rainbow was so beautiful.
It was so bold and bright!

So many shades of colors,
It was as fun to look at them hanging with others.

Once upon a time there was a rainbow filled sky.

Paige Meyer, Grade 4
Concord Elementary School

Relaxed/Stressed

Relaxed
candles, music
sleeping, laying, relaxing
calm, soft, loud, busy
running, calling, planning
noisy, tired
Stressed
Danyell Klinedinst, Grade 5
Claysville Elementary School

Ocean

Have you ever seen the waves?
I have how about you?
The white sand gets all wet
When the waves wash up on you

Have you seen the waves?
You have how about I?
I have seen the waves today
Passing, passing, by
Alexandra Toras, Grade 5
Boyce Middle School

Dancers

Dancers are like butterflies,
Leaping in the silent night.
So peaceful, but elegant,
They are a perfect sight.

A dancer is a feather floating,
With poise and graceful flair.
Always going with the flow,
For them to miss a move is rare.
Ayla Torchia, Grade 5
Bermudian Springs Middle School

My Reflection

Every time I look at you
You are looking back at me.
What is it you do?
What is it I see?

I walk left and I walk right.
You follow me all the time.
I have you in my sight
You don't even whine.

I see you in the daytime,
Yet miss you in the dark.
And when I go play,
You will leave a mark!

I look to the left and right
You are always in sight!
Nicole Wallis, Grade 6
Freedom Area Middle School

The Lost Friend

I lost a friend not long ago but I still see her in the halls
She never smiles or looks my way and she ignores my calls

We sort of had a silent fight, about a subject not quite right
She heard a rumor, spread some lies until tears came to my eyes

I couldn't bear the whispering, it hurt me so, way down within
But never did I let her see this pitiful sight of me

I hid my feelings, dried my tears put on a joyless smile
This painful strife seemed like long years when really was a short while

The days passed by, and then the months, they seemed so sad and slow
But I'm not hurting anymore for to that friendship, I've let go

Although I'm well, and over it, the memories bring some tears
I know now, what I hadn't then, some friends turn rotten over years
Emily Longenecker, Grade 6
Central Dauphin Middle School

The Pythagoreans

Pythagoras sailed from Samos' ports
To make Croton's farmers his cohorts
They gathered around him and asked, "Why are we here and how?"
He told them their reasons and they said their vows

They took up the cloak
For this matter was no joke
They studied math and philosophy
And became a true society

Their order had many virtues
One of them was to always be true
Their religion was based on numbers
And they each became humbler

They lived in silence
While their theories did advance
In the B.C. 500s
The bar of their achievements did glow red

In his life he made many advances
His and his followers' mysteries entrances
While many theories are lost
Their knowledge is worth any cost
Hunter Rex, Grade 6
Cathedral School of St Catharine of Siena

Reading

I hear the pages turning a mile a minute
I feel my eyes start to bulge when I get to a good part of the book
I feel anxious to skip to the next chapter, so the suspense will go away
I feel my mouth form all different shapes
I feel my heart sink when I finish the book
Jillian Craig, Grade 5
Newtown Elementary School

Demosthenes

Demosthenes' father died when Demosthenes was seven,
He couldn't recuperate until he was eleven.
This man moved to Athens after he was schooled,
Out of his inheritance, he was fooled.
Demosthenes created many orations,
Many of these caused great aggravation.
One of his lectures was the First Philippic,
This one, Phil did not predict.
Another of Demosthenes' speeches was On the Crown,
In this he said, "I do not want to be crowned."
Aechines was sent to exile,
And he was sent to live on an abandoned isle.
Later Demosthenes goes to exile too,
On the island he had a catch-22.
He decided to jump off a mountaintop,
And he landed with a bop, flop, pop.
To this day he is the best orator of all,
Only I wish he didn't fall.
His influence over many people changed their lives,
O woe! O woe! His suicidal nose dive.

Colin Miksiewicz, Grade 6
Cathedral School of St Catharine of Siena

Fun and Work

First, what is fun?
And what is work?
And are they really different?

Like if work is school, is fun recess?
Of if work is brussel sprouts, is fun dessert?

Or

What if you have fun doing work?
Like doing a project or making a cake.

In the end, I guess they're not that different.
But they're part of life
And life is just that.
So live it, fun and work.

Aaron Pernikoff, Grade 6
United Hebrew Institute

Florida Twister

It starts to rain, I am going insane.
The trees start blowing the sky stops glowing.
Bells start ringing birds stop singing.
The clouds look funny it's not that sunny.
It starts lightning it's very frightening.
The clouds start moving dancers start grooving.
It's a funnel hurry hurry!! Under the tunnel.
Oh no it's a twister we have nowhere to go.
It's ok hold on the metal bar so the twister won't take us far.

Felicia Romesburg, Grade 6
Freedom Area Middle School

Colors

Green is an M&M that goes crunch in my mouth.
Green is a leaf that drifted from a tree.
Green is the grass that I like to play on.
Green is the bush where I scraped my left knee.

Yellow is a sunflower that grows so tall.
Yellow is the sun that beams so bright.
Yellow is a banana that squishes in my mouth.
Yellow is the stars that twinkle in the night

White is a cloud that floats in the sky.
White is the snow that tumbles down so slow.
White is marshmallows that I gobble in my mouth.
White is a daisy that grows in a meadow.

Samantha Corradetti, Grade 6
Immaculate Conception School

Ode to My Dog

My dog is the best
His name is "Shadow"
He is small as an ant, and fluffy as a bunny
He has curly black hair

And he's as cute as a stuffed bear
My dog loves toys
He drifts away with the love of people
Because he's so spoiled
He always has attention
And he listens very well

Shadow barks only once
When he wants to go outside
Every time someone walks in the door
He always goes and greets them with a toy, or he'll go bananas

He's great at doing tricks
It's as cute as a bear whenever he comes and lays next to me!

Michelle LaBella, Grade 6
St Sebastian Elementary School

A Gray Heart

The tears of the sun fall into the sky making rain
The rainfall falls into your heart
Making you feel an emotion of darkness

Your heart feels empty
And you feel darkness all around you
Your heart stops
You stop to let it all out
But it is hard

The moon cries all night
But no one hears a sound
Have you ever heard the moon cry?

Taylor Harvey, Grade 6
St Rosalia Academy

Christmastime

Christmas trees stand all around;
Colorful twinkle lights abound.
Shivering carolers sing a song
While Christmas bells jingle long.
Gifts stand under the Christmas tree,
And children's faces are filled with glee,
Rejoicing in the past good year,
For a new one is almost here.

Ben Paget, Grade 6
Portersville Christian School

My Teddy Bear

My cute little teddy bear.
Rubbing softly against my hair.
Little, tiny, beady eyes,
Always there for when I cry.
Black, brown, white, blue,
Hugging him when I get the flu.
For, it is my soft teddy bear.
He will always love and care.

Amelia Nahum, Grade 4
Avonworth Elementary School

Juggling

Juggling
It is amazing
In the circus
They juggle torches,
chain saws, chairs, even people
Or just balls
But if you're new
and want to keep your hands
Please don't start,
with chain saws

Tommy Augenstein, Grade 5
Lincoln Elementary School

Waterfalls

Waterfalls, waterfalls,
Go outside city walls.

There are pictures of them
In people's halls.

Some people say,
"They overflow in May!"

Some look like someone is dropping
Sparkling diamonds down,
down,
down.

No matter how hard you look,
You'll never find one in Nicktown.

Sarah Gomish, Grade 4
Northern Cambria Catholic School

Rudeness/Respect

Rudeness
Offensive, cruel
Insulting, disregarding, savaging
Contempt, scorn, esteem, reverence
Complimenting, valuing, appreciating
Honorable, admiring
Respect

Logan Andrew Dietz, Grade 6
St Sebastian Elementary School

C Is for Cat

C is the little cat
Who sits all day
Watching the bowl of fish
She seems to know
Not to go
The little cat makes a wish

Caroline Farrell, Grade 4
Our Lady of Peace School

Toaster

I am a toaster,
I am sometimes very cheap.
And when your toast is ready,
I will tell you with a beep!

If your toast is stuck in me,
don't get it out with a knife.
If you do, you will get
the electrocution of your life!

Daniel Zinobile, Grade 5
McMurray Elementary School

Basketball

B earing with the heat
A very tiring pair of feet
S hoot the ball high in the air
K ids are screaming yay
E nough of this silly nonsense
T he score is very high
B askets are being made
A ll of us are yelling at bay
L oving the game
L ooks like we won

Cody Craig, Grade 4
Concord Elementary School

Sharks

Sharks
Predators, sizes
Catching, eating, sensing
There are many sharks.
Cookie Cutter Shark

Nicholas Musa, Grade 5
East Stroudsburg Elementary School

The Ocean

In the ocean waves crash,
Onto the shore the seashells dash.
As the dolphins glide by,
Seagulls fly in the sky.
The ocean is a good place to be.

Lindsay Randall, Grade 5
East Stroudsburg Elementary School

Football

F ast
O ne touchdown
O ne win
T ackle
B litz
A thletic
L earn
L ast

Juan Diego Saenz, Grade 5
East Stroudsburg Elementary School

Leaves

The leaves tickled my feet,
On the fall, cold ground.
Small and very petite,
They seemed to be earthbound.

Then rustling in circles and twirls,
'Til they touch the tree
Calming down to a swirl,
Hitting the ground as soft as can be.

Ryan Starner, Grade 5
Bermudian Springs Middle School

Wolves

Wolves can be different colors,
And they can be different sizes.
They look so cute and fun,
But there is an evil side to them.
Wolves may trick you many ways,
But don't forget their sweetie ways.
Wolves have senses just like us,
They can cause a lot of fuss.
People think that wolves are bad,
When they really aren't so bad.
That's what I think of wolves!

Shiloh Waltman, Grade 4
Watsontown Elementary School

Spring

Spring
Fun, warm
Playing, laughing, teaching
Spring is the best ever.
Season

Tiffany Conklin, Grade 4
West Branch Area Elementary School

Honda Is the Best

H ot engine after riding
O ff road riding every day just coming in to get warm
N ever doubt if you can get over something
D riving off jumps, over hills, and climbing rocks
A TVing is number one!

I n the air doing tricks
S tarting up every time

T rust your instincts when riding
H urrying to get home for dinner
E veryone can enjoy

B uying and selling ATVs to get better ones
E ntertaining like nothing else
S oaring through the air at 50 mph
T ime spent with family and friends

Reed Shuttle, Grade 6
Bridle Path Elementary School

What Is Green?

Green is grass.
Green is a ball.
Green is a clover.
Green is a leaf.
Green is a caterpillar.
Green is a tree.
Green is an apple.
Green is an eraser.
Green is a feather.
Green is a notebook.
Green is a shirt.
Green is a hat.
Green is a book.

Green is a door.
Green is a coat.
Green is a lunch box.
Green is a turtle.
Green is a book bag.
Green is a balloon.
Green is palm trees.
Green is a crayon.
Green is socks.
Green is a magnet.
Green is a necklace.
Green is a pencil.
Green is a marker.

What would we do without green?

Gabriella Benninger, Grade 4
St Leo School

Reading

In the evening
And pleasing
In a quiet house
I read and think
How beautiful the sunset is today
Are there more people who think the same
Nice, shiny orange balloon

Tyll Dinges, Grade 5
Wexford Elementary School

Matt and Pat

There once was a leprechaun named Matt.
He had a friend named Pat.
He liked to look for gold with mold.
One day Matt lost his gold and went to tell Pat.

Dakota Creek, Grade 4
West Branch Area Elementary School

Spring!!!

Spring spring is my favorite time of year
Spring spring it is finally here
Spring spring the weather is fine
Spring spring I wish it was mine
Spring spring it's a great time to play
Spring spring it's here from March to May
Spring spring it's awesome to me
Spring spring good-bye buddy.

David Russell, Grade 4
McDonald Elementary School

Spring Again

Ah, yes it's spring again,
That time of year when sorrows end.

No more crying, weeping, mourning, or being sad,
It's time to hang out with your family, mom and dad.

A time when flowers bloom and birds sing,
A time to rise up, like an eagle with wings.

Let the wind blow on your face, as you fly so high,
You can dream, be happy, or reach out and touch the sky.

At night you can look at the stars above,
And sit and reflect gracefully like an elegant white dove.

Brendon Griffin, Grade 6
Moravian Academy Middle School

The Long Walk Home

An angry blizzard I call this sight.
I trudge through the snow with all my might.
I'm bundled in my coat so tight,
Searching for my cottage light.

My wife and children are snuggled up there,
Awaiting my return with utmost care.
My wife in her rocking chair,
My daughter with her teddy bear.

My son, he's probably fast asleep,
But me, I'm struggling through the sleet.

Taylore Roth, Grade 5
Bushkill Elementary School

Computers

A mouse, a keyboard, a monitor and a CPU.
They all work together to help you.
With homework, with letters, and whatever else you need.
You should have no fear, because computers are here!
You can type the answers to your homework on them.
You can e-mail your friend, too.
Computers are the world's best friend.

Coleman Whiteley, Grade 5
Souderton Charter School Collaborative

Basketball

B alls being thrown around
A lways a battle
S neakers on the move
K eeping the ball is important
E xtra points for fouls
T imeouts are called
B alls thrown into hoops
A lways a good game
L ast minute score
L oser and a winner

John Kozak, Grade 5
Sacred Heart of Jesus School

Happiness, Love, and Memories

From your great-grandma
To your mom and dad
With your family reunions
To the memories you had.
The time that flows,
It flows so fast
You love them so much
And they love you back.
On Christmas Eve
You all get together
To give presents
To your Pollyanna.
From money to clothes
To a big teddy bear
You just can't explain
How much you care
The happiness
Love
Memories
You had
That's why family is there.

Katie Foley, Grade 6
Hillcrest Elementary School

Doctors

Doctors are like bandages,
They help us when we're hurt.
They clean our infections,
And wipe out all the dirt.

Doctors are like parents,
They are loving and do care.
They help us feel much better,
Because they are always there.

Doctors are like medicine,
They cure us when we're sick.
They always give us lollipops,
Everyone likes to lick.

Bryan Westerlund, Grade 6
St Valentine Elementary School

Gym Class

Gym class is like a pest,
That never leaves you alone.
Gym class is like an odor,
That never goes away.
Gym class is like a cold,
I just want to stop having it.
Gym class is like an itch,
It keeps coming back.

I hate gym class a lot!

Austin Shearer, Grade 6
Chambersburg Area Middle School

Spring

Springtime has arrived
Plants are now alive
Birds are migrating
Animals stop hibernating
Living things are revived

Clay Gannon, Grade 5
Pocopson Elementary School

Super Game

Indoor soccer
Fast, fun
Kicking, running, screaming
Aggressive, hustle, sweat, team work
Dodging, pushing, passing
Strong, quick
Champions

Dominique Dennis, Grade 4
Memorial Elementary School

I'll See Ya in Heaven

Standing in the trenches
Along with his buddy
Shooting at the enemy
Then he heard a groan
He looked beside him
His buddy was not there
Finally he looked down
There he was bleeding to death
He knelt down to see what he could do
Then his buddy said his last words
"I'll see ya in Heaven."

Brandon Moist, Grade 6
Strodes Mills Middle School

The Pearl

There once was a very slim girl
Who wanted to own a pearl
She went to the beach
Found her a leech
But there was no pearl for the girl

Kaitlyn Pendrak, Grade 4
Avonworth Elementary School

War

War is like a dead flower,
yet,
is still like a seed.
Death of one idea, birth of another.
Growing on ideas and plans.
Guns shooting
Bang! Bang!
Bang! Bang!
Bang! Bang!
A song of guns.
A cry for help.
People dying are seeds in the earth.
Motivation to go on.
Fighting,
Fighting,
War doesn't warm the women's hearts,
Or, their tears.
People crying,
Mothers weeping
Men shouting
Babies sleeping
Wives worrying,
Isn't it great?

Patrick Jones, Grade 6
Mount Nittany Middle School

Colors of the Rainbow

Black is for the night
Gold is for the sunlight

Red is for roses
Green is for garden hoses

Blue is the color of the summer skies
Brown is the color of my eyes

Orange pumpkins grow in fall
White snow makes great snowballs

Purple is in the rainbow
Yellow makes bad snow

Rainbows have the best colors!

Chris Houck, Grade 6
Cheswick Christian Academy

The Fire Rose

A single rose in a vase
the rose on fire the vase a blaze.
The people inside in daze
trapped in a hell-like maze.
To think it all started with a rose
the fire rose to be precise.

Will Schaeffer, Grade 5
Miquon School

Friends

Friends
Friends are there when you need them.
Friends keep your secrets
Play with them, laugh with them, share with them.
Friends are happy to be with you
They never put you down.
Friends are people who will last a month, to
a year, to an entire lifetime.
Cherish them, love them, keep them
Friends

Kristen Rohm, Grade 6
West Allegheny Middle School

Sean

Sean
Short, skinny, kind, and awesome
Son of Jimmy and Lisa
Lover of video games, board games, and hot dogs
Who feels sick of being grounded; I hate being yelled at
and tired on Mondays
Who finds happiness in my family, games, and friends
Who needs a hug, haircut, and care
Who fears mean people, violence, and bad dreams
Who would like to see Usher and Ciara
Who enjoys movies and games
Who likes to wear jeans and sweats
Resident of East Stroudsburg
McFarlane

Sean McFarlane, Grade 5
East Stroudsburg Elementary School

Amber

A very good friend.
M iddle name is Marie.
B est friends with Jessyka, Kelci and Wendie.
E nergetic.
R ight handed.

Amber Marie Menke, Grade 6
West Allegheny Middle School

A Great Place to Go

The beach is a great place to go
I don't have to worry about wind, rain, or snow
I love the warm, sandy ground
I can hear the waves crashing sound
The sun's heat is hot on my head
And I'm watching the seagulls all get fed
The ocean is like my own pool
It makes me feel refreshing and cool
I don't want this feeling to ever end
I hope the sun's light never ends
Wow, I really love it here
Hopefully I come back next year!

Mary Holmes, Grade 6
West Allegheny Middle School

The Dog

There once was a silly, silly dog.
Who went on a funny little jog.
He found a Pokémon named Seedot.
Who always hid in a little pot.
Then he found his way back through the bog.

Derrick Graham, Grade 4
West Branch Area Elementary School

Michele Kwan

Youngest of three children,
Began skating at five years old,
Michele Kwan's the greatest figure skater,
Or so I have been told.

Olympic and National titles,
She won on ice so cold,
Impressive leaps and flying twirls,
This girl's off to win another gold!

Hallie Papiernik, Grade 5
Villa Maria Academy Lower School

S Is for Shopping

S is for shopping
The stores are filled with elegant pink boots
I wish it would last all day
Maybe from July until May
Most people come carrying their loot

Sarah Wagner, Grade 4
Our Lady of Peace School

Spring

S ummer is coming
P eople are running
R ainy days are in the forecast
I mpressions of happy faces at last
N ights are still cold
G oing through the winter we have all been bold

Caitlin Lynch, Grade 5
Clay Elementary School

A Bird's Flying

Look, a bird is flying into the sky
Happily riding on the wind
And when it's getting very, very high
I see the wings are flapping, trying to find
A peaceful place to stop for a rest
Maybe for warmth or to set up a nest

How I wish to be like this bird
So I could rise high enough to see
All the world wonders I have heard
The mountains, the rivers, the sea
So I could sail with the clouds so high
Then to skim where the waves reach the sky

Bilyana Tzolova, Grade 5
Easterly Parkway Elementary School

Dogs/Cats
Dogs
Furry, cute
playful, loving, active
good, happy, excited, determined
Cats
Isabella Tomko, Grade 4
St Sebastian Elementary School

Rainbow
R eally cool
A wesome
I love rainbows
N ever ending amazement
B eautiful colors
O h! It's like crayons in the sky
W ow!

Alyssa Carson, Grade 4
Avonworth Elementary School

The Walls of Troy
The clashing of swords
The screaming of men
The tears of bloodshed
The walls of Troy falling to its knees
The king begged for mercy
But no pity was pleased
The men fought hard
And marched back to Greece
They marched back in victory
For the great nation of Greece
Nicholas Leonello, Grade 6
St Rosalia Academy

Hiding
Sometimes I feel like hiding in the
Shadows of the world.
I just hide cold and shivering
my mind completely blank.
Confused, just sitting there
nowhere to go or hide. I scream.
Nothing but echoes.
Ca'Nisha R. Howard, Grade 6
West Allegheny Middle School

Video Camera
I am a video camera
I can tape a funny clip
Maybe you can be on AFV
If you fall and trip.

I can also tape plays
Although they are boring
I might fall asleep
Don't mind my snoring.
Brenna Ramsay, Grade 5
McMurray Elementary School

Ginger
on **G** oing puppy who is full of joy, loves to play
w **I** th that ducky toy, gonna chase it
i **N** the kitchen when I get half way slam on the brakes to stop and
G et a drink, and for some reason whenever I blink it looks like I wink.
ev **E** ry day I need to run and when I get started I
R ant on and on.

Cody Ketter, Grade 6
H Austin Snyder Elementary School

Autumn Dancing in the Air
Sometimes falling like a star,
Leaves can go very far.
Falling leaves from the sky,
Meaning that they all died.
Leaves are a gentle song blowing in the wind.
Dancing swiftly through the air.
Colors flashing right and left.
An exciting time for animals to see.
Summer is gone, fall is here, yippee!
Drowning in leaves,
As bears go into hibernation,
Needing shelter for winter to come.
Getting colder by the day,
Put your sweatshirt on right away!
Woods are filled with animals and leaves.
As the night creeps in the moon shines on the leaves everywhere.
Kelly Wilson, Grade 6
Our Lady of Mount Carmel School

Freedom
Freedom is important; it should be all around.
Rosa Parks was one way that freedom could be found.
On buses then there were some rules for people who were black.
The white could sit in front of them, but black would sit in back.

Rosa Parks was black you see, and she sat in the front.
But one man said, "You can't sit here!" and made a tiny grunt.
And even though she should have sat in the back of that long bus,
She didn't move and now she's made some freedom for all of us.

Another way to freedom for all the rest of us
Was Martin Luther King, and what a hero he was.
He said these words and they are not as silly as they seem.
Those words he said to all of us were just, "I have a dream."

This dream of his was very great and what it was was that
A black would be the same as whites; not treated like a rat.
This man knew what he had to do and this is all it was:
He had to live his dream and in the end that's what he does.

One other way to freedom is its heroes of today.
And we can all be heroes in this one important way:
Just don't treat people like they're slaves and always try to do
What people of our freedom would and what they would say, too.
Samantha Mack, Grade 4
St Alexis School

Nature

Blue is raindrops on my head,
Black is saying "time for bed."

Red is the sun setting,
Green is the dollar bills flashing while people are betting.

White is the newborn seal,
Yellow is the mushy cornmeal.

Brown is wood, freshly cut,
Pink is a collar for a mutt.

Purple is a blooming flower,
Orange is the strong will of power.

Sophia Erb, Grade 6
Moss Side Middle School

Something Silly

Something silly, scary and strange
Something silly, is like the home of the range
Something silly I don't know more
But if you give me a hint I could do more
But if you know something silly
Then write a poem or 2
I know you will try it
I know you'll make it through
Today I'm tired, I'm sleepy and through
Tomorrow is another day for more something silly poems
(Don't forget to write 1 or 2)
Today I'm through

Mia Bennett, Grade 6
Independence Charter School

My School Day

At Neil Armstrong I go to science class,
Be careful not to cut yourself on the measuring glass.
Next it's math,
The substitute teacher was a psychopath.
Next I go to play the cello,
Mrs. Irwin always says "hello."
After that I go to lunch,
On some chips I shall munch.
Then comes one of my favorite classes of the day,
I quickly run off to L.A.
Then it's reading I travel to,
We're reading *The Giver*, are you?
Social Studies class is next,
Where we read a whole bunch of text.
Health is the Unified Arts I am in,
This is where we learn that smoking is a sin.
Then my school day ends, hooray, hooray,
I'll start all over another day.
When I say good-bye to all my friends
This is how the school day ends!

Nadia Cook-Loshilov, Grade 6
Neil Armstrong Middle School

Swim Meet

A flash, a splash, the race has begun.
I hear the cheering and chanting,
the screaming of my coach.
I look over to see my opponent.
I think to myself, "Go faster, or finish hard."
I want a better time, a faster time.
Each hundredth counts.
I strive to be on top, to beat my rivals,
please my coaches, be my best.
I slam my hand against the wall.
I finished. I look up,
jerking my head looking for the time.
I won!

Amanda Gannon, Grade 6
West Allegheny Middle School

Surprised

Surprised is yellow.
It sounds like a shout.
It smells like tropical flowers.
It tastes like pop rocks.
It looks like a Jack in the Box popping out.
Surprised is jumping on your bed and shouting Wow!

Sarah Wiley, Grade 6
Grasse Elementary School

The Green Fuzzy Monster

The green fuzzy monster
Shy
Broken
Sad
He is never ever mad.
He really craves to have a friend,
someone to be there for him
'til the very end.
He is not a horrifying fellow.
If you ask me,
he looks kinda yellow.
So next time you see this warm, fuzzy guy,
don't be terrified,
Just say hi!

Todd Saylor, Grade 6
Hillcrest Elementary School

Rainbow

The Irish stay
On a pile of hay
Looking at the wonderful slide.
That reaches the sky
And goes to a pot of gold.
The slide is colorful,
That it looks nothing but a bunch of crayons in a line.
The slide is a rainbow.

Costa Barlamas, Grade 6
Freedom Area Middle School

Jungle Rumble!
Elephants are mumbling
Mice are whispering
Birds are talking
It's a Jungle Rumble!
Monkeys are chatterboxes
Lions are scream-machines
Gorillas are laughmakers
It's a Jungle Rumble!
When the animals are
Waking, screaming, mumbling
Whispering, laughing, chattering,
It must be a Jungle Rumble!
Erin Redwing, Grade 4
Easterly Parkway Elementary School

Leaves
Leaves falling off trees
Sometimes orange yellow and green
Beautiful leaves
Casey Morris, Grade 4
East End Elementary School

Butterfly
As peaceful as the sea at sunrise,
As radiant as a rainbow in the sky,
As swift as a rabbit,
What I see is a butterfly.
Claire Remy, Grade 4
St Francis of Assisi School

Fall Leaves
They're in the trees.
They're on the ground.
They're in the air.
They're everywhere!

Leaves are big.
Leaves are small.
Some are crunchy.
Some make no noise at all.

Some stay in the trees,
Some fall on the ground,
But wherever you go,
Leaves can be found!
LeeAnn Streshenkoff, Grade 5
Concord Elementary School

Sammy Says
Sammy says she is so sick
of slimy snakes and Sprite
that she will even spend time
with scorpions in the state of
South Carolina.
Hillary Dietrich, Grade 6
Allison Park Elementary School

Fall Has Arrived
Bushes rumbling in the wind
Pebbles under my feet
Gliding me across the courtyard
Feel like roller blades
Under my shoes
Water in the old bird bath
Rising like waves in the ocean
Leaves clinging to the tree
Like a baby would to its mother
Wind whispering into my ear
Tickling my face
Feels like someone watching over me
When I enter the courtyard
Butterfly bush leaning
Like a willow in the wind
Now

Finally

Fall has arrived
Dana Billy, Grade 5
Lower Salford Elementary School

Winter
Cold, wet
Freezing, sleeting, blowing
Blistery, icy, slippery, windy
Falling, shivering, sliding
White, snowy
Winter
Kirsten Setzer, Grade 4
Memorial Elementary School

No School Today
Today at school was very
Boring no one was in homeroom
No one was in computer class not
Even a teacher.

When I went to lunch I
Could just smell old demerits.
And when I went down the
Halls I did not see anyone at all.

I went back to class still no one
There again. All I did was hop
Up and down the halls.
Finally I saw someone
The janitor.

He told me that yesterday was
The last day of school.
So I was the only frog at school.
Patric Fogelsonger, Grade 6
Chambersburg Area Middle School

Shopping
My mother took me to the mall today
the fees I got I cannot pay

I shopped and shopped until I dropped
until my wallet finally flopped

I bought a ton of shoes and clothes
and once again my wallet foreclosed

My mom said I'll have to pay her back
I thought that sounded kinda wack

And so now all those chores I do
will forever remind me of all those shoes
Shannon Sullivan, Grade 6
Carson Middle School

Mom
Mom
Nice huggable
Cleaning, buying, cooking
A really hard working person
Relative
Tyler Bizzarro, Grade 4
East End Elementary School

The Soldiers
Soldiers
responsible, fair
helping, serving, saving
The soldiers saved our lives.
Americans
Abigail Bumbarger, Grade 4
West Branch Area Elementary School

Life
L ike to have friends
I slands to have vacations
F lowers to enjoy
E very season and person
Logan Tirums, Grade 4
East End Elementary School

Poems
Waste bin full of paper
Words running through my head
Over and over
Sharpening lead
Write about a lake
Or a secret place
Maybe take a break
It that's the case
Poems are dreams on paper
Write about them later
Christine Simpson, Grade 5
East Stroudsburg Elementary School

Soccer

Soccer is my sport,
I run around the court.
Kicking the ball is fun,
But I don't play in the sun.

I got a soccer pin,
But we really didn't win.
I tried to cheer them up,
They wouldn't listen for a buck.

We finally made it to the championship game,
And everyone came.
We even won,
It was a pain, but fun.

Kayla Kashlak, Grade 4
Panther Valley Elementary School

He Is My Best Brother

He cried when I broke his toy
He stopped crying when I got in trouble for it.

He cried every time I won the game
He laughed every time I lost.

He cried when Mom said she likes me more
He stopped crying when Dad said he likes him more

He cried when I ate his last cookie
He laughed when he ate my last cookie

He's always jealous and annoying
And he thinks he's always right

But, do you know what?
He is the best; he is my brother!

Yoo Su Nho, Grade 6
Sacred Heart Elementary School

Seasons

Spring's flowers, autumn's breeze
Summer's warmth and my winter's sneeze.
Seasons pass through the year
As we know when each season is here.
Winter's cold and in our way
Although I don't mind a snowy day.
Now is spring as flowers bloom
I can finally come out of my room.
Summer arrives and what do you know?
The pool's are open — the water will flow!
Time goes fast and now it's fall
I need new school clothes at the mall.
Every season has its own style
And each will only last for a while.

Jennifer Buss, Grade 5
Vandergrift Elementary School

Ode to My Dog

She was as black as a night
With a new moon.
She was as vicious as a bear
Protecting her cubs.
She was friendly because
She would look for a pat on the head.
She was as pretty as a flower.
She loved me.
She also loved my family.
She would chug her water, and wolf down her food
After long walks
She would put her head on my lap and I would pet her.
She would wag her tail when I got home from school
She would play games with me
She would perk her ears when the garage door went up
She would chase other animals, like deer.
She protected me because she loved me.
She liked the color orange.
She barked at other dogs.
She liked sitting out under the sun.
She was my dog Addie and I loved her.

Michael Witt, Grade 6
St Sebastian Elementary School

Tree Hugger

I am a tree hugger
I am a tree lover
When our people cut the forests down
It puts a great frown on our society
Which is a great part of me
And you
And you and you and you

Now that our trees are disappearing
All our lost oxygen will not be reappearing

Right now the sky is blue
But it's turning gray
As the acid rain begins to spray

Paul J. Brandebura, Grade 6
West Allegheny Middle School

School Time

S chool is here five times a week
C an't help but weep and whine
H omework is tough every night
O h man it is homework time
O ur school bus is here to take us to school
L ong hours writing all day

T eachers expect hard work
I n time you will have fun
M ost of the fun is out on the playground
E ventually the day is done

Justin McKenney, Grade 6
Bridle Path Elementary School

Respect
Respect
Helpful, advice
It makes people feel good
It is nice to say or to do
Helpful
Courtney Santos, Grade 4
Penn-Kidder Campus

Snow
Snow is very cold
Very bright it's the
Opposite of summer night
It's like the beauty of a butterfly
The butterfly flies
And the snow falls Goodnight.
Michelle Perna, Grade 6
Haverford Middle School

Abhor/Respect
abhor
aweless, irreverent
insulting, disparaging, desecrating
outrage, neglect, admiration, courtesy
honoring, hallowing, hailing,
ceremonies, deferential
respect
Vicki Mustovic, Grade 6
St Sebastian Elementary School

Dog in a Tub
There was a big dog in a tub
who loved to get a good scrub.
He always would whine,
although he was fine
and would quit when he got a good rub.
Alessondra Treece, Grade 6
Bedford Middle School

Ice Cream
There's so many flavors,
So many choices.
I love them all,
So how will I do this?
I have to think fast,
Before the truck leaves.
I've made my decision,
And it shall be vanilla!
Yummy, good choice!
And when the truck goes,
I hear that silly song
I scream.
You scream.
We all scream.
…For ice cream!
Danielle Martin, Grade 6
Locust Grove Mennonite School

Ode to My Cat
My cat is like a man that has just been taken into a psycho clinic.
My cat likes boxes and the broom,
But when she goes outside she likes the foxes,
But hates the mushrooms.
She is a fierce lion,
She is a fast going,
Cute,
And also energetic.
She plays with air-soft BB's
With her shiny fur
Her brown and green eyes
And her different colored paws.
Her whiskers twinkle in the sunlight,
And her tail swaying back and forth across the ground.
Ham
Milk
Chicken
You name it,
My cat likes it.
Kevin Corcoran, Grade 6
St Sebastian Elementary School

The Truth
Some people go through their whole life wanting something,
Then when it's too late, you find out you had it the whole time.
Never claiming it; letting it pass by.

Some people live their whole lives by rules and regulations,
Just staying on the safe side and never doing otherwise.
Relax, God wants us to enjoy life to the fullest.

Some people wonder why angels aren't around today,
God sends angels to us every day through other people.
They're there, but, now we call them friends.

Some people ask the question "Why did this happen to me?",
when something goes wrong,
God will never give us something we cannot handle.
He believes in us; we just have to believe in ourselves.

Some people go through their whole life not knowing who they are,
God gave us an identity so we can make something of it.
Don't be fooled, stay true to yourself!
Victoria Vetter, Grade 6
Holy Family Academy

Mom
If I would fall down and cry my mom would be there sooo quickly
Would yours?
If I would get sick my mom always knew the doctor's phone number
Would yours?
If I was lost my mom would keep looking until she found me
Would yours?
I love my mom

Taylor Smith, Grade 6
Locust Grove Mennonite School

Life

Life goes fast when the cold rides past
Life is hard when you push it too far
When it comes to age 97 you might not be in Heaven
Days you win days you lose
There's always a chance for you

Jarrell Adams, Grade 6
Independence Charter School

Lily's Game

Lily was a girl,
Who was so very fast,
One day she gave b-ball a whirl,
And boy she had a blast.

She practiced day and night,
And soon got really good,
To watch her play was such a sight,
She could score no matter where she stood.

She tried out for the team,
All her shots went in,
Lily showed the team how to screen,
Which made the coaches grin.

When Lily made the team,
She always did play hard,
This really made her beam,
And was their first all-star guard.

Mary Catherine Curran, Grade 5
Villa Maria Academy Lower School

Christmas

C aroling around with friends
H appy to get presents
R ipping wrapping paper off presents
I love Santa Claus
S ledding down hills
T earing through the snow on a snowmobile
M rs. Claus is Santa's helper
A snowy night on Christmas Eve
S kate on the ice pond.

Austin Decker, Grade 4
Bushkill Elementary School

Nature

As the sun shines,
it makes a larger shadow.
I walk away because it seems to follow me.
As I run the leaves chase me.
I am safely in my tent for 6 days.
We come home and I need some city air,
I decide to take a walk to the park,
all of a sudden the grass hypnotizes me,
I'm back in my house and now I HATE NATURE!!

Ciera Coombs, Grade 6
Freedom Area Middle School

Darkness and Light

Darkness is like a broken friendship.
It is as your heart was crushed and trampled on.
Darkness is lifeless darkness is nothing.

Light is like a new friendship.
Light is as if your heart was lifted and singing.
Light is life light is anything.

Reginald James, Grade 5
East Stroudsburg Elementary School

The Human

A human that lived on the moon
he wished he could go back to earth soon
but the truth really is
he was scared of show biz
so he was hiding on the moon

Joshua Oldham, Grade 6
Bedford Middle School

Summer

I can't wait until summer,
but those bees are such a bummer.
I can't wait until the last day of school,
to go swimming in my pool!
Late nights, pillow fights, all of those mosquito bites.
Always going to the pool with Jess,
but she never wears a dress!
The ice cream man is coming soon
with snow cones and wooden spoons.

Rachel Link, Grade 6
West Allegheny Middle School

Friends

Friends are great!
Friends are true,
Sometimes friendships take time to grow,
Sometimes they come out of the blue,
Friends you may know since you were small or for just a day,
One thing makes them all the same,
Friends help you find your way.

Tara Koskulitz, Grade 4
Holy Family Academy

Rainforest

Exploring in the rainforest is the best,
Lots of tweeting birds in their nests.
Bunches of insects creeping around,
Picked one up from its sand mound.

The rainforest is wet and has lots of trees,
Sweet and cool in the summer breeze.
Lots of rabbits scampering all around,
Hippity-hopping all home bound.

Garrett Cook, Grade 5
Bermudian Springs Middle School

Big Fat "F!"

Big fat "F," the letter I hate. Especially when it's one of my grades. Oh no here it comes again on my little brother's homework, I hope we win, then he won't get in trouble. Oh yeah, sometimes I love the letter "F" because it's the beginning of the best words like, "Fashion," "Fabulous," and oh yeah I can't forget about the place of France the country of love. So bye bye now you've just heard about the one and only, big fat "F."

Shaquanna Leak, Grade 6
Independence Charter School

Color of Friendship

The color of friendship is like the color of love, faith, or anything else. The color of friendship can be blue, pink, purple, black, or white. It doesn't matter, just as long as you love them for who they are inside and not what's on the outside. The color of friendship is something you better hold on to in life. If you hold on to that color of friendship you will always be happy and always have a special friend. That friend will always stick with you through tough times and when you're feeling down they come and cheer you up. The color of friendship can build trust with your friends, but before you go tell special things to people make sure you build that color of friendship or you'll never be able to trust again. Hold on to that color of friendship. Never let it fade away!

Alyssa Kay Hughes, Grade 6
Bedford Middle School

Summer

The silent ocean waves to me: "Jump in! Summer's here!"
There will soon be children running wild and free, with nothing to be done but spend a day in the sun!
The shells on the beach are calling to me: "Pick me up and take me home to put on your shelf so I won't be alone."
Summer starts calling: "I'm here, have fun! With no school in the way, there's room to run!"
The wild children do cartwheels on the beach. The dunes are mountains, their tops beyond reach.
In the years to come, I will always treasure my summer memories.

Jenny LaPierre, Grade 5
Sol Feinstone Elementary School

Summertime

I open my eyes and I see the bright, blue sky looking at me like a giant camera.
I hear the birds sing like a sweet lullaby.
I smell the fresh cut green grass. It smells like a new day.
I can taste the cold, creamy, chocolate ice cream melting in my mouth like cotton candy.
I can feel the heat from the sun making me sweat.
Time to go for a dip!

Gabriela Albegiani, Grade 5
Easterly Parkway Elementary School

Boats

I enjoy looking at big and little boats. Some boats are for work and some are for play. Some run at night and some run in the day. Boats can be fast and boats can be slow. You cannot run a boat in the snow. You can run boats in a river or lake, even an ocean or bay. Boats bring goods every day. Boats can run in and out of forts, and help supply army forts. Some boats are famous and go down in history, and others remain a mystery. Some run on gas and other boats cannot go too fast. Some boats are strong and some boats are weak, some boats make a trip in a day, and others make it in a week. Some boats sail beside sea walls and other boats get caught in squalls. That is how some boats run some boats are for work and some boats are for fun.

Terry Plank, Grade 6
Strodes Mills Middle School

The Mountains

The mountains' snow is ice being shoved in hot chocolate,
The dirt is my chocolate powder and is being dumped in the milk,
The grass is mint in chunks and is being sprinkled in the mixture,
You might say that a mountain has nothing special, but in my mind it's a delicious snack!

Natalia Siguenza, Grade 5
Jenkintown Elementary School

Survivor Sallie

Survivor Sallie swam straight over several sharks,
still stinging from sunburn,
while slowly, but surely,
setting to a soft sandy shore.

Rachel Tucker, Grade 6
Allison Park Elementary School

After Fall, Before Winter

The air is as stiff as cardboard
pine needles on the great pine tree
as pointy as the toe of a women's fancy dress shoe
leaves on the bushes
are red, green and yellow
some are just downright orange
The birdbath looks like still water
showered with brown leaves
birdhouse has not
one single soul in it
whiskey barrels filled with wind dried plants
their summer colors long gone
birds in the sky
going south
headed for vacation
running from winter

Alyssa Santangelo, Grade 5
Lower Salford Elementary School

School Book

The school I am sitting in is a book.
Yes, a book with lots of information and stories,
but don't get any worries,
this book is not a bore.
The kids and teachers are characters,
playing their part.
The classrooms are the pages.
On each page there is always something interesting,
just like,
in each classroom something is always being taught.

Gabrielle Massi, Grade 6
Guth Elementary School

All About Me

Ashley Parks.
Shy, funny, nice.
Wishes to become a great person.
Dreams of going back to Texas.
Wants to travel around the world.
Who wonders what I will be like when I'm older.
Who fears upside down roller coasters.
Who likes to learn new things.
Who believes in almost everything.
Who plans to do new things.
That's me!

Ashley Parks, Grade 4
Bushkill Elementary School

Until You Cry*

You never know you miss something
Until you cry.
First, it's there and then it's gone.
And you wish it still would be going on;
So the next opportunity that comes knocking at your door,
Answer it and give it your full,
Give it all you've got.
PAX ET BONUM
(Peace and Good)

Olivia Kirsch, Grade 5
Northern Cambria Catholic School
*Dedicated to the cast and crew of "Dead Man Walking"

The Want to Skate

When she was eight,
she wanted to skate.
Her mother said no,
but they went to a show.

She wanted to skate,
her mother said when you're older than eight.
For now her mother said no.
She had to show her how it would go.

She asked once more,
her mother said sure.
Her mother was sad,
but she was glad.

Katherine Brittner, Grade 6
St Gregory Elementary School

Mother Nature's Right Hand Man

I nip at your toes,
I freeze your nose.
I put icing on the ground,
I cannot be found.
   Can you guess who I am?
   Jack Frost!
I am the Winter King!
   But in summer I'm not king of anything!

Christian Porto, Grade 4
Beaver County Christian School

The Rainbow

The rainbow has many colors in her heart.
She shines in sparks,
On a rainy day.
She's marked with all the colors in her mood.
She has many personalities like…
Red, orange, yellow, green blue, and purple,
She'll change her mood
From rain to sun.
She has pots of gold
At the end of her soul.

Elizabeth DeBerardinis, Grade 4
Lionville Elementary School

The Golfer

Tiger Woods
Smart and nice
Playing in tournaments
Hitting hole in ones
Winning the tournaments
Father, winner, golfer
Tyler Mark, Grade 5
Shafer Elementary School

School

Once I started school
I felt like I was a fool
I opened the door
To learn some more
Now I feel like I'm cool
Dakota Rollage, Grade 4
South Park Elementary Center

Robbie the Leprechaun

There was a leprechaun named Robbie
He had a special hobby.
He went to look for a rainbow,
Even though he walked very slow.
Then he drank green tea in his lobby.
Jeremy Trump, Grade 4
West Branch Area Elementary School

Whoopee Pie Cake

Whoopee pie cake
For goodness sake.
The sacrifice that I'll make
For some whoopee pie cake.
Whoopee pie cake you taste so good.
I love to eat, and I would if I could.
Whoopee pie cake you are like a dream.
Oh, what I'd do to taste your cream.
Remington Wright, Grade 4
Watsontown Elementary School

Recycle

The bees will sneeze if you don't recycle
The trees will be pleased if you do
So clean and clean, and take care please
The trees and bees will thank you.
Cody Cooke, Grade 4
Fishing Creek Elementary School

Butterfly

Butterfly
Peaceful, colorful
Fluttering, relaxing, amazing
They are all different
Insect
Jacqueline Palmieri, Grade 5
Penn-Kidder Campus

My Favorite Kind of Day

The grass is green the sun is shining,
I get my bike in perfect timing.
I ride up a hill. My legs are sore,
but I do it again two times more.
I go inside for lunch,
PB&J is what I'll munch.
I go to the pool,
I jump in — how refreshing and cool.
We came home after two hours,
Look! Here comes a thundershower.
Courtney Deems, Grade 4
Center Elementary School

Lucky

Lucky, you are my pet.
You don't like going to the vet.

You are so smart.
You have my heart.

You run so fast.
You will never be last.

You walk me to the bus each day.
You follow me around till I say, "Stay!"

You lay by my side all night.
I hope we will never ever fight.
Ian Farley, Grade 5
Cheswick Christian Academy

Bunnies

Bunnies, bunnies everywhere
Bunnies, bunnies cute little hares
Bunnies, bunnies have big toeses
Bunnies, bunnies wiggle their noses
Bunnies, bunnies nice little things
Bunnies, bunnies tiny babies
Bunnies, bunnies hop all around
Bunnies, bunnies don't make a sound
Bunnies, bunnies run and scurry
Bunnies, bunnies fuzzy and furry
Bunnies, bunnies in their cages
Bunnies, bunnies live for ages
Bunnies, bunnies lovely bunnies
Bunnies, bunnies do you like bunnies?
Christina Kulp, Grade 5
Brecknock Elementary School

Summer

Summer is fun
Summer I swim
Summer is fun with no school
And friends
Patrick Owens, Grade 4
Panther Valley Elementary School

Freedom to Appreciate

The American flag
Flies high and free
But how did this freedom
Come to be?

It wasn't easy
That's for sure
We fought and fought
In battles and wars

But now there's freedom
And oh, how great
Then again, it's something
To appreciate

For we wouldn't be free
If it weren't for those
Who could've been lazy,
But war was what they chose

So now when you pledge
To that flag, so grand
Think of our freedom —
May God bless this land
Ally Bartoszewicz, Grade 4
St Alexis School

Moon

With a light clouded vale
Small shadows all around
Timid animals squirming in the bushes
Floating up there
Pale as milk
The moon is shy
It doesn't shine like the sun
The sun shines brightly
The moon glows in the sky
Faint light casts o'er the land
Carrie Lindeman, Grade 5
Lincoln Elementary School

Hines Ward

Hines Ward here and there
Hines Ward up in the air
Hines Ward all around
Hines Ward up and down
Hines Ward always inbound
Hines Ward on the ground
Hines Ward down the field
Hines Ward railed in the ball
Hines Ward will never fall
Hines Ward he is so cool
Hines Ward in the Super Bowl
Nick Morena, Grade 4
Concord Elementary School

To Mom

I'm glad you're my mom.
I'm glad you're my friend.
I love you as a friend and I love you as a mother.
This is my way of saying I love you.
This is my way of saying I love you.
My emotions are true.
Yes, they're true
My emotions are for you.
It's time to stop talking
And if I may
I want to say
HAPPY VALENTINE'S DAY.

Renessa Alert, Grade 4
Easterly Parkway Elementary School

Stars

Stars are shining bright
like diamonds reflecting light
They are really high
jumping up you wouldn't reach them

Stars are like angels looking down at you
To reach them you would need a lot of trampolines
Stars are beautiful no matter where they are

Kellie Hirsh, Grade 6
St Valentine Elementary School

Nature

Something that is beautiful,
Having nothing to harm you,
Always getting to your heart with sounds,
Sounds of the beautiful nature hymn.
Locusts and birds working together
To make their song sound better.
Playing every night for campers' enjoyment.
Nature has so many wonders.
So adore the sounds of nature,
And listen to its every beat.
Because some day,
You will hear these sounds no more.

Dalton Deardorff, Grade 6
St Francis Xavier Elementary School

Trees

I was climbing our apple tree,
On a windy day.
It seemed as if the tree was moving.
It was, but then it wasn't.
I heard cracks from all directions.
I guess it was just little twigs,
Bending and breaking in the fierce wind.
Well, I slipped and almost fell that day,
But I recovered my balance.
I used my strength and got to the top again.

Matthew Ludwig, Grade 4
Northern Cambria Catholic School

Fear

Why do we have fear.
Do we really fear something
or do we just want to think something's wrong.
Fear, what is wrong with fear.
No one knows what it really is,
so find a way to break it.
Fear.

Michael Manson, Grade 6
Independence Charter School

Lost

Silence silence there is no sound.
I feel so sick as my tears hit the ground.
We lost we lost my aching chest.
I tried I tried I tried my best.

I feel so sick as my tears hit the ground.
My whole team disappointed they all frowned.
I tried I tried I tried my best.
That defeat aching like a pest.

My whole team disappointed they all frowned.
The other team is being crowned.
That defeat aching like a pest.
We failed and we failed we failed the test.

James Marrero, Grade 6
Grasse Elementary School

Spring Love

Spring, spring here it comes.
cause that's when the humming birds hum.
Spring, spring all around.
Spring spring on the ground.
Spring, spring flowers grow
Spring, spring rivers flow.
Spring, spring goes so slow.
Spring, spring that's when the fire flies glow.
Spring, spring warmth is here.
Spring, spring winter feared.
Spring, spring no more coats.
Spring, spring just as we hoped!

Nicholas Perry Hannan, Grade 4
Avonworth Elementary School

Nighttime

Night is a warm blanket that wraps you up tight.
Night brings you to a dream world filled with light.
Night has many dangers that will hurt you if they can.
But, night will always bring you home once again.
Night is the time when you go to bed.
Night is the time when stories are said.
Feel cozy and snug and loved all around.
Go to bed soon and to a dream world you are bound.

Marissa Flores, Grade 6
Bridle Path Elementary School

Breeze

Breeze
Cool, refreshing
Blows, whistles, shifts
So peaceful
Wonderful.
Chanise Davis, Grade 5
St Cyril of Alexandria School

Sunny Days

Puffy clouds in the sky,
Birds singing as they fly,
Laying in the bright green grass,
Watching the clouds as they pass,
Always nice and warm,
When there's a summer storm,
A dip in the pool,
Makes it nice and cool,
Lots of butterflies and bees,
Tripping falling getting scraped knees.
Playing with a friend,
Wishing summer would never end,
And there's only one rule,
There is no school!!!
Jennifer Messner, Grade 5
Fishing Creek Elementary School

Pizza

There once was a girl named Lisa
She had a piece of pizza
It had every topping sauce and cheese
After that she got really fat
and said no more pizza please
Tia Morouse, Grade 4
South Park Elementary Center

Break n' Free

Troy
Wildcat b-ball
Singing, dancing, b-ball
Likes to sing, start something new
Bolton
Raheem Greene, Grade 4
Penn-Kidder Campus

Summer Vacation

It's summer vacation.
Hot air all over.
Breezes blowing at you.
You like the summer, but fall is near.
The bright sun is shining.
Swimming, beaching, and fishing.
It feels like fun.
But when it's fall
You wish to go back to summer.
Cami Smith, Grade 4
Avon Grove Intermediate School

Fireflies

In early evenings in July,
I wait to see a firefly.
He and his friends put on a show,
With their beautiful twinkling glow.
The lightning bugs, they sleep all day,
And blink the rest of the night away.
At twilight time I get a surprise,
Of thousands of beautiful fireflies.
And when I glimpse their golden glow,
Summer is truly here, I know
Colleen Donnelly, Grade 6
St Hilary of Poitiers School

Black and White

Black
Dull, mysterious
Distracting, boring, dooming
Gothic, gloomy, vivid, bright
Gleaming, shining, lighting
Energetic, cheerful
White
Kaela Green, Grade 5
Penn-Kidder Campus

Thinking

Walking down the sidewalk,
Or frolicking in grass.
Thinking always happens,
Through time and in our past.

We think of things so little,
And things we think are tough.
We think about all people,
And think about all stuff.

If you cannot stop thinking,
It's common, can't you see?
If we could just stop thinking,
How boring life would be!

Just think about this poem,
And think about all things.
And then you'll pause and think about
What excitement thinking brings!
Jordan Williams, Grade 4
Lincoln Elementary School

Christmas

Christmas is full of delight
With gifts wrapped ever so bright.
Joyful carolers sing
About Jesus the King
And how He saved us all.
Jacob Young, Grade 6
Portersville Christian School

Sun

The sun is so bright
Now it fills the sky with light
Now I wait for night
Ashleigh Nadzam, Grade 6
Freedom Area Middle School

Useless Things

A school without a teacher
A church without a preacher
A horn without a beep
A ninja that can't creep

Mrs. Yukon without a good reputation
A hand without circulation
A body without bones
Ice cream without a cone

A splash without a splish
An ocean without fish
A pucker without a kiss
A target without a hit or a miss

A person without self-pity
A house without a kitty
A fat cat that is flat
A house without a welcome mat

A game without a rule
A world without school
A restaurant without a restroom
A bride without a groom
Matthew D. Janovich, Grade 5
Claysville Elementary School

Autumn

One hot autumn day
Leaves were blowing in the air
High above the clouds
David-Louis Browne, Grade 4
West Bradford Elementary School

Go Steelers Go!

Here we go, Steelers, here we go.
On our way to Colorado
We are going to beat you,
Because we have Polamalu.
Bettis charges like a bulldozer
That way we will roll you over.
Porter as sharp as a tack
That is how he sacks the quarterback.
Ward catches just like Velcro
And down the field he will go.
Big Ben throws as straight as a pin
That is why no one can win!
Michael Roberts, Grade 5
State Street Elementary School

Players

Shaun Alexander
Fast, small
Running, scoring, catching
Offense, running back, defense, free safety
Tackling, running, intercepting
Tough, tall
Brian Dawkins

Albert Innaurato, Grade 6
Holy Spirit School

I Am Alyssa

I am a shy girl
I wonder why people have so much to say
I want to have as they do
I hear people talking and laughing
I am a shy girl

I pretend like I know what is always going on
I feel happy when I do have something to talk about
I touch their shoulder to tell them it will be ok
I worry if they notice I don't have a lot to say
I cry because maybe I don't want to be like everyone else
I am a shy girl

I understand why people say I'm so quiet
I say I don't always like to talk
I dream soon they won't care if I'm so quiet
I try to have something to say
I hope I'll start to have more to say
I am a shy girl

Alyssa Alcindor, Grade 5
East Stroudsburg Elementary School

Fall Is Coming

Fall is coming
Strong, powerful winds
roaring with aggression
Honey-locust leaves scattering to keep warm
Bitter, cold, fall breeze numbing my hands
and pinching my cheeks
The sun is barely showing as it hides
on top of the white and gray clouds
A bird bath filled with leaves
but abandoned by birds
Fallen, dead leaves
twirling in a tornado
trying to rise to
their original branch
As the beautiful never-ending
honey locust and evergreen trees
reach to the clouds and turn fall colors
I know that
fall is coming

Tyler MacDougall, Grade 5
Lower Salford Elementary School

Shadows Play

Our shadows play with the wind
They play with the moon when we are asleep.
They depart with us at nighttime
to play with ghosts of the evening.
They only want to have fun.

Evan Hatton, Grade 4
Lincoln Elementary School

Blue

A color of the rainbow that stands above the rest.
Blue is water.
Blue is the color of sadness when sun turns to clouds.
On a nice and sunny day blue is wide open skies.
Blue is icy cold rain.
Blue is cheerful.
Blue is calm.
Blue is peaceful.
Blue is when kindness, happiness, and peace are in the air.

Nicholas Carter, Grade 5
Rolling Hills Elementary School

Spring

The first little flower pops up from the ground
Then the world starts to turn around
To a side where you can hear the birds sing
This side has to be spring!

Playing soccer and basketball
Really isn't bad at all
My birthday will be coming soon in May
For me that is one special day!

In spring school comes to an end
When we must say goodbye to our best friends
Looking forward to the warm spring sun
Brings delight to everyone!

Erin Lischerelli, Grade 6
Conemaugh Township Area Intermediate School

The River

I am a river
Quiet and cold
Fish slither and I shiver
Fishermen throw hooks in me and I hurt
Trees drop leaves on me when cold
Ice mantles over me while skaters skate in the frigid air
Come, hot children, swim in me to cool off
Animals drink me and I get small
But rain falls and I get large
I am a river
Very useful
Very large, yet very small
I am a river
Quiet and cold

Timmy Langton, Grade 4
General Nash Elementary School

Preposition

Out the door,
above the sky,
throughout my wings that I will fly,
to see the sights,
before I die,
as I soar,
above the sky,
in and out,
above a tree,
I will go,
beyond the world,
to see

Tyler Rivera, Grade 6
Grasse Elementary School

NASCAR

Jeff Gordon was running good
Until somebody smacked his hood.

He got turned around
The other car could not be found.

Finally when he caught the pack
Matt Kenseth knocked him back.

Nathan Hetrick, Grade 5
Cheswick Christian Academy

Birds

Hear birds' lovely chirps
See the birds fly while singing
Touch their soft feathers
Alexandra Greenberg, Grade 4
Center Elementary School

Fred's Phobia

Fred fears fire hydrants
On first, fourth, and fifth street.
Following four firemen,
Fred found the flesh of four fingers
Frozen to a flagpole on February 15.
Fred fainted.
Andy Pulaski, Grade 6
Allison Park Elementary School

Katherine

K is for Katherine my loving mother.
A is for always there loving.
T is for the best.
H is for helping, always helping!
E is for energetic, always running.
R is for really great!
I is for interesting.
N is neat and nice.
E is for exciting, always surprising me!
Michelle Bartha, Grade 6
West Allegheny Middle School

A Birthday Spectacular

Birthdays at my house are always lots of fun,
A decorated birthday cake with colorful icing for everyone.
Children laughing, games galore,
Parachute fun, friends, family and more.
Crafts to match the birthday theme,
And decorations from beam to beam.
Pizza, cookies, creamy ice cream too,
There are always enough presents for me, and treat bags for you.
Birthdays come just once a year,
So let's get ready, my birthday is almost here.

Dylan Almeida, Grade 6
Bridle Path Elementary School

Memories

What are memories?
Fading photos in an album filled with life?
Book marks in a book not yet finished…or is it?
What are memories?
Pieces of a puzzle that are already connected?
Mirrors reflecting the past?
What are memories?
Great moments left to savor, or flashbacks of guilt, pain, and sorrow?
Is memory a path that can be retraced, or nothing but an illusion?
Are memories like a familiar wisping breeze, or a cold, hard rain?
Are memories truth or lies, are they sincere?
Are they shards of life to look back on forever, made to share?
We make memories every day.

Kayla Marie Landis, Grade 6
Cocalico Middle School

Rico

I remember my dog Rico.
I remember when we used to play in the hot summer sun.
I remember when he always cheered me up when I was bored.
I remember when he used to follow me through the lush green woods.
I remember when we all learned he had hip cancer.
I remember the day he died and how very sad I was.
I remember my dog Rico.

Eric Nolin, Grade 5
Claysville Elementary School

Remembering the Children*

A land of few mountains and many rivers,
    where loaves of bread are served at every meal
    and people enjoy the game of buzhashi.

You may have been a miner
    who went down into the mines every day to collect gold,
    a foreign trader who went to the marketplaces every day to sell goods,
    or a hunter who collects winnings from Mother Nature every day.

I will be thankful for what I have,
as I remember you.

Jen Isaacs, Grade 6
Deibler Elementary School
In remembrance of the children in Afghanistan

Toni Teresa

Who likes to go on family vacations
Has a bad habit of biting my nails
Wonders if there are aliens
Plays guitar
Can't seem to stop listening to music
Laughs at everything
Likes to buy everything at the mall
Often uses an iPod
Wish I could fly
Still can't fly (I tried) or whistle
Is embarrassed when I trip and fall
Never saw anyone who looked like me
Is afraid of someone dying and spiders
Watches a lot of scary movies
Refused to leave all my friends forever
Someday hopes to be famous or find a cure for cancer.

Toni Teresa Mascaro, Grade 6
St Genevieve School

Pizza

Pizza
Fun to eat; a real treat
Tastes so good,
Eat all day I could,
Spectacular toppings
And marvelous crusts
That make your pizza delicious,
Pizza is like a thunderstorm
It's delivered and then it's gone so fast
Use different toppings,
Get a special taste each time,
People like pizza different ways,
That makes pizza enjoyable,
You can make it taste how you want
Pizza's my favorite food
It's so good I want to eat it every minute
Make your own pizza, or buy it at the store
It's always yummy to eat!

Shaked Retter, Grade 6
Mount Nittany Middle School

Remembering the Children*

A land of hard work
   where most people live on plateaus,
   and people make copper.

You may have been a football player
   who scores many touchdowns,
   a drummer who performs in front of an audience,
   or a singer who sings beautiful songs.

I will pay more attention to what's happening in the world,
   as I remember you.

Dan Grammes, Grade 6
Deibler Elementary School
*In remembrance of the children in Zambia

My Gram

My gram is someone I love
She is sweet, beautiful and all of the above
Although she suffers from Alzheimer's disease
She always seems to be pleased
Seeing her smile beats any other thing
She is more beautiful than a diamond ring
I wish she was better
But even though she isn't
She will be the best gram forever

Angela Albarano, Grade 6
Foot of Ten Elementary School

Football

The ball was snapped, and Jimmy ran
He got open and waved his hand

The ball was thrown down the beach
He saw the pass was out of reach

Jimmy leaped up and caught the ball
But before he knew it, he got mauled

Lucky for him, he crossed the line
Hallelujah, it was just in time

Jimmy got up, dusted off his pants
Spiked the ball and did a touchdown dance

Andrew Maust, Grade 5
Cheswick Christian Academy

Have You Ever...

Have you ever seen a sunset,
All the beautiful colors jumping out at you?
The brilliant yellow rays reflecting off calm, still, blue waters?

Have you ever smelled a red rose,
The enchanting, sweet aroma filling your lungs?

Have you ever touched a petal,
As gentle and soft as velvet
So delicate that it dissolves between your fingers?

Have you ever heard birds singing their marvelous songs,
Bouncing through the air and echoing through the trees?

Have you ever tasted fruit,
So luscious, delicious, and cool that it tingles in your mouth?

Powerful is the One who created humankind and nature
The One who is with us every day of our lives
the One and only Father who cares about us from above
who gave us these amazing gifts to teach us how to appreciate,
   love, and live our lives.

Catalina Escobar, Grade 6
Sacred Heart Elementary School

Muddy Day
I'm running in the rain
with a big shirt stain
thumping through the mud
squish squosh
slosh
squishy
squosh
Oh my gosh!
I'm muddy
mushy mashy
and
moshy
Entering my house
mud going everywhere
thud thump
thimp
thomp
stomp
Then I hear a yell it's my mom!
OH NO!!!
Daniel Black, Grade 5
Wexford Elementary School

Timothy
Timothy
Athletic, energetic
Hunting, fishing, running
Sports maniac
"Tim"
Timothy Gottshall, Grade 5
St Francis of Assisi School

Bailey
Bailey, Bailey all around,
His foot prints are on the ground.
Bailey, Bailey taking a nap,
He is sleeping on your lap.
He is playing on the sand.
He is always licking your hand.
My dog Bailey is my best friend,
Loving him will never end.
Olivia London, Grade 4
Avonworth Elementary School

Turtles
Turtles are green.
Some like to bite.
Some like to swim,
And some get in fights.
Turtles are slow,
And they don't take flight.
Turtles are green,
And they're a wonderful sight.
Danielle Healy, Grade 4
St Leo School

Rain
Rain clouds fill the sky
The rain fills the big pot holes
The rain fills the lakes
Ashley Sladisky, Grade 6
Cheswick Christian Academy

Happiness
Shines like the spring sun
making kids laugh
while playing tag
with the smell of blossoms
fill the air
while the birds sing
Maria Fareri, Grade 4
South Park Elementary Center

Clue
I found a clue
That was from Scooby Doo
It lead to a mystery
That was solved by history.
Alex Skivington, Grade 4
Fishing Creek Elementary School

Thunder and Lightning
He lights a candle
God is moving furniture
A storm is coming
Mercedes Ann Maze, Grade 5
Claysville Elementary School

The Difference
One small disagreement to tear us apart
That's all it will take
To break my heart
Just the difference in you and me
Look hard and you will see
It shouldn't be this way at all
A million differences
A million mistakes
When will we learn it shouldn't be
Fat or thin
Black or white
Tall or short, what will it take
To show the world it shouldn't be?
Kaitlyn Kurisky, Grade 5
Our Mother of Perpetual Help School

Cats
Cats
Fluffy, cute
Always adorable, awesome
Always hiding from you
Kittens
Natalie Snow, Grade 6
Freedom Area Middle School

Island
Natural and warm
People go on vacation
Full of trees and sand
Brittney Gellentien, Grade 5
Penn-Kidder Campus

Holocaust
Hide from the greedy
Work for the twisted dream
Die in the night
Live in the day.
Shawn McNew, Grade 6
Chambersburg Area Middle School

Where I Am From
I am from science and technology,
creating the world.
I am from dish washing
and eating play dough
because I thought it was fruit.

I am from the Jewish-Russians.
I am from Esther and Gregg.
I am from crazy family members at
gatherings having a great time.
I am from excitement.

I am from fun in the sun at
Ocean City, NJ.
I am from shopping and
buying every shoe.
I am from having great vacations
not wanting to end.
I am from fun in the sun.
Jessa Eskin, Grade 6
Haverford Middle School

Spring Freedom
Spring breeze
spring buds
the trees and their branches
Stretched
to admit
the long awaited sun

My hair
falling around
my face
My feelings
of freedom
released and carried

In the cool whispering air
Delia Scoville, Grade 5
Falk Laboratory School

Pandas

Pandas are black and white
Cute and cuddly, they're a happy sight

Endangered species from China they come
Lucky for us, the zoos have some

Climbing trees is what they do
For dinner, they have yummy bamboo

A grizzly or polar this bear is not,
Playful and fun is the manner they've got

Just an animal to some it may be
A panda is a very special gift to me

Madison Santella, Grade 6
Sacred Heart Elementary School

Colors Forever

Pink is for a baby girl
Brown is for a fluffy squirrel
Blue is for the ocean wide
Gold medals give you feelings of pride
Red is a color that is bold
Grey is Dad's mustache cause he's so old

The colors of the rainbow are a smile turned upside down!

Kayla Zboran, Grade 5
Cheswick Christian Academy

The Three Tasks

The Norwegian Horntail
They wonder why he's not in jail
It is oh so vicious
And thinks Harry's quite delicious
He flies high, he flies low
He goes as fast as he can go
Harry got the egg armed, but was harmed

The poor Harry Potter
Has to breathe underwater
And even though he begs
He still has to get fins for legs
He gets attacked by grindilows
And gets them off with a couple of blows
He saves Gabrielle and Ron, then he's gone

Harry entered the maze
He was in the third faze
Victor attacked Fleur
The first one out was Delacour
The next one out was Victor Krum
Who was really super dumb
Three are alive, but one won't survive

Susan Ekstrand, Grade 6
Bedford Middle School

My Swimming Experience

I went to the YMCA to take a dip —
Once I got in I took a big slip!
Help! Help! Everyone screamed
But the teacher was in the middle of a dream.

I felt like a nobody
Since the teacher didn't help.
I was very sad inside
And that is how I felt.

While everyone was screaming to the top of their lungs,
I guess they knew it wasn't fun,
The teacher didn't bother to look
I guess I was just off the hook

My dad had on his swimming trunks,
He came to save his daughter
Even when he jumped in the pool
I was still under water.

My dad was trying to save me,
He picked me up to my feet.
I didn't take swimming lessons anymore,
Didn't even bother to look back at the door

Essence Winder, Grade 5
Hamilton Elementary School

Charlie

I have a dog named Charlie
He is as fast as a Harley
He is a curious doggy with his fluffy wobbly ears
I have a dog named Charlie

Peter Landgraf-Kimball, Grade 5
Schnecksville School

Painting with People

People come in all colors
Like paint
Some people like red
Some people like blue
For people it is the same way
Some people are white
Some people are black
But from my point of view
Both colors mix

White is to black
As black is to white

People are like chocolate milk
White is the milk
Black is the chocolate

Without both ingredients you can't make it

Anthony Hirsch, Grade 5
Jenkintown Elementary School

Thunder

Thunder is screaming
Lightning, raining
It's too noisy
Please go away!

Wind is whistling
Snowy, windy
It's too cold
Please go away!

Sun is bright
Yellow, shiny
It's too hot
Please go away!

Leaves are falling
Red, yellow, orange
So many colors
Please, please stay!
Jaehyo Chung, Grade 4
Easterly Parkway Elementary School

A Walk Through the Woods

The whispers of the wind,
Between the tall trees.

The brown squirrel,
Scampers across the ground.

The silky green grass,
Underneath my tired feet.

The sweet taste,
Of black and red boysenberries.

The fragrance of the meadow,
Smells like sweet honeysuckle.
Daniel Cortese, Grade 6
Neil Armstrong Middle School

Night

You watch it come
You watch it go
Its darkness you may never know
The stars are bright on its dark pelt
The moon is so clear
It looks like bright yellow felt
It makes everything dark
So hard to see
It doesn't always fill you up with glee
You lay in bed at this time
Listening to your neighbor's wind chime
Then your eyes start to close
When you awake the sunlight flows.
Maddie Galler, Grade 6
Hillcrest Elementary School

I Am the Tide Pool

I am the tide pool
Where creatures splash around
And if you listen closely
You will hear that splashing sound

I'm home to starfish, anemone too
Sideways-walking pinching creatures
Some old, some new

I'm not as big as an ocean
But not as small as a pond
Where prey and predators will get along
If you wave your magic wand

I am the tide pool
I shelter many creatures
And as you can see,
I have many special features
Melissa Cubit, Grade 4
General Nash Elementary School

Winter

In winter snowflakes fall at dawn,
Sparkling snowflakes of white,
A blanket of white covers the lawn,
The grass is out of sight.

You rush down in snow clothes,
Mittens, coats, scarves, and a hat,
The cold wind nips your nose,
And winter happens just like that.
Sarah Prosser, Grade 5
Boyce Middle School

Athletic

A major part of my life is sports.
T he helpful part is that I am short.
H olly, our coach leads the way.
L oving the game reboots your energy.
E very other team loses their prize.
T he V.I.P. player always gets a surprise.
I ncomplete plays are challenged at last.
C ourageous players fight for the past.
Leann Gordon, Grade 6
Freedom Area Middle School

Spring

S ounds of the bees
P lace memories in my head
R unning and playing
I n what seems like the time
N ow to be free but to have
G rand, grand, springtime fun!
Amanda Dremsek, Grade 6
West Allegheny Middle School

Paper Airplane

A paper airplane
Soaring in the wind
Sometimes high
Sometimes low
Making loops and turns
Until it lands on earth
Like a two-year-old going to bed.
Ian Briggs, Grade 5
Jenkintown Elementary School

Red

Red is light
Red is tiger lilies after rain
Red is fear
Red is friendship
Red is love
Red is fire running towards you
Like jousting tournaments
Red can be sad
Red can mean happiness
Red is freedom
Red is power
Tayshon Shawley-Rutan, Grade 5
Easterly Parkway Elementary School

I Am

I am the wind, the trees, the water.
As the hermits say, this is me.
I am in a cave, on a cloud
I am the sand, the stars in the sky.
I live in the sunset, in the rain falling.
I am being.
I am.
Sarah Kravinsky, Grade 5
Jenkintown Elementary School

Violin

Violin
High, low
Small, moving, squeaking
Violins can sound high,
Violin

Cello
Low, lower
Vibrating, medium, squeaking
Cellos can sound low,
Cellos

Orchestra
High, low
Together, playing, moving
An orchestra is in tune,
Orchestra
Caitlyn Huebner, Grade 4
Indian Lane Elementary School

Deanna

Funny, short, nice, attitude,
Related to her mom, Tina and Ashleen,
Who cares about food, TV, and movies
Who feels very mad when she's with her sister,
Who needs to get rid of school
Who gives all of her effort in dance and cheerleading,
Who fears the color brown,
Who wants to see movies *Aquamarine*
And *She's the Man,*
Resident of Harvard Rd.

Deanna McCullough, Grade 4
Manoa Elementary School

Trees Are Terrific

Trees help us breathe because trees have oxygen.
Trees are very pretty.
They have beautiful colored leaves during fall.
In winter, trees have nothing at all.
In the spring, the flowers again grow,
but sometimes we watch them go.
Trees are strong; they survive, even when they get cut down.
But they can never frown.
In the summer they're cool and green,
and they always have to be seen.
Trees don't like fires in the woods
and they always cover it with their hoods.
Trees are terrific. Why let them go,
they don't do much except grow, and grow.
They're humongous, and they care for animals;
like birds, raccoons, squirrels, cats, dogs, and insects.
Trees are brown, green, and different colors, too.
I like trees.

Fadwa Fentis, Grade 4
Washington Heights Elementary School

Nature

Nature is a beautiful thing,
Every animal, every plant,
I love to hear the birds sing.
Trees that form a forest of peace,
Grass covering the ground like a blanket of fleece,
Nature is harmony and love,
The earth below, the sky above.
Nature is blue,
Nature is green,
Nature is every color that I've ever seen.
It makes you smile from ear to ear,
It's something you can see and even hear
Nature is living,
But can be dead,
Nature is everything from the toes to the head.
Nature is the winter,
Nature is the spring,
Nature is basically everything!

Colleen Wismer, Grade 5
Rolling Hills Elementary School

Summer!

Summer is so really cool,
Summer is the time, of no school,
Summer's my favorite of all four seasons,
And for that, I have, over 12 reasons.

1 is because it's a season of running,
2 is because the weather is stunning,
3 is because the people are kind,
4 is because I can rest my mind!

5 is because you can swim and hike,
6 is because I can ride my bike,
7 is because you can play basketball,
8 is because you can hang at the mall.

9 is because you can camp out at night,
10 is because I love a fish when you get a bite,
11 is because the kids play rover,
12 is because this poem is over.

Daniel Zambanini, Grade 6
Conemaugh Township Area Intermediate School

Cats to Dogs

Cats
furry, cuddly
loving, playing, meowing
whining, sweet, smelly, smart (sometimes)
furry, barking, playful
lovable, big
Dogs

Madeline Adamczyk, Grade 4
St Sebastian Elementary School

Thomas Jefferson's Fountain Pen

I am a very famous pen,
For I am Thomas Jefferson's special friend,
And without me he wouldn't have made it anywhere,
I am the most handsome pen of all,
You should trust me with your writing for I don't fade,
Even though Thomas doesn't give me much credit,
I am the king of all pens,
And I am very wealthy.

Brandon Murray, Grade 6
Freedom Area Middle School

Spring

Brisk winds
Bright colors
Light green grass
There are weddings in spring
People take spring break
It's nice and breezy in spring
It's nice to play outside

Marchella Pinno, Grade 4
Urban League of Pittsburgh Charter School

Candy

C razy
A pples
N utritious if no sugar
D ynamite flavor
Y ummy!

Serenity Smock, Grade 4
East End Elementary School

Barbecue Wings

I like barbecue wings.
They ring me up.
They set me on fire.
Barbecue wings are what I desire.
I really like them saucy.
I really like them spicy.
I feel like I'm in flames.
I eat French fries with them.
I would drink ice-cold Coke.
To set out the fire.

Alec Felix, Grade 4
Watsontown Elementary School

Atlanta Falcons

F antastic offensive players
A wesome defensive lineman
L ikes to win NFL games
C an beat any team, especially the Eagles
O utstanding on offense and defense
N ike sponsors the Falcons
S uper good playing football

Brad McGinn, Grade 5
Robeson Elementary School

Staples

Silver, shiny and gray
You use them every day.
Sharp, small and thin
They are made of metal, wire and tin.
Hard, tough and strong
They'll last the whole day long.

Kathleen Reid, Grade 6
St Maria Goretti School

Hero

There was a big flood,
And people watched as,
Everything was washed away.

One man stood tall when the
Water smashed against him.

But he stood very tall and strong.
He put the dam back together.
He was the hero of the town.

Joseph Frontino, Grade 4
Northern Cambria Catholic School

Spring

Spring is in the air, children laughing and playing,
Bare trees are replaced with a gown of new born leaves,
The stingy cold days of winters replaced with a calm
Warmth that thaws the coldest hearths
Not only with the heat of nature
But, with a feeling of a rebirth of nature itself
As blue birds sing their happy little songs,
The bears and other animals come out of their hiding,
One forgets their sorrow,
The beauty of spring is not the superficial dress it puts on to impress,
But, its ability to captivate even the loneliest souls
Into a sense of happiness.

Kunal Atit, Grade 6
Montgomery Elementary School

Jr. High*

Last night while I lay thinking here, some what ifs crawled inside my ear,
And pranced and partied all night long, and sang their old what if song:

What if I get bullied?
What if I'm a bad goalie?
What if I oversleep? What if I eat sheep?
What If I get in a fight? What if I fear with fright?
What if I'm shy? What if I cry?
What if I get drunk? What if I flunk?
What if nobody likes me?
What if my teacher goes on strike?
What if I get D-hall? What if I can't play b-ball?
What if I'm a jerk? What if I forget my homework?
What if I get held back? What if I start to slack?
What if I get a bad teacher? What if I see a bad creature?

Everything seems swell, and then the nighttime what ifs strike again!

Julie Reese, Grade 6
Foot of Ten Elementary School
*Patterned after "Whatif" by Shel Silverstein

Purple

Purple is majesty, ready to be crowned.
The way to life, the way to death
But without a path.
Emptiness and confusion are purple's way of lost.
But be prepared for sorrow.
The way to darkness, the way to light.
Purple is mystery,
Neither good, nor bad.
Purple's turf covers the sky.
Purple's choices will make you scream or even cry.
The way to life, the way to death,
Purple is proud of all its choices.
But in a wisp of smoke, it's gone without a trace
Since purple gave up on you no one else will give you a place to stay.
This is purple's way, didn't you know?

Shawn James, Grade 5
Rolling Hills Elementary School

Baseball

I stepped up to the plate,
bases loaded,
two outs,
down by three
and the count was 2-2.
I was facing the best pitcher in A-ball, Freddie Greene.
It felt like butterflies were fluttering in my stomach.
Here we go!
And the pitch…
"Ball" yelled the ump.
The count was 3-2, we needed a hit to win.
and the pitch…
POP.
Back, back, back — gone!!!
Yelled the announcer.
We won, we won because of me;
We won!!!

Sam Haberstroh, Grade 6
Mount Nittany Middle School

Families

Families help you when you're in need,
Always there for you, when you have greed,
To love and to shelter you, to give you
Confidence, to feed you and raise you,
You need one to live, you need one to love
You need one to protect you,
You need one to hug,
Families.

Jacob Gonzalez, Grade 5
East Stroudsburg Elementary School

Dad

Who doesn't like their dad?
I love mine
He spoils me a lot
He helps me with my homework
He gives me whatever I want when I want
He is 33 years old
Meet my dad, Roy Jones
Amondai Alexander, Grade 6
Freedom Area Middle School

Violet

Wind is Violet
when it is sunset.
When two people
have just met.
Just as new silk is smooth,
Violet can leave you in a peaceful mood.
Jelly is Violet, fruit is Violet,
But I must say, that the violent Violet violins
will screech vigorously.
Bethany Kelly, Grade 5
Peebles Elementary School

A Hunter's Dream

Wouldn't you love to be sitting in a tree stand,
when a monster buck walks right out underneath you?
When you pull your bow back,
and then you feel the excitement.
Then let go of the string
and you got your first buck.
What a hunt!

Thomas James McGarry, Grade 6
Curwensville Area Elementary School

My Imagination

My imagination is a vast creation.
It's a huge sensation.
It's full of color and life.
It's as keen and sharp as a knife.
My imagination expresses me.
Its soul is wild and free.
It's also caring and able to love.
It is similar to a dove.
Flying around, spreading wonder to all.
It will never fall.
My imagination never thinks of bad things.
It thinks of angels and their beautiful wings.
Soaring in the sky.
Those are the visions that go by.
Its heart is red and bright.
It loves and cares day and night.
It will never stop.
It is a mop,
getting rid of all the bad things.
My imagination is a vast creation.
It is a huge sensation.

Abby Hendricks, Grade 5
Hopewell Jr High School

Bill Cosby

Bill Cosby was born July the 12th
And left high school to help in military health
His patients got bored like they were learning astronomy
So Bill would cheer them up with some old fashioned comedy
He left Temple University in 1962
To pursue a TV show dream that actually came true
In life he went through many tangled cords
But it all paid off when he won 3 Emmy Awards
On *The Cosby Show* he played a man named Cliff
And he made it funny because he was never stiff
Before all this he appeared in clubs in Vegas and Tahoe
And did many commercials for sponsors such as Jell-O
Now Cosby is living a beautiful life
Living in rural New England with his wife
Who knows what he's doing at this time and place
But he might be putting a smile on a face
If you need a smile look for him around the bend
That's my story The End

Nicole Colon, Grade 6
Christopher Columbus Charter School - South

Snowball Fights
Cold, wet
Hitting, smashing, running
Fun, Messy, Freezing, Enjoyable
Throwing, falling, aiming
Compact, chilly
Snowball fights
Becca Drucker, Grade 4
Memorial Elementary School

Sidney Crosby
Sidney
best player
scoring, skating, passing
best rookie in the NHL
Crosby
Kellen Carleton, Grade 4
Avonworth Elementary School

Concentrating
Concentrate is what I must do
To write a poem to give you
I need quiet and dark would help too
Is it hard for you to concentrate too.
Concentrating will help you in school
It will help you at work too
Concentrating will really help you
Bennet Clark, Grade 5
Wharton Elementary School

Right Now
Right now
Someone is saying good night.
Right now
Someone is saying good morning.
Right now
a child was just born.
Right now
Someone has passed away.
Right now
Someone is crying.
Right now
Someone is laughing.
Right now
Is your choice to do whatever you want
Chloe Ali, Grade 6
Locust Grove Mennonite School

Friends
Friends
Special, wonderful
Helping, loving, caring
I need my friend very much!
Buddies
Cheyenne Moore, Grade 4
West Branch Area Elementary School

Spring
Spring sky appears.
Flowers come when rain pours down.
Spring is fantastic.
Timmy Paciello, Grade 4
Colonial Elementary School

Springtime
Winter is over
And we watch it go,
Finally no more playing
Out in the cold snow.

Now we get muddier
Each time we go out,
And when we get back in,
We receive a stern shout.

When it rains,
We feel terrible pains,
That we can't go out,
We only know there won't be a drought.

Each day we awake,
Into the beautiful sun,
And know that spring
Has just begun.
Mitchell Miller, Grade 5
Fairview Middle School

The Big, Puffy Pumpkin
The big, puffy pumpkin,
is round and bulgy out,
The big, puffy pumpkin
is orange, no doubt!

The big, puffy pumpkin
can weigh 1,000 pounds,
which has even more weight
than two hounds!

The big, puffy pumpkin,
the jack-o'-lantern gives a scare,
so when people pass by,
they must take care.

The big, puffy pumpkin,
even though it can't glide,
it'll go really far
when it goes down a slide.

The big, puffy pumpkin
inside it has a seed,
the big, puffy pumpkin,
it can feed.
Neilesh Vinjamuri, Grade 4
Lionville Elementary School

Christmastime
Christmastime is cold
The snow shines like gold,
People eat nuts by the fire
While the kids read Christmas fliers.

Relatives come from far away
Together they sing and gently sway.
Carolers sing at the door,
While babies play on the floor.
Andrew Niederlander, Grade 6
Portersville Christian School

Alone
Alone
Alone
with no one by my side
not one soul to keep me dry

It was only last night my parents died
no more food to eat
So I have to creep, creep, creep

Finally a nice, warm home
with loving people to keep me dry
no longer
no longer
I stand alone

Now I have a nice, warm home!
Rachel Cable, Grade 6
West Allegheny Middle School

Skiing
Skiing down a mountain
In the winter at Jack Frost
I ski down the mountain
Left, right, left, right I go down
Faster, faster I sped down
Kevin Irwin, Grade 5
Newtown Elementary School

Halloween
Trick-or-Treat
Pitter, patter, patterns of little feet.

Door to door,
How many more?

Witches and bats
Clowns with hats

What a pair,
What a scare!
Abigail G. Kline, Grade 4
Northern Cambria Catholic School

The Very Happy Girl
There's this girl I know that is as happy as a butterfly,
She is always jumping and singing,
As a frog, or bird,
She is like a smile that always smiles,
She is like dolphins on warm summer nights,
She is as happy as a grateful grandma,
She's always laughing and is very playful,
As a cool breeze,
She is as happy,
As the heavens above.

Shannon Golden, Grade 6
Neil Armstrong Middle School

Pink
Pink tastes like cotton candy at the fair,
sprinkles on top of an ice cream sundae,
and Bubbliscious bubblegum.

Pink smells like strawberry lollipops at the circus,
colorful flowers in a gorgeous garden,
and watermelon body lotion.

Pink sounds like shoes dashing on the ground,
a zipper being closed on a backpack,
and beautiful birds chirping.

Pink feels like soft rose petals gently blowing in the wind,
relaxing after a long hard day,
and a cozy sweatshirt on a cold winter day.

Pink looks like the sun setting in the nice cool sky,
a pretty dress that sways in the wind,
and a pink Eagles jersey that shines in the bright light.

Jamie Langzettel, Grade 4
Indian Lane Elementary School

Ode to My Bunny
He's brown like a Hershey's bar,
My bunny that licks cereal from my hand.
He loves the attention he gets from my family.
When he is brushed he turns soft as silk.
Sweet swirls of buttercup eyes
Surround Foo's cute, little face.
Small with a cotton balled tail, cute as can be,
He tries to take bows off his fluffy, feathered ears.
Chewing on my clothes, putting holes in them,
Makes this sweet little bunny twitch his nose.
Playing outside, running around, eating the grass,
Will make a cute photograph.
Seeing the way he hops and runs will make you laugh.
Eating, drinking, and sleeping are a few of his favorites.
His softness, cuteness, and being cuddly
Will remind you of a teddy bear.
Oh, how I love my Lil' Bunny Foo Foo!

Meghan Brown, Grade 6
St Sebastian Elementary School

Earth Wakes Up
The wind blows and gives me a chill.
When I look at the branches blow, they look like hands.
You can smell spring coming.
When the wind blows, the leaves go with it.
You can hear the birds calling
Grass begins to grow.
And this is when you know.
Earth wakes up.

Brianne Hughes, Grade 5
St Ambrose School

Fall Is My Season
I love fall.
It begins to get chilly and the trees look silly,
they have lost their clothes.

Fur is growing,
mammals are eating,
and soon will be sleeping until the snow goes.

I can hear the lightly
dried leaves falling
all the way
to the ground
from the trees.

Now you really know
why fall is…
my favorite season.

Is what I said enough of a reason?

Jessica Rissell, Grade 5
Robeson Elementary School

If I Were in Charge of the World*
If I were in charge of the world
I'd make everything free
Stickmen would be real
And baseball practice would be every day
If I were in charge of the world
There'd be no hot days
No smoking
And no mean people
If I were in charge of the world
You wouldn't have to go on long trips
You wouldn't have to do jobs
You wouldn't have to go to school
Or clean up your room
And a person who sometimes forgets to go to baseball practice
And sometimes forgets to feed the dog
Could still be in charge of the world.

Andrew Kriebel, Grade 5
Souderton Charter School Collaborative
*Patterned after "If I Were in Charge of the World"
by Judith Viorst

Dogs

Most people like them and some do not
They will smell really bad if they get hot
Dogs will not let you down
They might not even let you drown
Mitchell Tasker, Grade 5
Rhawnhurst School

Turkeys

T urkeys are tasty
U sually very fat
R oasted in the oven
K luck, kluck, kluck
E very Thanksgiving I eat one
Y ummy in my tummy
Ryan Manhoff, Grade 6
Moravian Academy Middle School

She Won't Be Here

In about a year
She won't be here.

Could it be
That she will soon leave me?

I'll miss her more
Than I ever did before.

I know she must go,
But in my head I'm thinking no.

My sister must go to college
So she can gain knowledge.

Where she will go?
I do not know.

But, in about a year,
She won't be here.
Nora Sweeney, Grade 6
Sacred Heart Elementary School

Cupid

Cupid has white wings.
Cupid loves getting valentine things.
Cupid loves to sing.
Cupid loves to sing in the spring.
Kaleb Quick, Grade 4
West Branch Area Elementary School

Beans

B ean is my last name.
E ven though I don't like them.
A mushy gushy thing in my mouth.
N o! Never I won't eat them.
Kari Bean, Grade 6
H Austin Snyder Elementary School

Fire

Fire
Fatal, destructive
Bursting, smoking, destroying
An extremely horrible sight
Flames
Stephen Kurus, Grade 5
Penn-Kidder Campus

Christmas

Christmas was a wonderful night,
When the kings had a star in sight.
The star was shining so very bright,
Baby Jesus was bundled in light.
Gaige Pavlocak, Grade 5
Verna Montessori School

A Little Seed

A little seed,
turns into a tree.
Apple tree
orange tree
pine tree too!
Depending on the seed,
what tree will it be.
Christine Briggs, Grade 4
Pittston Area Intermediate Center

Panda

They are black and white,
And big as a tree,
Some eat grass,
And some eat trees.
Also lives in rain forest
And endangered.
Alton Eidem, Grade 4
Panther Valley Elementary School

Snow

Snow
Cold, frosty
Flows, blows, swirls
The Lord's gift
December.
Alanna Tucker, Grade 5
St Cyril of Alexandria School

Red Zinnia

Old red zinnia
Shriveling up and dying
Just lying on the grass
Still beautiful
The petals fall off
With the gentlest touch
Vanessa Ondo, Grade 6
St Rosalia Academy

Ghost Ship

I heard a sound, a mournful sound,
aboard my westbound ship.
I strained to see what it could be,
aboard my westbound ship
and what I saw
could drop your jaw.
I blinked and looked again.
I saw a ship, a haunted ship,
the ship began to moan.
The moaning sound
I soon found out
was coming from inside.
A haunted ship,
a haunted crew,
what could this ghost ship mean?
The ship moved on,
toward the setting sun
leaving me, myself and I
to wonder what the sight had meant
and why they caught my eye.
Jacob Cordell, Grade 5
Easterly Parkway Elementary School

My Little Sister

I have a little sister
her name is Evelyn.
She is a special gift from
Heaven with
her little squeak that
she does every
week…my little sister.
Patricia Sorg, Grade 4
Immaculate Conception School

Recipe for an Angel

You need 1 cup of sugar
2 gallons of sweet
100 feathers, 2 cups of power,
and a toga, harp, sandals
Then put it in a cloud for 10 days
When it's finished let it free.
Luke Bauer, Grade 4
Avonworth Elementary School

Spring to Winter

In spring the flowers come up
They are like little pups
The way they flow in the wind
It's a beautiful sight

Before you know it, winter comes
It sends upon a terrible fright
Few by few the flowers die
At the end, their job is done
Jake Rostek, Grade 6
St Rosalia Academy

Independence

Independence is a gift to all
The British no longer rule us
In Boston we dumped the British tea
The king made many unfair taxes
The colonists prepared to fight the king
General Washington led the troops
George Washington was a great leader
Many battles were fought by the troops
Philadelphia was the capital
Thirteen colonies became states
Our first flag had thirteen stars and stripes
Ben Franklin helped gain our freedom
George Washington became president
Independence gives us all freedom
We are now free to govern ourselves
Its birthday is every July fourth
We all celebrate as one nation
Our nation chooses its own leaders
Independence is a gift to all
We cannot forget our independence

Rachael Kenetski, Grade 4
St Alexis School

Snowflakes

Wintertime hath come again.
The air is turning crisp.
There are snowflakes lying on the ground.
People make snowmen and some knock them down.
But when they break the irreplaceable snowflakes,
the world cannot see their beauty.
So when you tread on the snow,
make sure that you know,
you are breaking irreplaceable snowflakes.

Austin Berbaum, Grade 5
Souderton Charter School Collaborative

School

When it is 6:00 am,
I don't want to get up.
My mom yells and yells until I get up.
Now that I am ready, let's go eat.

So now it's 7:15,
I have to eat before I leave.
Now that I am done with breakfast,
Must brush my teeth so they are white.

Get my coat on hurry, hurry,
Here comes the bus.
"Good bye Mom!"

Oh look it's Mrs. Chrobak greeting us at the door,
"Hi everyone!"

Taylor Walsh, Grade 6
St Gregory Elementary School

Discourteous/Respect

Discourteous
rude, impolite
unjustified, disparaging, undeserved
disrespectful, irreverent, polite, decorous
middling, respecting, separating
good, fair
Respect

Rosie Coppola, Grade 6
St Sebastian Elementary School

Harmony

The cows are in the pasture chewing on their cud.
The sheep are in the meadow bleating at the sun.
The horses are in the valley drinking from a stream.
And together they live in harmony…
Or so it seems.

Sarah Poliski, Grade 4
Our Mother of Perpetual Help School

Skateboards

Bam is cool.
He likes to ride a skateboard.
He didn't like school.
The board was called rayboard.

Bam broke a record.
But Tony did not.
Bam went to Eckerd.
And boy he fought.

He kicked Tony Hawk in a match up.
And beat Ryan Shecklers score really bad.
And beat a guy named Ashton Shupp.
Then boy was Shupp sad.

Michael O'Connell, Grade 4
Panther Valley Elementary School

The Woods

Sitting quietly
In a stand
Listening,
Watching,
Waiting.
Wildlife slowly waking
To the bright yellow sun
Rising to begin their day.
Snakes slither slowly to sun on smooth stones.
Foxes find food from fields to feed their families.
The deer wake up to a cloudless sky
Where the birds begin to fly.
Noisy squirrels making a racket
While I'm shivering inside my jacket.
So many great things to sit and see
That's why the woods are right for me.

Jayson Lottes, Grade 6
Chambersburg Area Middle School

Ocean

Relaxing water
Cold, salty, waves, splashing hard
Refreshing and calm
Josh Hertzog, Grade 5
Penn-Kidder Campus

Road to Detroit

Big Ben back to pass,
As their defense ran out of gas.
Their offense was bad,
Which made Steeler fans glad.
Black and gold sparked the night,
When our team put up a fight.
Seattle we will play,
To make our day.
One for the thumb,
To make Pittsburgh number one.
Go Steelers!
Patrick Mittereder, Grade 6
Carson Middle School

Water in the Wild

In the woods
A soft stream
Water falling off a hill
Splashing like rain drops
Except more of it
And much prettier
Trees surrounding it
Moving swiftly into a lake

Faster and faster
People come to me
Fish in me
I move into the ocean

People come to me on vacation
life guards watch
I have a current
I have fish and sharks
I am deep and dark
I have
I am a lake
a waterfall
and an ocean
Tori Contoudis, Grade 5
Jenkintown Elementary School

Friends

Friends
Caring, great
Running, chatting, dancing
They are giggling
Buddies
Erin Salerno, Grade 5
Penn-Kidder Campus

Lavender Beach

Lavender is the beach that shines with pride,
with a beautiful haze flowing in the morning sky
I desperately inhale to smell the generous flowers
The beach is like a mural on a city street wall,
painted gracefully with bright colors of the rainbow
that makes a smile on your face
I skidded through the sea,
with water skis on, not knowing what direction I'm going on and on
Stephanie Abreu Barros, Grade 4
Lincoln Elementary School

Easter

Easter
Eggs of many colors
The beautiful smelling flowers of spring
Church bells ringing
Yummy are the treats and chocolates nesting in children's baskets
Feeling the grass underfoot as we search for eggs
Easter
Carli Kohler, Grade 6
St Maria Goretti School

Ode to My Cats

Cats, oh cats, I simply enjoy having you.
You are fun to watch when you pounce on anything that moves.
I enjoy seeing you run as fast as a race car when you hear the treat bag open.
It is cheerful to hear you meow.
Your purr when you are petted is as calming as a sunset.
It is funny to see you chase your tail and trying to escape outside.
You are as still as a statue when you are sleeping in the sunlight.
Your black and white shade is a silhouette to behold.
I idolize your bravery when you explore the "unknown."
You jump as if you were on a trampoline when you are spooked.
You are adorable when you curl up to stay warm.
Your stealth movements surprise us all.
Ode to my cats, that are more than just pets to me.
Joseph Vais, Grade 6
St Sebastian Elementary School

Totoro*

Totoro is like a big furry ball that has a big mouth and a deep roar of lions.
His eyes widen when he hears a thump or some tinkling on the umbrella
that he was given by a girl on a drop! Drop! Rainy afternoon.
He enjoys loud noises and his eyes get as big as an orange.
He has two shelf-short feet and arms.
He is a lovable and kind creature that only can be seen by children.
His claws clank on the sidewalk
and his breathing is a deep groan of excitement and sometimes relief.
His ears are like triangular, furry spoons
and his nose is as leathery as a leather coat.
Totoro loves nuts just like children crave gum and candy.
I wish every child experienced such a treasure
only if it were true.
Milana Manuilov, Grade 6
Mount Nittany Middle School
*Based on "My Neighbor Totoro" from Studio Ghibli Hayao Miyazaki.

Michael Jordan

As a rookie Michael Jordan went to the All-Star game
Soon after everybody knew his name
He was a slam dunk artist and skilled at handling the ball
He was known to make some of the greatest fall
When the fans saw Michael go to the hoop they felt inspired
The fans were sad when he finally retired
When he returned fans cheered on
Three more championships Jordan led on
The MVP of the '96 All-Star game
It seems after retirement Jordan remains the same

Taleek Workman, Grade 6
Christopher Columbus Charter School - South

My Dog Shadow

My dog is so sweet, so soft, so cuddly.
My dad says she is as soft as a tiny bunny.

My dog loves to play fetch when it's warm or when it's cold.
I hope we both love to play catch when we're old.

My dog at night when the sky turns black,
She sleeps all night on my heavy backpack.

My dog is faster than a Lamborghini
She could beat a Ferrari or even my dad's new car,

Like a dog in a picture laying on the floor,
My dog is peaceful and loves to lay near my door.

My dog can jump as high as a deer.
She begs for food and catches it in midair.

Robert Oeler, Grade 4
Philipsburg Elementary School

Winter

Winter is cold
Winter is white
Winter can be a fright,
Winter has cold days and nights
Winter is a wonderful sight.

Erin Rodgers, Grade 6
West Allegheny Middle School

Friends

Friends are people who care about YOU.
They stayed by your side,
Comforted when you cried.
They helped when the going got tough,
Or when you have just had enough.
Friends are loyal people who listen and care,
They tell you it will all be okay if you are in despair.
They stand up for you if you are down,
They are your clown when you have a frown.
Friends are priceless people who never let you down.

Samantha Shepherd, Grade 6
West Allegheny Middle School

Ten

One wacky wimp waved wide weapons.
Two tall trees tell tales of two timbers.
Three trees grow too tall to talk.
Four fat fairies frequently fall fast.
Five freaks forgive five fat fairies.
Six sneaky snakes slither into school.
Seven seals swam so slow.
Eight eagles eat some eels.
Nine nerds nibble on Nerds candy.
Ten terrible turkeys torment two two-year-olds.

Cody Jones, Grade 5
Claysville Elementary School

Where I'm From

I am from my mother's womb,
From the umbilical cord.
I am from the pretty violet sheets
(flowers all around me)

I'm from the rose bush
The Japanese maple tree,
Whose short limbs remind me of my own.

I am from blinis and lobster
From Estelle and Jay.
I am from my brothers,
Who shoved me all around.

I'm from the Estberg and Lord branch,
The sea shore and the Gulf of Mexico.
From the hall of fame basketball plaque of my grandfather.
From the Harley Davidson my father loved to ride.

In the cedar chest in my parents' room
Comes baby blankets,
Calendars of old,
A christening gown of mine and my grandfather's
These are memories all boxed up in one little chest.

Haley Lord, Grade 6
Haverford Middle School

Salmon

Salmon is the feeling of a soft, fluffy blanket
when you are at a friend's slumber party.
It is the smell of laundry after it has just been washed
on a friendly summer day.
Salmon is the sound of wind when it is not evening or not night,
but the time of day when the sky is happier than ever
and the clouds are pinkish-orange.
Salmon is as sweet as the cheeks of a laughing baby.
It is the taste of a soft pink apple or a ripe strawberry.
Salmon is a beautiful shade of pink
and is also a sign of friendship.

Deanna Offner, Grade 5
Peebles Elementary School

Ice Hockey

On the ice, you can feel the freezing cold air brushing against your face as you are going dangerously fast down the ice.
You can hear the crowd roar as your beautiful shot goes sailing over the goalie's shoulder and into the back of the net.
You can see hats flying onto the ice when you score your third goal to complete your hat-trick.
You can smell the butter on the delicious popcorn when the game is tied up at three.
You can taste your green shock doctor mouth-guard as you are going on a breakaway.

Sean Wacker, Grade 4
Colonial Elementary School

Summer Days

The fresh pine scent fills the air.
Barefoot in the grass without a care.

The big bright sun lights up the day.
The children play in the yard.

The BBQ smell makes my taste buds water.
The sweet juices of the watermelon slide down my throat.

You can hear the voices of the football fans in the crowd.
The noisy chatter of the squirrels in play sounded like hundreds of clocks ticking all at once.

The soft touch of the grass felt like a cushion under my feet.
The sun felt like an electric blanket on my skin.

Trevor Mang, Grade 6
Neil Armstrong Middle School

Green

Green is a crawling caterpillar climbing a leaf.
Green is the dark green sea that rolls over, jumps into the air and comes down with a crash.
Green is the beautiful sound the grasshopper makes when he buzzes his wings.
Green is the bright green lollipop you lick while playing with your friends.
Green is the sweet aroma of fresh cut grass on a warm summer's day.
Green is the best color in the world.

Jacob Martin, Grade 5
Peebles Elementary School

face to face with life

poetry can make you fall in love or rip your heart into shreds, life is too short so organize your time properly, you wonder how or why we fall in love so all those boys and girls don't procrastinate in life, now we are face to face with life and we can't run or hide from the rumors or the truth, there is no mother or father to protect us now we're our own person,

we're face to face with life.

Toni Marshall, Grade 5
William C Bryant School

Taught Not Instinct

Hatred of a fellow man taught not instinct.
Hatred learned from experience, sound, sight and deep down in the slightest piece of your uncontrolled mind you know that this isn't your opinion this isn't your voice.
Your judgment is clear until you hear things and you become influenced and it becomes a sort of poison that sweeps through your entire mind and later, takes complete hold of your judgment.
You're now wondering that, the things you were told, were they true?
Your mind now craving the answers you finally realize that what you know and heard was not your choice it was influence now you start to develop your opinion.

Devan Gordon, Grade 5
Shafer Elementary School

Art

Art may fill many desires
For some it may just inspire
Them to move toward fulfilling their dreams
Even as dark and as lonely as it seems

Art may be used to express yourself
To get rid of bad feelings
It may be used to get rid of
The pain and hurt you've been concealing

Some may use it for fun
And others just to take up time
Some create art on a rainy day
Or sometimes even in the sunshine

Sometimes keeping art from the past may
Even help you remember
The fun you had as a young child in the summer
Or when you started school in September

Whatever you use art to get
Peace, serenity, or joy
It inspires lots of creativity
So when it comes to art, never be coy

Anita N. Bynum, Grade 5
Eden Christian Academy

Popcorn Delights

I can't think of anything but popcorn,
It comes from a cob that looks like a horn,
I make it in the microwave,
But how could you not leave a bag to save,
Although I have a strange obsession,
I know for a fact it cures depression,
We all know it's sweet and buttery,
But it's so light it's kinda fluttery,
And now you know how I feel about it,
So, I'll make a bag before I throw a fit!

Alicia Via, Grade 4
Watsontown Elementary School

Obnoxious, Popular, and Wonderful

Obnoxious
Deplorable, nasty, strange
Obnoxious people are very insane

Popular
Cherished, admired, beloved, adored
If you are popular, your life is no longer a bore.

Wonderful
Marvelous, remarkable, extraordinary, striking,
Wonderful things are simply astonishing.

Caroline Clark, Grade 5
Doyle Elementary School

The Earth

The Earth is polluted with gasses and such.
Because we use that stuff too much.
The Ozone is melting away.
So now we all have to pay.
For all the gasses we use.
But we don't use we abuse.
But now the Ozone's what we lose.
'Cuz we don't just use we abuse.

Emma Wagner, Grade 6
Freedom Area Middle School

Corvettes

Corvette, Corvette
Shiny and green
Body shape long
Motor sounds mean

Vettes, Vettes
My favorite cars
When one passes by
I see stars

If I had a Vette
I would drive like the wind
Zipping past
It would make your head spin

Vipers and Spyders
Just don't compare
When you have a Corvette
You are all the way there

Blue, black, and red they are all cool
It doesn't matter what color all Corvettes rule
There is just one problem I can see
Dollars lots of dollars a Corvette is going to cost me

Ethan Mummert, Grade 6
Chambersburg Area Middle School

My Dog Ben

I love my dog, Ben, he's really funny.
He chases cats and the bunny.
He gets real happy when we come home.
Because now he knows he's not alone.

He can speak, sit, and give paw.
But he likes it best when we play ball.
Ben really likes it when we give him our food
It really sets him in a good mood.

He likes to sleep in my bed.
And sometimes snores right by my head.
Without him I would be real sad
Because with him I am really glad.

Eric Onofrey, Grade 4
Elizabeth Elementary School

BLT Sandwich
When the person in front of you
orders a BLT sandwich,
did you ever think?
Could BLT mean big lardy toot,
or bananas love Timmy?
Maybe Bobby likes Tara sandwich?
I don't know.
I think we should stick with
bacon lettuce tomato sandwich.

Aubrey Schmeider, Grade 5
Center Township School

School Days
S is for scientific science
C is for calculations
H is for homework
O is for outstanding
O is for ominous tests
L is for learning

D is for dictionary
A is for an A+
Y is for yesterday's test
S is for SCHOOL

Gabrielle Davis, Grade 4
Concord Elementary School

Day and Night
Day
bright, new
tanning, running, swimming
sun, pool, quiet, soothing
watching, sitting, sleeping
sparkling shining
Night

Kylie Jo Taylor, Grade 4
West Branch Area Elementary School

My Pet Rock
R owdy ambitious dog
O utside playing on his chain
C onstantly aggravating me
K issing and licking me always

Erin Lohr, Grade 5
Wharton Elementary School

Football and Baseball
Football
Fun, exciting
Glee, faith, trust, devotion
Pitching, hitting, fielding
Thrilling, amazing
Baseball

Alex Bloom, Grade 5
Our Lady of Grace Elementary School

Friendship
Friendship is as sweet as flowers,
Sometimes like an evening shower.
It is like birds that sing,
Friends are like a diamond ring.

If you don't think that I'm right,
Just wait until you're in a fight.
And on that day, you'll realize,
Having a friend is a gift in disguise.

Lauren Shearer, Grade 5
Bermudian Springs Middle School

Useless Things
a table without chairs
a tree without pears
a hat without a head
a man without a bed

a dog that doesn't bark
night without dark
a buck without a horn
an earth without its core

a piece of bread without jelly
a man without a belly
a truck without a motor
a boat without a boater

a head without a body
a house without a potty
a hen without eggs
a man without legs

a chip without dip
a drink without a sip.

Brent Blacharczyk, Grade 5
Claysville Elementary School

Teamwork
T eam
en **E** rgy
A gility
me **M** ber
W in
O utstanding
awa **R** ds
wor **K** ing hard

without teamwork
we would have no team,
without a team
we would have no games,
without games we would have no fun,
teamwork is great!

Michael Gottstein, Grade 5
Holy Family Academy

Basketball and Football
Basketball
striped, orange
shooting, dunking, fouling
jersey, shorts, helmet, pads
tackling, catching, passing
injured, laced
Football

Mike J. Pennington, Grade 4
West Branch Area Elementary School

Dog
A dog who did nothing but dig,
dug a hole that was so big.
The gaping hole
was bigger than a pool,
just to find a missing twig.

LeAnn Grimes, Grade 6
Bedford Middle School

Seth
Seth
Fun, energetic
Helping, whipping through things, caring
Happy, mad
Friend

Harrison Ajemian, Grade 4
West Bradford Elementary School

Homework
H ow do we do it?
O h, so boring!
M oaning and groaning!
E asy, but hard
W ork, work, work
O h help me!
R ipping it up is what I want to do…
K illing my brain!

Alec Wentzel, Grade 5
Robeson Elementary School

Spring Plaza
Spring, Spring, here it comes.
Humming birds start to hum
Robins dig for worms,
But they sometimes squirm.
Spring beats winter at his own game,
Hurray, hurray, spring has fame!
Kids playing with friends,
Bears coming out of their dens.
School's out,
Everybody all about.
Spring is almost over, hurray!
Summer is on its way!

Thanna Oddo, Grade 4
Avonworth Elementary School

Garrett

G oing, going, going, always doing something.
A lways ready for anything.
R eady for almost everything.
R eally fun to be around.
E veryone thinks he's awesome.
T otally doing something.
T welve years old.

Garrett Browning, Grade 6
West Allegheny Middle School

Easter

Easter is full of joy,
Candy is so tasty to every girl and boy.
Eggs are colored and oh so sweet!
My dress is pretty and very neat.
My basket is full right to the top.
The bunny is funny and likes to hop.
The Easter egg hunts are awesome and a treat.
The boxes of chocolates are so sweet.
Even if the eggs should crack,
We're still so glad that Easter's back!

Jamie Thomas, Grade 4
Daniel J Flood Elementary School

My Loved Labrador Dog

My loved Labrador dog
who always eats like a hog
and loves to play
yes play at the bay
she loves to lay in the hall
and loves to play with her old tennis ball.
That's my loved Labrador dog.

Amy Weakland, Grade 6
Bedford Middle School

Fall

Fall is almost over.
So put away the shorts and T-shirts.
Get out the snowsuits and sweaters.
Heat up the hot chocolate.
It's time for sledding and snow-boarding.
I can't wait for winter.
It's my favorite season of all.

Michelle Leszunov, Grade 6
West Allegheny Middle School

Lovey My Lovebird

I remember Lovey soft and sweet
I remember when his beak chipped
I remember when he was old enough to breed
and had little red feathers on his head
I remember when he learned to get out of his cage
I remember when my sister's cat got into my room
And I remember when his life was lost to that darn cat

Shannon Teed, Grade 5
Claysville Elementary School

Spring's Whisper

The whispering wind is saying "Spring, spring, spring."
The trees even seem to be moving in its own mild rage.
Buds seem to be getting life from the robin's call of beauty.
Brush seems to create a barrier to keep things at peace.
The wonderous aromas of spring's newly bloomed flowers
to give spring its colors of light and beauty.
What this is, I said before, is spring's whisper.

Sean P. Conway, Grade 5
St Ambrose School

The Trees

Crinkling, crackling, crunching of leaves
Under the feet of walking children.
Snapping, popping, and cracking of twigs
Under the feet of walking children.
The soft sound of birds chirping in the distance.
The writing of pencils and pens upon paper.
The soft gentle sound of the whispering trees.

They talk to the horses, the plants, and the ground.
To tell them to listen to people around.
"Listen, listen," say the pine trees.
"Pay attention," say the young plants to the parent above.
The trees may not talk nor make any sound,
But they sure do listen to people around.

They talk to the grass.
They talk to the stars.
They talk to the pine trees
And the leaves that have fallen before.

Though we cannot hear them, they still do talk.
They talk through the wind that whispers on by.
It weaves through the trees that stand in their spot.
But no one ever knew that they could talk.

Erin Alcorn, Grade 6
Verner Elementary School

Ocean

As fierce as a lion.
As calm as a lamb.
In summer it lends a cool helping hand.
Tense and gentle.
Wise and old.
With a hint of blue it is rather bold.
A mysterious place.
Full of wonder, danger, and wide open space.
It is a pool of beauty that the world adores.
With wonderful colors and endless shores.
The depth of it marvels oh so many.
Sometimes it beams like a new copper penny.
With a dash of shimmer and a touch of glaze,
I think it is truly a sight to behold.

Carolyn Quinn, Grade 6
Our Lady of Mount Carmel School

Mirror

Like a conscience.
All knowing,
Uncovering the truth.
Detective,
Of your wrongdoing.
Revealing your secrets,
And lies.
It is a bearer of bad news.
Helps you make choices.
In the time of despair.
It never stands in the way,
Of your choice.
Even if it's the wrong one.

Michele Paulosky, Grade 6
Our Lady of Mount Carmel School

Midnight

M iraculously sweet
I rresistible
D ream horse
N onchalant
I ntelligent
G rateful
H ero
T ough, fast

Aubrey Smith, Grade 6
H Austin Snyder Elementary School

Seasons

The winter is cold,
In the winter it may snow,
The winter is white.

In spring it is warm,
There are blossoming flowers,
Spring is in the air.

The summer is hot,
There are bees buzzing around,
Let's go in the pool!

In the fall it is cool,
Leaves are falling to the ground,
Welcome back to school.

Mary Williams, Grade 4
Sacred Heart School

Winter

Fluffy, white snow
Sledding, skiing, snowboarding
Cold, flaky, freezing, icy
Blistering, blowing, flurrying
Strong winds, bad roads
Winter

RoseMarie Lauck, Grade 4
Memorial Elementary School

Friends

They are crazy but sometimes sweet,
They never leave they always stay,
Sometimes you're in a muck your friends will help get you unstuck,
Sometimes you will get mad but don't mope,
They're always there for you like the sun and moon,
Your friendship will not die or dry,
They're almost always around,
They'll come back that's a fact,
They just need some time to think,
Just be brave and behave,
Then you're all back together and friends forever.

Linda Lutz, Grade 6
Neil Armstrong Middle School

Ghazal of the Border Collie

Our new puppy arrived one January night.
Her fur was like a child's painting in black and white.

I named her Lacy, which rhymes with Casey,
my dad's old dog who was black with no white.

Like me and Lacy, Dad and Casey romped and watched the Yankees.
But my TV is color. His was black and white.

When we took Lacy for walks she sniffed the snow,
speckling her black nose with flecks of white.

We spread newspapers inside the house,
and she learned to pee on black and white.

Once she escaped and took off like an eagle in flight.
She was a blur of black and white.

Now she's big and gentle and never bites.
She's a 50-pound lapdog in black and white.

Nathan De Prospo, Grade 6
Charles W Longer Elementary School

Remembering the Children*

In remembrance of the children of Sierra Leone
a land of high mountains, swamps and sandy ground
where rice, cocoa and peanuts grow
and children are in the military fighting for their lives

You could have been a devil dancer as your chief gets crowned
a diamond miner
or a repairman for commercial boats

I will be thankful that I'm in school and not fighting for my country
and that I'm eating food all day long and always seem to want more
and not starving to death every day of my life
as I remember you.

Mikaela Fritz, Grade 6
Deibler Elementary School
*In remembrance of the children of Sierra Leone

California

California is a special place
Where the sun shines brightly on your face.
The mountains are really tall
And the ocean is the biggest of all.
There are sea lions lying in the sun
And trolley car rides which are such fun.
The beautiful valleys are covered with vines
Grapes grow on them, of all kinds.
Mansions and movie stars are in Hollywood,
I'd be in a movie if I could.
California is a great place to be
Disney, adventure, and so much to see!

Josh Brown, Grade 5
Chalutzim Academy

The Beach

Foamy blue waves crashing up on the beach,
The white caps are dancing out of my reach,
Salty warm waves pushing me toward the shore,
I grab my surf board and swim out for more.

Playing in soft sand that is sparkling white,
Sun shining brightly not a cloud in sight,
A blanket of hot sand piled up on me,
The beach is always a great place to be.

The sun fades from yellow to orange to red,
I'm still at the beach when it goes to bed,
Exploding fireworks make showers of light,
Bright crackling bonfires burn in the black night.

Sarah Francis, Grade 5
Edgeworth Elementary School

Summer

Summer is the greatest of all four seasons.
I've got plenty of reasons.
During the summer you can play many sports.
You can even wear shorts.
You can ride bikes in summer.
It's really not a bummer.
Every day in summer it's very nice.
There is definitely no ice.
In the summer you can enjoy almost anything.
You can even hear the birds sing.
In the summer you can run around,
And get grass stains from the ground.
In summer it seems you can do anything at all,
Especially anything that deals with a ball.
My poem is coming to an end,
But we can all pretend,
That summer is right around the bend.
I am really not teasin',
Summer is the greatest of all four seasons.

Robert McConnell, Grade 6
Conemaugh Township Area Intermediate School

Different

I'm so much more different than everyone.
My face isn't the same as theirs.
My color isn't their color.
They try to make me like them but,
I keep my own vibe and I stay me.
I stay different.

Jasmin White, Grade 6
Independence Charter School

Brilliant Dream

I'm living the life with my very best friend.
I never want this day to end.
We're so rich and we love to shop in the mall.
Shoes, purses, bags, we have it all.
Suddenly I see a very bright light.
Am I crazy, is everything all right?
I don't really know what this means.
But then I realize that it was one of my dreams.

Shakera Kelly, Grade 5
East Stroudsburg Elementary School

The Amazing Amazon

I can see the vivid colors of marvelous birds
and enormous trees surrounding me

I hear the sound of courageous animals screeching
and flying amongst the leaves of the towering trees

I can smell the delectable aroma of mangos and fruits
hanging in the fanning trees above me

I can taste the cold water rushing in the glistening
Amazon River

I can feel the cool breeze slowly and swiftly flying
through the canopy of trees,

For I am a graceful butterfly swooping through the
Amazon Rain forest

Maxie Ehrlich, Grade 4
Colonial Elementary School

Halloween

I see the pumpkins, Jack o' Lanterns and
Lots of kids in costumes.

I smell the delicious candy when I open it.
I taste the yummiest treats in the world.

I touch the bony fake skeletons in my
Dad's front yard.

I hear the scary sounds and kids saying
"Trick or Treat" at every door.

Erika Komp, Grade 4
Colonial Elementary School

Night

The sun has set,
The stars are bright,
The end of day,
And start of night.

The crickets chirp,
The frogs croak,
The children fall asleep,
Under the wind's graceful stroke.

But as the sun comes up the hill,
The peaceful night seems to stand still.

The sun wakes those,
From silent sleep,
And comforts those,
Who tend to weep.

And soon begins another busy day,
When adults work and children play,
But every day just has to end,
Then the cycle begins again.
Madison Chafin, Grade 5
Boyce Middle School

My Dog

My dog Soccer is very sweet,
The things she does are so neat!
Sometimes she plays with balls,
But other times she tears apart dolls.
My dog is the best,
No other dog could beat her
on the best dog examination test!
Kathleen Stanus, Grade 4
Christ the King School

Moving

Boxes being packed
Things getting lost and broken
Must say goodbye
Frustration and stress
Olivia Canny, Grade 4
Bushkill Elementary School

Alanah

She's a sweet friend to have.
She always loves to play.
She's always excited.
She's never sad a day.

She's always nice to us,
And helpful to others.
With her sensitive heart,
Her name is Alanah!
Ashley Irish, Grade 5
East Stroudsburg Elementary School

A Person

There is a person that I really treasure
We had happy times together.
But one day
He went away,
And I never saw him again
For he was in Heaven.
Josh Waxman, Grade 4
Lower Gwynedd Elementary School

Sand

Glistening golden
Shiny irritating grains
Flowing into dunes
Shannon Green, Grade 5
Penn-Kidder Campus

Deer Season

Through the woods to kill a deer,
Quiet as a mouse you go.
Wait for the deer to magically appear,
You really want a doe.

Look through trees and what do you see?
An animal with brown hair.
It's not a doe, but what can it be?
A man-eating grizzly bear.
Curtis Laughman, Grade 5
Bermudian Springs Middle School

Friends

Friends are nice
Friends are cool
Friends fight
Friends rule
Friends are kind
Friends are trouble

But friends should always try
And stay humble.
Emily Simpson, Grade 4
Panther Valley Elementary School

A Scary Ride

Have you ever ridden a scary ride?
That sends shivers up your spine.
Did this ride make you wary?
All this ride was very scary.

I heard a scary noise in that ride.
And I didn't scream for joy that time.
I cried for mom, but she wasn't there.
I wished I could not be scared.
I will never ride this ride again.
Shayla Pringle, Grade 6
Freedom Area Middle School

Winter

Winter is my favorite time of the year.
There's never animals that you can hear.
They're tucked away in their nice house.
No one's out, not even a mouse.

I just love winter when it's around.
Especially when snow's on the ground.
I can play in that white stuff.
Until I think I've had enough.

No, it's almost time for spring.
When the birds come out to sing.
Goodbye winter, goodbye fun.
Now I will go out and run.
Leonard Ogozalek, Grade 4
Panther Valley Elementary School

The Sun

The sun is gentle.
Hot, sweet, not sour or bitter.
Rays of light on me.
Emma Longstreth, Grade 4
Marlborough Elementary School

Books

I open my book,
As words jump out at me.

I begin reading quickly,
As thoughts swim through my mind.

I read until the end,
Until I'm fast asleep.

Dreaming of the story,
Right beneath me.
Allison Campbell, Grade 6
Christ the Divine Teacher School

Dog

Dogs
can
get
crazy

They bark
and they
can get
Quite loud

Boy! They
Will chase you —
run around in
circles
Logan Gardner, Grade 4
Fishing Creek Elementary School

Me, Emily Boak

My name is Emily, I love my family,

An artist or author, I'd love to invent,
I sure hope I don't get stuck in cement!

Two things I love are horses and cats,
I don't like to eat many sweets and fats!

I fear death, I'm artistic and kind,
There always is something on my mind!

I like to do pottery, I ski and draw,
My imagination is big, but it started real small!

I like to write and weave,
And here is something that I believe,

If you are always truthful and always kind,
A caring friend you'll always find!

Emily Boak, Grade 5
Bushkill Elementary School

Weekend

Every day I go to school.
It may be boring but it's cool.
If the bell doesn't ring I will shout.
Bell please ring and let school out.
In the amusement park line I stand,
I ride the rides and watch the band.
It's time for school I must go in.
But I can't wait for the next weekend to begin.

Bridget Brumbaugh, Grade 4
St Maria Goretti School

Spring

It's springtime
Clear blue skies above
Grass covered fields below
Like a whole new world.

April showers have come and gone,
Bringing new life to the land.
This is a fantastic dream after winter's harsh touch
What a wonderful time of year!

The wind is whispering in your ear,
The sweet perfumes of flowers all around.
Sound of birds and bees everywhere
Buzz, Chirp, Buzz

Such beauty, beauty, beauty
Everywhere you turn.
We have paid the price of winter's toll,
Let us now enjoy the spring.

Nora Adams, Grade 6
Mount Nittany Middle School

The Rocky Road

Mint chocolate chip is as good as can be
And cookie dough is as good as it seems
Now don't forget vanilla it just tastes so amazing
And always remember that chocolate drives me crazy
Peanut Butter Cup seems like you're walking on the Milky Way
And I could eat Bubble Gum flavor every single day
The coffee flavor just tastes so yucky
And the banana flavor reminds me of a yellow rubber ducky
Sherbet ice cream tastes a little funny
The white kind reminds me of a big fat bunny
Ice cream is so good to eat
And ice cream is very sweet

Kelly O'Donnell, Grade 6
Churchville Elementary School

Summer

The white sandy beaches
The blue crystal water
The distant blazing sun

The smooth velvety feeling of a flower petal
The soft warm breezes
The hot sun warms me

Eating ice cream all the time
The cold sensation of a vanilla milkshake
The sweet and sour taste of barbecue

Laying on the couch
Smelling the lovely aroma of freshly baked cookies
Smelling barbecued chicken, ribs, and hot dogs

The birds chirping
The drip, drop of the rain
The crackling sound of twigs as you run

Kelsey Dundon, Grade 6
Neil Armstrong Middle School

Pops, My Grandfather

Pops was the father of ten,
Four girls and six men.
He married a woman named Sue,
And his name was Lou.

For his company, he was the starter.
It was clear he'd have to work harder.
That doesn't mean he wasn't a great dad,
Though his kids sometimes made him mad.

Now that he has passed away,
We miss him every coming day.
Whatever he is… granddad, husband, dad,
Knowing that he's my "Pops" will always make me glad.

Madeline DeVlieger, Grade 5
Villa Maria Academy Lower School

My Grandmother

In 2001,
In a place that I knew not,
My grandmother lay,
Slowly drifting off,

On a long slow journey,
To a place,
Far, far away,
Where everyone may go,

Will you take this journey,
Like my grandmother,
To face death head on,
Or will you escape to the graveyard?
Sarah Roberts, Grade 5
Wexford Elementary School

Flyers Game

Hockey player,
energized goalie,
shot comes,
glove save,
covers up,
face off,
we win,
the hard,
face off,
travels up,
pass up,
to a fast player,
pass again,
sonic shot,
goalie misses,
back twine,
we score,
we win,
YAHOO YIPPEE,
good time,
Flyers game!
Matt Fegley, Grade 6
Grasse Elementary School

Love

Love is like a dove.
Captured by one, free by rest.
No air to breathe in.
Victoria Robles, Grade 6
Allison Park Elementary School

Pyramid

Mysterious, huge
It's beautiful and sacred
Breathtaking, ancient
Alexander Stephen Ta Bois, Grade 5
Penn-Kidder Campus

Wolves

W atch for prey
O ut at night hunting
L eaving dens in winter
V ariety of wolves hunt for food.
E xtremely intelligent
S o hard to spot
Jesse Zubik, Grade 4
Avonworth Elementary School

Rain

The rain came down,
All over the wet town,
And now I'm really mad,
But at the same time sad.
Ellen Mook, Grade 4
East End Elementary School

Crocodile Jim

Crocodile Jim
will see you swim
out there in the water.
You'll be caught by him
Crocodile Jim,
caught just like an otter.
With a snap of his jaws
you will be gone
disappear for a while.
But it's pretty sad
that you've been caught
By a hungry crocodile.
Martin Taylor, Grade 4
Concord Elementary School

Spring Is Here

Spring is here.
It is a time to play.
The flowers are blooming.
Birds are singing.
Spring is here
Blue skies
Green grass.
The air is fresh
Everyone rushes to go outside
Spring is here
Summer is coming too
We go and swim
Spring is here
I love spring
I just can't wait
Spring is here
What a wondering feeling
Winter is the past
Winter is history for a while
Spring is here
Lindsey Bodiker, Grade 6
West Allegheny Middle School

Rapids

Playing their everyday game.
Rocks after water,
Dodging,
Splashing,
Never resting —
Never sleeping —
Always playing their game.
Aaron Gunderson, Grade 5
Franconia Elementary School

They...

Frogs hop
Dogs plop
Frogs swim
Dogs grin
Skyler Phillips, Grade 4
Fishing Creek Elementary School

Good and Evil

Good,
Kind, nice
Generous, cheerful, happy
God, teachers, Hitler, devil
Crushing, destroying, killing
Vicious, treacherous
Evil
Davis Wayne, Grade 5
Our Lady of Grace Elementary School

Faces

Faces are very nice
Features on each are quite precise

They sometimes have a shade of blue
At other times, not having a clue

Sometimes a face looks red with anger
Especially when hit with a hanger

A face can be green with confusion
On a day when having quite a delusion

Faces make the world go 'round
That is why they never frown.
Andrew Clinger, Grade 5
Vandergrift Elementary School

Dogs

Dogs
Different sizes
Barking, playing, eating
Friend of deep mystery
Puppies
Emily Leight, Grade 4
Hereford Elementary School

Life

Life isn't always fair
But you have to take what you get.

Life can be easy
Life can be hard
Life can be simple
Or like a sweet tart.

Life is beautiful art;
The goodness of life comes from the heart.

Crystal Washington, Grade 6
Independence Charter School

Made to Fly

I fly my plane,
The one I made
The one I bade farewell
For the point was for it to fly well indeed.
But not into a great big tree!
Boo hoo!
That was but the best plane for me.

Now school, a bore,
Has come around
I can't wait till I get out!
But not until three.
Sigh

Yippee!
I'm out! I could fly
away, fly home, fly home
to make another plane,
a better one for me!

Finally I'm finished. Let's fly.

Peter Bartholomew, Grade 5
Falk School

Spring's Spell

The spring breeze that blows through my hair,
To leave my spring garden I do not dare.

Birds that sing their lovely tune,
Soon the sun turns to new moon.

Spring showers of the skies clear tears,
Melt the ice and all winter fears.

The flowers break the winter spell,
Shall it be back again? Only time will tell.

As the leaves fly and the grass grows green,
I hope that spring is not only a dream.

Mallory Zondag, Grade 6
Moravian Academy Middle School

Rainbow

Orange is as bright as the sun
Silver must bore everyone

Blue is as bright as the sky
Red is the color of some color dye

Brown is the color of an autumn tree leaf
Green is a color I look at brief

Pink is a girl's new shoe
Teal is a very nice color too

Purple flowers bloom in the spring
Gold makes a good wedding ring

Do you like colors as I do?

Tyrone Klump, Grade 4
Bushkill Elementary School

Starry Night

I am a starry night sky
Just shining so bright
And I have a big galaxy full of stars
And beautiful brightness.
The beautiful stars in my big huge night sky
Glitter and shimmer their beautiful brightness.

Tilynn Heavens, Grade 6
Freedom Area Middle School

My Family

I love my family.
They can be strange at times,
but when you know them they're special.
My brother was adopted,
but if he was not here I would not be me.
I love my family.

Rachel Miller, Grade 4
Bushkill Elementary School

Nature

Leaves with colors everywhere
dancing their way through the air.

Grass swaying side to side,
hearing birds sing as they glide.

A rabbit hopping through a log
covered with a morning fog.

Deer jumping over twigs;
Their fur looked like a giant wig.

This is what happened on this wonderful day.
As the trees and leaves begin to play.

Katie Holohan, Grade 6
St Ambrose School

When You Find a Leprechaun

When you find a leprechaun
on St. Patrick's Day
ask him where
his large pot of gold lay.
Guarded by a bee
or under a tree
find where
his large pot of gold lay.
If it be at the end
of a rainbow
with a shamrock inside
or a place where
no one can find,
find where
his large pot of gold lay.

Georgette Covasa, Grade 4
Easterly Parkway Elementary School

Life

What is life?
An unfair cruel thing
A lot of problems
Life can be quick and short
A painful thing
A scary thing
With smiles
With frowns
Something that is a joy
Full of glee
That is what life means to me!

Zehavit Kabak, Grade 5
Rolling Hills Elementary School

Milk and Cookies

In the land of milk and cookies,
the clouds are made of candy.
Cookies float in all the milk,
in the land of milk and cookies.

Sugar birds fly slowly by
as bubble gum rainbows
bless the Jell-O sky.

Good-bye!
milk and cookies
Good-bye!

Mila Tamminga, Grade 4
Easterly Parkway Elementary School

Woodstock

Loves to take baths
In her cage
All day long
Because she loves to feel pretty

Sabrina Moyer, Grade 5
Newtown Elementary School

Remembering the Children*

A land of mountains and plateaus,
    where 15% of all children go to high school,
    and people have homes of stone blocks, and mud.
You may have been a rich farmer,
    who grew the finest rice,
    or a fisherman who caught the largest fish on the coast,
    or a miner (a digger) who mines the most valuable diamonds in the country.
I will be grateful for all I have been given,
as I remember you.

Kari Andersen, Grade 6
Deibler Elementary School
*In remembrance of the children of Sierra Leone

School Food

School food cannot be described in just few simple words,
they feed you stuff you dare not eat like mice or squid or birds.

Vending machines have pop or chips on which most kids depended,
except some kids who are total dips (even PETA was offended).

Sometimes it crawls in frenzied rage or snarl or spit or scowl,
sometimes you put it in a cage because it's on the prowl.

It may be brand food (that's a nice change) so be glad don't sneer or stifle,
otherwise you'll need a 50 yd range on a G-13 sniper rifle.

Whether it's nice and tasty or mediocre and crude,
never be off-guard or hasty when it comes to school food.

James Imbrie, Grade 6
Neil Armstrong Middle School

The Big Game

The day I woke up
I could feel it in my blood
Pumped up and ready to go
As I'm sitting I'm thinking about the big game
Can't stop the adrenalin rush
Diving into the end zone for the winning touchdown
I could hear the crowd chanting my name
When I got up the whole team ran to me
They put me on their shoulders
It was my senior year, and everybody was hugging
To lighten up the moment I said save the hugging for the lockers

Kenny McClain, Grade 6
Freedom Area Middle School

The Magic Garden

When you go through the magic garden you'll see many things,
    like diamonds and golden rings.
If you turn to the right door your wish shall come true.
But if you go through the wrong door your bad luck will be due.
So choose right,
    don't fight.
And discover the magic garden!

Heather N. Krzywicki, Grade 6
Fairview Elementary School

What Real Friends Can Do!

They can be so nice
They can be so mean
They change their moods
They can change their look
They can make you angry
They can make you want to pull your hair out
They can be
They can try to convince you not to do drugs
They are not "real friends" if they can't do just about anything
What real friends can do

Kasey Davies, Grade 6
Grasse Elementary School

Pictures

Pictures show memories
Both good and bad
They could show you a dead relative
Which could make you sad

They show you a place where you had happy times
Like our old house with the green wind chimes
They show you when you had a lot of fun
With family and friends or with anyone

They'll show the fear on your face on your first day of school
Or the joy you had when you got your first set of tools
They show us events we can't remember
Such as the first day of preschool in September

They show you sitting on the couch with your dad
Or sitting in time-out because you got mad
Some of those things will make you sad
Others will often make you glad

Because, remember, pictures show memories
Both good and bad.

George Farmer, Grade 6
Sacred Heart Elementary School

Summer

Birds are singing
Swing hinges are ringin'

Chipmunks running
Kids playing

Cool breeze hitting your face
Grass tickling your feet

The taste of ice cream melting on your tongue
Water cooling you down

The bonfire is smokin'
And the chlorine is soakin'

Randi Hudson, Grade 6
Neil Armstrong Middle School

Dance of the Dolphin

When the moon shines bright,
Look out on the ocean.
Look straight into the moon's reflection.
The water will sparkle but don't be deceived
Because what awaits you is under the sea.
Diving right into the ocean blue,
I swam over to the sparkling moon.
Then all of a sudden I was hoisted up,
And I felt my heart taking off.
When I crashed back down to the water,
I did not drown for a friend was near.
I opened my eyes and all that I saw,
Was the most handsome dolphin of all.
He started to swim in a circle around me,
And then started to do a new little dance.
He jumped, spun, and flipped through the air,
It seems so simple to him because he didn't have a care.
Then he included me in his graceful dance,
And soon I was dancing his dance.
Now to this day I will never forget,
The Dance of the Dolphin in the ocean's depths.

Courtney Bickel, Grade 6
Strodes Mills Middle School

My Letter to Santa Claus

I wrote a letter to Santa,
I wrote with all my might,
I never stopped to take a break,
And wrote it all that night.

I asked him for a video game,
I asked him for a football,
I asked him for a pet dog,
Or anything at all.

I never told him one thing,
A thing that he should know,
I wanted to wake up Christmas morning,
And see nothing but falling snow.

When I woke on Christmas morning,
I rushed to the window and saw,
My special Christmas wish had come true,
It was the whitest Christmas of all!

Joseph Anzur, Grade 6
Holy Spirit School

Cash

There once was a man with a lot of cash,
He threw it all in the trash,
A little boy showed it to his mommy,
She showed her husband Tommy,
There went the cash right out of the trash.

Samantha Cunningham, Grade 6
Freedom Area Middle School

Jewell

J em, Jewell
E qual in all ways
W ins everything
E nergy all the time
L oyal to students
L oving to students,
if she says she will be there she will

Nicole Dixon, Grade 6
H Austin Snyder Elementary School

Gatorade

Tasty, liquidy
Bottled, colored, capped
Good for fun sports
Cold
Mike Sardella, Grade 4
Manoa Elementary School

Different Feelings

When the wind blows by
words pour in your head
about what you did wrong
But when the breeze goes away
then the thoughts go away with it
You now think about your future
with honeysuckle on the fence
and in your future more decisions
you come towards
a little old house
at the top of the street
with the prettiest garden
that you put together
You would have never thought
it would be your life.
Alana Anselmi, Grade 4
Lincoln Elementary School

A Rainy Day

Grass is green
Sky is blue
Hopefully you are not blue, too.

If it is a rainy day,
Grab a hat and go out to play
You'll be having fun anyway.

Finally now, the sun shines through
It's still wet, but there's lots to do
Hopefully you can come out, too.

Grab your shoes
Grab your gear
All types of weather
Are sure to appear!
Thomas Rupert, Grade 5
Vandergrift Elementary School

Frank the Crank

There once was a crank named Frank
Who noticed that he shrank
He began to worry
So he called his friend Murray
And then he walked the plank
Nichole Sluga, Grade 5
Mount Jewett Elementary School

Why, God, Why?

I cry
You dry my tears.
I hurt
You make the pain go away.
Why, God, Why?

I'm mad
You calm me.
I'm confused
You make me understand.
Why, God, Why?

Why God,
do You do,
all of this
when I don't deserve
any of it.

Could it be
because You love me
or because You have to.
So one question,
Why, God, Why?
Shannen Snyder, Grade 6
Bedford Middle School

Shy Is...

Shy is...
Scary,
Timid,
Fear of others.
Shy is...
Annoying,
Embarrassing,
Slinking away.
Shy is...
Afraid,
Amazed,
Scared to be wrong.
Shy is...
First,
Not last,
And wondering why,
I'm always shy.
Rebekah Willson, Grade 4
Beaver County Christian School

The 4th of July

Boom, boom, crack
The sound of fireworks everywhere
Pirouetting in midair like
Dancing ballerinas
Falling in graceful cascades
Sparkling jewels in the sky
Clouds of smoke hanging in the
Hazy, hot, humid sky
Brilliant, beautiful bursts followed
By booms and bangs
Amazement swelling in your chest
As pride for your country
The lights, colors, and sounds
Of the red, white, and blue
A celebration of freedom for
Everyone to see
John Peterson, Grade 6
Mount Nittany Middle School

Basketball

I love to play basketball
Although I am small
I've used the triple threat
To beat players I've met

Although I am small
I can dribble the ball
To beat players I've met
I can use skills that I get

I can dribble the ball
Around players short and tall
I can use skills that I get
To win many, I bet
Carter Peters, Grade 6
Grasse Elementary School

One Woman*

One woman on a bus
Changing the lives
Of millions of people.
By not giving up her seat,
She changed history.
Now we honor her
By walking
Where she was arrested.
She defended their freedom,
And now we thank her.
Rosa Parks,
First Lady of the Movement,
We honor you,
Only one woman.
Sami Kovacs, Grade 6
*Inspired by the walk
commemorating Rosa Parks.

Friends and Dreams Come True

Friends are friends and never apart,
Maybe in distance, but never in heart,
Friends forever and never to change,
You may love, you may hate,
You can cry, you can change.
Dreams are wishes, straight from the heart,
Love is something,
That will never be apart,
And always remember,
It's not all about keeping promises,
It's about following your heart.

Chelsea Bilger, Grade 6
Strodes Mills Middle School

My Reflection

I look in mirrors and I see,
Black shadows are so small,
Not always staring back at me.
Sometimes it's quiet, sometimes it will call.

When I see myself, I would scream
And never let my fear out.
When scared, my insides feel like cream,
When I let my fears out I do not doubt.

My reflection looks back at me,
As I stared back at it.
When I did look back I saw me.
Not liking what I see, I want to spit.

I look in my eyes I feel shy,
I am like this but why?

Elise Burkett, Grade 6
Freedom Area Middle School

Summer

Summertime is the best,
There are no teachers chasing you for a test.

No books, no pencils and no more school
Time to jump into the pool.

Time to have fun and enjoy the sun
Walk, jog, or enjoy a run.

No more leaves, snow, or sickening chills,
Riding your bike up and down the hills.

If summer were here every day
I know exactly what I would say!

Summertime is finally here
It's the best time of the year!

Alexa Griffiths, Grade 6
Conemaugh Township Area Intermediate School

I Love to Write

I am Julia and I love to write,
I can do it all day and night.
I do it even when I'm sad,
It calms my nerves when I'm mad.
I love it when people read my writings,
As much as I love people hearing my reciting.
I wrote this poem all about me,
I can't wait to write the next one,
Just wait and see.

Julia Aldrich, Grade 5
Sacred Heart of Jesus School

By Myself*

When I'm by myself
And I close my eyes
I am a dirt biker landing a hard trick.
I'm a skateboarder who landed the Indy 900.
I'm a super fast racecar driver.
I'm a gold medalist street bike racer.
I'm a black belt in karate.
I'm a brave navy seal.
I'm a skilled air force pilot.
I'm a super good doctor.
I'm a billionaire.
I'm a whatever I want to be,
And anything I care to be.
And when I open my eyes,
What I care to be
Is Me!

Connor Conti, Grade 5
East Stroudsburg Elementary School
*Inspired by Eloise Greenfield.

Summer

Temperature rises and school lets out,
No one is crying, not even a pout.

Soccer season starts with a blast,
As we all hope our winning will last.

Tournaments start and we have fun all day,
Our team will laugh because of what we all say.

Swimming outside in the sun's bright light,
We'll keep on swimming until it is night.

Vacation away to see something new,
Friends wait to hear what happens with you.

Camps bring new friends, who teach something new,
Now we begin the end of summer blues.

Next school year begins, yes, summer flew,
We wait for next summer to have more fun too.

Lindsey Buncich, Grade 6
Conemaugh Township Area Intermediate School

Leaves

Leaves
Floating to the ground
Soft, warm, and moist on your cheek
Drifts on the spring breeze
Olivia Rauktis, Grade 4
St Sebastian Elementary School

Springtime

A time of change
Cocoons bursting open
Flowers blooming
Robins returning home
A time for new beginnings

Spring is like a rainbow of colors
Different sounds being heard
Bees buzzing
Birds chirping
There is magic in the air

Seasons come and go
But spring is by far
My favorite time of year
Dana Stabryla, Grade 4
Concord Elementary School

Spyro the Dragon

Spyro the dragon has a spiral tail
When he's mad he blows a fiery wail

Spyro the dragon has pointy horns
He will charge at you, he never warns

Spyro the dragon has lots of fun
But when the day is over he is done
Ian Krzyzanowski, Grade 5
Concord Elementary School

School Is Out

School is out,
It's time to shout,
Yippee, yippee,
Hooray for me.

It was so fun,
But now it's done,
The days flew by,
Now say good-bye.

Summer comes next,
No more projects,
It's time for fun,
Work? None!
Meredith Meyer, Grade 5
Reidenbaugh Elementary School

The Colors

Red — courage, hardiness, boldness
White — purity, innocence
Blue — vigilance, perseverance, justice

These colors are familiar
Aren't they?
Well they're not just colors,
They mean a lot.
They mean the wars
And the veterans
That risked their lives in them
Just to save us.
So not just those colors mean a lot
So do the veterans

Thank you veterans!
Savanna Lorah, Grade 5
Robeson Elementary School

Riding

When I am on a horse,
    I feel like I am flying through the air.

When I am on a horse,
    My hair blows in the wind.

When I am on a horse
    The horse and I feel fine.
Taylor Rake, Grade 4
Northern Cambria Catholic School

Battles

Bulldogs beat bulls
in battles while
bumping balloons
beside benches.
James Macek, Grade 6
Allison Park Elementary School

Italy's Food

Italy
Italy's food
tastes so good
pizza, pomegranate, parmesan cheese
and tiramisu for desert please
Joey Recktenwald, Grade 4
South Park Elementary Center

Snow

Snow
Fluffy, white
Icy, soft, fun
So fun to play in
Outside
Allison Steffy, Grade 5
Clay Elementary School

Cats

Cats
quick, purrs
runs, meows, sleeps
lives in a house
Cats

Kittens
small, squalls
soft, purrs, sleeps
lives in a house
Kittens

Felines
fast, purrs
meows, sleeps, runs
lives in a house
Felines
Kaitlyn O'Brien, Grade 4
Indian Lane Elementary School

If Friendship

If friendship is like a bread box,
    Regard me as a crumb.

If friendship is like a chain,
    Think of me as a link.

If friendship is like a rug,
    Remember me as a thread.

If friendship is like the ocean
    Think of me as a minnow.
Colette Gress, Grade 5
East Stroudsburg Elementary School

Flag

Falls to the ground in war and battle
Lightning strikes it day and night
Although it goes up without a fight
Gushing blood of red and white
What am I?
Neal Khaisman, Grade 5
Jenkintown Elementary School

The Moon

The moon is an eye
watching over us.
It sees far and wide.
Knowing how we do things
our own way.
Peacefully inspiring us,
it blankets the sky
with wonderous colors.
Kaylin Vickinovac, Grade 6
Freedom Area Middle School

Creatures

Lady bugs are very small.
They're red and black and climb up walls.

Butterflies have colored wings,
Which cling to almost everything!

Birds built nests up in oak trees.
They love to soar through the warm breeze.

Bumble bees make buzzing sounds.
They fly above the busy towns.

All these creatures make me smile.
They each display a different style!

Sarah Chorle, Grade 4
Philipsburg Elementary School

Cleaning

wiping, spraying
that's what I do
cleaning, clearing
reaching for days, months, years, and centuries
the dust spreads like wildfire
I dust

Celeste Kirkland, Grade 6
Luther Memorial Learning Center

Friends

Some are big and some are small
Either size I love them all.
This goes out to all my friends,
We'll be together until the end.
Through all the tough times
And the happy ones too
You make me feel like I can make it through.
So here's to my friends this is about,
I love you guys without a doubt!

Elizabeth Horst, Grade 6
Locust Grove Mennonite School

Summer Day

Wind flies through my face, cold
Blistering winds surround me
With darkness closing in.
The moon beats down on me like there's no way to get out.
I hold myself tight knowing it will be o.k.
The bitterness of the wind makes my cheeks freeze.
Suddenly it stops.
The warm sun dries my hair,
The sun shines like a golden airplane ready to take off.
My eyes can hardly open.
I twirl around happy in the sun
I start to laugh and chase myself in the meadows
And roll down the hills

Mika Rubinstein, Grade 4
Lincoln Elementary School

Doughy Boughy

There once was a guy named Bo
He liked to make lots of dough
So did his pet crow
One day Bo and his crow ate all the dough
Whoa yelled Bo we ate all the dough

Gunner Goldie, Grade 4
Avonworth Elementary School

Snowfall

Beautiful, white flakes glistening in the yard.
When combined with rain and cold,
Can become very hard.
Dangerous and slippery,
So you better be careful!
Many in snowsuits find it delightful.
When it falls, my brother and sister love to play.
Sometimes they stay out and play in their sleds all day!
It is uncontrollable, yet gentle and soft.
Mother Nature drops it flake by flake from aloft.
Snow is small ice crystals falling to the ground,
Silently and gracefully landing without a sound.
Fresh and sweet smelling,
Like a crisp autumn morn.
Santa's best friend, to lift off his sleigh.
Different shapes and sizes, yet unique in every way.

Caitlin Moran, Grade 6
Our Lady of Mount Carmel School

Spring

The beautiful day,
Oh sunshine so bright
The river sparkling with joy,
As a ray of light
The breeze racing with speed,
Clouds white as can be,
Making shapes all so differently
Flowers that bloom in the morning sun
Birds chirping together 'till the day is done.
Oh, I am having so much fun!
Soon I will have to go inside,
But at least this beauty will be waiting for me,
The next time I'll come out.
You'll see!

Darina Kronin, Grade 5
Easterly Parkway Elementary School

Victory

Victory is the color gold
Victory is good sportsmanship and honor
Victory feels like championship
Victory tastes like pizza
Victory looks like big gold trophies
Victory sounds like people cheering

Andi Pranvoku, Grade 5
Rhawnhurst School

Picklepie

I had a pickle
It really tickled
I had a pie
With color dye
Now I have picklepie that tickled

Ivan Rodriguez, Grade 4
Moscow Elementary Center

Beautiful Rainbows

Beautiful rainbows
are like colors
hanging
in the sky.

Sometimes
they seem to dance
like how the stars
are twinkling.

Whenever I look
at them
it seems nature
has entered my mind.

Beautiful rainbows,
beautiful rainbows
they are the pure beauty
of nature.

Lining Wang, Grade 5
Lincoln Elementary School

Jell-O

J ell-O is jiggly
E specially when it isn't in a cup
L ike when it's on a plate
L ovable Jell-O brings a
O ne of a kind snack

Bradley Felt, Grade 6
H Austin Snyder Elementary School

Spring Flowers

Spring flowers,
rise up,
after April's long showers.

Along with every flower,
after every shower,
comes up a new power,
of new memories.

Bright warm weather,
birds grow new feathers,
and take off,
ready to soar.

John Mullan, Grade 6
Nazareth Area Middle School

The 7 Piglets

There were 7 piglets sitting on the steps, on a hot summer day.
The first piglet just complained.
The second piglet went to the beauty shop to get a pedicure.
The third piglet went to take a dip in the pool.
The fourth piglet went to Sears.
The fifth piglet went to Rita's and bought a water ice.
The sixth piglet went to an agency office to arrange a flight in Alaska.
The seventh piglet went to Save-a-lot and sat inside the freezer.
That hot sunny day was too much for these 7 little piglets.

Chelsey Chachoute, Grade 4
Children's Village

About Me

Maureen
Who likes to play sports
Wonders about what my mom's mom was like
Believes in God
Works hard to accomplish my goals
Gets annoyed when I get blamed for what my brother did
Sometimes feels nervous before swimming
Laughs at everything
Tries to include everyone
Wishes she could make her dad better
Understands how to take care of younger children
Still can't believe that my aunt died last year
Daydreams about boys
Is embarrassed when my mom sings in the car
Worries about what I look like in the morning
Is shy around some parents
Is afraid of squirrels
Is self-conscious when my hair looks too thick
Watches my brother play sports
Doesn't understand why some girls have to be mean to each other
Maureen

Maureen Leis, Grade 6
St Genevieve School

My Backyard

My backyard is like heaven for us because we can be free.
It's a dreamland where everything comes to life.
Within the fence there is only our swing set that I got for my sixth birthday
And the empty space to imagine anything you would like.
As we jump in the crunchy leaves during the fall nothing will stop us
Until we hear the ring of the dinner bell.
In winter when we wake up and see the snow everywhere,
The only thing that will stop us outside is when the air
Becomes very cold and our toes become frozen.
In spring the first place we turn to play is the backyard
Because we can prance around in the wet and cold rain
In summer I have my friends over and we build forts
That we stay in until it gets too dark to see.
When we are outside the first place we look is the backyard.
I love my backyard!

Ryan Day, Grade 6
Our Lady of Mount Carmel School

Cafeteria

Pack your lunch! Pack your lunch! Or you'll be sorry!
Eat the candy and your stomach will turn into a rock quarry.
Batwings, eyeballs, dead armadillo skin soufflé.
Mom gives me a "living food detector" on Halloween Day!
Now on the bus today I ask you to come to my funeral.
Since mom forgot to pack me, now I'll have to eat the casserole!

Ethan Simmons, Grade 4
Avonworth Elementary School

Fourth of July Fireworks

Boom bang! The fireworks have started.
Red, white, and blue! Each of the colors.
Orange, yellow, green! Those fireworks are big.
Sizzle, bash, roar! Wow aren't they loud!

Purple, gold, silver! What a sight!
Pop, bing, ting! Look at those fireworks spiral.
Shimmer, shimmer, crack! Those fireworks sparkle.
BASH, BOOM, BANG! Such different shapes.
Hiss, rumble, whistle, wheeze! All multicolored.

Boom, bang, sizzle, bash, roar, hiss, whistle, rumble, wheeze,
Purple, gold, silver, orange, yellow, green, pop, ting, bing,
Shimmer, shimmer, crack, fizzle, BASH, BOOM, BANG,
Red, white, blue! OOOOOHH, AAAAAHH!!! The grande finale!

William Ament, Grade 6
Neil Armstrong Middle School

My Love for Pink

Pink tastes like…
　　The soft, creamy strawberry ice cream
　　The chewy, crunchy M&M's
　　The bunches and bunches of sprinkles

Pink smells like…
　　The soft, sticky cotton candy I get on the fourth of July
　　My very good smelling shampoo I use
　　The sweet smell of roses in the spring

Pink sounds like…
　　The crumpling of paper when I mess up,
　　The runt-like squealing of a piglet
　　The joys of laughter when I put a sticker on my desk

Pink feels like…
　　The gooey, mess of paint
　　The soft, warm feeling of Kaity's sweater
　　The awesome, cool feeling of Colleen's backpack

Pink looks like…
　　My ever so cool smiley face sticker
　　A barking poodle that I see at the pet store
　　A jeweled rhinestone bracelet

Cassandra Santiago, Grade 4
Indian Lane Elementary School

The Moon

Slowly being unraveled
The Moon is a ball of yarn.
It is used by Mother Nature
And Father Time alike.
To weave and stitch all of our lives
One by one and to bring us closer
Until its thread is gone.
Yet our lives continue
Because they replenish what they take away,
So we can be happy and rejoice
With the Moon above.

James Kappas, Grade 6
Freedom Area Middle School

Sun and Moon

The sun is a shine that lights up the street.
The moon appears when you want to sleep.
The sun is a time to run and play.
The moon is when you dream up your next day.
The sun is a candle that lights the sky.
The moon is when that light starts to die.
You never see both at one time.
One fades and the other is sublime.
Sun is day, moon is night.
Sun you can see, moon you lose sight.
The moon is like the sun's reflection.
The sun and moon have a connection.

Zach Jones, Grade 5
Rolling Hills Elementary School

Where I Live Pennsylvania!!!

P ennsylvania is the perfect place to live
E ven better than Florida
N ow I live in Farmington on the mountains
N o other state is better
S o if you come and live here
Y ou won't regret it
L iving here is one of the best things that happened to me
V ery special to me
A nd if you don't, you'll regret it
N ow I love it here and
I will never want to live
A nywhere else and if you come you won't either

Suzanne Wolfe, Grade 5
Wharton Elementary School

Staircase

Life is a staircase.
It has its ups and downs.
Sometimes you don't know who your true friends are,
Or who you can really trust.
Sometimes you don't know which way to go,
Or where your life will take you.
Life is a staircase.

Casey Avery, Grade 6
Freedom Area Middle School

I Want to Fly
I want to fly
So high in the sky
Above all the animals, people, and trees
I want to fly with the birds and bees
Watching children play below me
As they run, jump, and scrape their knee
Seeing families having barbecues
And people praising God in pews
I want to say hi to the sun
That sure would be fun
I want to fly
So high so high in the sky
Jessica Woltemate, Grade 6
St Hilary of Poitiers School

My Precious Kitty
My cat's fur is as black as coal,
His yellow eyes shine like the moon.
He meows until I fill his bowl,
Mornings, he wakes me up too soon.

My cat is a fierce, wild beast,
His paws are quick and strong.
He dreams about his next, big feast,
While sleeping all day long.
Lorenzo DeVita, Grade 5
Bermudian Springs Middle School

Why Am I Different
People look.
People stare.
People say things, but I don't care.
Why am I so different?
Like a human so normal, and nice.
But not me.
I just love me.
Why can't they just like me?
For me!
Stacey J. Brucker, Grade 6
West Allegheny Middle School

Frozen Delight
Ice white as snow
Tasty frozen delight
Silent like the night
Amy Eisenhofer, Grade 4
Benchmark School

My Cat
My cat
is very fast
as prowls slowly and
then starts meowing for food,
but stops and sits.
Ryan Karns, Grade 6
Bedford Middle School

Video Gaming
Gaming
Fun, exhilarating
Playing, winning, upgrading
Maybe challenging, but exciting
PS3
Andrew Ahlquist, Grade 6
Bridle Path Elementary School

Lunch Time
The fruit juice is from outer space
Here to poison the human race
The apple sauce don't dare to try it
The potato chips once caused a riot
The milk is moldy and so bad
The tuna salad makes us mad.
The way they cook here is a crime…
But lunchtime is still my favorite time!
Amrita Singh, Grade 4
Falk Laboratory School

A Is for Airplane
A is for airplane
High in the sky
Up, up, and away
Be back in a day
You'll need a sharp eye
To spot us in the sky!
Christopher Connor, Grade 4
Our Lady of Peace School

Summer and Spring
Summer
hot, sunny
walking, playing, swimming
flowers, rabbit, blossom, bird
playing, planting, cleaning
warm, nice
Spring
Jennifer Medzie, Grade 4
West Branch Area Elementary School

The Beach
Waves crash
Children dash
Seagulls cry I wonder why
Looking for bait
They'll have to wait
The sun's warm rays upon my face
The beach is such a wonderful place
Crabs scurry
As I eat my McFlurry
Badababababa
I'm loving it
Nora Watson, Grade 6
St Hilary of Poitiers School

Chocolate
Chocolate is good.
Chocolate is sweet.
Sometimes it can be bad to eat.
But if you eat it and take a chance.
Don't get up and do a *silly* dance.
Jessica Loudon, Grade 4
Panther Valley Elementary School

Winter
Wintertime
Wintertime is fun
I like to go sledding
I like to play out in the snow
Snow time
Jesse Arrington, Grade 6
Freedom Area Middle School

Dancing
I started when I was 4 years old
A local studio is where I danced
I took ballet, tap, and jazz
The teacher liked the way I pranced.

It was hard and it was fun
I practiced every week for years
When it was recital time
My mom would always shed some tears.

Improving as the years have passed
I really have turned into something
Hard work and practice has paid off
A competitive dancer I am becoming.
Kayla Raber, Grade 5
Wexford Elementary School

Spring
Fancy flowers from below,
All around they start to grow.
Trees shoot up from the ground,
Buds are blooming all around.

Out of the sky, come golden rays,
Bees are buzzing out to play.
Over the sky, the birds they flutter,
Gliding over the clouds like butter.
Hayley Boyer, Grade 5
Bermudian Springs Middle School

Dinner
Thanksgiving
smoky, juicy
chomping, chewing
giant turkey, luscious filling
delicious
Gary Holmes, Grade 5
Southside Elementary School

Apples

It seems as if people are apples
Some are sweet like Red Delicious
And some are sour like a Granny Smith
Plenty are big and tall.
Plenty are small and short.
But when you bite into them
They're all different on the inside.
Some apples don't fall far from the tree.
And one bad apple can spoil them all.
Many apples stand on their own, and become simply unknown.
While others like staying in the crowd.
A couple of apples are slower to grow.
And some just like to go with the flow.
Unfortunately, apples get put into these cliques.
And all these groups do are make conflicts
Why not put that red one with that green one.
Though don't leave one out and leave it upset.
Sometimes SNAP! One more apple falls
But it can be picked up off the ground by someone else
So if you can see, us "humans" and apples are really the same!

Gabriella McDannel, Grade 6
Mount Nittany Middle School

Hockey

Hockey is hard handling the puck,
and lifting the cup.

Centers shoot, score,
skating to the very end.

Defense stop, slam,
hitting 'til their bodies bend.

Wingers help the center there's a left and a right,
they help the center light the light.

Goalie is a dangerous position,
desperately diving, making tough decisions.

I love skatin' on the ice at 7 a.m.,
the fog and the sound of skates digging in the ice.

When we are done we feel exhausted,
pads are torn, hockey pays off for hard work.

Handling the puck and hoisting the cup.

Alex Blum, Grade 6
Neil Armstrong Middle School

A Dog Named Bacon

There once was a dog named Bacon
who thought that his bone had been taken.
He looked all around and soon he found
that he was foolishly mistaken.

Bethany Brenneman, Grade 5
McMurray Elementary School

A Chocolate World

A world full of chocolate would be so grand,
I would scoop it and eat it
With my left hand.
I would be covered in chocolate
From my head to my toes,
I might get a stomachache,
Who knows?

Billie Patterson, Grade 5
Fairview Middle School

The Colors of the Sky

Blue is the color of a clear sky.
Yellow is the color of the stars so high.

Orange comes out at dawn.
Black nights make you yawn.

Red is when the sun sets.
Purple reflections make you want to get wet.

Pink is rarely found.
White is the color of a passing cloud.

Dark gray clouds are a bad sign.
Flashing yellow lightning is not far behind.

The colors of the sky can tell you many things.

Brittany Strand, Grade 6
Cheswick Christian Academy

Green

Green is like the pointy pine needles rubbing against your arm.
The sweet fragrance of maple and mint.
Like ocean waves crashing on a warm summer day.
And the taste of your birthday cake on the day you turned one.
The joyful feeling you get when you look at green,
Because it reminds you of Christmas day.
A glorious goose guessing the time of day.
And a gleaming grape falling on a glorious green floor.
The trees wave hello to a kid walking to school.
And the grass was going swimming in the morning dew.
Green is glorious!

Shannon Jaecke, Grade 6
Peebles Elementary School

Spring

The cool air in the morning
The cool air at night
The beautiful flowers and fresh air.
The sounds of birds and animals coming out of hibernation
The trees whispering in the wind
The sounds of spring
The sounds that are heard.

Temmy Reilly, Grade 6
West Allegheny Middle School

Harry Potter's First Year

If Harry Potter's parents never had died. Hagrid would not have to place him in Dumbledore's hands.
Placed on his aunt and uncle's doorstep. To occupy he was given cans.

A few years later a letter came in the mail.
Addressed Mr. Potter #4 Privet Drive. His uncle screamed and cried with a great wail.

On the night of his 11th birthday a giant came to fetch him
His aunt and uncle astonished. Hagrid told him he was a wizard, quite dim.

On his way through Kings Cross Station Hagrid left him stranded right there.
Then he meet Ron after Hagrid left him. Stranded, they ran into a barrier and disappeared to where.

He rode the Hogwarts Express to Hogwarts. A giant castle on a high hill.
Millions of kids in tables of four. A silly old hat with a circle bill.

At the end of the year a dangerous task three were in store to protect the stone.
Voldemort on the back of Quirrel's head. Lord Voldemort dies at the end with a scream and moan.

Kayla Mende, Grade 6
Freedom Area Middle School

Spring

Spring is nice, it is fun. It's nice to play outside. It's fun to take a ride in the car with the window open. It's also fun in the sun, playing with your friends. You see many flowers coming up all around you, yellow, pink, purple. They smell very nice when you walk past them. You can hear crickets at night when the sun goes down. You never know what's going to happen next but that's what is so great about SPRING.

Dylan Roach, Grade 4
McDonald Elementary School

The Snow Is Falling

As the snow falls gently to the ground, my spirit rises as the cold wind resounds.
I run outside to the beautiful sight, and look up in the sky at the crystal light.
I hurry inside in my nightgown and bare feet, hoping school is canceled so I can play in the winter treat.
I watch the news, KDKA, to see if school is canceled or at least delayed.
"I can't believe it!" I say as I jump up and down. School is canceled and the snow has completely covered the ground.
I dashed up the stairs and jumped on my sister's bed, and repeatedly said "Wake up! Get out of bed!"
She looked at me, still weary and half asleep and said, "What's wrong with you? I'm trying to sleep!"
"Get up and get dressed," I started to say, "School is canceled and it's snowing, let's play!"
She looked out the window in disbelief. The snow is so white and beautiful, now three to four feet deep!
We got dressed in a hurry, fearing the snow would melt and made a snowman with a hat of felt.
"What do we do next?" I asked excitedly. "I know let's go sled riding, follow me."
As I walked towards the big hill I looked around. The trees are so peaceful with all of their sound.
"Come on! Get in! We don't have all day." I climbed in the sled joyfully, now we can play.
One, two, three and we went flying around the bend, hoping our fun will never end.
We ran back home, soaking wet from the snow. My mother said, "Come on it's late! Time to go!"
I ran inside. I was home at last, taking one last look at my winter past.

Christin Folwarczny, Grade 6
State Street Elementary School

My Thoughts, My Feelings

When you look into my eyes what do you see? You usually see a girl with no problems. If that's what you see you are wrong. Behind my eyes are secrets you do not see. The truths I have never told before. Disrespects I have towards people. Feelings I keep locked inside of me. But one of these days the secrets, truths, disrespects, and feelings are going to come out of me. I will reveal all my secrets. I will tell the truths I have never told. I will not disrespect people. My feelings will be fixed in a flash.

Mary Fitzwater, Grade 6
H Austin Snyder Elementary School

Sky

The wide open view
Seen from every direction
With clouds that rain, rain, rain
And visions that portray moods
With the pink of sunsets
And the black of nights
With stars as spotlights on a dance floor
And the view of a flower beginning to grow
The way it holds the sun close and lets it shine
To throw upon the wandering people below
The beautiful gift of light
Stand, sit, or stare
At the amazing sight of sky

Ciera Hall, Grade 6
Mount Nittany Middle School

Advice from an Ice Skate

Glide through,
Take your time,
Don't rush,
Be graceful,
If you fall, don't be afraid to try again,
Forever bonding with the ice skates,
Never give up,
Always try again,
Remember the skates,
You'll never forget the first time you touched the ice,
Ice skating is the best!!!

Tara Braunsberg, Grade 5
Robeson Elementary School

All About Me

Angela
Who likes to play the clarinet
Wonders about the future
Has a habit of biting my nails
Believes in God
Works hard to get good grades
Plays basketball
Gets annoyed when I can't succeed at something every time
Sometimes feels like I have too much to do
Feels guilty about yelling at my parents
Laughs at jokes
Tries to be a good person
Likes to buy clothes
Understands other people's feelings
Is trying hard to get along with my sister
Is embarrassed when I mess up in front of a big crowd
Is shy around people I don't know
Is afraid of bugs
Is self-conscious when everyone is staring at me
Refuses to do things I don't want to do
Someday hopes to become a better basketball player

Angela Boccuti, Grade 6
St Genevieve School

My Lazy Friend Ted

My bus driver once said to Ted,
You'll do nothing but sit in bed,
But he got up right here and there.

And then Ted's mother got him out of bed,
By the smell of a skunk,
That was so dead!

So that day
Ted got out of bed,
Just to play with his old friend Ned.

His mother did say that,
Ned was so merry,
And looked like a bright red bouncing cherry.

So one day Ned,
Got Ted out of bed,
And so that's what happened,
To my lazy friend Ted.

Dylan Shaffer, Grade 4
Mount Vernon Elementary School

Trees

Tall and brown against the wind,
Stand firm before the storm.
From seed they grow to give us shade
Their leaves come and go in the season.
Using their bark that has no sound to help
Brace for the oncoming world.

Stephen Pappas, Grade 6
Chalutzim Academy

The Sides of Love

Love is, always everywhere around us,
Love is, in the park, or on the school bus

Love is, what brings us together,
Love is, remembering each other forever

Love is, there when we are mad,
Love is, the therapy when we are sad

Even though love is with us each and every day,
People don't know that love can turn the other way

Love is, equal to envy,
Love is, equal to tragedy

Love is, what can leave an emotional mark,
Love is, tears that are shed in the dark

Love is, rejection that tears us apart,
Love is, always to remember that it may break your heart

Luke Meyer, Grade 6
Sacred Heart Elementary School

Shoo-Fly Pie

Shoo-fly pie
Just the thought I could die
So tasty and delicious
But I have to say it's not nutritious
Good for a snack or dessert
But I must assert
It is so great
I can't believe how much I ate

Abigail Yenser, Grade 5
Schuylkill Valley Elementary School

Poems

When you write a poem,
It does not matter what you do,
And these are some examples for you:

You can read them for fun
You can write them for someone
You can play with them for fun

You can send them to a contest
You can write them just for you
You might write to a friend
Or to someone in your family too

You can write down your feelings
You can write it as a letter
You can write it as a song
Or as a project for school

Whatever you do just remember,
That it does not matter how you write it
As long as it's from you!

Shani Estikangi, Grade 6
United Hebrew Institute

Computers

They save your memories
You upload your pictures
And save them for eternities
You can ignore the lectures
You just look it up on the internet
Computers are the best inventions yet

Bajaan French, Grade 6
Independence Charter School

Land and Water

Land
Grassy, dirty
Living, growing
People, buildings, fish, seaweed
Raining, splashing, refreshing
Wet, liquid
Water

Justus Kirschner, Grade 5
East Stroudsburg Elementary School

Where Is Heaven

Where is Heaven, up or down?
Is Heaven beneath me or maybe above?
Do I walk down to Heaven?
Or do I walk up?
What road do I take?
What sign do I listen to?
What is Heaven, will I see God and angels?
I wonder what it is like,
Golden Gates as high as the sky, stormed with clouds like the stars
that float through the night.
Will I go to Heaven, has my life been holy?
Will I see a great shining light?
Will someone be waiting there?
Maybe
My family, friends, and relatives?
What road do I take to get to Heaven?
Up
Or
Down?
What sign do I listen to?

Vinny Postiglione, Grade 6
Our Lady of Mount Carmel School

Camp!

A different life!
Exploring new places.
Full of unbelievable adventures!
Developing bonds that last a lifetime!
Wonderful new friends.
Drinking bug juice.
Sports all the time!
Anxiously awaited camp fires, funny stories, mouthwatering smores!
An overnight bunk in the woods.
Eight weeks to have freedom from my parents!
Independence to just take a chance to improve on my skills!
Happiness is what I go for at Pine Forest Camp!

Sloane Beil, Grade 5
Rolling Hills Elementary School

Ali

Ali was a boxing champ
And after he hit an opponent the opponent fell down with a cramp
Ali acted clever in the ring
And he became the knockout king
Do not step in the ring
Or you will feel a sting
Ali had a very good life
They said his punches hurt like a knife
When it was time to fight
He got ready that night
I like Ali because he is kind and my favorite boxer
When he punched the man he gave him a shocker
He wore the belt for a long time
That's why he had a great mind

Semaj Pinkard, Grade 6
Christopher Columbus Charter School - South

Ode to the Beach

The waves dashing down to shore,
Exploding into sand castles.
The shells make a sound of whales,
Riding along the salty water.
Clothes getting soaked,
From the flashing water.
The soft, silky, smooth sand,
That's up against bare feet.
The current of the water pushing back,
Still going back for more.
The sun bursting a bare back,
Making it light up like fireworks exploding in the sky.
The wavy seaweed dashing to shore,
Like an athlete racing to win.
A boat drifting in the water,
Look down and see crystals of smooth sailing water.
The saturated sand,
Up against bare feet.
The mystifying wonders of the beach,
Just waiting to be discovered.

Janki Patel, Grade 6
Hershey Middle School

Softball Championship

Bonk, Bang as the ball is hit,
Clink, Clank as the first baseman catches the ball.
Dink, Donk as I hit the ball,
Slush! Slosh! as I run to first base.
Cheer! Cheer! we got a run!
Scream! Scream! you got a homer!
Yes! Yes! get the out.
Crack! Smack! there goes a popup.
Strike 1, Strike 2, Strike 3! You're out!
Go! Go! one more…WE Win!!!

Meghan Schmidt, Grade 6
Neil Armstrong Middle School

Spring's Glory

I see in the mountain tops, so, so high;
I hear the bird's song within the soft blue sky.
I feel the wind go softly through my hair;
As I look at the branches, they look so bare.
Not for long will I see the empty branches of the winter trees.
For they'll be filled with design.
And beautiful colors that will be for everyone to see.

Connor Holohan, Grade 5
St Ambrose School

The Moon!

The moon is a jack-o-lantern,
Shining on Halloween night.
A face carved in the surface,
Sparking our imagination.
What mysterious, wonderful stories lie behind it?

Jonathan Ellsworth, Grade 6
Freedom Area Middle School

Mom

Mom
Beautiful queen
Cleaning, helping, working
The greatest mom alive
Special

Charlie Yang, Grade 5
Rhawnhurst School

Sadness

The sun's tears make the world dark
They make the moon cry
They kill all the happiness
The world is in darkness for now and forever

The moon is like a crying angel
Its gloom is always there with us
Everything reminds you of its mournfulness
It can never go away

Reagan Adams, Grade 6
St Rosalia Academy

Pickles

Pickles are fantastic,
Pickles are amazing,
Pickles are salty clouds of greatness,
Slowly they slither down your throat,
In slices or as a whole,
Like a small rock being enveloped,
By a wave barreling from the ocean,
Its salty greenness being consumed by your gigantic mouth,
Along with,
Sandwiches,
Burgers,
And whatever else you hunger for that day,
In all different sizes,
Big,
Small,
Thick,
Thin,
Pickles are fantastic,
Pickles are amazing,
Pickles are eaten,
CHOMP!!!

Martin Silberberg, Grade 6
Hillcrest Elementary School

Everything Like You

You are my sunshine, my beam of light,
My glass of water, my full delight,
My cute puppy, my backyard,
You are everything I enjoy and like,
From my stuffed animals, to my cubby case,
I like you best of all in case you haven't noticed.

Taylor Blasko, Grade 5
Schnecksville School

Eye

Eye
round, shiny
searching, scanning, moving
Different colors all around
Eye

Lashes
hairy, soft
moving, blinking, dusting
Close when you're tired
Lashes

Face
soft, hairy
moving, talking, chewing
You can have accessories
Face
Kristen Zulli, Grade 4
Indian Lane Elementary School

My People Are Strong

My people are strong,
Because we have faith,
We hold hands,
We care for each other,
We stand as one.

My people are strong,
Because we don't betray,
We help each other,
We sing together
We stand as one.

My people are strong.
Because we have fun.
We gather 'round,
We smile at each other.
We stand as one.

My people are strong
Because we have love,
We boycott together,
We eat together,
We stand as one.
Suryá Watkins, Grade 6
Independence Charter School

Spy

Spy
Undercover, enormous
Shooting, disguising, hiding
Finding out military secrets
Agent
Dylan Long, Grade 5
Penn-Kidder Campus

Fire

On the fire pit
Streaks of orange and yellow
Burst into the air
Christopher Smith, Grade 4
West Bradford Elementary School

Dog/Cat

Dog
furry, lovable
barking, whining, biting
colorful, playful, lazy, nice
meowing, purring, licking
cute, cozy
cat
Molly Greb, Grade 4
St Sebastian Elementary School

My Dog, Mocha

My Mocha dog, you are so cute,
You never bite, you aren't a brute.
You run so fast, quick as a flash,
Run into something, it goes clash!

You come to me when I call,
And you love your little ball.
You love to squeak your little carrot,
Then you bark loud as a parrot!

When dinner comes, you are a hog,
During your nap, you're lazy as a log.
You always seem to want to please,
When you rest, there's finally peace.
Ethan Klersy, Grade 5
Bermudian Springs Middle School

Happiness

Happiness is bright yellow
It tastes like a very sweet lemon
It smells like a beautiful lotion
It feels like a huge hug
It sounds like beautiful music playing
Happiness is a gorgeous sight.
Mara Shank, Grade 4
Fairview Elementary School

The World's Best Dad

The world's best dad never gets mad.
He is the dad that is so rad.
The world's best dad is so cool
he tries to keep his calm and rule.
He cheers you up when you are sad
and doesn't yell when you are bad.
The world's best dad is the sweetest.
He is the best above all the rest!
Rachel Jackson, Grade 4
Immaculate Conception School

Summer

Is summer here?
I love that season
Warm air and green trees.
The bad thing is the bees
Green grass blue skies.
At night even fireflies
Friends outside to play with.
Stories to tell some are myths.
Nicholas Hill, Grade 6
Freedom Area Middle School

My Cousin Jacqueline

My cousin's name is Jackie
She's only six months old,
She's very small and pretty.
This is what I've been told.

I saw her last September.
I got to hold her first.
She was oh so cute and tiny,
It just made me want to burst!

She's coming again in February
Oh, I just can't wait,
I need to get a calendar
I need to mark the date!
Lucy Ciarlone, Grade 5
Villa Maria Academy Lower School

The Glide of Your Life!

When you hang glide you fly
Way up in the sky.

While you're up in the air,
You haven't a care.

Flying into a cloud,
It's peaceful, not loud.

To my ears, as I float,
It's a musical note!

I want to sing
As I'm carried by wings!

The higher I glide,
The greater the ride!

I have lots of fun
Flying in the sun.

Gliding over the sand,
I don't want to land!
Michael Coyne, Grade 6
Portersville Christian School

Alopecia

One morning waking up in my bed
To find that there was something not on my head
I went to go look in the mirror and saw
My hair was falling out, I was so appalled
I ran downstairs to tell my dad
He looked surprised and kind of sad
My dad brought me to the doctors quick
The doctor told me it might be able to be fixed
I was happy to know that it was not serious
Even though I was still a little delirious
We met a nice woman who had it too
She said "I could make a wig for you"
I lit up with joy and bliss
I wanted to give her a big giant kiss!
Now I'm happy to know that this is me
This is who I am and who I want to be

Rikki Bocchinfuso, Grade 6
Bridle Path Elementary School

In My Classroom

Six tables and chairs
stacked high above ground.
Pencils and paper
that have been thrown around.
The squeaky chalk writes fast
kids never pay attention.
I stare at my paper
and try to pretend I'm in a different dimension.
The teacher's grumpy voice
talking away.
But I say to myself
I wish I wasn't here today.

Hannah Adelsheimer, Grade 5
Falk Laboratory School

Summer

Summer is my favorite season,
I find it rather pleasing.
Rolling and playing in the grass,
But all the time goes so fast.

Running and jumping into the pool,
Although some people think we are fools.
Sports are always the way to go,
Except the times you stub your toe.

Footballs grasped running fast,
Leaving the enemy in the past.
I wish we could only have more time,
But it as short as this rhyme.

Playing and yelling all day long,
I hope that you enjoyed this song.

Eric Ewing, Grade 6
Conemaugh Township Area Intermediate School

A Day with My Dog

I went outside to play basketball
But I couldn't remember where I left it at all.
So then I took a walk with my dog
And she couldn't stop growling at bullfrogs.

As we were walking down the street,
We started to look for something to eat.
She was tired, so I gave her a rest
She then tried to keep up, she was doing her best.

We were finally home when I saw
My dog look at my mother in awe.
She was suddenly in a great mood
When she saw my mom holding a pan of dog food.

Emily Irwin, Grade 6
Our Lady of Grace Elementary School

The Christmas Story

One day an angel named Gabriel
Was sent from the Holy One,
To tell the Virgin Mary
That she would be bearing God's Son.

"His name will be Jesus," said Gabriel.
Then Mary asked, "How can this be?
As you see I am still a virgin,"
She said on a bended knee.

"The Holy Spirit will be upon you.
All things are possible with God."
"I'll do as God commands," she answered.
He smiled and left with a nod.

Awhile later Joseph and Mary
Came up from Galilee,
To be taxed in Bethlehem
As Caesar Augustus decreed.

God's Son was finally born
And placed upon the Earth,
By a faithful woman of God
Through a miraculous birth.

Ashley Hoban, Grade 6
Portersville Christian School

The Grasshopper's Tune

Not a sun or a moon
But a grasshopper's tune
A silent night sky
Above the hammock where I lie
Alone by the grass
As the fireflies pass
Listening to the bumblebees hum
Wondering when the morning sun will come

Kira Farrell, Grade 6
Bridle Path Elementary School

Books, Books

Books, books, there are so many books.
Nonfiction, fiction, science fiction,
There are a lot more too.

If you don't yet read,
And you like picture books,
The library even has those too.

Ask a librarian to help you find
A book that's just right for you.

Did you know authors even get
Awards for their books?

There are so many books,
There are cookbooks,
There are even books about cooks!
Natalie Bukowski, Grade 6
Northern Cambria Catholic School

Winter

Some say winter
Is a season of love
A season of romance
Truly from up above

Others say winter
Is a season of care
A wonderful season
For the whole world to share

Others say winter
Is a season of fun
A time for snowball fights
A season that's number one

Others say winter
Is a season of giving
An incredible season
For all of the living

I think winter
Is all of these four
It's all of these four
And yet so much more
Zoe Turnpaugh, Grade 5
James Buchanan Elementary School

The Shirt

There once was a girl named Jane.
She had a shirt with a plane.
The shirt disappeared.
She had a great fear.
She found she had no one to blame.
Hayley Eckhardt, Grade 4
South Park Elementary Center

Snow

Snow
Shiny, white
Falling, sparkling, laying
The best winter day
Flakes
Kirsten Hamilton, Grade 5
Villa Maria Academy Lower School

Baseball and Soccer

Baseball
Fun, hard
Hitting, pitching, catching
Bat, ball, goal, goalie
Running, kicking, blocking
Black, white
Soccer
Luke Monica, Grade 5
East Stroudsburg Elementary School

Oh Dear

Oh dear I missed the bus,
   what a fuss.
Mom said she won't take me,
   so I have to watch the baby.
Anyway, why go to school
   all I ever do is drool.
I'm watching TV,
   oh yippee dee.
Nothing good on,
   I wish I was gone.
Renee Thorwart, Grade 4
St Leo School

Angela

Angela
Mom, organized
Adorable, supporting, gentle, active
Relaxing, loving, friend
Gel or Mommy
Kellyann Ho-Sang, Grade 5
East Stroudsburg Elementary School

Kelsey

Kelsey
Funny, crazy, girl, tall
Related to Robbie, Abbie, Johny, Marissa
Who cares deeply about animals
Who feels happy
Who needs more stuffed animals
Who gives kindness to her cats
Who fears her brother
Who would like to see no animal cruelty
Resident of her house
Krista Vandetty, Grade 4
Manoa Elementary School

My Reflection

What I see in my reflection,
Looking in the big sea,
Causes me to feel rejection,
Because it is scary looking at me.

I see myself in many ways,
Changing, moving around.
I like the way the water sways,
Yet many ways I look just like a clown.

Every day the pictures change,
They give me quite a scare.
Sometimes the water is so strange.
I cannot help but sit and think and stare.

No matter what I seem to see,
I'm really still just me.
Matthew Schneider, Grade 6
Freedom Area Middle School

Soccer

Soccer
Joyful, fun
Shooting, passing, scoring
Always is a blast!
Football
Benjamin Aiello, Grade 6
Our Lady of Grace Elementary School

A Creepy Man

Black beady eyes
at night
crooked yellow teeth
long
ugly nails
dark
mysterious hat
scaring everyone in sight
Whitney Ballash, Grade 4
South Park Elementary Center

The Real Christmas

Christmas is a time of cheer
When friends and family gather near.
Young and old cherish this season
Because they know the real reason:
Jesus came to Earth
By a sacred birth.
Kings, angels, and shepherds were there
Witnessing God's love and care.
He sent His Son, the King of Kings;
His glory shines as truth He brings.
This season is a time of joy
For young and old, girl and boy.
Rachel Calhoun, Grade 6
Portersville Christian School

Spring

Rain will fall in April,
Beautiful flowers will bloom in May,
Which is always perfect timing,
So you can give them to Mom on Mother's Day,
Birds will start singing in the morning,
The sun will start to warm the air,
Plants start sprouting all around us,
Bringing out the animals including hares,
School soon will be out,
With summer vacation on its way,
Every kid can't wait until the day comes,
Each one of them are counting each day,
This is the season where the weather starts to get warmer,
Where everyone starts to change into shorts,
Most kids do not need sunscreen or sunglasses yet,
But some can start to skateboard,
Most people enjoy spring very much,
But not as much as summer, you know,
Usually people use spring as an excuse,
To pack up for vacation and be ready to go.

Nicole Vecchio, Grade 6
Wendover Middle School

Remembering the Children*

A land of freezing weather,
     where people are starving,
     and people eat Kim chi.

You may have been a governor
     who makes laws,
     a farmer who would grow food for a market,
     or a manager who runs a small restaurant.

I will remind people about you,
as I remember you.

Jack McMenamin, Grade 6
Deibler Elementary School
*In remembrance of the children in North Korea

School

Knowledge gives us brain power.
We grow in intelligence like a tower.
Special subjects and gym are fun,
They keep me exercising and on the run
Recess with my friend is a joy,
In elementary school, we can even play with a toy.
Social studies is amazing and exciting
Language arts with reading and writing is enticing.
Math and science are educational to me,
As I grow smarter, it is easy to see.
Computers and technology are the best,
They keep evolving and improving more than the rest
School is educational and exciting each day,
"So stay in school and go to college," is what I want to say.

Jeffrey Marmur, Grade 6
Churchville Elementary School

Harriet Tubman

Harriet Tubman was a girl born a slave.
She cooked and cleaned all day long.
Her life was very grave.
When she was sad she'd hum a song.

Harriet was hit by a two pound weight,
Sleeping spells were a result,
Bad scars were her fate.
A trustworthy woman she did consult.

"I want to be free," she said all her days,
While sweeping and plowing in the field.
She thought over plans in many ways.
When she crept away she used night as her shield.

She stayed with a farmer, and traveled "underground."
She went in carriage, and to a shoe shop.
Harriet did all this without a sound.
Only once in Pennsylvania did she stop.

So this woman is truly a hero.
Now her life on Earth is done.
She showed us that black's account for more than zero.
Her life was a trophy she had won.

Madeline Smedley, Grade 5
Villa Maria Academy Lower School

Butterfly

Here come the butterflies.
I love to watch them fly up high in the sky.
It's fun to see the butterflies that come around me.
The colors are so beautiful that I see,
There's pink, purple, blue, yellow, and green.
The butterflies are beautiful as you can see,
They love to fly all around me!

Evelina Kozub, Grade 4
Daniel J Flood Elementary School

The Wetlands

I am the wetlands marshy and muddy
Shelter is provided in my grass
Swimming in my puddles, you will pass
Otters, ducks and squirrels too
These animals will not eat you
There are snakes, crocks and mosquitoes too
Careful these animals might hurt you
You always want to check your back
Because they might attack
There are a lot of trees in the wetlands too
Here are some I'll name them through
Spruces, Black Gums and Cottonwood trees
Which blow in the soft breeze
I am the wetlands marshy and muddy

Timothy Doerr, Grade 4
General Nash Elementary School

Campfire Singing

When the man said, "Let's sing
A campfire song."

The fire started to sing,
So did the wolf and bear.

The tent started to sing,
So did the log and fish.

Everything in camp sang,
And I joined in.

Michael Amsdell, Grade 4
Northern Cambria Catholic School

Bacon

Bacon, bacon it looks so brown.
I like to buy it downtown.
My food goes great with toast.
Bacon, bacon I like the most.
It tastes a little like pork.
A good thing is you don't need a fork.
My food smells fresh and hot.
I like it so much my mom makes it a lot.

Dixie McCoy, Grade 4
Watsontown Elementary School

Browns

B est team
R ocks
O utstanding
W orldwide
N aughty
S uper bowl hopefuls

Cody Dille, Grade 4
East End Elementary School

I'm Home!

Arthur is walking in the door.
John is on the floor.
Liz is on the computer playing.
Mom is at the table working.

Arthur Armington, Grade 5
Easterly Parkway Elementary School

Love

Love is like a lilac flower,
Love has certain kinds of power.
A heart is a symbol of deep love,
Another symbol is a white dove.

On Valentine's Day, your heart, it booms,
With love and happiness that blooms.
When you're in love, you can float,
Through the river on a dreamy boat.

Nicole McLearen, Grade 5
Bermudian Springs Middle School

A Dragon's Wrath

Time to face the dragon's wrath.
Destroying cities in his path.
Prowling on the things he meets.
He throws away bones and feet.
Do not get in his way,
For he will make you his own prey.
He eats servants day and night.
To find more food he takes his flight.
He flaps his wings with all his might,
Flying 'till he reaches his highest height,
Eating anything and everything in his sight.
Then, he begins his adventure once again.
Please listen, I really do not want to leave you hanging on a limb.
BEWARE of this dragons wrath,
Or maybe next time you will be the one in his deadly, destructive path!

Umaru Davis, Grade 5
Russell Conwell Middle School

The Game

The ball goes, up she tips it to me,
I dribble halfway down the court,
she's open, I pass, she makes the shot!
Does anyone know how many points we've got?
I'm on defense looking her straight in the eye,
someone sets a horrible pick, and then, of course, I trip.
The ref calls a foul, oh my what now?
The ball is out of bounds, is anyone open, will they make the shot to tie?
The ball goes SWOOSH! right through the net,
but they haven't caught up to us yet.
I drive right down the lane to the hoop,
I take the shot, I missed, oops!
My teammates behind me rush right down
the other team is following
the rebound is ours, it goes back up
2 more points to our score have been added up
the first, second, third quarters go by,
2 seconds are left
the ball sails high
the opposing team loses to us
27 to 25.

Andrea Groves, Grade 6
Neil Armstrong Middle School

God's Creations

God created the Earth that we live on.
God created the sun that gives us warmth.
God created the flowers to smell nice on spring days.
God created the trees to give us shade.
God created people to look out for each other.
God created the oceans, rivers, and lakes so all animals could survive on.
God created the hills and mountains so all land wouldn't be flat.
God created the grass to lie on in the summer.
God created a world of people to look out for each other and follow His will.

Christen Sedlak, Grade 6
Sacred Heart of Jesus School

The Frog and the Fly

The frog jumped up and caught a fly
Way, way up into the sky
When he landed on the lily pad
He realized it was a bee he had

The bee stung him in the mouth
And he decided he would move down south
When he got there it was warm
And all the flies were at the farm

All he wanted was one fly
If he didn't have one he would cry
He decided he would have some pie
And in the pie he found a fly

Jamie Gerber, Grade 5
Greenock Elementary School

Invisible

My shirt is invisible and so am I
I'm really unlike the normal guy
It's very informal
But I won't lie
The cause is unknown, but I'll tell you why
It's invisible because it was worn by a radioactive guy
It was said to be toxic, but I stood them up straight
They said it had to be the food that I ate.
I outgrew it one day
That invisible shirt in which I played
Uncomfortable I put it on
And they said something was wrong.
Unfortunately it was small
I had gotten just too tall
I cried and frowned
I sobbed until the sun went down
One day Mom came home with a bag
In the bag there was an old rag.
Something else caught my eye,
"A bigger shirt," I cried.

Andy Schlosser, Grade 5
Edgeworth Elementary School

LBI

LBI
Is the place where time just flies by
And before you know it the sun is falling down
And the quietest thing in the town
Is the moon rising up from the ground
And the people sneaking down to the sea
Where the moon looks like a dream
Sitting and waiting for the sun to come out
To light up the day in a relaxed way
To cheer up the old and relinquish the new
I think Long Beach Island is the place for you

Emily Evancho, Grade 6
Good Shepherd Elementary School

Remembering the Children*

A land of many forests of trees,
    where animals,
    and people find food and shelter.

You may have been a ranger
    who searches for new animals in the world to tame,
    a doctor who helps patients at a hospital,
    or a tourist guide who shows tourists around the land.

I will think of all the hard things you have gone through,
as I remember you.

Eric Grzesnikowki, Grade 6
Deibler Elementary School
*In remembrance of the children in Madagascar

I Wish…

There was peace on Earth
I could fly
All hate and war would cease
I lived in a paradise
I could fly
I could eat dessert for every meal
I could buy things and not pay for it
We did not have to go to school
The night was gone and it was always day
We would have time machines
I could learn to drive
We had houses that could do anything for you (mansion)
Everyone was a good person
No one would get hurt
Everyone in the world spoke the same language
There was no jail because there was no crime
My good dreams would come true
I could be famous
I could go to the beach every day
It snowed whenever I wanted to

Diandra Krupek, Grade 5
Schnecksville School

The Race

Driving to the towering mountains
Pondering how the fluffy snow feels
Lurking outside a frozen fountain
Soo Soo chirp the bright red cardinal kneels

Trudging along the snow covered road
Tilting to sides on my dark blue boots
Leaning against the barren tree showed
The great white puffed up owl while it hoots

Climbing the towering mountains at night
Wind brushing hard fiercely at my face
At the top a wonderful sight
Sun is going down, 'tis time to race!

Olivia Poppenberg, Grade 5
Edgeworth Elementary School

Clouds

The clouds cry,
The rain falls,
The rain sings,
The rain calls,
The rain jumps,
The rain splashes,
The rain comes,
The rain goes,
The clouds laugh.

Laura Johnston, Grade 6
Christ the Divine Teacher School

Spring

Spring is great
Although it comes and goes
It will come and pass
Summer comes next
With sunshine so bright
You can jump and swim,
Leap and fall
Spring is great
So is summer

Kira Rinehart, Grade 6
West Allegheny Middle School

Guitar

G reat songs you can play
U seful for making awesome sounds
I ncredibly loud
T wenty-one frets on each string
A n amazing instrument
R ocks my soul

Bobby Pavlovsky, Grade 5
Rolling Hills Elementary School

The Flag

Flag
red, blue
waving, celebrating, amazing
I see a flag waving in the light.
Banner

Fayeanna Tarner, Grade 4
West Branch Area Elementary School

Spring

Spring is here
Time to cheer
Hear the birds
Without fear
Hear the spring birds
Not one tear,
Come on everyone
Spring is here!

Julie Applegate, Grade 6
Fairfield Private Academic School

Spring Is Here

Spring, Spring is on its way.
Geese are landing in the bay
Every day after showers
On the ground lay flowers
Grasshoppers hop
Kids are licking lollipops
Bluebirds are singing
Church bells are ringing
On the ground are worms
Every day one squirms
All the thing above
Are things that everyone loves

Katie Rudzik, Grade 4
Avonworth Elementary School

Mexico and Antarctica

Mexico
Hot, sunny
Swimming, playing baseball, fishing
Spanish, country, continent, mountains
Sledding, fishing, climbing
Cold, snowy
Antarctica

Matt DeCello, Grade 5
Our Lady of Grace Elementary School

My Pets

I have a slick, slithery snake,
If you look closely, you see it shake.
I found this snake out-of-town,
When I saw this snake, it was brown.

I also have a little lizard,
I named this tiny creature, Blizzard.
When he eats his daily meal,
Slurp! How good it makes him feel.

I have a tiny, friendly frog,
I found this frog in a bog.
This frog lives in a stinky shoe,
This little frog is very dark blue.

These are all of my animals,
Some eat fruit or are cannibals.
This is the story of all my pets,
I hope I don't need the help of vets.

Forrest Evans, Grade 5
Bermudian Springs Middle School

Friends

Funny, dependable
Laughing, playing, talking
Always there for me
Buddies

Jenna Masciantonio, Grade 4
Manoa Elementary School

Rain

Rain
wet and cold
great for farming, planting, and growing
great, fun, flooding, high winds
damaging, destroying, dying
dangerous, awful
hurricane

Patrick Sennott, Grade 4
St Sebastian Elementary School

My Brother Jason

Jason
Athlete, smart
Football, baseball, fishing
Doesn't cause any problems
Jay

David Menist, Grade 5
East Stroudsburg Elementary School

Springtime

Tulips, hyacinths, daffodils
Soon will be blooming among the hills
Yellow, pink, lilac too
Colors, bright for me and you
Sprouting so pretty with all of their frills

Erica S. Albright, Grade 6
Bedford Middle School

Lightning

Falling like a rock
From the great gray cloudy sky
Lightning strikes the earth.

Justin West, Grade 4
West Bradford Elementary School

Summer Is…

Hot days
Big waves
Flip-flops
Belly flops

Day camps
Bike ramps
Lemonade
Stayin' in shade

Wake up at noon
Tanning at lagoon
Boardwalks
Long walks

Tan lines fade, but
Memories last forever…

Syd Tustin, Grade 6
St Genevieve School

Christmas

"Rip, Wrap" go the presents as the kids open them.
"Flick, Flock" go the light switches as the kids turn them on.
"Bang, Boom" go the pans as they get smashed together.
"Boing" goes the bouncy balls banging off the walls.
"Meow" goes the kitty as he plays with his yarn.
"Ding" go the gingerbread men coming out of the oven.

Michele Rectenwald, Grade 6
Neil Armstrong Middle School

Colors

Green is the grass
Red is the sunset

Pink is the baby's rosy cheeks
Gold a beautiful color of a ring

Yellow a color of the sun
Silver a color of a beautiful diamond

Blue a color of the sky
Gray is a color of a thundercloud

Colors are very cool, you see them every day
How many colors do you like?

Morganne Andrukaitis, Grade 4
Bushkill Elementary School

Winter

The sun fades in the endless sky
As white and puffy clouds go by
Dropping snowflakes, small and white
Billions dropping, what a wondrous sight
All of the rooftops are covered with snow
The same as the hard ground and objects below
Young ones are ice skating, covered up tight
So they won't come down with a case of frostbite
The kids are quite cheerful, but the adults are not
'Cause they have to shovel the whole parking lot
It's getting very cold, so you better come inside
And warm yourself up — the door's open wide
So grab some hot cocoa, make it a delight
'Cause it's December 20th, and winter comes at midnight

Thomas Hart, Grade 5
Brecknock Elementary School

Tropical Islands

Puerto Rico
          Palm trees billowing everywhere.
Hawaii
          Pretty flowers in your hair.
Florida Keys
          Warm with amazing beaches.
The Bahamas
          Nice, pretty braids in your hair.

Michelle Sabastro, Grade 4
Avon Grove Intermediate School

The End of Summer

It's the end of summer and the beginning of fall
It's when the leaves on the trees start falling down
It's when the grass begins to be yellow
It's when the river is cold as snow
It's the beginning of fall

Miar Yousef, Grade 5
Jenkintown Elementary School

Broken

Forgotten unloved unhappy
Wants to know if anyone cares
So sad heart that's trapped, ripped up stepped on and smashed
Rejected unwanted not knowing where to go
Has feelings but not knowing if anyone knows
Not happy
Only
Broken and smashed

Becca Lladoc, Grade 5
East Stroudsburg Elementary School

The Redskin Victory

It was a stormy day,
But nothing could keep us out of the way.
We were playing in the Super Bowl vs the Jets.
Even though we didn't have the bets,
It turned out that we won.
That night the team had lots of fun.

Alexander Lyons, Grade 6
H Austin Snyder Elementary School

My Friend, Winter

Swoosh, swoosh, swoosh,
Down
    The hill
      I go
Feeling the wind's icy fingers inside my jacket
And the mountain's coat of packed snow under my skis.

Down,
    Down,
      Down
Faster and faster I go,
Pushing my legs right and left as I turn,
Hearing my skis carving down the belly of the slopes.

Brrr, brrr, brrr!
I remember hating the winter
And being nipped by winter's wrath.
Now I welcome the feeling of
Gliding
    Down
      The hill
Laughing because winter has become my friend.

Logan Rose, Grade 6
Portersville Christian School

Greenhouse
Tropical, scented
Made of glass, keeps plants from harm
Sprinkling water
Tatiana Anaya, Grade 5
Penn-Kidder Campus

Snow
Snow is frozen flakes,
Coming to the ice cold ground.
Winter wonderland!
Erin Murphy, Grade 4
Sacred Heart School

Brightly Shining
Like a light in the sky,
Brightly,
Brightly shining oh so high,
The farther it gets,
The darker the night,
But the closer it gets,
The higher the tide,
A silver dollar in the sky,
Half or whole or fingernail shape,
So brightly shining through the drapes,
That is what the moon shall be,
For now and ever eternity.
Matt Sullivan, Grade 6
Our Lady of Mount Carmel School

My Closet
When I am mad or sad
I go to my place.
My own place.
It may not be amazing
But it is mine
All mine.

No one knows where I am
I am hidden
In my place
I am alone
In my closet
My place

It is small
But I think of it as snug
Clothes on my face
It is my special place

When I feel better
I jump out
Like a new bird
From my special place
And act like nothing happened.
Molly Aigeldinger, Grade 6
Guth Elementary School

Train to New Mexico
Train rumbling and shaking
New Mexico on its way
Train cars moving
Snack bar closing
Mom drinking tea
People talking
Hakeema Sayles, Grade 5
East Stroudsburg Elementary School

Bathroom
I knew a girl called Sue.
She had to go to the loo.
She went to the mall.
And picked out a stall.
And that's what she had to do.
Lily Read, Grade 4
Lower Pottsgrove Elementary School

Soaring
To be
like the majestic eagle
that spreads its wings
and glides
above
the rocky canyon

To be
like the mythical dragon
that stretches its long neck
and flies
over
the rugged landscape

To be
like the free spirit
that spreads its invisible wings
and rides
through
the mountains of the mind

To soar
Joy Wang, Grade 6
Hillcrest Elementary School

Tuna Casserole
Tuna casserole, tuna casserole,
How I love you tuna casserole.
When my dad burns it, I like it best.
Next to the crackers, it does rest.
But not for long, I've got to eat it.
It's my favorite, you better believe it!
Soft and mushy, it's so slurpy,
Eat too much, and you might burpy!
Robbie Hemphill, Grade 4
Watsontown Elementary School

The Big Bore
There was a little boy who was a bore,
He made his dear old mom snore.
If he got an X-BOX 360,
And beat SSX Tricky,
Then everybody would adore.
Josh Tinklepaugh, Grade 6
Freedom Area Middle School

The Black Cat
He swipes, he purrs
Oh, that black lovable cat
He is here, he's there.
Matt Mamros, Grade 5
McMurray Elementary School

Soccer
Soccer
Sportive, playful
Running, kicking, playing
Happy, fun,
Sport
Allie Buckalew, Grade 4
West Bradford Elementary School

Trees
Trees
Big, tall
Still, shaking, falling
Rough bark, smooth wood
Redwood
Devon Nowark, Grade 4
Hereford Elementary School

Alyssa, My Friend
Alyssa is sweet as icing
Alyssa is as bouncy as a bunny
Alyssa is as fast as a cheetah
Alyssa is as neat as a filing cabinet
Alyssa is as funny as a clown
Alyssa is as smart as an encyclopedia
Alyssa is as athletic as Mia Hamm
Alyssa is as quiet as a mouse
Alyssa is as playful as a dog
Alyssa is as pretty as a tulip
Alyssa is as helpful as a nurse
Ciera Bretz, Grade 5
Newtown Elementary School

Puppy
P ets
U nbelievable
P erfect pets
P uppies are cute
Y oung
Kelsie Sutton, Grade 4
Manoa Elementary School

Green Is

life and the feeling of home and freedom
vigorous, healthy and natural
a peaceful forest with birds singing in the daylight

grass swaying in the country breeze
pines, evergreen trees, valleys and hills
joyful children running outdoors

Ben Seligsohn, Grade 4
Benchmark School

My Favorite Sport

I like to play baseball all day,
That is so fun.
But if you are bad you pay,
The year goes so fast that it is done.

I like to hit the ball,
When I hit the ball it goes far.
We play in the fall,
When we win you can hear the beeping of the car.

I like to run the bases,
But you might trip and fall.
So make sure you tie your laces,
So that's why I like to play ball.

Colton Black, Grade 4
Panther Valley Elementary School

Brown Tastes Like

Brown tastes like…
    Fresh pie right out of the oven
    A nice chewy cookie
    A chocolate chip off a warm cookie

Brown smells like…
    A new football out of its bag
    A smelly monkey swinging back and forth
    The trees in the park

Brown sounds like…
    A wickedly rock breaking into little pieces
    A squeaking football
    A creepy crawling squashed bug

Brown feels like…
    The smooth grip of a football
    The rocks from the slimy ground
    The leaves flowing thru the nice refreshing air

Brown looks like…
    The dusk that comes once a day
    The sunset in the morning
    The smooth and flat dirt

Brent Roller, Grade 4
Indian Lane Elementary School

Bittersweet Memories

Bittersweet memories riding off into the distance
Leaving sad, but sweet memory trails going off
    in the wind like a swishing tail.

Sometimes crossing, meeting and switching paths.
Wandering to a different place every time they journey.

Every moment different, every trail different,
    Never knowing where the trail will lead you.
    Bittersweet memories,
    Bittersweet trails at night.

Matt Horrigan, Grade 4
Lincoln Elementary School

Freedom

I live in a country that is free
I can be whatever I want to be,
There is a statue called Lady Liberty
She holds a light for all to see.

I live in a country called the United States
I think my free country is just great,
I thank the Lord for my fate
Because for many people they must wait.

My country has been through many wars
They have helped open many doors,
People have come from distant shores
To enjoy the freedom of owning their own stores.

My country believes in equality
For people of every nationality,
It was not always this way you see
For my country once had slavery.

There was a man named Martin Luther King
He wrote a speech called, "I Have a Dream."
He often said, "Let freedom ring."
This message we will forever sing.

Matthew Ruwe, Grade 4
St Alexis School

The Haunted House

The story grew, with a witches brew.
A knight came to fight a ghost who lived in a castle.
He was a wanton ghost for 100 years,
And a haunting spree started when he was three.
He was reading a book about *Ghosts* by: Marget Boast
He scared the knight by saying "Boo,"
But who was really reading,…
You!

HA!
HA!

Madison Zaccagnini, Grade 6
Moss Side Middle School

Fury

Fury is vivid red.
It tastes like salt water.
It smells like rotten eggs.
It's as hot as boiling water.
It sounds like a charging elephant.
Fury is a scorching desert day.
Bailey Frye, Grade 4
Fairview Elementary School

Snow

The snow is falling,
little drops of cotton,
falling slowly on the ground,
it's snowing all around.

The snow is laying on the grass,
a big blanket covering it all,
so white and fluffy,
a cloud, so puffy.
Carly Arbes, Grade 6
Freedom Area Middle School

Goodbye

We wait inside an empty house
Hearing our voices echo
We start to cry
We say a silent prayer
Then we turn towards the door
Then we say our sad good-byes
The van starts moving very slowly
We wave goodbye as we cry
Now our friends are gone, gone far away
We wait and wait to see them once again.
Mary Milligan, Grade 5
Brecknock Elementary School

I Have a Dog Named Spot

I have a white dog
Whose name is Spot,
And she's sometimes white
And she's sometimes not.
But whether she's white
Or whether she's not,
There's a patch on her ear
That makes her Spot.

She has a tongue
That is long and pink,
And she lolls it out
When she wants to think.
She seems to think most
When the weather is hot.
She's a wise sort of dog,
That's named Spot.
Matthew Scott, Grade 5
Trafford Elementary School

Camp Men-O-Lan

At Camp Men-O-lan,
We all got a tan.
We were in the stream,
we found some shaving cream.
To make the cookies was very easy,
they turned out to be very cheesy,
and everybody was queasy,
while we were sitting by the fire,
we stood and sang like a choir.
When we went through the obstacle course,
we learned a lot about a code called Morse.
This was the funniest part of all; when we learned about pond life,
we saw Mr. Jameson use a jackknife.
Kelly Tran, Grade 6
Grasse Elementary School

Surfing

When I am on the sandy land of the seas with my board,
I feel like I am in heaven.
When I am in the water,
I am waiting for a wave.
Now the wave is coming,
It's huge,
I am swimming up to it,
I catch the wave and I surf.
It feels like the heaven's clouds are drifting me closer to the heavens then,
The wave is gone.
When the wave goes away,
I wait for another,
And when I catch another,
It feels like the story starts again.
Bianca Dixon, Grade 6
Hillcrest Elementary School

Nature's Call

At night when you're asleep
One by one the animals creep
The mice dance to the crickets song
The birds clap and chirp along
The spider rebuilds her web because the children knocked it down
And the city cats come to get away from the noisy town
Here come the deer and around they prance
Then come the stray dogs with what food they found by chance
Out come the foxes so fast and sly
Bunny rabbits appear cute yet so shy
Here comes the skunk these are his friends he will not spray
There is the turtle coming slowly tired from all day
And then the eagle swooping down, he is the best well known
Somewhere in the distance they hear the wolves howls and moan
If you stay up late and watch your lawn
You'll see all of the animals up until dawn
So go out and watch the animals have a ball
See the animals, see them play
Stay awake and witness natures call
Kali Yext, Grade 6
St Ann Elementary School

The Ocean

I like to watch the ocean
It's like a magic potion

With hues of blue and green
And all the colors in between

I like to see the seagulls flying overhead
But I hope they don't land on my best friend's head

Nate Brocato, Grade 4
Bushkill Elementary School

Me

In the year of 1994
I was born and I was now a little baby.
In Lewisville, Texas on one Halloween night
I didn't have much hair but it was blonde
and I had big blue eyes.

When I came home everyone thought I was so cute
they just wanted to hold me.
I had a problem with my foot…
So I had surgery on it and had a cast.
But I finally got it off and I was so happy.

I grew up to be a tall, blonde girl
And I've done a lot of things.
Now I can't wait till I'm even older…
To see what more things I can do.

Ashley Hulbert, Grade 5
Wexford Elementary School

The Eye of Nature

Nature is such a calm, beautiful thing.
Up to the mountainside,
Down to the river's flow.
With all this beauty
Where all the creatures roam,
From the lakes,
To the sky,
Nature is such a wild thing.
Down to the underground,
Up to the skies above,
Where creatures roam this side.
Nature is a scary thing,
But a cool place.
So, explore around the mountain grounds
Where all the creatures roam.

Bree Muoio, Grade 4
Washington Heights Elementary School

Napping Ned

Sleepy, tired, fatigued, snoozing and drowsy
When you try to talk to him your outcome
is lousy!

Douglas Benton, Grade 5
Newtown Elementary School

Remembering the Children*

A land of volcanic desert
    where temperatures are deadly
    and people are unemployed.

You may have been a farmer
    who tried to grow food for your starving country,
    a religious leader who spread faith throughout a city,
    or a herder that lead animals across the desert.

I will hope to get an education,
as I remember you.

Cassidy Crawford, Grade 6
Deibler Elementary School
*In remembrance of the children in Djibouti

Listen and You Will Hear, Watch and You Will See

Every day
we walk by people
we do not even know.
But one glance seems to show
who they can be.
This is the truth I speak of but it is a grim one.
When they talk we do not listen.
When they act we do not watch.
God made us in the image of himself, but is this God?
He created us to love, but can we call this love?
We seem not to think, not care,
not listen, or watch.
If we took the time to look past the words,
the looks, and the riches.
If only we could be God.
If only we could love.
If only we took the time to listen when they talk
and watch when they act.
This is the truth I speak of but it is a grim one.
For if you listen you will hear.
And if you watch you will see.

Elizabeth Yoder, Grade 6
Blue Mountain Middle School

A Recipe for Making Heaven

Take two cups of beauty,
add five cups of happiness,
a pinch of play and
tons of love.
Mix on high until well blended.
Pour over packs of fluffy, white clouds.
Mix in everything you could ever want.
Bake at perfect temperature for ten minutes.
Take it out and sprinkle with sunshine.
Then ice it with God!
Take a bite and you'll smile forever.

Hannah Logan, Grade 4
Avonworth Elementary School

Waterfall

In the forest
Swiftly flowing
High and long
White as snow
Calm and green when touches bottom
People gaze
Cliffs with it
Green as an emerald
Rushing through
Loud as drums
Beating on the emerald
Trails for people
I am a waterfall

Kevin Lynch, Jr., Grade 5
Jenkintown Elementary School

Friendship

Friendship is
A never ending movie

Friendship is
A pot of truthful
Clear water

Friendship is
A singing bird

Friendship is
My love for friend.

Shaiza Khawaja, Grade 5
East Stroudsburg Elementary School

Neslia

Neslia
Strong, generous
Swimming, eating, playing
Video game master
"The Nester Machine"

Nestle Milan, Grade 5
St Francis of Assisi School

The Swimmer

There was a skinny swimmer,
who swam the seven seas.
He got all of his energy,
from eating all his peas.
He had to swim the seven seas,
after falling off his ship.
He broke his foot,
he broke his toe and even cut his lip.
After that he swore and vowed,
he'd never sail the seven seas,
and he might quit eating peas.

Jordan Al-Mukhtar, Grade 6
Neil Armstrong Middle School

My Best Friend

V arious
I ntense
C aring
T errific
O utstanding
R eliable
I ncredible
A wesome

Lauren Schichtel, Grade 6
H Austin Snyder Elementary School

Sunshine!

Sunshine is the best
She likes to build a nest
She does not quack
And does not lack
A wink of sleep!

Gina Casato, Grade 4
South Park Elementary Center

The Sun and the Moon

Sun
Shining, steaming
Glimmering, turning, darkening
Dusky, frigid
Moon

Mary McFarland, Grade 5
Bushkill Elementary School

Happiness

Happiness is light blue
It tastes like a juicy strawberry
It smells like a red rose
It feels like a soft cloud
It sounds like a lullaby bird
Happiness is a field of roses.

Renee Raymond, Grade 4
Fairview Elementary School

Birds

cardinal
fluffy, pretty
flying, diving, eating
chickadee, blue jay, finch, snow owl
hovering, swerving, landing
hover, land
chickadee

Zach Corbin, Grade 5
Southside Elementary School

Reading

When a book is read
An imagination's touched,
Also, someone's heart.

Amanda E. Hampton, Grade 5
West Branch School

The Hawk

Over the trees in the soft blue sky,
I saw a hawk and heard its cry.

Step by step through morning dew,
The hawk above me cried as it flew.

I wished that day that I could fly
And be beside that hawk so high.

Connor Holohan, Grade 5
St Ambrose School

Raindrops

Rain falls drop, drip, drop.
Huge, little, big, small.
Rain falls all over
drip, drop, drip, drop.
The sun is out
it needs
but to dry.

Nicholas Estrada, Grade 4
Easterly Parkway Elementary School

Easter

Easter
colorful, fun
laughing, jumping, hunting
Easter is my favorite holiday.
holiday

Tosha Hahn, Grade 4
West Branch Area Elementary School

Best Quarterback

B est in the NFL
I ntelligent Quarter
G ood guy all around

B iggest baddest Steeler of all
E asy to see
N atural Quarterback

Thomas Daniels, Grade 5
Wharton Elementary School

Bee's Hives

B arbaric
E vil
E xtraordinary
S tingers

H elping
I ndestructible
V ile bees
E xecute
S tinging Hornets

Atta Ebrahimi, Grade 5
East Stroudsburg Elementary School

Oh! Chips…

My favorite snack food is delicious chips,
If I didn't eat any I would probably eat a ship,
If I met the person who made chips I would probably die,
I like them better than tomatoes or a ham sandwich on rye,
I like them better than old chicken legs,
I know I wouldn't like them if I ate hard-boiled eggs,
They're better than a sandwich four feet tall,
To me chips have it all!

Evan Simpler, Grade 4
Watsontown Elementary School

Spring Has Bloomed

Look around spring is everywhere,
The scent of flowers in the air.
Bees are buzzing all around,
Grass is growing on the ground.

Birds are soaring in the sky,
Like a tree's branches reaching high.
Fish are swimming in the water,
In school children are growing smarter

Children keep on running running,
Their feet keep on thumping thumping.
I hope that spring will never close,
I shall always know the scent of a rose.

Zane Hawk Travis, Grade 4
Avonworth Elementary School

Donner the Goner

There once was a reindeer named Donner,
Everyone knew he was a yawner,
Riding shotgun when he fell from the sleigh,
No one knew if he was okay,
Now poor old Donner is a goner.

Cody Lambert, Grade 6
California K-8 School

The Island of Dreams

The island of dreams,
Lets you relax, let out stress, and swim in never ending streams.
You can build a sand castle a mile high, and a mile long.
Whatever you say there, will never be wrong.
The water is rich chocolate, that you can drink anytime
There's even talking trees, and each says a rhyme.
So make yourself comfortable don't worry at all,
At the big palm tree, there's a huge shopping mall.
Golden lemurs everywhere
In the trees, and in your hair.
Silver flowers blooming one by one,
And some grow so big, they almost weigh a ton.
Half of the island's warm, and half is cold.
As long as you stay there, you'll never grow old.

Rachael Hunter, Grade 5
Newberry Elementary School

The Puddle

Slish, slosh, mud and mash,
Step in a puddle, and it'll go splash.
It may be hot, or it may be cold,
Puddle won't care, if you're young or old.

Stepping high or stepping low,
Keep your feet happy as they go.
Jumping across or side to side,
When I fell in, you know I cried.

Hannah Kerr, Grade 5
Bermudian Springs Middle School

It's Our World Too!

It's our world too!
We little kids are always getting pushed around.

It's our world too!
Older kids get $20 for allowance
and we don't even get $5.

It's our world too!
We would be lucky to bat 9th
in a 9 man batting order.

It's our world too!
They get to stay out late
and we have to be in by 5.

It's our world too!
If we need to go to practice.
They already have mom's car.

It's our world too!
But guess what,
"Son, you're going to have to baby-sit tonight."

Richard Stephenson, Grade 5
Concord Elementary School

My Dog

My dog is named Stinky I'm sure you know why
He eats stink weed and smells like a fly
One day he rubbed all over my clothes
And I ended up with an infection in my nose
He chases skunks especially when they spray
He pees on my shoes almost every day
I'm sure you now know that my dog is quite gross
He's the dog that stinks the most

Nathan Ehnot, Grade 5
Robeson Elementary School

Water

As I walk through the water
It swallows me as if I were food,
And it says, "I wish I had a friend to play with."

Meghan Obusek, Grade 6
Christ the Divine Teacher School

North Pole

Jagged blue icebergs
Polar bears catching salmon
White cap on water

Jimmie Newbern, Grade 5
Penn-Kidder Campus

Leaves

Leaves are so pretty,
falling in the smooth cold air
they are so much fun.

Nicole Miller, Grade 4
East End Elementary School

Dakota

Dakota
Furry, big
Jumping, howling, barking
Loves to chew bones
Malamute

Katrina Iobst, Grade 4
Christ the King School

Ed

There once was a cat named Ed
She liked to roll on her head
When she did it for the first time
She looked like a mime
So now she just lays in bed

Melanie Geer, Grade 5
Mount Jewett Elementary School

The Pumpkin

The orange pumpkin
Was quite round
With seeds
Inside
That go
All the way
Down.

It's a jack-o'-lantern
At Halloween.
It's a turkey
At Thanksgiving.
It's a decoration
All year round.

It's seedy.
It's slimy.
It's hard.
It's smooth.
It's squishy.
It's just plain
EWW!

Courtney Flach, Grade 4
Lionville Elementary School

Friends

When you are friends, you should be friends for life.
When you are friends you just don't go and tell anybody your friend's secret.
You'll stand up for them in their troubles
And help them face the world beyond.
That's what true friends do.

Angelica R. King, Grade 6
H Austin Snyder Elementary School

Approaching

The sun is gleaming through the trees
beating down on my skin
The wind is a soft breeze
blowing my hair
pine tree leaves are getting browner and browner
while I look at them
The bushes are bare
Except for a couple of stray leaves
looking so lonely and abandoned
The breeze is picking up the speed,
the air is getting colder
leaves are changing colors
The leaves are dancing like a baby
who has never danced before
The shadows on the walls are jumping with joy
I can tell winter is approaching!

Shannon Nace, Grade 5
Lower Salford Elementary School

Aqua Green

Aqua green is glistening water and a new rainbow and is relaxing like home.
Aqua green is the taste of blue raspberry candy.
Cherry Icee and vanilla ice cream smell aqua green.
Playing at the ocean on a warm day makes me feel aqua green.
Aqua green is the sound of birds singing and the ocean waves.
Aqua green is Rose Garden Pool, all of summer, and fun on a rainy day.
Playing at night just before sunset is aqua green.
Aqua green is the color of happiness.

Jake Floyd, Grade 5
McMurray Elementary School

The Sky

I am the sky
Way up high
While I stay still, the clouds go by
I strike lightning that attracts to metal
And if you're near me you better run or put your foot to the pedal
I make slow winds and strong winds that make hurricanes
That can drive people really insane
So next time if you're in a plane
You better watch out for me or maybe even a hurricane
I am the sky
Way up high
While I stay still, the clouds go by

Anthony Cubbage, Grade 4
General Nash Elementary School

Nature Is Beautiful

As I look down into the beautiful wild,
I see the trees are swaying in the wind.
The red and yellow leaves spin around,
as the wind travels by.
As I gaze down into the bright rivers,
I see animals drinking out of the fresh water.
The green grass sways in the wind,
that the animals walk in.
Almost everything is big and green,
the color of nature it must be!
With the animals everywhere, we must make sure
that we keep everything beautiful and clean.
There are the farms that keep the animals fed and clean,
by not littering, and keep America clean.
We must do these things,
nature is beautiful in so many ways.

Olivia Stewart, Grade 4
Washington Heights Elementary School

Homerun Harry

Homerun Harry came out to play,
On this beautiful blue skied day.
He picked up his bat and went to hit,
Everyone was excited and could not sit.

The ball hit the bat and took off like a shot,
Homerun Harry knew it'd never be caught.
He circled the bases and tagged home for a run,
He couldn't remember when he'd had so much fun.

Rebecca Babincak, Grade 5
East Union Intermediate Center

Summer

Summer is when it is hot.
It is when kids play in the parking lot.

Summer is when you drink a lot of water,
It's when mothers pend time with their daughters.

Summer is when you have fun,
It's when you have a hamburger on a bun.

Keighlyn Oliver, Grade 4
Daniel J Flood Elementary School

Best Friends Forever!

We are always on top of each other's lives
Wondering what they're doing and why!
We will always remember the good times and the bad
As all six of us walk together in the sand, hand in hand
As we breathe in, we breathe out.
Some have doubts and take different routes.
We will grow up and apart keeping in touch,
With only our friendship to keep us as one.
We'll be best friend forever, keeping each other forever.

Marina Burdge, Grade 6
Greencastle Antrim Middle School

Dogs and Cats

Dogs
Big, small
Running, barking, walking
Poodles, Golden Retriever, Siamese, Tabby
Jumping, scratching, leaping
Soft, furry
Cats

Anjali Regan, Grade 4
Easterly Parkway Elementary School

Light Blue

Light blue tastes like
  Blueberries in my mouth,
  Snowflakes landing on my tongue,
  A blue M&M melting in my mouth

Light blue smells like
  Chlorine in a pool,
  Fresh air just outside,
  Lilacs that just bloomed

Light blue sounds like
  The waves of an ocean,
  The crunch of blue sprinkles in my mouth,
  The joy and peace all around

Light blue feels like
  The silky slippery skin of a dolphin,
  Raindrops on my head,
  Being sad and happy at the same time

Light blue looks like
  Tears dropping from people's eyes,
  The sky that is so high,
  The never ending ocean.

Colleen O'Brien, Grade 4
Indian Lane Elementary School

Beach Beauty

The waves roll in with a gentle rhythm
They crash upon the shore with a mighty force
I see people on the beach at play
Children are running about like little birds scurrying for food
A blazing sun beats down
A beautiful blue sky is above
We walked along the shore, my friend and I
Hearing sounds of seagulls hunting for food
They were as free as kites in the wind
Baby sandpipers scattered as we approached
The waves tickled at their feet as they ran
We watched the big boats bob in the distance
The deep bellow of their horns signaled their approach
Our shadows grew long as the sun set in brilliant colors

Kelly DiMuccio, Grade 6
Mount Nittany Middle School

I Wish…
I wish I got everything that I wanted for Christmas.
I wish I could make the rules and laws.
I wish candy was considered nutritious.
I wish no one ever had to do anything they didn't want to.
I wish no one ever had to die.
I wish I could control the weather.
I wish I was tall.
I wish everything was free.
I wish everything was voice activated.
I wish everybody had a Disney World in their backyard.
I wish everybody was born smart and athletic so they didn't have to go to school or practices
or so they don't have to be made fun of.
I wish everyone got along.
I wish everyone had fairy godparents.
I wish for peace, no war, and everybody was always in a good mood.
I wish nobody ever had bad dreams.

Brady Gallagher, Grade 5
Schnecksville School

Hereth Comes Winter
"Away, away," the bluebird calls, "before the snow so gently falls."
Down below the lonely wolf waits, watching the sky, dark as slate.

All the others under the dark slate sky, knew Winter's breath was on the fly.
Those who would stay, under sky dark as slate, knew time had come to hibernate.
So squirrels, rabbits, rats and voles all began to search for holes.

On a day that seemed just the same, forward with a bang Old Winter came.
He got down to work and blew his breath over, pansies, lilies, chrysanthemums and clover.
Then the Old Man spread his dark cloak, over pine, maple, hemlock, and oak.
Commandingly Old Winter rose up high, tiny white snowflakes fell from the sky.

One day in March that seemed just the same, down with a breeze young Maiden Spring came.
Up on her gentle breeze the Maiden did fly, swiftly gone away was the dark slate sky.
So squirrels, rabbits, rats and voles all began to climb out of their holes.
Spring came to the forest's delight, it was the Young Maiden who ended the long Winter's fight.

But though they are harsh, we must learn not to hate, Old Man Winter and the sky, dark as slate.

Liana Venezia, Grade 5
Audubon Elementary School

Helen Keller
At age four Helen got sick, it certainly wasn't a disease she'd pick.
The doctor said she'd become blind or deaf, that very day no hearing or eyesight was left.
Her mom kept saying she isn't dumb, but everyone knew her senses grew numb.
Her mom wanted to prove Helen was smart, so she looked around 'till she found the right part.
Then one day Anne came, so it never was the same.
Helen's first word was water, her mom knew she had a special daughter.
The smarter she grew, kept her right on cue.
Soon she got an education, it certainly was no vacation.
It was hard for her to do it, soon Helen's light bulb lit.
Every day Helen grew smart, now her brain missed no part.
Helen Keller proved them wrong, even though it took her so long.
Helen's mom was so right, she proved Helen was intelligent and bright.

Sarah Jansen, Grade 5
Villa Maria Academy Lower School

The Blue Snake

The river is a blue snake
winding its way through the rolling green hills.
Slowly crawling along.
Its tail flowing out of its home,
the ocean

Maria Cristina Landschoot, Grade 6
Park Forest Middle School

My Best Friend

A couple summers ago
I saw you up at camp
I thought you were some little boy
Playing under the street lamp
I didn't know who you were
And you probably didn't know me
I had seen you in the woods
Hanging on a tree
I wanted to introduce myself
And find out your name
I wanted to be your friend
And I hoped you'd feel the same
And then 3 years ago
On that labor day
I knew that I had a chance to ask and say
Hi! My name is Laura I'd like to be your friend
Then you said my name is Jeff just tell me where and when
So little did I know 3 years ago what was waiting for me
I found my very best friend
And his name is Jeffrey

Laura Moeller, Grade 6
Elizabeth Forward Middle School

Stuck!

When I went to take my shirt off to get into my PJ's,
It got stuck on my head, and I was whirling different ways.
I ran around my room, and I couldn't see a thing,
And at that very moment my phone started to ring.

So, then I tried to get it, but I ran into some chairs,
But after I got up, I fell all the way down my stairs.
I rolled all the way to the bottom, and landed with a THUMP,
And I landed on my head, and I could feel a bump.

So I tried to get my shirt off of my head,
But when I tried to do that, I fell and landed on my bed.
I screamed and I wiggled, all around my room,
Then I got back on my bed, and I fell down with a BOOM!

And then it was at that moment
I realized one crazy thing,
It would have been much easier
If I unbuttoned all the rings!

Danni Morgan, Grade 5
William Penn Elementary School

Summer Days

Oh, how I love hot summer days
Cooling off by the pool and having lots of fun
Hours spent swimming and playing with friends
Off on a bike ride or an early morning run
Oh, how happy I am that school is done

Sean Slaby, Grade 6
Sacred Heart Elementary School

Friends

A friend is someone you can look up to
Someone you can believe that they don't let you down
A friend who likes you for being you
And someone who stops you from being a clown

A friend is always with you once they pass you by
Someone who is always so sweet and so nice
Comes with you on the roller coaster ride
And someone who always has good advice

A friend is someone who helps you all the way
And cheers you on at your softball games
Who hangs out with you from day to day
And says you have an awesome name

A friend says that you are Number 1
Who helps you sing your favorite song
A friend celebrates with you when you've won
Who stops you from doing something wrong

A friend like you who is so true
And comes to you just like a dream
Makes you feel happy when you are blue
And show you what true friendship means

Simone Coleman, Grade 6
Sacred Heart Elementary School

Tree

A tree is like a person
growing every year.
A tree loses its leaves in winter,
But don't worry have no fear.

In spring the tree will grow
new leaves all green and lush
If a tree could, I'm sure
A tree would blush.

When people are near
they admire your height and beauty,
even when they are sad, mad, or moody
then when you are old
you spread your seeds, your children.

Then they will grow and repeat the process again.

Joshua Rutta, Grade 6
United Hebrew Institute

Sunflowers

The first day of spring
you smell a scented flower

Walk outside what do you see
a big tall yellow flower waiting for you

A cracking sound what could it be
endless possibilities

A kid is eating sunflower seeds
ask to have a handful

He says yes but beware
of the nice salty flavor

Pick it up it seems so smooth
that lovely sunflower seed
Jessica Murray, Grade 6
Neil Armstrong Middle School

Why Not Peace

Wouldn't the world be great
If no one would hate
There would be relief
To all grief
No one would annoy
No one would destroy
No one would bring down
The ones around
That would take your breath away
But yet again that's far away
Taylor Schlegel, Grade 5
Schuylkill Valley Elementary School

The Boy with Bad Habits

Once there was a boy with bad habits,
He always had to snack on rabbits.
Once he ate sixteen,
He would turn all green.
And then he stopped those bad habits.
Jordyn Andrews, Grade 4
West Branch Area Elementary School

i made a mistake

i went to the pond to get a fish
i made a mistake and got a dish
i went to the store to buy some bread
i made a mistake and bought a snake
i got to the park to play some ball
i made a mistake and forgot my ball
i went to the airport to catch a plane
i made a mistake and caught the rain
i got to my house to go to sleep
i made a mistake and saw the end
Jeffrey He, Grade 5
Newtown Elementary School

Soccer

Soccer
Use feet
Running, throwing, catching
Fun, breathtaking
Energetic
Colleen Walsh, Grade 4
West Bradford Elementary School

Microwave

I am a microwave.
And have a food crave
For macaroni and pepperoni.
They'll put it in my cave.

Sushi is no good.
I would try if it I could.
My owner thinks it is yummy.
But I think it's crummy.
Heather Simpson, Grade 5
McMurray Elementary School

Bubbly Delight

Snap, crack, pop.
The fun doesn't stop.
Taste is sugary and sweet.
A fun and favorite treat.

Sticky and pink you can chew,
Squishy, soft and rubbery too.
Blow a small or giant bubble.
Not in your hair, that's trouble.

Blow pops, Bazooka, and Bubblicious,
They're all so special and delicious.
More than gum, not quite candy,
Bubble gum is sweet and dandy.
Anna Corch, Grade 6
St Ann Elementary School

Monday Morning

Alarm clock rings on a Monday morning
loud as a freight train
racing down the track
the thought of just turning it off
and going back to bed
sounded pretty good to me
I woke up
did my morning routine
I was still tired
and I definitely wasn't inspired
my long school week has just begun
here we go again
and it was only Monday morning
Cory Jackson, Grade 6
Mount Nittany Middle School

Bunny's Adventure

A bunny once saw a hole
And came face to face with a mole
They rubbed noses
They made different poses
And found the mole was a friendly soul.
Anthony Donatelli, Grade 4
South Park Elementary Center

Lion

Lion
Big cat
Jumping, killing, eating
Peaceful when it's sleeping
Feline
Dane Cessna, Grade 4
East End Elementary School

Waterfalls

Some waterfalls are breezy,
Some are magical illusions,
A lot are refreshing rapid rivers.

Whenever I see one,
I see a rich golden fountain
With rapid crystal blue water
Pacing with the wind.

Closing my eyes so I can think,
No noise just silence around me,
I listen to the cascade of the water,
It sounds like swish, swish.

I feel the mist on my face,
It's like nobody is around me,
Just me and the waterfall.
Mikaela Mooney, Grade 6
Mount Nittany Middle School

Football

What is football?
Fierce game!
Respect!
Love!
Bone-breaking tackles!
Touchdown dances!
Super Bowl!
Sweat!
Team effort!
Pride!
Screaming!
Home crowds!
Hype!
Best game ever!
That is football
Tyler Rosenblatt, Grade 5
Rolling Hills Elementary School

Myself

My hair is like a thin piece of yarn.
My eyes are blue as the sky.
My fingers are like worms coming out of their holes.
My arms are like the equator.
My heart is filled of happiness
that is yellow as a smiley face.

Reilly McDermott, Grade 4
Avonworth Elementary School

So Cute

From my face I am cute
Even though I play the flute
People say I should mute
Because they say I'm not cute
Because I have tons of loot
But in their minds I know they think I'm cute

Sydney Sullivan, Grade 4
South Park Elementary Center

Spring

I wake up in the morning,
at the window the sun beaming,
It's going to be a hot day
while the sun is steaming.

My garden was crowding
with all the colorful flowers blooming.
While the bumble bees are buzzing around,
I see a caterpillar crawling on the ground.

As the sun was setting in the night,
I need to water the flowers before I lose sight.
Cannot forget to pick some for the vase,
The flowers' scent lasts throughout the days.

Nicholas Orliw, Grade 4
McDonald Elementary School

Messy Lockers

Lockers…a binder, a book, a little tiny storybook
Why don't I take a look
Up and down heard a sound
Day by day
When can I hire a maid?
My locker is like a jungle
Two little monkeys in a bundle
As dirty as a dump
Oh, my gosh, it's 12:00!
I will find my lunch
I will find my coat
There are my notes!
Time to go, time to leave
Where is my key?
There is something I have to say,
Maybe I will clean my locker the next day!!!

Samantha Westpy, Grade 5
East Stroudsburg Elementary School

Dad

One who shares, and one who cares.
One who promises he'll always be there.

When I'm older I'll understand,
He's just trying to be the best man.

No matter what I do, his love I see,
Don't you wish you had a dad like me.

There's a place in my heart no one can see,
Because, (Dad) it's reserved for you and me.

Nicole Conley, Grade 5
East Union Intermediate Center

Spring

The birds come out
Swooping and swinging from tree to tree
Swooshing in the air,
as they fly by
Chirping letting everyone know
a new spring is about to arrive
Crickets squeaking at dusk
telling everyone don't worry tomorrow might be better
Quack go the ducks as they enter the ponds
sploshing, and splashing about
in the new fresh blue water
Sizzle goes the sun against the water
Spring, what a beautiful time to go and smell the roses

Briana Cole, Grade 6
MMI Preparatory School

Independence

England had a powerful king.
He liked to control everything.
Since this king was not so grand,
People left in search of new land.
They traveled many miles across the sea,
To find a land where they would soon be free.
Thirteen colonies began the new nation.
The British did not like this new creation.
To keep control the king taxed their tea.
The colonists got mad and threw it in the sea.
The king tried to take away their rights.
Colonists prepared an army for fights.
George Washington led our troops to victory,
And helped our country earn its liberty.
The Declaration of Independence was written.
America is finally free from Britain.
We now are a country of our own.
The American flag is now sewn.
Betsy Ross made our flag red, white, and blue,
A symbol of independence for me and you.

Leah Stauber, Grade 4
St Alexis School

Squirrel Hill

I am a squirrel
That lives on Squirrel Hill.
Like my friend
My name is Ben.
Ben and I ran real high up a pine
We saw a guy
He said, "hi."
But we were mad
The guy did something bad
He littered
That is against the law
He heard Crow caw.
Crow said don't be bad
Pick up that bag.
Thanks,
Please don't litter on Squirrel Hill
Steve Morgan, Grade 4
William Penn Elementary School

Colors

Red is the bouquet of roses
Orange is the glow of the sun
Purple is my birthstone
Blue blankets the clear sky
Green is the tall grass

Colors make the world beautiful
Janice Amy, Grade 4
Bushkill Elementary School

Dreams

Dreams are things that
Walk in and out
Never stops whispering
About impossible things
They seem as if
They just can't happen
They are the ones
That speak the truth
So follow your dreams
And never let go
or they'll fly away.
Zachary Shenfield, Grade 5
East Stroudsburg Elementary School

Diana Ross

Diana Ross
Kind and nice
Singing on the stage
Working hard in every way
Caring for people
Brave, nice and kind
Brianna Negron, Grade 5
Shafer Elementary School

I Want to Be

I want to be a bird,
Flying through the sky.
I want to be a cheetah,
Running on the ground.
I want to be a fish,
Swimming in the ocean.
But the one thing I want to be
Is me!
Jenny Hineman, Grade 4
Chadds Ford Elementary School

Brother Trouble

Brothers at 12 are cool
Brothers at 16 are mature
Not fun to be with
Not fun to live with

My brothers are cool, though
BB guns
Water polo
Tall, strong blondes!
Computer
Playstation
Cars, girls, yuck!
Active acting
Fun, fun, fun
That's how cool my brothers are
Chet Bickhart, Grade 4
Benchmark School

Sister/Brother

Sister
happy, graceful
loving, caring, doubting
daughter, girl, son, boy
hitting, helping, working
tough, rough
Brother
Bradley Howard, Grade 5
East Union Intermediate Center

Birds' Wind

Gusts of all nature.
Birds are chirping instantly.
Side by side they fly.
Brittany Sembower, Grade 4
Center Elementary School

Star Is Life

The star is life
Blooming in the night
Dying in the day
Making pictures in the sky
Telling stories that we cannot hear
Stephanie Stewart, Grade 6
Freedom Area Middle School

Summer Time

Summer is nice
Like sugar and spice
I always stay cool
When I jump in the pool
Vacationing in the sun
Having never-ending fun
Playing all day
Everything joyful and gay.
Summer Time
Carly Wickham, Grade 4
Worcester Elementary School

Springtime

Spring
Playing, running, exercising
Spring is my favorite season
Weather
Amanda Hubler, Grade 4
West Branch Area Elementary School

Erving*

My cat Erving is the best
Everybody has confessed
He's cute and funny
You'll agree
He even has a pedigree
He likes to play and chase my hand
He is very, very grand
When he sleeps he makes a snore
But even then
He's not a bore
He's orange and yellow
He's a lovely fellow
He's cute and sweet
And loves his treats
Surely he'll scratch if you try to play
But don't start to cry
Because he'll run away
Erving will always comfort you
Whenever you are very blue
Rachel Kish, Grade 4
South Allegheny Elementary School
*Dedicated to Erving

Star

A bright flash of light
far in the night
cold air
hot but moist
like a boat
floating
twinkling like light
Amanda Quinn, Grade 4
South Park Elementary Center

Little Freddie

Little Freddie, Little Freddie how I miss you
How I wish people could still kiss you
In the hospital you were doing so good
You and Mom were about to move out the hood
Your Mom is cool
She wouldn't have raised you to be a fool
I miss you so dear
You guys were moving close to here
Your Mom wanted to take you to see the Nile
She would do anything to see you smile.

Anthony Tomasino, Grade 4
Avonworth Elementary School

Wolves

Their fur as soft as new fallen snow,
In the night their eyes glow,
From white to yellow, to gray to red,
Each hair on their back is as thin as a thread,
They live all over from the east to the west,
All in all wolves are the best.

Sarah Moses, Grade 6
Grasse Elementary School

Spelling Bee Nerves

When I was sitting at my spelling bee
I was nervous, that you see
As I wiped my hands on my desk
I wasn't sure I'd pass my test
How do I know what the word will be?
The girl beside me — am I as smart as she?
I sat there and sat there until I was called
I pulled so much hair out, I probably look bald.
Sweat is dripping down my face
Can I still escape this crazy place?
It's my turn, my word is said
Can I spell it, "cavalcade?"
I took in my breath, and started to spell
And what do you know, I did it well.
I didn't take first, but I did take third
Can you believe all this for a word?!?

Myaunna Lawhorn, Grade 5
Vandergrift Elementary School

The Amazon Rain Forest

I am the largest forest in South America.
My trees grow in several different layers.
I have infertile soil.
Tens of thousands of plant species live in me.
My enemy is a lumberjack company.
About 10 percent of me is destroyed.

I am the Amazon Rain Forest.

Jeremy Hull, Grade 6
Our Mother of Perpetual Help School

Active

A lways playing with my friends
C limbing trees is what we do
T ill the time comes
I nside we go
V ariety of things to do
E verything was fun today now it's time to go

April Travis, Grade 6
Freedom Area Middle School

Stars

The stars tell the story of our universe afar.
You wouldn't really know it if you were driving in a car.

Some nights you must wonder, why are stars meant to be.
Some map or adventure just waiting for me?

Stars are our guides, our givers of light.
You must know how to use them without any fright.

Some night when you're lost, just look at the north star.
If you trust it, I bet you will go far.

Victoria Pierson, Grade 6
Pittston Area Middle School

Happiness

Happiness is the color baby blue.
Happiness feels like a fluffy pillow.
Happiness tastes like chocolate covered strawberries.
Happiness smells like fresh picked flowers.
Happiness looks like people having fun.
Happiness sounds like kids laughing.

Megan Shay, Grade 5
Rhawnhurst School

I Wish It Would Be Summer

I wish it would stop snowing,
It snows most every day,
That snow and heavy wind,
Prevents my playing outside today.

I wish it would be sunny,
So I could see outside,
And watch those pretty bluebirds
Flying in the sky,

But I can't 'cause it's been raining,
Now most every day.
I wish that it were summer,
So outside I could play,

Without freezing to the core,
Or left with my teeth chattering like a beaver,
So far all have agreed,
Save for those with hay fever.

Nicholas Gude, Grade 5
Souderton Charter School Collaborative

Night Fades

Night fades.
It's lost in the sky.
It has forgotten where to go.
Night fades.
We're still waiting.
When will it come?
Night fades.
The sky is gray.
A light shower falls.
Night fades.
It has found the trail again.
Rising above the clouds.
Night has faded.

Elizabeth Holesa, Grade 5
Southside Elementary School

A Girl from Milk Street

There once was a girl from Milk Street,
Who did not walk on her two feet.
She waved with her toes,
To all that she knows.
It was a funny way to meet.

Amber Mendez, Grade 4
Penn-Kidder Campus

Spring

One day I went downtown.
When I was there I met a clown.
He said to me, "Look who's coming."
I looked and saw a honeybee humming.
Then I saw some flowers bloom.
In the sky I saw a moon.
There are people skating by.
There is a blue bird in the sky.
When the rain was pouring.
I went inside and it was boring.

Sarah Schuchman, Grade 6
Moravian Academy Middle School

The World Around Me

The world around me
With the drink like tea.
People always sick
And getting beaten with a stick.
Wanting it to stop
Always needing a cop.
Is always in pain
With nothing to gain.
Always bad music
And funny names like Nic Ric.
Helping out as much as you can
Also having to watch every man.
Wishing to go to the old ways
Instead of looking at the future days.

Dillion McCutcheon, Grade 6
H Austin Snyder Elementary School

A Day in My Life

My whole family is so important to me
If I didn't have them I wouldn't be me
My cousins and I are like peanut butter and jelly
We are like a million peas in a pod
I have six aunts and six uncles
I have twenty-one cousins
Sometimes we fight
Like cats and dogs
My youngest cousin, Brandon, always cries waah-waah-waah
My oldest cousin, Jessica, works at a cash register ka-ching ka-ching
My cousins range from five months to twenty-five years
I always look forward to the holidays
I think I'm really blessed
This is the perfect family for me
So this is my life

Emily Schindler, Grade 6
Mount Nittany Middle School

Lovable Lime Green

Lime green is palm trees and lily pads.
Lime green is the taste of green apple candy and mint chip ice cream.
Flowers smell lime green.
Lime green makes me feel relaxed.
Lovable lime green is the sound of fireworks and bubbles.
Lime green is the park, my room, and a coral reef.
Lime green is seashells.
Lime green is also the rain forest.
Lovable lime green is exotic.

Jessica Dowd, Grade 5
McMurray Elementary School

Clear

Clear is the cool feeling of rain on a window when you touch it.
Clear is the smell of dew on the freshly cut lawn.
Clear looks like the ocean against the horizon on a cool, breezy day.
Clear tastes like the ice cold water you're about to drink.
Clear sounds like the April showers on the wavy ocean.

Colby Haas, Grade 4
Watsontown Elementary School

Basketball Team — B

The ball beating on the ground is what causes our hearts to pound
The sound of moving feet is our lives' natural beat
Many games have been won either indoors or under the Pennsylvania sun
Crazy as it may seem, we are proud to be the B-team
As the ball hits the backboard I send a prayer to the Lord
"Let it go in" to make the game another win
Call that foul or the crowd will howl
Control the temp-o to let everyone know
The play being called. Don't let the pass be lulled
On the ground, wrestling for the ball or until the ref whistles a call
Listening to the crowd jeer won't distract us from why we are here
Listen to what we say because we're here to play
Basketball is our sport. Meet us on the court

Katie Roach, Grade 6
Carson Middle School

Rain

Rain drops in gracefully
Like a dancing cat.
It falls in with coolness
All over the world.
And prances away as magnificent as ever before.

Rachel Style, Grade 6
Southern Lehigh Middle School

My Friend Julia

I don't know how to tell you. I just want to say.
You changed my life in so many ways.
Without you how could I have survived?
You make my spirit fly. You keep my soul alive.
You know what I'm thinking. You don't have to ask.
When I'm with you, I don't need to hide behind a mask.
A mask full of lies that I thought would protect me from life.
When I was down, you lifted me up.
You helped me off the ground.
When fear tried to break me,
You didn't forsake me. You shared my laughs.
You felt my pain and stuck by my side through sunshine or rain.
I could tell you my secrets and know they would not be told.
Our friendship is true it can't be bought or sold.
I just want to let you know all you have done.
You have been my guidance and so much fun.
I hope we never grow apart.
And I say these words with all of my heart.
For everything you did and still do:
THANK YOU!

Annie Lowenthal, Grade 5
Chalutzim Academy

My First Day in Disney World

It was early in the morning —
It was so exciting.
We were going to Disney World
I was with my cousin.
We packed stuff that was frozen —
We had a lot of it.
It was kind of rough all being in the car,
But it was great so far.
I was so happy, nothing can stop me.
I was wishing we were there.
But my sister didn't even care.
When we finally got there
We went to the candy store
I wish I could have eaten,
More and more and more.
After that we went to a roller coaster
And my mom got me in a picture.
We had a lot of fun and I was so hyper,
I ran, I ran, I ran, I felt like a windmill cutter.
My cousin and I were so happy that day
I wouldn't change it any way.

Mark DeLeon, Grade 5
Hamilton Elementary School

The Land

If I had one wish, just one,
It would be for everyone.
The one wish would be…
For everyone to take care of the land
as if she were our family.

At one point in time
We almost destroyed the land
For our economy to grow.
Until many people saw
We would have to be more careful
Or we wouldn't survive.
And those people were right.

We have destroyed the land
As if she is an enemy.
Even though she just wanted to help.
Thanks to our caring, courageous, and colorful world…
We can survive.

Adam Langton, Grade 6
Mount Nittany Middle School

Granddad

When I was two my granddad died,
Everyone in my family cried.
My parents said it wasn't my fault,
His heart came to a sudden halt.

His heart attack was a scary thunderstorm,
Now his body is anything but warm.
On a sad winter's day, we buried him on a hill,
It wasn't just the cold, that gave us a chill.

He'll never know how much he meant,
I cherished all the wonderful times we spent.
As the sad days slowly went by,
I tried to be strong, but I just sighed.

'Till this day, I can still see his face,
As his heartbeat went at a slower pace.
His death was like a big, black hole,
But I'm happy because God took control.

Shianne Fisher, Grade 5
Bermudian Springs Middle School

Freedom

Freedom is the color of a rainbow
Freedom feels like hands joining together
Freedom tastes like a cinnamon bun
Freedom smells like sugar
Freedom looks like millions of flowers
Freedom sounds like R&B

Jessica Orr, Grade 5
Rhawnhurst School

Spring

Spring is like a renewal to nature.
Life comes back.
The gentle sun in your hair.
The wind whispering in your ear.
The smell of flowers blooming.
Wet showers come.
Birds singing like pianos.
But they're never out of tune.
March comes in like a lion.
And out like a lamb.
Spring is gentle.
Spring is warm and cool.
Spring is the waiting room for summer.
For the very end of school.
Melissa Jacobs, Grade 6
Our Lady of Mount Carmel School

The Basketball Game

Dribble, pass, shoot
Twelve seconds on the clock
Score is only 3-3
Now's no time to talk

Set a pick and then slide left
7...6...5...4
The game is almost over now
And victory's at our door

And then I get the ball in hand
The board reads 3...2...1
SWOOSH! The games is over now
And 4-3 we won
Victoria Szafara, Grade 5
Immaculate Conception School

The Princess

The princess who fell in a moat,
Was surprised there was no boat.
The servants in the castle,
Thought she was a hassle,
And hoped that she would not float.
Sydney Samuel, Grade 6
Bedford Middle School

Spring

Spring is one of the best seasons
It is when the flowers bloom
It is when the birds sing a tune
It is when you can play outside
And let your hair sway in the wind
You can play basketball
And volleyball too
Spring is one of the best seasons
And I'm not teasin'.
Madelyn Royer, Grade 6
Strodes Mills Middle School

Autumn Is Soaking In

The wind is whipping me in the face
Coldness soaking
into every inch of my body
White pine
towering over me and the school
Its pine needles
glistening in the sun like icicles
Honey locust tree leaves
dancing wildly
down to the ground
Wind hissing
in my ear like an angry snake
The leaves piled on the ground
look like golden brown snowdrifts
Autumn is soaking in
Noah Reifsnyder, Grade 5
Lower Salford Elementary School

Tennis Friend

A tennis ball
Is a new friend
A tennis ball bounces to you boing boing
A new friend laughs at your jokes haha
A tennis ball is waiting to be hit
A new friend is waiting to be played with
A tennis ball
Is a new friend
Tamar Schejter, Grade 4
Easterly Parkway Elementary School

Black

Black
is a dark night
with no stars
Black
is my cat's fur
around the white
Black
is a black stallion's coat
that glistens
Black
is a river
at midnight
Black
are my feelings
at times
Black
are the mysterious shadows
playing off objects at night
Black
is my
favorite color
Snezhana Karpova, Grade 5
Lincoln Elementary School

Ode to Baseball

America's Pastime
The best game ever
Summer nights
On a lit up field
A full count
The bases loaded
The crack of the bat
Hearing the crowd boo or cheer
Parents yelling in the stands
Having a catch with dad in the backyard
Throwing until your arm is dead
The feel of crushing the ball
Going to a game
The field perfect like a picture
The tense feeling during playoffs
Screaming at the TV
Watching the curse get broken
Seeing a curse get made
The magic of baseball
Jordi Shapiro, Grade 6
Hershey Middle School

It

It is nasty.
It may bite.
It will smack,
With all its might.

It will come.
It will go.
It will start
To grow and grow.

It should come
Very soon.
It should come
Around noon.

If you were listening
To what I said
Then you know
It comes before bed.

That would be my hunger!
Olivia Cerroni, Grade 4
St Leo School

School

S chool is fun
C oncentrating on
H ard work
O ften pays
O ff
L ike winning a trophy
Carly Carolla, Grade 5
Wharton Elementary School

Sadako: A Real Life Heroine

Sadako died,
Her mother cried.
She was on her 644th crane,
And the rest I will try to explain.

In 1945, the atom bomb was dropped
Which is why Sadako's life had stopped.
Leukemia was the cause.
I think she deserves a round of applause.

Jennifer Hite, Grade 5
Schuylkill Valley Elementary School

Christmas Time

Bells are ringing everywhere we go,
Icicles are hanging on every building.
Children are running, laughing and playing in the snow.
Carolers are singing through the town.
People are picking Christmas trees in the cold air.

We enjoy the aroma of pine trees in our homes,
As we fill them with lights and ornaments.
Fragrant hot chocolate warms us up.
We place the nativity scene near the burning fire.
And we anticipate Jesus' birthday.

We wrap presents for those we love.
We put gifts under our tree.
We soon go to sleep,
While Santa Claus brings presents down the chimney.
At last, we open gifts and thank the people who gave them to us.

Thus we celebrate God.

Hannah Trout, Grade 4
Verna Montessori School

By Myself*

When I'm by myself
And I close my eyes
I'm a football player.
I'm a dog chewing a bone.
I'm a billionaire donating 6,000,000.
I'm an author writing a book.
I'm a chef cooking for the president.
I'm the governor of Pennsylvania.
I'm an artist drawing a beautiful picture.
I'm a musician playing the trombone.
I'm a cop arresting bad guys.
I'm whatever I want to be.
An anything I want to be
And when I open my eyes what I care to be
Is me.

Brandon Haag, Grade 5
East Stroudsburg Elementary School
*Inspired by Eloise Greenfield

Night

Going through the darkened night
It hurts to see when the sky gets bright
As the night sounds fill the air
My body shivers from the things that stare
And when the things stop staring at me
I just walk home happily
But as I get home the sky gets dark
And over again I feel the dart
So fear will rise but I just don't care
Because some of the night is in the air
And when the air begins to creep
I slowly lay down and go to sleep

Aly Kratzer, Grade 5
Southside Elementary School

Snow

Snow, snow everywhere.
Lying on the ground.
Where, oh where?
Going 'round and 'round.
See, see here it is!
Falling from above.
Why, why is it so white?
I do not know.
Snow, snow everywhere.
So silently falling.
No one knows.

Spencer Thurman, Grade 5
Christ the Divine Teacher Catholic Academy

The Hungry Hawk

I stare I glare I am the hawk.
I'm looking over the wonderful meadow,
Searching for rodents
You better hope I don't see you,
Or you will be in my stomach!

AJ Heastings, Grade 6
Freedom Area Middle School

Old Friends and New Friends

In the year 2005,
I met new friends.
I was shy at first, but not anymore.
I thought they would just ignore.

I would miss all my friends from Rowan Elem.,
I would cry all day and think of them.
Maybe I can meet them someday,
And tell them about my new friends.

Now that I have new friends,
I will be okay,
But I can write letters and call them.
I will try every day.

Justine Oh, Grade 5
Wexford Elementary School

Dragonfly's Death

In the pond I see my face
Filling with a lot of laughter
There is a dragonfly in the air
I'm swatting it with all my might
All there is now
Is just a bit of silence

Matt Coupe, Grade 5
Nether Providence Elementary School

Osama/Respect

Osama
Mean, cruel
Killing, shooting, beating
Unruly, anarchy, cooperative, conformity
Helping, listening, self-disciplined
Nice, kind
Respect

Kevin Kenny, Grade 6
St Sebastian Elementary School

Cats and Dogs

cats
skittish, colorful
hiding, jumping, peering
claws, teeth, paws, tails
running, chasing, barking
happy, friendly
dogs

Breanna Lincoski, Grade 6
California K-8 School

Ode to Notre Dame

At the bookstore
Trying to find out what to buy
Shorts, shirts, sweaters, and sweatpants
Or maybe standing in a Quad
Watching some people play croquet
Or buying some barbecued items
The smell of things on the grill
From one of the houses
Watching the water polo team
Trying to sell something
In their swim trunks
Or marching down the street
With the band playing
Loudly like an elephant's trunk
Scaring the other team
Already practicing in the stadium
Listening to the crazy fans
Who are cheering at the big game
For the home team
Notre Dame

Jonathan Schupper, Grade 6
Hershey Middle School

Puppies

Puppies are brown
Puppies feel like a cuddly blanket
Puppies taste like chocolate
Puppies smell like candy
Puppies look like the cutest babies
Puppies sound like a whistling howl.

Maryana Zakharkiv, Grade 5
Rhawnhurst School

The Best Baseball Kid

There was a super kid named Mitch.
He could really throw a good pitch.
Then he wore weird socks.
His friend's name was Lock.
He had a teacher named Miss Klitsch.

Mitchell Peters, Grade 4
Penn-Kidder Campus

The Fun in the Sun

May
fun, sunny
running, jumping, swimming
in May it's my birthday.
Month.

Gerika Gallaher, Grade 4
West Branch Area Elementary School

Wild Horse

Wild horse,
how your black coat
glistens in the sunshine
and your mane flaps so wildly
as you run.

Jolene Nave, Grade 6
Bedford Middle School

Cats

Crawling crying
are many cats.
Very catastrophic
little brats.

Daniel Lis, Grade 6
Allison Park Elementary School

Star Wars

S ith
dea **T** hstar
d **A** rth vader
at- **R** t

W ookie
A nieken
R 2d2
S kywalker

Brendan Matthews, Grade 5
East Stroudsburg Elementary School

My Best Friend

He is funny
He is nice
He is loyal
He is very playful
He is the greatest in the world
To me he is the best
He is soft and furry
He is my dog Sam

Shannon Klimpel, Grade 6
H Austin Snyder Elementary School

Basketball Player

Basketball's the game
I love to share
With all of my friends
Because I am a player.

Before each game
We say a prayer.
Then I show the crowd
That I am a valuable player.

We shoot, we miss.
But things get grayer.
They shoot, they score.
"Hey coach, he's no player!"

I think the ref's calls
Are really unfair.
But sportsmanship is key
To an honorable player.

I shake their hands
To show I care.
Maybe I really am
A valuable player.

Paul Brasavage, Grade 6
Holy Family Academy

School

I am sittin' in the classroom.
I am almost out of time.
My teacher says that I have to write
a poem that will rhyme.
I am thinkin' of some words
that will make my teacher proud.
I am hopin' that I will not
have to read this poem aloud.
I am writtin' all the things
that I really want to say.
I am tryin' to do my best
so that I will get an A.

Ellen Funari, Grade 6
Chambersburg Area Middle School

Pencil

A dancing stick, pulled by hands,
Leaving many long and short footprints.
When he misses a step, he dances upside down,
And the footprints are gone.

Allison Laseau, Grade 5
Jenkintown Elementary School

Music

Music is a thing of infinite glory.
It can tell you a tale or a story.
It can help you when you're down.
It can make you feel like you have the crown.
Music

Ryan Glover, Grade 6
Westmont Hilltop Middle School

Tiger, the Cat

Tiger acts like a dog and is big too,
Cat door is too small, he can't fit through.
Not even into a small hole,
He's a big fat butter roll.

Likes to drink out of the toilet bowl,
His stripes are as black as coal.
Lies around and eats all day,
Wants my chicken, I push him away.

But as a horse, weights fifteen pounds,
Loves to eat, gobbles many rounds.
Rolls on his back, so you rub his belly.
When you do, it jiggles like jelly.

Rachel Raymond, Grade 5
Bermudian Springs Middle School

Friday Night Lights

Friday night lights
A time under the football lights
With my friends and having fun
Watching the game with some buds
Walking under the lights on Friday night
Walking with my friends to watch the game
Hanging out up on the hill
After that we eat some food
Half time half time is the players' break
Half time half time is crazy time
After the half time I watch some more
With my friends and strangers and all
Rooting for the team I want
Just walking and chilling out the same time
When the Friday night lights go out
We give the players high fives
I say goodbye to the field
It was a good wasted night
Under the Friday night lights

Dallas Walls, Grade 6
Strodes Mills Middle School

Spring

Spring, Spring, Spring, I love you so,
Flowers and trees just grow, grow, grow.

From animals to plants, everything blooms,
It makes you forget about winter's glooms.

The sun comes out to show itself,
It makes you want to put everything back on the shelf.

The birds are singing on this very day,
They almost forgot they had to go away.

Children laugh and play from east to west.
Spring, of course, is always the best.

Elana Morgan Lowell, Grade 6
Moravian Academy Middle School

Recipe for a Football Player

First add 5 pounds of toughness,
Next mix in some fastness,
Then blend some catching skills,
If you want him to be a QB stir in throwing skills,
Pour in a cup of energy,
Let it cook for an hour and a half,
and you have a football player.

Zach Kreutzer, Grade 4
Avonworth Elementary School

A Leprechaun's Gold?

There once was a leprechaun that was cold.
He ran into a pile of gold,
He took the gold and ran away.
He said I had a good day.
Somehow his gold turned into mold.

Bethany Pepperday, Grade 4
West Branch Area Elementary School

A Journey

We're going on a journey; we'll go so far
We'll find hidden places, wherever they are
We'll sail stormy seas
Fly through the trees
Journey through the Sahara, trudge through the snow
Oh, all the places we can go
We can go far, we can go near
Glide like a bird, prance like a deer
Explore like a cat
Hang like a bat
Shine like the sun, glow like the moon
Go from bitter days of February to lazy days of June
We've gone through these adventures so quickly it seems
Probably because all these adventures are our dreams

Maggie Sullivan, Grade 6
St Nicholas St Marys School

Spring

Spring is in the air
You can see it everywhere
The flowers are so sweet
The birds go tweet, tweet
The sun is in the sky
The clouds go rolling by
We wear short sleeves
There are lots of green leaves
It is almost summer
That is a bummer
Because I love spring
So I could just sing
Miranda Steinkopf, Grade 5
Central Elementary School

Nature's Waterfall

She flows all the time
Grass shimmers from the cool mist
Water flows with joy
Rocks beneath cleansed from water
Yet fish and frogs swim below
William Haunstein, Grade 5
Bushkill Elementary School

Candy

Candy is a really sweet treat
It is very, very sweet.
It can be yellow, red, or blue
And white like peppermints, too.

Gumdrops, taffy and Nestle
But what goes with candy bestly
Is no one asking to share
And you? I don't care!
Connor Fees, Grade 5
Lincoln Elementary School

Science

S ome projects are fun.
C ool.
I t is an awesome class.
E very day is fun.
N eeds a lot of thought.
C reative class.
E very day is hard.
Joe Kozemko, Grade 6
H Austin Snyder Elementary School

Matt

There once was a boy named Matt
He did a big Kersplat
It was on a field
And Matt peeled
That was the boy named Matt
Kathryn Neville, Grade 4
Moscow Elementary Center

Ode to My Cat, Smokey!

My cat is as gray as smoke.
My cat is as fast as lightning.
My cat is stronger than most cats.
My cat is as affectionate as couples in love.
My cat loves milk as much as a dog loves water.
My cat loves the warm as a polar bear loves the cold.
My cat loves me as much as I love sports.
My cat lies next to a teddy bear like a baby lies with a blanket.
My cat enjoys jumping on a TV as much as I like shooting baskets.
My cat will play with string like a girl plays with makeup.
My cat is sometimes lazy like my sisters always are.
My cat's eyes are as bright as the moon.
My cat's paws are a sharp as knives.
My cat's whiskers are as long as an elephant's nose.
My cat is as soft as cotton.
My cat is as smart as a human.
Alex Wright, Grade 6
St Sebastian Elementary School

About Me

Precious
Short, funny, kind, and neat
Daughter of Mary
Lover of writing stories and reading
Who feels happy on Fridays, tired on Saturdays, energetic on Sundays
Who finds happiness in friends and family
Who needs a friend or pet to be with
Who gives courage to people if they need it
Who fears snakes and bees
Who would like to see Mary Kate and Ashley
Who enjoys riding my bike, swimming, and playing
Who likes to wear pants, a sweater, and a shirt under it
Resident of East Stroudsburg
Coardes
Precious Coardes, Grade 5
East Stroudsburg Elementary School

Freedom

Don't you think we'd feel guilty if we owned another man?
Only for one reason just because we can
How would you like it if you were that slave?
All the work that you would do, the food that you would crave
Do you think it's really fair for them to do all that work?
While all that we do is poke them with a pitchfork
And that's how they treated the slaves; how brutal and cruel!
When all the owner would do is give them a job and a tool.
Why did we go to war over such a silly thing?
When the chances of them winning was thin as a string
Why would they even try when they had no chance of winning?
And what were they thinking since their ammunition was thinning
The North worked very hard because freedom isn't free
And the slaves were glad there was no more slavery.
Thomas Murphy, Grade 4
St Alexis School

Memory

See there's this place,
Where I see a familiar face,
I see a woman,
Who may never sin,

I see a boy,
Who I wish would play with an old toy,
I see a young man,
Who learned to make me laugh, and trust me, he can,

Then I see her,
The one who takes me in when I say brr,
She's the one I miss the most,
I sometimes miss her yummy roast,

Finally there are the friends,
Some of them have forgotten me,
And soon I see,
That I am too behind,

But they say they miss me,
And when I see them, we're both filled with glee,
This place I speak about,
Just happens to be my old house.

Shelby Gill, Grade 6
Sacred Heart Elementary School

Summer

Summer at last! It's finally here,
Kids drink lemonade, and adults drink beer

Soccer and baseball and lots of fun,
And heat beats down from the blazing sun

Flip-flops, Frisbees, and swimming pools,
School is out, no teachers, no rules

Summer is my favorite time
But this is the end of my summer rhyme.

Jake Speicher, Grade 6
Conemaugh Township Area Intermediate School

St. Patrick's Day!

It is St. Patrick's Day!
Hip! Hip! Hooray!
It's when little leprechauns go out and play.
And Irish people dance and sway.

The people feast on Irish stew.
And good Irish beer they brew.
One day a year we can be Irish, too!
St. Patrick's Day is for me and you!

Jarrod Polk, Grade 4
Immaculate Conception School

Easter

Easter is coming!
Children swarm the streets.
Easter is my favorite,
Come on let's all get treats!
We all get chocolate,
We all get special things.
There is something more important than all of this,
It is the rising of Christ that makes this day what it is!
I love Easter,
I love Christ!
This is the best day of all!

Mary Pettit, Grade 6
St Boniface School

I've Never Been as Scared in My Life

I've never been as scared in my life as I run out onto the field,
I knew the pressure will not yield.
The pigskin ball in my hands,
All you can hear is the cheering of the fans.
As I wait for the hike,
I think that no teammate is alike.
I throw the ball as I'm sacked hard,
It felt like my helmet was reduced to shards.
The faithful receiver does his job,
Just barely catching my lob.
As he runs for the end zone,
I know that he is not alone.
Oh no he was tackled,
Our hands might as well been shackled!
Fourth down and fifteen seconds to go,
For the last time in the game I throw.
He catches the ball for a touchdown,
Then I fall to my knees on the wet muddy ground
Just to hear my name being screamed all around.
I've never been as scared in my life.

Tyler Miller, Grade 6
Strodes Mills Middle School

Madness

Madness feels like black as darkness.
Madness tastes like rotten eggs.
Madness smells like a skunk spraying.
Madness looks like angry elephants in a stampede.
Madness sounds like fire rising up.

Anson Paul, Grade 5
Rhawnhurst School

Open Range

Out on the open range
the fields of tall grass seem to sway themselves in the wind.
The rolling hills and clear blue sky seem to connect.
The storms are like every strike of lightning is hitting you.
It feels like you are the only one there,
and that you are alone, but at the same time peaceful.

Caroline Davis, Grade 5
Wexford Elementary School

Why Do I Cry?
I look out my window
And wonder why,
Why, oh why
Do I always cry?

I cry every day,
I cry every night.
I even cry
When the sun's shining bright.

I cry in the fall,
I cry in the spring.
I even cry
When the birds start to sing.

There's a tear in my eye
When holidays come.
There's a tear in my eye
When the bumble bees hum.

So, here I am,
Looking into the sky.
And wondering
Why do I always cry?
Ryleigh Blakley, Grade 4
Brecknock Elementary School

Flying
F rightening
L ifting
Y es, interesting
I nedible peanuts
N o end
G oing places fast
Zachary Cole, Grade 6
H Austin Snyder Elementary School

Family
Parents
Nice, warm
Helpful, respectful, strict
Makes us feel loved
Moms
Giemaly Soto, Grade 4
Christ the King School

The Mall
The mall is like an ant hill,
No one in there stays still
People purchasing,
Little kids playing and running around
Whenever you are in there,
You'll hear all sorts of sounds
The mall is like an ant hill.
Thomas Michael Sullivan IV, Grade 6
Guth Elementary School

Desert
Dehydrating, hot
Tall, razor sharp cactuses
Enormous, sandy
Nyssa Diaz, Grade 5
Penn-Kidder Campus

My Feelings About School
I
Love School
Newtown Elementary
Nine a.m. to three thirty p.m.
So I can see my friends, to learn and to
see my nice teacher, Mrs. Sharp!!!
Robert Wallace, Grade 5
Newtown Elementary School

First Things First
First the morning, then the breakfast
First the Prom dress, then the necklace
First things first.
First the mother then the kid.
First the bottle then the lid.
First things first.
First the key slot then the key
That's the way it had to be
First things first.
Brittany Mancini, Grade 5
Claysville Elementary School

Mountain Slope
A
Big
Rocky
Ledge
Steep, tall
Motionless
In a forever sleep
Quiet like the clouds
Loud as a clap of thunder
Claire Lippay, Grade 5
Jenkintown Elementary School

Martin Luther King Jr.
He was nonviolent
He was not silent
Unlike any before,
Determined, you can't ignore

An inspiration to any race
He encouraged all to find their place.
Unfortunately he passed away
But his dream, is here to stay.
Jack Marcrum, Grade 5
Edgeworth Elementary School

War and Peace
War
Dreadful, horrible
Killing, crying, hurting
Sadness, hatred, love, cheerfulness
Smiling, cheering, returning
Contented, joyful
Peace
Jon Carlo Patton, Grade 5
Our Lady of Grace Elementary School

Every Day
Every day I wake up and wash my face.
I run around in a certain pace.

I brush my teeth with a brush,
And always get dressed in a rush.

I go to school and learn a bunch,
And talk with friends during lunch.

Teachers rock, all day long,
But giving homework is very wrong.

My book bag hurts my back a lot,
And a couple boys are very hot.

That's why every day I'm mean,
And cause a very dramatic scene.
Alyssa McKee, Grade 6
State Street Elementary School

Triangles
T
ri
ang
les h
ave thr
ee sides.
Sometimes t
hey are equal.
Scalene is my fa
vorite type of triangle.
Alex Schultz, Grade 6
St Maria Goretti School

Singing
Singing is fun,
singing is cool,
especially when you
get to do it in
school.
You can join the
choir, that is true;
It lifts your spirits, all day through.
Zachary McKenna, Grade 4
Immaculate Conception School

I Am a Girl

I am a girl
I wonder why the world is not peaceful
I hear birds chirp and sing
I see trees, birds, and families
I want to see people be nice to each other
I am a girl

I pretend to be happy
I feel scared
I touch pencils, tables, and people
I worry someone will get hurt
I cry when I am sad
I am a girl
I understand what I can do
I am a girl

Ashley Acevedo, Grade 5
East Stroudsburg Elementary School

Moon

The moon is a flashlight in the dark,
it is a bright light bulb,
it is the only thing you see in a pitch black night,
it is the brightest diamond in the sky.
Sara Carpenter, Grade 6
Guth Elementary School

The Prairie

I am the prairie long and wide
A lonely stream runs up my side
It feeds the animals of all different kinds
Who live in my fields far and wide
The sun beats down upon my skin
Shining on seeds to help them begin
Since I've been here I saw so many things
Animals, plants, and mountains too
But the strangest thing I ever saw
Did not bite, chew, or gnaw
It laughed and played upon my skin
They treated the animals as if they were them
I am the prairie long and wide
A lonely river runs up my side
Justine Yeh, Grade 4
General Nash Elementary School

Trees

Trees and the wind are beginning to dance
Is this on purpose, or by chance?
How Mother Nature would smile to see,
The beautiful waltz of the wind and the tree.

Moving with elegance and flowing grace,
Slow and gentle is the pace.
Wind will stop, trees won't bend,
This lovely waltz will come to an end.
Alexis Phillippi, Grade 5
Bermudian Springs Middle School

Our Freedom

Our freedom just amazes me
The freedom that was meant to be
Our fighters went into war
Some had never been there before
George Washington led his troops to fight
They fought until they saw a light
A light that said "Now you have won
So go and rest; lay down your gun
Just go home and have some fun
See your kids; play in the sun"
They gathered 'round and packed their things
They would hear their families' greetings
From then on we all were free
The freedom that is now in me
So think about what I just said
Even if you're lying in bed
Thank the troops that fought that year
The troops that fought like angry steers
This is how we became free
The freedom that was meant to be
Annie Roble, Grade 4
St Alexis School

Fall Is Here

In the courtyard
Wind blowing
making me cold
Leaves on the honey locust tree
a shade of buttery yellow
dropping and running across the concrete
The wind bending the plants halfway over
The bird houses vacant
waiting for an occupant
pebbles scattered everywhere
On the pine tree
new growth is a different shade of color from the old
Kids playing on the playground
all bundled up because they're cold
Fall is here
Dan Bedell, Grade 5
Lower Salford Elementary School

Hot Fudge Sundae

On a hot summer day I went to the store to buy a sundae.
I wanted to build it on my own.
I liked it so much that it made me moan.
Just like loving the chocolate fudge.
I don't have to be a judge.
I also love the vanilla ice cream.
The flavor makes me scream inside my dream.
It's creamy, sweet and cold.
I will eat it until I'm old.
Jacob Shultz, Grade 4
Watsontown Elementary School

Cows

Cows grazing in the fields
Eating delicious green grass
In the cool, cool shade
Slowly wander into the barn
Jessica Whitmore, Grade 6
Chambersburg Area Middle School

Snake

S naps at your fingers
N ips at your nose
A ttacks everybody
K ind of mean
E ats mice and rats this is a guarantee!
Matthew Lang, Grade 4
Easterly Parkway Elementary School

Tori and Lorrie

There once was a girl named Tori
She wanted to be like Lorrie
Tori was clever
Lorrie found treasure
Then along came a boy named Corey.
Julius Santana, Grade 5
Rhawnhurst School

My Sister the Pig

When my sister eats
she's like a pig,
she attacks the food.
She's a pig.
Her room is a dump
and under her bed
is a dirty mess.
There's dolls, dirt,
and even some pigs.
Under her dresser
is like a bathroom.
It's so dirty.
Under her covers
is like a mud puddle.
It's so brown.
I saw some dirt there.
THAT'S MY SISTER THE PIG!
Clark Handel, Grade 4
Easterly Parkway Elementary School

Baseball

Baseball
Catching, sliding
Bunting, hitting, running
Catching, pitching, curve ball, home run
Winning
Charles Trovato, Grade 4
Penn-Kidder Campus

Flag

Colorful, beautiful
Waving, reminding, enlightening
God blesses the USA
Stars and stripes
Alicia M. Brooks, Grade 5
Penn-Kidder Campus

I'm a Hot Roasted Turkey

I'm a hot roasted turkey,
Each second hotter,

I'm a hot roasted turkey,
Boiling in water.

I'm a hot roasted turkey,
Already stuffed and fried,

I'm a hot roasted turkey,
Oh well, I tried.

I'm a hot roasted turkey,
Ready to be eaten in a feast,

I'm a hot roasted turkey,
They think I'm a beast!
Kaitlyn McGrath, Grade 4
Lionville Elementary School

Spring

To smell all of the flowers
roses, and daisies

the feel of the sun shining lightly on you
the sight of rabbits, and deer

the taste of ice cold lemonade
iced tea, and ice cream

hearing birds chirp in the early morning
and animals singing

the sight of little animals
playing in the sun all day
Kai Tainaan, Grade 6
Neil Armstrong Middle School

Emotion

Happiness seems yellow
I see friendly kids play in the park
I hear the laughter of children
I smell the cookies in the bakery

I touch the soil of the earth
I taste a little bit of Mom's cookies
Connor Keller, Grade 4
West Bradford Elementary School

Spring

S uper most best time of the year
P arents going on vacation
R ainfalls coming near
I nside out it's beautiful
N othing is wrong with tanning
G o outside and have fun
Nicole Conn, Grade 6
West Allegheny Middle School

Dusty, My Best Friend

I have an old dog named Dusty,
At times his movements are rusty
He used to be fast and quick,
Lately things don't seem to click
He is a small tan Chihuahua,
Not often will you hear him bow-wow
He's small enough to go through a log,
He could get lost in a morning fog.
Dusty gives me a lot of joy,
A blue ball is his favorite toy
He sits up when he wants a treat,
Sometimes he gets under my feet
I wish he could do one more trick,
My face he always likes to lick
If I lay, sit, squat, or bend,
He'll come running, my best friend.
Robert E. Muckel Jr., Grade 6
Smith Middle School

Farming

Farming
To be a real
Real farmer,
You think smart,
Drive nice shiny
Equipment,
work hard, and of course
You've got to
Get dirty.
Luke E. Hershey, Grade 6
Locust Grove Mennonite School

Night Sky

Stars are like twinkling tear drops,
Hanging from the sky.
When I look up to the moon,
It was a face of a guy.

When I gaze into deep space,
I see dark, dangerous clouds of fear.
But I know that in the morning,
The sky will be bright and clear.
Morgan Anthony, Grade 5
Bermudian Springs Middle School

Please Come Back to Stay

I knew I was asleep,
Because right there you were,
Standing right before me,
Looking like you did back then.
I know I was asleep,
Because the last time I saw you,
Was when you were dead asleep in that wooden casket.
I couldn't believe it,
Was I really seeing you?
You still looked the same,
Your hearing aid and,
All your gray hair,
The thing running through my mind
Was I really seeing you?
Then I knew I really was seeing you!
Then all of a sudden I woke up right before I could say,
Pappy I miss you so please come back to stay.
So good morning for now and I will wait for tonight
  when I can say,
Pappy I miss you so please come back to stay.

Cassie Irvin, Grade 6
Strodes Mills Middle School

In the Morning

In the morning the sun rises
And then the moon becomes unseen
We all awake to the sun's bright light
Then yawn, stretch, and get ready for our day

In the morning
The lawns thirst is quenched
With dew and frost
The sight is enchanting
As the sun rises in the far East

The long stretch of life slowly appears
As the day begins its start
In the morning life begins a new day
Just to do the same tomorrow

Madalynn Collins, Grade 4
Concord Elementary School

Candle's Glow

Let the silent echo creep its way up
to the slim gloomy glow of a glazing candle.

The tiny pieces of smoked ash
roughen the top of the soothing candle wax
as the ash sinks into the creamy silk

As the long slim glow of fire gets blown out by a child's blow
the world has turned off until another match is lit

Stephen Sramac, Grade 4
Lincoln Elementary School

Nothing

I'm going to write nothing
But I'm writing something
I don't know what that something is,
  but that something isn't anything.

That something is a something that is a very special something,
  but of course that very special something isn't anything.
That something is something in my heart that is something.
It is very special to me.

That nothing has got to be something
I can feel that very special something that is in my heart.
I wish I could figure out what that nothing is.
I hope it is very special.

It could be everything.
I wish that nothing, something was everything.
That nothing could be my family.
Maybe that very special something could be my family.

MY FAMILY
I decided that my very special something is my wonderful family
I'm so glad I figured it out.
My very special something is MY FAMILY!

Baylee Fee, Grade 4
Lionville Elementary School

Autumn

The wind blew deep,
So deep that tables and chairs flew.
The darkened mist layout as a creep,
In the night, waiting for the right moment out of the blue.

People waking,
Trying to stay warm from the cold.
Heaters running, ovens quickly baking,
Logs crackling in brightly burning fireplaces of old.

The changing leaves,
Swirling round, blowing through the air.
Wildly flying up into the eaves,
To softly float down, all scattered through my hair.

The fall air's cold,
Makes me feel extremely bold.

Miranda Pfeiffer, Grade 6
Freedom Area Middle School

Bears

Big black and bold
Eats everything
Aren't as mean as they look
Really small at birth
So don't be scared the next time you see one

Amy Boris, Grade 5
Sacred Heart of Jesus School

Ted and Fred

There once was a boy named Ted,
He had a friend named Fred,
Ted and Fred went to make stew.
But it came out to be goo,
And so they stood on their heads.

Samantha Peterson, Grade 5
Mount Jewett Elementary School

A Girl's Story!

The board I may not see.
I may talk to a tree.
And that doesn't mean I'm crazy.
But I'm totally free.
I have no friends.
I could use some helping hands.

Lydia Glover, Grade 5
State Street Elementary School

Family

Family is love between people you love
People to fight with, but for them
To know you'll always love them
People that live with you and share
The everyday life with and share holidays
With them to show you love them.
Family

Dennis Gregory Rocher, Grade 5
East Stroudsburg Elementary School

Death Is…

Death is…
Sad,
And death is being torn from a family.

Death is…
Cold,
And alone.

Death is…
Tearful,
And silent.

Death is…
Awful
And unnerving.

Death is…
Terror,
Or fear

Death is…
Black,
And terrible.
But death is not the end.

Madelyn Smith, Grade 4
Beaver County Christian School

Green

Green tastes like crunching crackling smooth lettuce in my mouth,
a green sour apple fresh from the tree on a nice spring day,
and the sweet and sometimes sour chewy gummy LifeSavers.

Green smells like fresh cut grass on a soccer or maybe football field,
the stench of old gushy rotten pepper,
and boiled vegetables next to a filleted juicy fish.

Green sounds like rushing water crashing down from a waterfall,
a frog's low pitch ribbit, and the roaring Eagles stadium.

Green feels like oozing slime out of a monster's ear,
the smoothness of a bowling ball on a cool Saturday night,
and the rough scales on a snake's back.

Green looks like the army camouflage from a testing ground,
a large juicy watermelon on a hot summer day,
and the tiles at a fancy hotel at midnight waiting for New Years.

Hunter Seufert, Grade 4
Indian Lane Elementary School

What If

What if you were a lone black dot
In a sea of white
Watching white people cut in front of you while you stand in line
What if you were walking down the street
Seeing "White only" signs
And "Colored only" signs
Over bathroom doors and doctor's offices

What if you go outside each day
And hear your mother say,
"Don't go near that white girl when you go outside to play"
And as you go outside you hear your white neighbor say
"Don't go near that colored girl when you go outside to play"

What if as you walk into town that white girl who lives next door
What if that white girl
Asked you to be her friend
What if…

Maddy Griffin, Grade 5
Jenkintown Elementary School

Laser Lemon Yellow

Yellow is newly waxed taxi cabs and school buses filled with excited children.
Yellow is cheerful and bright.
Yellow is the taste of yummy lemon meringue pie.
Flowers and scented candles smell yellow.
The sun makes me feel yellow.
Yellow is the sound of squeaky rubber duckies and hungry newborn chicks.
Yellow is beaches, a hayfield, and a hay barn lit with sunlight.
Tanning on a bright beach is yellow.
Watching the sun go down is yellow.
Yellow is a bright patch of daisies.

Melanie Morgret, Grade 5
McMurray Elementary School

Adventures with Laura

I have a friend named Laura McGarry.
She has a dog that's very hairy.
Laura thinks of fun things to do,
But sometimes I get bored boo-hoo.

Once we played a game called "Trouble,"
Then I won and she played double.
But the thing we do the very best,
Is drive our parents to distress.

We went on vacation to Cancun,
Last year during the month of June.
Our families went to Chichen Itza,
Which my dad called chicken pizza.

We took a trip to Niagara Falls,
And made our way down the halls.
The ride we took on the Maid of the Mist,
Was the very first thing on my list.

Laura and I have traveled together,
In many different kinds of weather.
Now you've gotten to take a look,
At some of the journeys that we took.

Stephanie Prohaska, Grade 5
Villa Maria Academy Lower School

Cafeteria

The cafeteria at lunchtime sounds like a rock concert
until the teachers calm us down.
The tables look like trash dumps
where skunks would hang around.
Our lunches are unhealthy like chocolate ice cream
it makes the teachers just want to scream.

David McCreesh, Grade 6
Guth Elementary School

Colors I Like

Black is my favorite color ink.
Des'Tyne really likes the color pink.

Orange is the color of my favorite leaf.
Brown is the color that reminds me of beef.

Green is the color of my garden hose.
Red makes a pretty rose.

Abby's purple pants are so awesome.
White is the color of a blossom.

Blue reminds me of the sky.
Yellow is the color of a fry.

Colors rock!

Laura Kilgore, Grade 6
Cheswick Christian Academy

Winter!!!

Winter is the time of year
The time when you see all the deer
It's time to cheer
"Yay winter's here!"

Oh, come on Pop!
Let's go outside
Let's play tag…
I'll go hide

My hands are cold, my nose is froze
My nose is runny and I look funny!
It's my favorite time of day
Time for hot chocolate, I pray!

Audra Zaman, Grade 6
Conemaugh Township Area Intermediate School

Hershey Park

On my way to Hershey Park,
My sister spotted the parking lot.
Couldn't wait to get some candy
But my dad said I could not.

When my dad wasn't looking,
I went off on my own.
I went looking for a stand,
Thought I heard a moan.

Holding my cotton candy,
I'm looking all around.
A stranger tries to talk to me,
But I don't make a sound.

When I got away —
From that weird stranger
I was really crying,
I thought I was in danger.

Finally I saw my mom and dad,
Over by the merry-go-round.
At last I was feeling happy,
'Cause I didn't have to keep looking around.

Benjamin Nogueras, Grade 5
Hamilton Elementary School

Montana

Come to Glacier Park see all the sights.
You will become so bright.
Black Bear, Grizzly Bear what more could you want?
Plains of flowers all around.
Can't believe there could be so many on the ground.
Water falls so high they almost reach the sky.

Scott Mealey, Grade 5
Immaculate Conception School

Secret Hunting
There are many secrets just waiting to be discovered. Yet you can't reveal their vivid wonders unless you search for them; but some of them are meant to be left under the surface. You must contain the knowledge to know which to tamper with in order to go "Secret Hunting." If you don't you could make a big mistake!

Kaji Goode, Grade 6
Independence Charter School

Ode to My Hamster
Her fur is as brown as the sweetest chocolate.
Her pudgy black eyes are dark pits of doom.
Her little white belly is a pure white snow pile.
Her sharp claws are weapons of steel.
She loves her yellow ball, spinning like a top.
The little red boot toy where she likes to stay is her fairytale castle.
Her litter box is one of her favorite places to play and she plays in it like it's her most treasured hideout.
She loves her fruit and nut treats shoveling them into her mouth as if they are the sweetest thing on Earth.
She pops out of my hands like she is a fugitive running from the cops.
She talks and stares as if she was hypnotized.
She digs in her food dish spewing out a mountain of food.
She bathes like she is fixing her hair for someone important.
She is so athletic and boxes with her sister, fighting like they're in a boxing ring.
Scraping the bars on her cage.
She eats the paint until her teeth turn yellow.
She also enjoys eating the bedding like it was some sort of treat.
My hamster is like no other.
She is sweet like the chocolate and never is bad.
I love my hamster and she loves me.

Madeleine O'Neil, Grade 6
St Sebastian Elementary School

Summer
The flowers burst into a beautiful array of color.
The trees open their buds, some releasing a peaceful aroma.
Birds, magnificent, the word that describes these creatures.
The sun casts a crimson shadow on the darkening sky as it sinks below the hilly horizon.

David Mark Hedinger, Grade 6
Chalutzim Academy

I Remember
I remember when my soccer team went to Cape May.
I remember the time my soccer team won the league championship.
I remember the first time I made the Parkland United primer soccer team.
I remember the time my soccer team got killed at Hempfield and played team ranked in the top 5.
I remember the time my soccer team beat my brother's team at Iron Lakes.
I remember the time when my soccer team pushed the coaches into the pool.
I hope I can remember all these memories.

Steven Guetzlaff, Grade 5
Schnecksville School

Football
Football is fun, the glory of falling in the mud, it's funny flipping around on a cold fall day, your heart beats so fast when you come out of the tunnel, and the crowd cheering, and the music loud, you feel like butterflies are in your stomach when you knock someone down, and when they look back at you like "what just hit me", after you get back there and do it again and when you get knocked down you just get back up, the pressure of a blitz you have to throw it fast before you get sacked, or else your coach is really mad you look up at the scoreboard and you're down by seven you have to keep trying even if you're dying.

Blake Hodder, Grade 6
Neil Armstrong Middle School

Friends Forever

Friends last forever,
They never let you down,
And they always make sure that your frown is upside down!
They're there when times are glad,
They're there when times are sad,
They were even there when those times were bad.
So it doesn't matter how far you may be apart,
You'll know they'll always be in your heart.

Rebecca Casner, Grade 6
Strodes Mills Middle School

Untitled

Moisture, seeping up through the ground
Soaking the leaves
Clothes damp, actually soaking wet
Like the Atlantic fell on them
Leaves walking down the street
Trailing water behind them
As they're blowing
Down and down until they come to an end
Where tornados are growing
Making leaves arouse
Just because the scent of food is here
And smelling great
But as they're disappearing
Sadness is growing, such a disappointing sight to see
Trees crying, flooding ground around them
Because the sight of their children going
Wiping tears with the wind as their handkerchief

Morgan Wambold, Grade 5
Franklin Elementary School

Ode to the Penguins

They're black,
As the sky at night,
Eating the fish,
That they love so much,
Waddling everywhere they go,
When they get tired they'll slide on their bellies,
Males sitting on the egg both day and night,
Swimming as fast as they can go,
Kind of like mini-submarines,
Shivering in the winter cold,
Feels like it will never be summer,
Sitting in huddles to stay warm,
They're used to the freezing temperatures,
And even more to the snow,
Dreaming of splashing in the water once more,
They're funny looking to most of us,
With their chubby bellies,
Looking like a plum,
Eating fish all day long.

Nick Rittle, Grade 6
St Sebastian Elementary School

Cats

As amusing as a story that makes you smile,
As contented as a clown that makes you laugh,
As playful as a bouncy ball,
Are my friends that are special to me.

Aleksahdra Lilic, Grade 4
St Francis of Assisi School

Dreaming

Dreaming is a happy thing
And you never know what it will bring

Sometimes you dream of marshmallows and candy
Sometimes you dream of a beach oh so sandy

In San Francisco or LA
In a boat, or by a bay
You can dream

Every person can dream, anytime, anywhere
Dreaming is in everyone, everywhere

Ericka Clayton, Grade 6
St Ann Elementary School

Rain

Some people like rain, but I think it's a pain.
You play outside and the sky is wide and then,
It starts to rain.
It rains and rains but it doesn't reach the drain,
and it starts to flood and makes mud.
I don't know why some people like the rain,
and that's the pain.

Daniel Henry, Grade 6
West Allegheny Middle School

Pink

Pink tastes like yummy cotton candy at a county fair,
delicious strawberry ice cream melting on a hot summer day,
and sweet bubblegum popping after I just blew a bubble.

Pink smells like freshly cut grass on a warm spring day,
hot tea on a cold winter night,
and tulips in a newly planted garden.

Pink sounds like happy voices at a party,
a butterfly's wings gently flapping through the air,
and water slowly rippling down a stream.

Pink feels like velvet pillows after playing in the snow,
the happiness after you win a game,
and an energetic rabbit hopping through a garden.

Pink looks like Easter eggs scattered around the yard,
roses in a glass vase,
and wet tulips shimmering in the sun after a rain.

Elke Hess, Grade 4
Indian Lane Elementary School

TV Blues
I have the no TV blues.
Moving pictures are no more
I'm down to doing chores.

My brain's not mush.
And everything's a hush,
With the no TV blues.

Cartoons are nowhere to be found.
I want to track them with a hound.

I'm grounded from the TV.
Because of messy me.

I lay here upon my bed.
With my hands on my head,
Because of the no TV blues.

That big dark screen is calling my name.
I wish I didn't put myself in shame.
Janine Krench, Grade 6
H Austin Snyder Elementary School

Little Red Tulip
Many tulips,
But just one stands alone
Watching, waiting.
Taylor Jones, Grade 5
Pocopson Elementary School

Feelings
Happiness
Happy, Cheerful
Loving, Caring, Smiling
Thoughtfulness, Pleasure, Pain, Hurt
Crying, Moping, Sobbing
Quiet, Unhappy
Sadness
Adrienne Blice, Grade 5
Our Lady of Grace Elementary School

Spring
Flowers, flowers blooming everywhere.
So many for us to share.
Spring, spring is full of sun.
It gives us more time to have fun.
Bees buzzing in the flowers.
Trying to avoid April showers.
Kids can now play outside.
And there are lots of bikes to ride.
You may be able to fly your kite.
But keep it in sight.
Birds are flying from their nest.
I think springtime is the best!
Megan McCloskey, Grade 4
McDonald Elementary School

Sports
Rookie
young, inexperienced
growing, thirsting, maturing
strikeouts, errors, doubles, home runs
hitting, fielding, leading
MVP, athletic
Superstar
Dan Saunders, Grade 5
East Stroudsburg Elementary School

Planets
Planets
Magnificent, colorful
Revolving, rotating, orbiting
Traveling through space slowly
Solar System
Jesus Varrone, Grade 5
Penn-Kidder Campus

Lightning
The laughter of rain
when thunder is in shame
A lantern in the sky
Kind of looks like a firefly.
A streak of light
so quick it's out of sight.
A mix between yellow and gold
whichever you choose, makes it bold.
Lightning fills me with fear
because I know it might be near.
But that doesn't mean you should run
staring at lightning is quite fun.
Tyler Martin, Grade 5
Rolling Hills Elementary School

Wolves
Gray wolves
race along hills
in the spring's bright colors
while pups prance clumsily with them
through grass.
Amanda Hooker, Grade 6
Bedford Middle School

Cold/Hot
Cold
frigid, nippy
freezing, cooling, icing
playful, frosty, fiery, toasty
burning, sweating, scorching
sunny, humid
Hot
Andrew James Crawford, Grade 5
Claysville Elementary School

I Am
I am a kid
I am a student
I am a sister
I am a daughter
I am a niece
I am a grandchild
But most of all I am Sara Leach
Sara Leach, Grade 5
Jenkintown Elementary School

Koolkat Kallishia
K oolcat
A lways active
L oving
L aughing all the time
I am loyal
S weet
H igh on life
I n the room
A lways watching TV
Kallishia Joseph, Grade 5
East Stroudsburg Elementary School

Brian's Winter
Great Hunter,
Lonely boy,
One hatchet,
Excellent book.
Colton Hewitt, Grade 6
Grasse Elementary School

Colors
Yellow is for the sun so bright
White is the color of the light
Pink is a girl's favorite dress
Green cafe food looks like a mess
Silver is the color of bells
Gold is for royal wells
Red tells us apples are ripe
Black are a zebra's stripes
Blue jays fly
Brown is for the color of rye.

Colors are wonderful!
Rachel Sew, Grade 5
Cheswick Christian Academy

Disappointment
Disappointment is pale gray
It tastes like moldy cheese
It smells like rotten eggs.
It feels like spider webs
It sounds like people crying
It looks like hearts are breaking.
Olivia Fye, Grade 4
Fairview Elementary School

Here Comes Winter

I look up at the trees
I see leaves falling
like twirling ballerinas,
tumbling gymnasts,
or candy falling from a piñata
I feel like a snowman
with cold air sending chills down my spine
my nose is as rosy red
as Rudolph's nose
the wind whips at a frightening speed
like a tornado
I sit quietly and hear the wind
pebbles moving when children walk by
branches smacking together
like claps of hands
I hear ooo's from the wind
whispering in my ear
here comes winter

Jennifer Brown, Grade 5
Lower Salford Elementary School

Amazing Flowers

Red, white, blue, pink as roses.
Flying petals on a spring day.
Love brings them all together into a violet.
Outside you will see me looking at all the flowers.
White as melted marshmallows.
Eight amazing Lilies around the sun.
Roses as red as blood.
Sunflowers seem to attract people by their beauty.
All the amazing flowers are here, there, everywhere so go look.

Cara Camesi, Grade 4
South Park Elementary Center

Dragons

Breathing streaks of blue fire
Anyone caught, their situation dire
Poisonous fangs the size of a pen
Eats young children, women and men

Hoards treasure in a cave
If you're caught and live you'll be their slave
Lives in mountains, oceans and the rain forest
The ones who survive are the best

Giant creatures from the north, west, south and east
Anything they catch will be an excellent feast
Tails with huge knife like spikes
The only ones who can defeat them are brave knights

Stealing damsels in distress
If you fight them it'll be a mess
Glowing eyes that pierce the night sky
1000 years until they die

Brandon Griggs, Grade 6
Bridle Path Elementary School

Ode to Excuses

Don't tell me your cat ate your homework;
And your spelling words went down the drain;
That you can't decipher your math work;
Because it got soaked in the rain.

I'm not buying excuses;
I have my own crisis right now.
It will kill me to have to say this, but;
I left the day plan at home.

Erica Michel, Grade 6
Sacred Heart Elementary School

Red

Red is the color of hunger.
Red is the smell of fresh pizza.
Red is the taste of ketchup.
Red is the sight of fire crackling over the log.
Red is your face after you mess up.
Red is like the lava of a mountain calling you.
And finally it's the rosy red city of Redsville.

Ashrith Balakumar, Grade 5
Peebles Elementary School

Walking Tall

I was walking tall
down the hall
at the mall
my friends were frightened
because I talk funny with my braces on

Walking tall is something brave
especially when your mouth is full of metal
and your smile's weird
it is really hard to be brave
when I wake up and feel like a geek with braces

Dan Park, Grade 5
Mount Jewett Elementary School

Oreo Ice Cream

I like eating ice cream,
It tastes really good and it is not steamy.
Ice cream is real cool,
So when you eat it do not drool.

Ice cream is one of my favorite foods,
My favorite kind is Oreo,
Oreo ice cream looks like the earth,
The white vanilla is the water and the brown Oreo is the land.

When I eat it I feel real special,
I feel like I'm in food heaven,
When I eat it, it is creamy like a mouth full of whipped cream.

Gregory Dongilli, Grade 6
St Valentine Elementary School

My Dearest Pumpkin
My dearest round pumpkin,
Which is usually round,
Has grown up from deep in the ground.

My dearest stout pumpkin,
I picked it myself.

My dearest carved pumpkin,
I carved it myself.

My dearest hollow pumpkin
I'm touching the sticky inside.

My dearest old pumpkin,
I think it has died.

I'm using it now
As a scarecrow's head.

Oh, my dearest round pumpkin
I miss it so.

But papa said there's always a day,
When you have to let go.
Gabriella Porri, Grade 4
Lionville Elementary School

Fat Kangaroo
There once was a big fat kangaroo
He is covered in sloppy goo
He always had a break
So he ate steak
And he is located at the Pittsburgh zoo.
Jake Paff, Grade 4
Avonworth Elementary School

All Be Free
The way I see we are not free.
People walking down the street.
Seeing the true me, you are afraid.
Your mom told you not to judge
a book by its cover,
So why do you judge?
Look into my eyes,
So you can see what I see.
Just so we can be free.
Will Biggs, Grade 6
West Allegheny Middle School

China
Mountainous, radiant
Misting, relaxing, amazing
"China is so majestic"
The great wall
William E. Chapin III, Grade 5
Penn-Kidder Campus

My Messy Locker
My messy locker is like a quest. A quest for the items you seek.
I tried to find my pencil. I did it for a week.
I tried to look for my homework. I looked and looked and looked.
But all I found was my old chapter book.
One day I showed my friend my locker.
He said that it looks likes a tornado hit. Books everywhere.
I still can't find my pencil. Maybe it's…wait, where?
Kaleb Nix, Grade 5
East Stroudsburg Elementary School

The Girl and the White Horses
Quietly lurking through the shadows
Making little ripples in the water
The moon shines down on their soft white fur

When out of nowhere there came a sound
Not just any sound but a soft whisper.
Like the whisper of a little girl.
She said, "Come here I won't hurt you,"
and in her hand were carrots.

It was dark yet the horses saw the girl and she saw the white horses.
She loved horses very much.
She took a step closer and the horses stood still
and then she took a few more and then she could touch one's mane.

She fed a carrot to each one and hopped on one and rode into the dark night.
Just her and the white horses, they became good friends.
Just her and the white horses.
Danielle Gehr, Grade 6
Locust Grove Mennonite School

Ode to Soccer
The ball raises high almost out of sight.
The team in their ocean blue uniforms.
A smile on our face,
And eyes set on the goal.
Laughing, smiling, having a good time.
While we pass the ball and make the score even.
Running back to our places spirits high.
The wind blowing through our hair,
And the sun beating on our necks.
The whistle is blown and everyone
runs toward it like a pack of wolves.
Growling and grunting to get
To the ball and dash down the field.
Almost as if we are flying because my feet barely touched the ground.
We make a great shot but not good enough
The whistle is blown and the game has ended
Yes we lost but we never gave up that is the important part.
This determined, delightful and defensive game has
Something about it that causes sheer enjoyment to the participant.
Meghan Donegan, Grade 6
Hershey Middle School

The Christmas Tree

We all went looking for the perfect Christmas tree.
I found the right one, and my eyes filled with glee.
Then I yelled to my family to come take a look.
We all agreed it resembled one from a storybook.
My father and brother had to cut the tree down.
Both dropped to the floor and started sawing to town!
As my mother and I watched them do so,
We giggled and murmured and hoped it would snow.
When they were done cutting the trunk,
We took it inside avoiding the junk.
Ornaments, tags, and bows crowded the floor,
We could barely even open the door.
We lifted it up with all the strength we still had,
Wishing and hoping we'd always be glad.
My brother and Dad put the flamboyant lights on.
Then favorite bulbs were added by me and my mom.
At last it was done, and with a great sigh,
We all said "voila" as we turned out the lights.

Stephanie Miller, Grade 6
Connoquenessing Elementary School

Christmas

Christmas is full of cheer,
Church bells ringing you can hear.
Children happy, very glad,
Giving presents to Mom and Dad.

Children sledding in the snow,
Having fun, down they go!
Carolers sing outside the door,
Songs of Christmas we've heard before.

Christmas is full of love.
It comes swiftly from above.
Seeing presents under the tree,
Fills the children full of glee.

Families come to gather round,
Love and joy fill up the towns.
The snow falls down from hazy skies,
There is peace and joy, and no one cries.

Isaac Watson, Grade 6
Portersville Christian School

Odious/Respect

Odious
hateful, rude
disgusting, gruff, sickening
indignant, hypocrite, honorable, kindness
enlightening, caring, cooperating
dignified, loyalty
Respect

James Lewis, Grade 6
St Sebastian Elementary School

The Beach

The beach is breezy, blue, and cool
Swimming and splashing in the surf
Sculpting sandcastles in the hot sand
White-capped waves washing our cares away
Sunny days scorch our skin
Finding shells in the salty sand
Umbrellas on the beach look like a box of colorful candy
The rolling rhythm of the tides freely flow
Walking on the warm sand
Feeling the sand between your toes

Victoria Sarver, Grade 6
Neil Armstrong Middle School

Moving

The year 2000 was the year we moved,
To a new neighborhood, new and improved.
New neighbors and friends to lighten the load,
We're easily found on Militia Hill Rd.

The house was built by my Uncle Kevin,
A beautiful place for a family of seven.
I have my own room for me and me only.
Which sometimes is fun and other times lonely.

Switching schools can be hard you see,
But not when you go to OLMC.
New friends I have met and come to adore,
It's more than I could ever have hoped for.

Our house is a greenhouse so open and bright,
With lots of great windows to let in the light.
This house is now a home, filled with happiness and love,
Just like the heavens up above.

Megan Oczkowski, Grade 6
Our Lady of Mount Carmel School

The Burning Building

Red is a flame of a burning building,
Orange the sun glaring down on the fire.
Blue is the sky above the burning house,
Green is the grass outside,
Pink are the cheeks of the nervous family running outside,
Black's the ash of the building after the fire,
What would you do?

Laken Henry, Grade 4
Bushkill Elementary School

Spring Is in the Air

Spring is the best time of year
The flowers are blooming and the birds are singing
The sun is shining and the sky is clear
Once you see those things you know spring is near
All the animals are grazing, and the wind is blowing
The water in the creek is so loud you can hear it flowing.

Katie George, Grade 6
Sacred Heart of Jesus School

The Great Depression

In 1929,
The faces were looking for places.
Looking, searching for empty spaces.
The Great Depression's coming.

They don't want it to come near,
But they all know it's here, it's here.
Broke, fearful, and scared.
People losing hair.

They try to fight,
They try for the pin,
They even try to steal the win.
It's over, it's over, thankfully, they cheer,
It's over!

Tyler Siegrist, Grade 5
Wexford Elementary School

Water and Soda Pop

Water
Blue, clear
Washing, drinking, gurgling
H_2O, ocean, cold, Sprite
Bubbling, fizzing, sparkling
Carbonated, frothy
Soda pop

Jimmy Barbuto, Grade 5
Our Lady of Grace Elementary School

Aircraft Carrier

Aircraft Carrier
Very big
Floating airfield, transport
Part of a battle group
Warship

Thomas Blackburn, Grade 4
Hereford Elementary School

How a Plant Grows

From earth and seed a plant
will grow.
Some in rain
some in snow
Many will bear food
to eat.
From earth and seed
a plant will grow.
Many trees will give
us beautiful autumn leaves.
While others give us oxygen to breathe.
From earth and seed a
plant will grow!

Breanna Malburg, Grade 4
Concord Elementary School

Amanda

Amanda
Athletic, talkative
Dribbling, dancing, pitching
Good sport player
"Mandy"

Amanda Hess, Grade 5
St Francis of Assisi School

Army

A merica
R eal dangerous
M onstrous tanks
Y elling

William O'Rangers, Grade 4
Manoa Elementary School

Harley Arly

Harley
Playful, suspicious
Running, playing, learning tricks
He's man's best friend
Arly

Dakota Becerra, Grade 5
East Stroudsburg Elementary School

Goalies

Protecting the goal line,
wearing goalie gloves, giving
their all and going all different
ways at once.

Zachary Hamilton, Grade 6
Allison Park Elementary School

The Fire

You can hear the fire roaring,
Trying to snap at someone like me.
It is popping and glistening,
Can it really, possibly be?

That the red, hot flames,
Could burn you to the stake?
You can hear its screeching pain,
When you douse it with the lake.

Ashley Hennon, Grade 5
Bermudian Springs Middle School

Right and Wrong

Right
Agreeable, suitable
Rewarding, enlightening, surprising
Correct, true, disagreeable, mistaken
Misguiding, misleading, unexpecting
Incorrect, unlawful
Wrong

Megan Roseman, Grade 5
Penn-Kidder Campus

The Horrible Day

There once was a boy named Nick
Who went in the woods and got a tick
He had an ache
Because he licked a snake
And now he is very sick.

Nicholas Horton, Grade 5
Mount Jewett Elementary School

Flower

As sweet as the smell of honey
Some you can eat
As pretty as a sun tan
They sway like grass on a windy day
As colorful as a rainbow
Their seeds blow away in the wind
As beautiful as a butterfly

Alexandra Hathorn, Grade 5
Jenkintown Elementary School

Honey

Honey is sweet just like Pete.
Honey is good like you should be.
Honey is sticky, sticky as can be.
Honey is healthy for you.
Honey is made by bees.
Honey comes from hives.
The hives are in a small building.
Honey, honey, honey.

Allen Wilson, Grade 6
Strodes Mills Middle School

Homework

Homework is a drag,
I would rather play it-tag.
All the tests are on the same side,
so I hope we get a study guide.
The teachers always give too much,
thinking goes on and on and such.
If I don't get a break,
my head will start to ache.
I hope that we won't get a lot,
if we do I'll hire a robot.
Once I start it I want to stop,
I would much rather shop.
There's so much math,
I might as well do it in the bath.
I could just watch tv,
but I have homework it just has to be.
There's always so many problems to do,
I wish I was sick with the flu.
If we didn't have any ever again,
I could always hang out with my friends.

Cosi Jackson, Grade 6
Neil Armstrong Middle School

The NFL Playoffs

The playoffs are today, today is do or die,
If you win you move on, if you lose you say good bye.

The Steelers beat the Bengals who didn't play very rough,
Next they play the Colts who are supposed to be tough.

On 4th and 1 kick a field goal, don't take a gamble,
If you don't make it the defense will ramble.

There is one second left and you're going for a hail Mary,
You go to throw and it is caught by your friend Larry.

It's the playoffs bring all you have because it's now or never,
And if you win the Super Bowl you'll be remembered forever.

Adam Dodson, Grade 6
Neil Armstrong Middle School

Tears

Tears are undecided,
I may cry because I am sad.
I shed tears that fall off my face
like the rain falls from the sky on a rainy day.

I may cry because I am happy.
Then the tears symbolize joy
in something that I see or do.

Sometimes I cry due to laughter.
I laugh as much as a 4 year old in a candy shop.

No matter what feeling I feel,
tears are undecided,
they are unexpected,
neither you nor I can hold them back,
without tears you can show almost no emotion.
Tears are beautiful in all ways.

Cheyenne Winley, Grade 5
East Stroudsburg Elementary School

Checker Pieces

Red and black, usually round
Move to the other side
Checkers is the game
It's a zig-zag ride

24 pieces in all
People have various skills
Jump your opponent as much as you can
It can be a thrill

Have a watchful eye
So your pieces don't get taken away
When you get across the board
"King Me" is what you can say

Elizabeth Blosky, Grade 6
St Maria Goretti School

Friends

Hanging out at the mall
Playing your favorite sport basketball
Having parties everywhere
You always play "truth or dare"

Writing letters every day
You always have something to say
Helping you with homework
Your other friend is becoming a jerk

Now this friend is the very best
She always helps you with the important test
Friends help you all the time
It is never a crime

Stephanie Hetrick, Grade 5
Westmont Hilltop Middle School

Fall Has Arrived

leaves skipping on the ground
wind blowing my hair
kids screaming like it is the end of the world
sun is shining through the trees
leaves blowing around like tornados
summer is gone
fall has arrived
rocks getting kicked like soccer balls
leaves crunched up like shells
on a sunny beach day
birds chirping
leaves dropping to the ground like rain drops
in slow motion
red
yellow
orange
leaves blowing in the air
trying to jump back
onto their branches
before the wind blows them
away from their home

Sydney Pienkowski, Grade 5
Lower Salford Elementary School

Thanksgiving Dinner

You say grace then everyone digs in
The turkey is scrumptious the lobster is great
The slice of steaming pumpkin pie on your plate
Your dog begs for food and you sneak him some stuffing
The mashed potatoes are everything but still on your plate
Mixed vegetables are devoured and gravy is gone
Dishes get washed and you feel really full
It's dark outside and you watch the football game
Later you sleep in your bed

Matthew Bair, Grade 5
Southside Elementary School

The Guardian Moon
Mountains standing tall
Against the clear, cloudless sky
The moon watching them
Steven Silverman, Grade 5
Pocopson Elementary School

100 Grand
May I,
have another
crispy, crunchy, chewy,
milky delight chocolate bar?
Yummy!
Alexis Snock, Grade 4
Stackpole Elementary School

Rain
Rain drops are
reflections of distant
memories.
Falling,
falling,
falling,
then finally hitting the ground —
splash.
Then they form a puddle —
a mirror showing your memories,
your fears,
your hopes,
your dreams,
all in one single moment:
then it all just
fades away,
never to be seen
again.
Caitlin McKenna, Grade 6
Mount Nittany Middle School

Christmas
Christmas
Lights gleaming
So many presents
Under the glowing tree

Celebration
Michelle Acker, Grade 6
McKinley Elementary School

Austin
A lot of fun
U sually crazy
S ometimes mean
T alented in football
I ndependent
N ice
Austin Pahel, Grade 4
East End Elementary School

Grandpa
Poppop
Loving, caring
Rest in peace
Sadness, anger, loss, emotional
The old man
Kaylen Policino, Grade 5
Rhawnhurst School

Spring
The final traces,
Of winter, slipping away.
Spring has come at last.
All the birds are back,
From their winter vacation.
Their song fills the air.

The clouds miss the cold,
And cry down torrents of rain,
So strong buds wake up.

Buds age to flowers,
With colors of the rainbow,
That wave in spring breeze.
Brandon McCracken, Grade 6
West Allegheny Middle School

In My Little World of Wonders
In my little world of wonders,
It hardly ever thunders,
The dogs say neigh,
And the horses say hey,
The wind never whips,
And the paper never rips,
The leaves never fall,
No one ever runs in the hall,
The planet is square,
All the animals share,
Everyone can hear,
No one drinks beer,
It's never in blunders,
In my little world of wonders.
Bethany Herb, Grade 5
East Stroudsburg Elementary School

Winter vs Summer
summer
hot, sunny
swimming, playing, picnicing
sun, beach, ice, snow
skating, skiing, sledding
white, cold
winter
Zakary Kubala, Grade 6
California K-8 School

It's a Bird
It's a bird
here it comes,
tweet,
tweet,
flap,
flap,
swish,
swosh,
boom!
O no!!!
It hit a tree!
Thomas Siegrist, Grade 5
Wexford Elementary School

A Living Machine
A light gray shark with teeth so sharp,
Sits on my counter and opens cans up.
I place in his mouth a giant tuna,
He tears it open so I can begin to feast.
Just like a good old fashioned beast.
Joseph Bello, Grade 6
Neil Armstrong Middle School

My Dog
My dog is the best
I love my dog so very much
My dog is so nice,
But she runs up in the woods
Nadja Kathrina Bryant, Grade 4
Fishing Creek Elementary School

Let Me In
Boy, it's bitter.
Can't see my litter,
'Cause all these flitters of snow.
Mom, let me in from the snow!
I've got to get bolder
'Cause now it's getting colder.
Mom, let me in from the snow!
I'm sittin' on a tire.
Wish I had a fire.
Mom, let me in from the snow!
Mom lost the key.
I'd rather pay a fee.
Than sit out here in the snow!
Abby Caviston, Grade 5
St Ann School

I Love Winter
I love winter.
What I like best,
Is all the snow just lays in rest.
I love winter with its sparkling snow.
I just wonder where does it all go?
Claire Grazioli, Grade 4
St Leo School

Advice from a Teacher…

Dear friend,
Don't judge a book by its cover.
Treat everybody equally.
Be respectful and they will be respectful back.
A book may be thick but it still has a heart.
Do good things and something good will come back to you.
Take the world as it comes.
Everybody's different no one is like you.
Try and do your best.
Never give up.

Brianna Higginbottom, Grade 5
Robeson Elementary School

Orange

Orange is the sunset and citrus and it is warm and soft.
Orange is the taste of hot chicken noodle soup.
Peppers and fall smell orange.
Smoky fires make me feel orange.
Orange is the sound of Country music and kicking a soccer ball.
Orange is the beach, my house, and my bedroom.
The soccer field is orange.
Sand in your toes is also orange.
Orange is like winning a challenging soccer tournament.

Alexandra Simon, Grade 5
McMurray Elementary School

Ch Lo

Ch Lo
Friendly, intelligent, curious, kind
Daughter of Lori
Lover of my mom, clarinet, math
Who feels happy, encouraged, determined
Who fears heights, bugs, thunder
Who would like to see Florida, California, my teacher do a flip
Resident of Tulip Circle Ephrata
Miller

Chloe Miller, Grade 5
Clay Elementary School

Snow

Snow is as soft as a feather and tastes like water,
But is as cold as ice.
Snow is a white blanket covering the earth.
It brings joy to some hearts but not to others.
You hear and see many things when it's snowing.
You hear children laughing when snow is flying,
And plows and snow blowers plowing through the heavy snow.
Oh how I wonder where it came from,
No less how it's made.
You can only see it in the winter,
And that's why winter is some people's favorites.
Oh, I love the snow.

Morgan Berry, Grade 6
Our Lady of Mount Carmel School

Valentine's Day

It's coming! It's coming! Run away!
It is almost Valentine's Day!
Close that window! Lock that door!
If you want safety, wait! There's more!
Don't want a kiss?
They can aim but they'll miss.
I don't want a mushy valentine.
I don't want to see the words "you're mine."
So hurry! Hurry! Run away!
It is almost Valentine's Day.

Patrick Hislop, Grade 4
St. Anastasia School

Summer

The air is warm,
and full of the scent of freshly cut grass.

Kids play baseball and football,
with bloody noses and sweat running down their faces.

It's a perfect day for a picnic,
under a tall tree in the park.

Go to the beach and feel the sand in your toes,
swim, surf, build a sandcastle, fly a kite, throw a frisbee.

Eat juicy red watermelon,
and get a popsicle from the ice-cream man.

Camp in the woods and pitch a tent,
smell the smoky campfire with toasted marshmallows.

Catch fireflies,
and see them glow in a jar.

But summer will end,
and you will have to go back to school.

Nick Cvetic, Grade 6
Neil Armstrong Middle School

Skipping Rocks

A sunny day
I went to the pond.
It was a breezy time in May.
I sat by the pond.
The rocks were all long.

The pond was glistening.
I picked up a small and long rock.
I tried to skip it.
It made a plop and squirted me.
I tried again, the same thing happened.
When I was about to give up, the pond stopped moving.
I tried it again, and it worked.

Meaghan Bogush, Grade 5
Brecknock Elementary School

Love

My love for you is very strong
So please don't go I have one song
My sweetie pie but if you have to go
Just tell me that you love me so
I'll be happy in my soul
If you tell me that you love me so

Emmie Leed, Grade 6
H Austin Snyder Elementary School

A Meadow

Wisping trees tall grass.
Big bright flowers, tall oak trees.
A peaceful quiet place.

Bradley Dierolf, Grade 4
Marlborough Elementary School

Newborn Seed

I will look through my past
that will never last

As I'm leaving all the things behind
I try to get things off my mind

It will never be the same
No friends calling my name

Deep in my heart
The feelings are getting apart

I look at myself in the mirror
Which reflects back with a tear

But I must proceed
Like a newborn seed

I want to fly high
Knowing everyone's under the same sky

Heejung Koh, Grade 6
Sacred Heart Elementary School

Poland

P artitioned
Sl **O** vic
Meta **L** making
W **A** rsaw
Mi **N** ers
Worl **D** War II

Tara Rakiewicz, Grade 6
Our Mother of Perpetual Help School

Friday Football

Football on Fridays
is fun because you
fight furiously for first.

Kyle McLaughlin, Grade 6
Allison Park Elementary School

Chinchillas

Chinchillas jumping in the fields oh, how wonderful!
They're eating tulips and doing whatever they want to do.
Thousands of chinchillas, mostly different colors.
They're gray, they're white, and some are even black velvet.
They are soft and furry, but I don't ever want to wear one as a coat!

Daniel Bortle, Grade 6
H Austin Snyder Elementary School

One for the Thumb

In the year 2006
The Steelers when to the Super Bowl.
They were playing the Seahawks.
They wanted a win for Jerome Bettis and a ring for their thumbs.

All the fans cheered when they stepped on the field
They fought and they fought
and for all their hard work
They had a lead going into the fourth

After 15 minutes it was clear…
The Steelers won! The Steelers won!
Hines Ward MVP;
They got one for the thumb

Nathan Murslack, Grade 5
Wexford Elementary School

Purple…

Purple flower, purple candy, purple backpack, purple room.
It is the sound of the ocean on a warm sunny day,
outdoors on a fall morning, hip-hop on a summer night,
and sizzles like little pop rocks.
It is the taste of wet grapes after it had rained, dull like dry paint,
salty like board walk fries, and sweet like a candy bar.
Purple feels like soft sheets under the night skies,
like a fuzzy scarf on a cold day, sticky piles of candy on Easter Morning.
Purple can paint my room, sing a great song,
Purple can cheer you up on a rainy day, and color a wide rainbow.
Purple cannot be green.

Chelsea Miller, Grade 6
Chambersburg Area Middle School

Victoria Serrano

Victoria
Funny, nice, cool, Puerto Rican
Daughter of Keisha and Armando
Lover of dancing, art, and R+B
Who feels bored on Mondays, happy on Fridays, and playful on Saturdays
Who finds happiness shopping, and playing outside
Who needs an advance in allowance and a puppy
Who gives my baby brother hugs and friends confidence
Who fears spiders, bears, and wasps
Who would like to see Chris Brown and Bow Wow in person
Who enjoys jumping rope, roller-skating, and shopping
Serrano

Victoria Serrano, Grade 5
East Stroudsburg Elementary School

Charging for Home

Smack!
"Go, Dani"
"Whooo!"
Here comes first,
Already at second,
Making my way to third,
Charging for home!
Other team throwing the ball in, trying to beat me there.
Before I knew it, I had crossed the plate!
"Way to go Dani!"
"High five"
"Good job"
"Great homer!"

Danielle Leidig, Grade 6
Chambersburg Area Middle School

Braces

When I was getting my braces
I was so scared
I hoped I'd have a miracle like
Something exploding in there.

Everyone would be evacuated
From the burning building,
I already knew that
It was never happening.

Awhile later, they called my name
And lead me to the chair.
They poked my mouth with a wire
So they certainly didn't care.

After they put in my braces
My teeth were sore for days.
My parents told me to take care of my teeth
For they still had a lot to pay.

Over the five months with my braces
I had a huge fit,
But after I got my braces out
It was all worth it.

Johanna Arias, Grade 5
Hamilton Elementary School

Sun

The sun is bright.
It makes you want to eat ice alright.
When the water runs down your chin
it will make you want to shiver thin.
Go get that hat so rays will not beam on your face.
Florida is a hot place.
The sun is not cool
because it tries to break all the cool rules.
So when you see the sun go jump in the pool.

Deazia Hutson, Grade 5
Urban League of Pittsburgh Charter School

Life in America

A cold breeze passing
You feel the joy and peace in your heart
In the air the taste of a fresh apple with juice filling your thirst
Bells ringing in your ear
The feel of freedom to not be ruled
A crisp smell of being alive
Happiness and laughter filling the streets
Then each moment you know
That old lives are ending but new ones are just beginning

Sydney Abrams, Grade 4
Benchmark School

The World to Me

You are the world to me
You are the only one my eyes love to see

You are the only person I can trust
So please never leave unless you absolutely must

Whenever I see you, it brightens up my day,
I feel so alone when you are far away

When I see you, my problems just drift off somewhere
And the world does not at all seem unfair

Please don't ever leave, oh, can't you see
Because you, yes you, are the world to me.

Brooke Warner, Grade 6
Sacred Heart Elementary School

Life Is Good and So Is Candy

Ah, so
Creamy candy
Vanilla alongside
Chocolate all at the
Same time
Hershey's

Andrew Knox, Grade 4
Stackpole Elementary School

Don't Give Up

If you fall
Don't give up
If you try and nothing's right
Don't give up
If you've tried, try harder
And one day you will succeed, but if you don't
Don't give up
Don't give up on your dreams
Don't give up on yourself
Whatever you do
DON'T GIVE UP

Vanessa Jimenez, Grade 4
Avon Grove Intermediate School

Water

Water rolling down the creek,
It was beautiful so to speak.
Splashing, sparkling down the hill,
Going down past the mill.

Fished living in a stream,
Swimming, singing like a dream.
Oh, how I love the summer days,
Listening, whistling in many ways.

So much fun it would be,
To go swimming by the sea.
Soon, sunny days are at an end,
Like water flowing around the bend.
Sydney Kauffman, Grade 5
Bermudian Springs Middle School

Pickle Party

Yummy pickles,
so tempting,
want to,
eat them,
not allowed,
so mad,
oh well,
sneak away,
all gone,
yum yum.
Laci Turfitt, Grade 6
Grasse Elementary School

Hot/Cold

Hot!
Warm, Torrid
Scorching, searing, sizzling
Angry, fierce, indifferent, hard-hearted
Freezing, chilling, frosting
Icy, frozen
Cold.
Jonathan Knab, Grade 4
Beaver County Christian School

Thumper

Thumper is a rabbit.
He's very cute indeed.
Though he has a habit
Of scratching his fleas.

On days that it rains
He stays in his house.
Oh yeah, he's litter box trained
And he might be afraid of a mouse!
Elise Pura, Grade 4
St Leo School

California

Come to California for some food,
Yummy, Yummy!
Even go to the beaches.
Come to Hollywood,
See some famous stars!
There's also…
Disneyland!
Come on, come on,
What are you waiting for?
Come to California, don't wait too long!
What are you waiting for?
Jennifer Benoit, Grade 5
Immaculate Conception School

Saddam/Respect

Saddam
Vicious, cruel
Combating, fighting, unrelenting
Iraq, bombs, heaven, angels
Calming, loving, accommodating
Good, natured, kind
Respect
Mike Sieber, Grade 6
St Sebastian Elementary School

The Hot Corner

They call it the hot corner,
I really don't know why,
Batter's up,
"Hit, hit!" the crowd calls,
"Catch the ball!" the coach calls,
Hear the crack,
Move so fast,
Move like lightning,
To first,
To second,
You get the two,
You won the game,
You walk off in glory,
You know that's third base,
And that's where you belong.
Curtis Weston, Grade 6
Strodes Mills Middle School

Christmas

C ookies are being made
H ot cocoa we drink
R eindeer on the housetop
I cicles on the tree
S anta Claus on his sleigh
T ons of snow in the house
M illions of presents all over the world
A ngel on the treetop
S tove is working overtime.
Kayla Woolley, Grade 4
Bushkill Elementary School

Ode to Sailing

Sailing is soft, and swift.
A trained sea glider,
A sense of peaceful travel.
A kiss of salty air,
A splash from the water.
The rocking,
The mainsail,
Catches the wind,
Like a child catches a butterfly.
An almost invisible tranquilizer.
When the sea gets rough…
The calm breaks.
Using all your force,
To steer into the right direction.
Switching positions from side to side.
Beginning to gain power,
Began to also gain speed,
Feels like you are flying.
Then the boat takes an,
Unexpected turn to capsize.
Sailing is scary and suspenseful.
Sarah Preston, Grade 6
Hershey Middle School

Flying Squirrel

There was an old Albino squirrel,
Who loved to go through trash.
He had red eyes and white fur,
But when he flew he crashed.

He landed on a black squirrel,
He landed on a bank,
He landed on a shed,
He even landed on poor Frank.

He didn't hurt the black squirrel,
He didn't hurt the bank,
He didn't hurt the shed,
But he killed poor old Frank.
Emma Cassidy, Grade 6
Haverford Middle School

Mustangs

Small fast,
Tough gritty,
Good racers,
Last long,
Very special,
Multiple colors,
Mean sounding,
Nice looking.
Mustangs
Ridge Foltz, Grade 6
Grasse Elementary School

Sharing

I have shared everything with you
I will never forget those memories with just me and you
Do you remember all those times?
And I really thought you were mine

All the times we had shared
Disappeared into thin air
How could disappear so fast?
Have you never remembered the past?

Sharing all those moments together
Planning to be friends forever
You said you loved me whatever I do
But maybe that was not really you

How could you leave me behind?
Because now I have to get you out of my mind
Every time I think of you I start to cry
You did not even say good-bye

Radhika Bajaj, Grade 6
St Francis Xavier Elementary School

Holocaust Victim

H ow far will they go
O h I don't want to know
L asting forever going on and on
O r stopping tonight and getting it done
C an't help but complain
A ching back, aching pain
U nder the watch of Nazis' eye
S o hard to be strong when you just want to cry
T he Lord will watch over me night and day

V ictims being chosen every which way
I n my heart I know there is hope
C hasing dreams may be hard but I know I can cope
T he option of giving up is not allowed
I n the end, I'll stand tall and proud
M y life will be long, and very renowned

Karli Coppens, Grade 6
Chambersburg Area Middle School

Storm

Thunder beat, in the sky.
Rain tapped upon the roof,
Lightning cracked.
Waves in the bay crashed upon the dock
Winds of the hurricane whistled around
The rushing river pulled itself up and over the banks.
Then, it all stopped,
Life was silent,
Until tomorrow's storm.

Lauren Miller, Grade 4
Avon Grove Intermediate School

The Story of Larry

There was a boy who was all alone,
If he had a name it was unknown.
Him still being alive was so incredible
For to everyone else he was practically invisible.
He wanted to be recognized by at least a few people,
And treated like a celebrity and not a cripple.

The thought of him being noticed was nonsense,
Unless he stood up in his defense.
So in front of a crowd he ate something highly hypoxic,
But he showed the world it was really nontoxic.
Now he is known and has been given a name,
His name is Larry, which means brave and tame.

Megan Mortensen, Grade 5
Edgeworth Elementary School

Wishes

My wishes are as deep as my heart.
They come and go when my family doesn't care.
I have to think of new wishes to start.
My wishes are grand until I decide to share.

Nichelle Bauernfeind, Grade 6
Freedom Area Middle School

Most Fantastic Me

I'm as strong as a gorilla beating a tiger.
I have brown hair like the shiny mud.
I have eyes like the golden desert.
I'm as good at passing in soccer as a bear is at climbing trees.
I'm as great at throwing a football as a tiger is great at running.
My bouncy ball collection is as huge as an elephant.

Marcello Mastromarco, Grade 4
Stackpole Elementary School

A Joyful Christmas

C hrist was born on Christmas day
H ot cocoa's on the table
R acing down a snowy hill
I see candles in the window
S tockings are hung by the fire
T ests are over for the holidays
M any gifts are under my tree
A n angel is on my Christmas tree
S eeing gifts everywhere on Christmas day.

Noel Mangino, Grade 4
Bushkill Elementary School

Spring

S is for swimming.
P is for pretty spring has sprung.
R is for ring around the flowers.
I is for Irish flowers.
N is for the nice things that my teacher does.
G is for the things that God does for all of us.

Jennifer Merithew, Grade 4
Daniel J Flood Elementary School

Spring
Spring is very happy fun,
Said the flower to me,
Everyone is happy,
Even the willow tree!

The willow tree is always sad,
His leaves are hanging down,
He never gets to grow so tall,
To try to see the town!

But now he is so joyful,
Like a bird with flapping wings,
The forest is so happy,
And it's all because of spring!
Brenna Diehl, Grade 4
McDonald Elementary School

Fun in the Sun
Spring is a wonderful day
The flowers come out in May
Now go and celebrate
Or go roller-skate
To have a fun day and play.

There are warm winds
That love to sing
When we go to the park
We hear the fireworks spark
The winds are like spring bling.

Today I saw the sun,
I had so much fun.
Humming bird are everywhere,
Giving flowers love and care.
Jenna Galuska, Grade 4
Avonworth Elementary School

Snow
When it snows or begins to sleet,
You can hear the children's feet.
As they play in the snow,
You can see their faces glow.

The snow is like a great white sheet,
Softly falls and hits the street.
Snowflakes are diamond drops that fly,
Like crystals falling from the sky.
Zach Stroup, Grade 5
Bermudian Springs Middle School

Sun
The sun rising up
Like a yellow scrambled egg
Waking the surface
Grace Brandstetter, Grade 5
McMurray Elementary School

Christmas
Plop! Plop! Plop!
Snow falls down
as I jump out of bed.
Thump! Thump! Thump!
Running down the stairs.
I reach the tree.
Rip! Crumble!
Presents torn open.
Excitement unleashed!
Woo hoo! Yeah!
Celebration, elation.
Yawwwn, snooore
we lie in the rubble.
Alex Barndollar, Grade 6
Neil Armstrong Middle School

Colors
Red as the bow on my head
Pink is the color of my bed

Green as the grass on the ground
Orange as my basketball that is round

White as the clouds in the sky
Blue is where the birds fly high

Black as the night
Yellow as the stars so bright
Jennifer Gereshenski, Grade 6
Moss Side Middle School

Snow
Cold, gleaming,
Swishing, flaking, freezing
Wet, slippery, light, shiny
Blistering, swirling, blowing
Melting, watery
Snow
Megan Wynings, Grade 4
Memorial Elementary School

Almost Brown
It is like an old penny

A worn out book
Makes me feel sad
Like a penny without any friends.
A bronze
Medal in the Olympics.

A burnt piece of wood
Almost brown.
Edward Goldhill, Grade 5
Jenkintown Elementary School

First Things First
First the dinner, then the ice cream
First the whisper, then the scream
First things First
First the winter, then the mittens
First the cat, then the kittens
First things First
First the car, then the key
That's the way it had to be
First things First
Kelsey Donahoo, Grade 5
Claysville Elementary School

Love
Once you find true love,
Don't play or gamble with it.
Just hang on real tight.
PJ Tatano, Grade 6
Allison Park Elementary School

Poconos
I love to go to Poconos
We own a house up there
We go up for vacation
It's so much fun
In the sun
There's a pool
And there's a lake too
My dogs love to swim in the lakes
I love to go kayaking too
So much fun in the summer
Kacy Edelmayer, Grade 6
Grasse Elementary School

Spring, Fun!
Spring is so much fun,
Just playing in the sun
Going swimming in the pool,
Or just relaxing all cool
No school, isn't that great?
So every night we stay up late
Spring is so much fun,
So enjoy it, it's all most done!
Lance Johnson, Grade 6
West Allegheny Middle School

Friend
There's a silver flash
Hidden in the trees
The wolf glares at you
But he isn't fierce
He's injured you see
Give him some care
Soon, you'll have a friend
He's one that'll stay
Trisha Harper-Brown, Grade 6
H Austin Snyder Elementary School

My Tomb

The wind weeps,
the floor creaks,
I awake in the cold nothingness of my tomb,
where I creep down the halls,
and where there are padded walls,
My tomb is where I live,
where the sorrow that I give.

Forester McDonald, Grade 6
West Allegheny Middle School

My Dog Ben

My dog's name is Ben and he's as big as a horse.
His fur is not soft it is very coarse.
He is still a puppy but you would never know.
He's never tired. He's always on the go.
He likes to play the game of tug of war.
He always wins that's for sure.
He tries to play with my cat Cole.
But he finds out quick cats rule.
sometimes he's bad and starts to whine,
But I'd never give him up he's all mine.

Cassandra Cush, Grade 4
Immaculate Conception School

The Little Lemonade Girl

Alex was the name of a little girl
who once had black, cute hair with curls.
She had Leukemia a type of cancer.
They were searching for a cure but found no answer.

She thought and she thought of a way,
to raise money soon someday.
"A Lemonade Stand that's it!
I'll raise money bit by bit."

She sold lemonade about twelve dozen.
Her friends and family bought it, even her cousin.
She raised about five million dollars,
after that she had lots of callers.

She was brave and true
but who knew?
She had changed the world
just one girl.

Annie Rodden, Grade 5
Villa Maria Academy Lower School

I See

I see frozen ice ready for me to take the first step on it.
It is the air that I breathe.
It is my passion to take place between the red pipes.
It is the love of the game.
I try my best every game to get a win.
I see the ice rink.

Robbie Stock, Grade 5
Schnecksville School

The Pacific Ocean

I'm the Pacific Ocean, salty and blue
Where boats float and fish glide smooth and true
People swim along with the waves,
While seagulls fly above and crave:
The sandwiches, crackers, and snacks
That mom and dad decided to pack
The crabs, lobsters hunt on my sand
While little kids struggle to stand
I'm on the west coast,
And it's hard not to boast:
Ha, ha, ha I'm the biggest ocean in the world
I'm always getting twirled by the moon
It's almost high tide soon
Tide pools are what I create,
When not a creature is awake
I'm the parent of rivers,
Who are just little slivers to me
Some people get the shivers
When sharks swim near the rim
Of the boat that they're in.

I'm the Pacific Ocean, salty and blue.

Nicholas Bonsignore Jr., Grade 4
General Nash Elementary School

Don't You Just Love Spring Floating in the Air?

Flowers growing everywhere.
Clouds floating in the air.
Kids hug their teddy bears.
Don't you just love spring floating in the air?

Butterflies fly about,
They will fly in and out,
Everything is growing with care,
Don't you just love spring floating in the air?

Spring is blooming
Clouds are booming
A garden in a shape of a square
Don't you just love spring floating in the air?

Hannah Lapiska, Grade 4
Avonworth Elementary School

Fig Newton

Is it a cookie or a cake? My teacher asked me.
I don't know I answered, but it tastes good with tea.
It's gooey on the inside and soft cake on the out,
My mom gives it to me when I put on a pout.
It's a fruity little treat and is shaped like a square,
If I don't eat one every day I act like a bear.
Is it a cookie or a cake? I'm not sure,
But once you take a bite, you'll love it I can reassure.

Justin Stover, Grade 4
Watsontown Elementary School

First Time on a Plane

Went for a ride on an airplane —
It was my first time.
Thought the plane was going to crash —
I was really nervous.

There were people all around me,
No one seems to care
That we had to put our seat belts on,
When we took off in the air.

As the plane is taking off
The sound hurts my ears.
My mom told me to suck on a lollipop,
So then I forgot my fears.

After the plane has taken off,
We're in the middle of the air.
I was feeling O.K. and calm
And then I was scared.

Finally the plane had landed,
We're ready to get off.
I really enjoyed riding it
I want to go again.

Ryan Frey, Grade 5
Hamilton Elementary School

Odyssey

Odyssey is a journey
beyond your wildest dream.
Odyssey is nice
you know what I mean.
All I want to say is
an odyssey is a big, big dream.

Amirah Grasty, Grade 6
Independence Charter School

Matthew

M onster at basketball
A good friend
T errific
T hankful
H ates chicken stirfry
E ats pizza
W inner

Tony Bowers, Grade 4
St Sebastian Elementary School

The Bad Dictator

There once was a bad dictator
Who did not like Ralph Nader.
He hated his guts
Because he ate chestnuts
And he would destroy him later.

Brett DiCello, Grade 5
McMurray Elementary School

Listening to Noise

Listening is very important, you can learn a lot of things,
if you listen closely you can even hear a bird sing.
When you walk out the front door,
noises from all over lead you to what you live for.
Noises can teach you a lot of things you didn't know before,
like planets and even more.
Listening to noise can take you anywhere if you just imagine.
Noise is precious, and there are many noises to listen to.
You can even make noise with a little tap tap with your shoe.
Without noise the world would be silent, you don't want that do you?

Lauren Perry, Grade 5
Brecknock Elementary School

Nebula

A beautiful nebula is shining like a beacon of light in a cold, dark world.
Flashing its colors like a bird of paradise.
While I hear comets racing by,
I feel the cold, dark emptiness of space behind me.
But I feel at home,
As the nebula turns into an ocean of cold, fresh water.
As soon as I touched the water,
It turned into a beautiful flower.

Eric Guaracino, Grade 4
Lionville Elementary School

Winter

Is winter fun to you?
It's my favorite season of all
Days off from school, and snowboarding
Freezing cold weather and playing with my friends is what I like to do

Sledding down the hill
Faster and faster we go
Enjoying every minute in the cold wet snow
Hated by many and loved by few, I love winter isn't it fun to you?

Lauren Barrett, Grade 6
Freedom Area Middle School

The River

Winding down the mountainside is a river.
It has been there for as long as I can remember.
Its bottom is made out of tiny pebbles,
glittering in the sun.
Its waters are crystal clear and as cool as an ice cube.
The sun filters through the trees,
letting its light brighten the world.
Flowers line the river's banks,
opening their faces to the sun.
Rabbits hop nearby and a hedgehog peers from its home.
A majestic buck and his family come to drink,
bending their great heads down for dainty sips.
This is my river. It has been here for as long as I can remember.

Natasha McCandless, Grade 5
Easterly Parkway Elementary School

Nature

N ature is a beautiful sight
A nimals live here
T igers and bears eat here
U nderground habitats for animals
R ain falls here
E xquisite place for humans and animals.

Hunter Phelan, Grade 5
Wharton Elementary School

Depressed

Depressed is black.
It sounds like a groan.
It smells like black tea.
It tastes like plain white popcorn.
It looks like a tear stained face with eyeliner running down.
Depressed is laying with heavy metal blaring in the background.

Amanda Tardiff, Grade 6
Grasse Elementary School

The Best

My mom is nice
So very cool
The best in the world
She really rules
She's super awesome
Very funny
My bestest friend
As sweet as honey
Dinner and dessert, she cooks all
When she's in the room, I'm having a ball
I love her and she loves me
Because we are family

Johana Barxha, Grade 5
Rhawnhurst School

All About Me

My hair is as brown as the bark on a tree.
My eyes are as brown as coffee beans.
I'm as tall and skinny as a pine tree.
In karate, I can defend myself like a lioness defends her cubs.
I can jump as fast as a cheetah can run.
I can gobble up information like a hungry bear cub.

Danielle Cusumano, Grade 4
Stackpole Elementary School

Summer

S wimming in the sun
U npacking the suitcases from vacation
M aking time to read a book
M aking friends at summer camp
E ating ice cream in the summer to stay cool
R iding my bike in the park

Caprice Tarallo, Grade 4
Immaculate Conception School

Shirley Temple

Who is the girl with sparkling eyes?
Whose singing and dancing take the prize?
She was a star at only three,
The youngest person on TV!

Her talent shown out pure and simple.
And every smile displayed a dimple.
Princess or orphan she could play,
To cheering fans both night and day.

Her name was praised up to the skies,
Her day would start before sunrise.
Shirley Temple could truly be,
The greatest star in history.

Taryn McFadden, Grade 5
Villa Maria Academy Lower School

Spring

Spring is fun
Spring is great
It's something to appreciate
It's warm
And breezy
Also sometimes sneezy
But still fun to run in the spring sun
With the tulips, daisies, pansies
And all the other spring flowers
Spring is fun
Spring is something to appreciate
It comes once a year and is a time of cheer!

Nicole Procell, Grade 6
Newtown Elementary School

I Made a Mistake

I went downstairs to bake a cake
I made a mistake and baked a snake

I went to the library to get some books
I made a mistake and came back with some looks

I went in my closet to get my coat
I made a mistake and pulled out a goat

I went to my room to go to bed
I made a mistake and bumped my head

I hit the ball to run some bases
I made a mistake and broke my braces

I went to the dentist to pull my teeth
I made a mistake and went to a thief

I went in my kitchen to get a snack
I made a mistake and ripped my hat

Josh Josephs, Grade 5
Newtown Elementary School

Fall

Fall is coming. Maple trees with their
big bright wings glistening in the wind.
Fall is coming.
All the beautiful leaves coming.
Fall is coming.

Eamon Trebilcock, Grade 6
West Allegheny Middle School

Basketball

Basketball
Dribble, shoot
That's a dunk
He shot a three
Swish

Brock Adams, Grade 6
Freedom Area Middle School

Puppies

Jumping playfully
All around the living room
Barking and screeching
Puppies prancing everywhere
I stare into a wild blur!

Claudia Erb, Grade 5
East Union Intermediate Center

Lou

There once was a guy named Lou
Who really hated his shoe
When his toe stuck out
He started to shout
And now he and his shoe are through

Randy Ginkel, Grade 5
Mount Jewett Elementary School

Fun on Ice!

Ice skating is really fun,
It is better than being in the sun.

Twists and twirls,
Spirals and jumps,
Skates on, skates off,
Finally a triple Lutz.

Ice shows, competitions,
And much, much more,
It's a lot of work,
But the reward is gold!

Ice skating is really cool,
Glitz and glam, spotlight too,
It is fun for me and everyone.

Katie Pavlick, Grade 4
Media Childrens House Montessori

Someone

I am 10
I am a student
I am a learner
I am flesh and bones connected
I am a maze with no end
I am a book on a shelf of many to pick
I am someone

Calvin Steinhauer, Grade 5
Jenkintown Elementary School

A Flower

I am a flower who was small
Every day my petals are smooth
When the wind blows you smell
My sweet scent of roses
When in the winter my petals fall off
All I am is a lonely stem.

Mackenzie McGurgan, Grade 6
Freedom Area Middle School

Seasons

Spring is almost gone,
Leaving winter in the past.
Summer will be here soon,
Days are going by so fast.

I can't wait to get out of school,
Swimming, running, summer fun.
Jumping in the freezing pool,
Playing in the blazing sun.

But soon enough,
Summer will leave,
Bringing fall into sight.
Now I'll play in leaves instead,
Everything's lookin' quite all right!

Emily Pia, Grade 6
West Allegheny Middle School

Summer

no **S** chool
f **U** n
freedo **M**
riding **M** y bike
fri **E** nds
th **R** ee on three hockey

Chris Hughes, Grade 6
West Allegheny Middle School

The First Day of Spring

The first day of spring
Geese are coming back today
Other birds are making way
Landing back on the water's spray

Andy Matson, Grade 5
Pocopson Elementary School

Parent

Parent
Peaceful, funny
Loving, caring, protecting
My parents are funny
People

Brandon Dumas, Grade 5
Penn-Kidder Campus

The Project

Bubble gum,
delicious fun,
big project,
girls crazy,
science project,
due tomorrow,
not finished,
messy table,
many papers,
scattered around,
no more
room, no
more time,
running yelling,
screaming fighting,
finally done,
now time,
to run.

Victoria Garner, Grade 6
Grasse Elementary School

Infinity

A pitch-black cat
With golden rings;
It isn't Halloween,
But he doesn't care.
His sleek fur tuxedo
And deep crimson eyes
Tell you his gift
Of immortality.
He speaks to those
Who are unafraid:
"Take me home,
For I am Infinity."

Becca Dohmen, Grade 6
H Austin Snyder Elementary School

Beast Feast

There once was a big old beast.
He terribly wanted a feast.
He had some turkey.
And then beef jerky.
He didn't want to move in the least.

Abigail Sims, Grade 4
Avonworth Elementary School

Remembering the Children*

A land of dirt roads and fertile soil,
  where homes are made of brick
  and people eat sweet potatoes.

You maybe have been a farmer
  who works all day in the hot sun,
  a miner who digs all day looking for graphite,
  or a merchant who tries to succeed at selling goods.

I will finish all the food on my plate,
  as I remember you.

Zach Midgett, Grade 6
Deibler Elementary School
*In remembrance of the children in Madagascar.

Stars

I watch the stars,
Thinking how far away they are,
Just staying there full of gas.
I gaze out there thinking,
That there must be some other life form,
Out there just waiting for us to discover it.
I thought about what it would be like,
If I was the first person on the moon.
I would be just standing there,
Amazed and proud at the same time.
I would think that it would be so much fun,
Just to stick the United States flag in the moon.
All of that just happened when I looked out my window.

Alexis Harman, Grade 5
Shafer Elementary School

Santa's Elves

Elf
Making gifts
Working for Santa
Living at the cold North Pole
Small

Ryan Ciocco, Grade 4
Cathedral School of St Catharine of Siena

Givin' Some Back

I'm giving some back to Mom,
She helps me with it all.
I'm giving some back to Dad,
He teaches me how to play ball.
I'm giving some back to Connor,
He plays football with me.
I'm giving some back to Mat,
He shows me how good best friends can be.
I'm giving some back to Grandma,
She helps me when mom's not around.
And I'm giving some back to Pap,
He picks me up when I am down.

Taylor Williams, Grade 6
Haine Middle School

The Sky

The sky has many colors and shades.
Black, pink, yellow: colors the sky holds.
Sometimes I look up at the sky
And wonder if its magnificence ever ends.
I imagine myself lying on one of those giant puffy clouds.
Then getting up and jumping from one cloud to the next.
I come back to Earth relaxed and undisturbed by other things.
I looked out my window, up at the sky and its colors
And I thought to myself, "I was there!"
And I think, "Thank you God who made the sky!"

Ari Chernoff, Grade 6
Chalutzim Academy

Your Dream Could Be

Your dream could be to do something amazing
To invent something new
To stop world hunger
Or just to do something for you
To become a singer or maybe an actress
Or to model the prettiest dress
Whatever your dream is, make it come true
The world would be a better place
With that special dream by you

Kelsie Kidner, Grade 5
Boyce Middle School

Winter

Winter, the cold, crisp air.
Sheets of fluffy white snow cover the ground.
Christmas and Hanukkah, presents all around.
"WHOOSH!" Sledding down a huge hill.
"Slurp, Slurp!" Gulping down delicious hot chocolate.
Cuddling under a blanket reading your favorite book.
Winter comes and winter goes.
The sun comes out.
Spring is here.
Fall follows summer.
I can't wait for winter to return.

Shelby L. Gallant, Grade 5
Rolling Hills Elementary School

Chocolate Bars

I will smile, I will not frown.
When I eat a chocolate bar that's brown.
My food sounds like a crunch.
You must eat them in a BUNCH!!
If you eat them, you get hyper.
They taste better than a windshield wiper.
It is very delicious candy.
It can come in very handy.
Chocolate bars are the best.
If I don't get my chocolate, I'm a pest.

Emily Willow, Grade 4
Watsontown Elementary School

Harry Potter

Lived with his aunt and uncle, until something happened that changed his life.
He was going to Hogwarts School of Witchcraft and Wizardry,
The wizard world was dangerous because people wanted to kill him with knives.

His first year there was a mess, he almost got killed by a dark wizard.
The stone was destroyed but all for the best, then he left Hogwarts for the year.

During his second year he got trapped, in a dark and mysterious chamber.
He had to fight a monster in a place that was unmapped, he succeeded and returned to Hogwarts after a horrible summer.

His third year he left his house and ran away, he met his godfather.
Together they defeated a deatheater, he was once again victorious and left Hogwarts to return the next year.

Dark and dangerous things flooded his life in his fourth year, someone was murdered and others cursed.
Everyone shed many tears, after his emotional stay he left to return with no clue of what would happen.

In his fifth year he lost such a great friend, there was a vicious battle in which people got hurt.
The headmaster wanted to see Harry yet Harry did not want to attend, he waited for his destiny which was ravenous.

Kira Vander Lippe, Grade 6
Freedom Area Middle School

My Dog, Mago

```
m                                          s t friend
 a                                        e speedy barkative
  g                                      b shoelace lover super pup
   o pit bull pet her bite playful puppy wet nose kiss Labrador retriever five weeks old
   love jumpy lovable sleepy cute tiny brown white nippy dog
    Chihuahua fun fussy out door top dog run monkey carrot lover happy
     scary trick master cage dangers not really
        m       m       m       m
        a       a       a       a
        g       g       g       g
        o       o       o       o
```

William Jarrett, Grade 5
East Stroudsburg Elementary School

Independence

Independence means to me the idea of being free
Why I think slavery is bad is because it makes a person very sad
I just don't understand how a human being can be sold to another man
If you believe in slavery you do not believe we should be treated equally
Slave owner's idea of a great day is to make their slaves work for very little pay
In the fields slaves work all day which gives them very little time to play
Deep in their eyes you can see their sadness; how could our nation have been part of this madness!
Abraham Lincoln is a hero you see, he was responsible for the slaves being set free
He took on this fight many years ago which caused the fight for freedom to grow
I would have been on his side you see; I am so against the idea of slavery
My idea of doing some good would be to help free every slave I could
I'd go from house to house you see fighting to free every slave I see
At this time slavery is not seen at all because it is against the law
I am so glad to live in our country where people are treated equally
How lucky we all should feel to live in a country where freedom is such a big deal!
When I think what God would want life for us to be I'm sure He would want every person to be free

Taylar Boeh, Grade 4
St Alexis School

Daybreak

I feel the warm sunbeams on my face.
I hear cute little birds chirping on the living room window.
I smell mommy cooking a delicious breakfast.
I taste a toasty waffle dunked in syrup.
I see my peppy little dog begging to go outside.

Tessa Kerpan, Grade 4
Colonial Elementary School

My Guitar Talks to Me

As I thrash through songs,
With heavy distortion,
My guitar speaks to me.
It says, "Play longer. Don't stop,
Play me until your fingers bleed.
Play me until your fingers have cracked.
Don't stop. Don't quit."
As if in a trance, I keep on playing.
As I sit there, I sometimes forget that I am playing.
Then my brother comes downstairs, and finds me
Sitting there, swaying.
He gives me a look like I belong in the cuckoo hut.
But I don't care.
Not one bit.
He doesn't understand
What type of a stage I'm in.
So I keep on playing.
I'll play 'till I die.
Then I'll get up and play some more.

Thomas Austin Detrick, Grade 5
East Stroudsburg Elementary School

My Favorite Animal

My favorite animal is a rabbit,
For them eating carrots is a habit.
Rabbits are very cute and furry,
But always seem to be in a hurry.
To be a rabbit would be fun,
Just hopping around in the hot, hot sun.
Rabbits are a great gift to get,
Especially if you want to give your kid the perfect pet.
For rabbits it is easy to hear,
Because they have such long ears.
Rabbits are cute and cuddly,
They're the best pet for anybody.
They're very easy to take care of,
All they need is a lot of love.
A baby rabbit is called a bunny,
Remember never to feed them sugar and honey.
Rabbits like to join other rabbits in races,
The best part about rabbits are their cute faces.
The best name for a rabbit is Hoppy,
Some rabbits ears are long and floppy.

Christine D'Agostino, Grade 6
Sacred Heart of Jesus School

Narnia

Numerous creatures everywhere
Aslan the king is always there
Read all 7 books to find more about it
New rulers are kind to all the animals and creatures
Icy cold mountains are beyond the land of Narnia
Aslan is a good loyal lion and protects the new land of Narnia

Elizabeth Sprowls, Grade 6
California K-8 School

Bear Scare

There once was a boy named Gary,
Who thought going to sleep was scary,
He woke in the night,
With quite a fright,
'Cause he thought he saw something hairy.

Gina Cassel, Grade 4
Marlborough Elementary School

Wars in the World

Wars are happening everywhere
In Iraq or here or there.

Wars are happening everywhere
Some people watch, some people stare.

Wars are happening everywhere
Try to watch them if you dare.

People are lying on the ground
You are the only living thing around.

You walk to school and there's a fight
You run away in terror and fright.

You get home and your mom greets you
Then you wake up and that nightmare leaves you.

Hannah Strauch, Grade 6
Strodes Mills Middle School

Families

Families are good companions through and through,
They give us love and happiness, too.

They help me when I need assistance,
They encourage me to have persistence.

Families are for love and sharing,
My family is full of caring.

My family is there when I'm down,
They turn my frowns upside down.

They love me in each and every way,
I love them more every day.

Jayme Gorham, Grade 5
East Union Intermediate Center

Books

Books are the color of a rainbow
Books feel like a soft paper
Books taste like paper
Books smell like plastic
Books look like a colorful rainbow
Books sound like the ocean.

Tori Chen, Grade 5
Rhawnhurst School

Summer

The summer is warm
I play outside every day
I love the summer.

Patrick Laudenbach, Grade 4
Bushkill Elementary School

Animals

Animals, animals everywhere,
some are big
and some are small,
some are short
and some are tall,
some are mean
and some are nice,
some have spots
and some don't,
some are black
and some are white,
some eat meat
and some eat plants,
all of these animals
are different, they are
all unique in a way
all of them are a part of
God's creation.

Leah Kucenski, Grade 4
St Leo School

Snowfall

Snow falls from the sky,
Making the ground crisp and white,
Freezing all the land.

Snow is beautiful!
It falls from up in the sky.
Snow is wonderful!

When it's cold outside,
Icy snow falls to the ground,
Making the land white.

Snow falls to the ground
Not having the slightest sound.
You know, winter's come!

Isabel Nelson, Grade 4
Sacred Heart School

Blue

Blue is like the calmness of the sea,
It's the juicy sweet berries that can be eaten right off the branch.
Indigo is the dew-filled petals of a bluebell plant.
See the cloudless sky over the rolling hills and valleys.
I hear a wolf cry in the blue bathed forest of the moon.
Feel the cool seaside breeze against your face.
Blue is the emptiness of the space around you.
Smell the ocean foam spraying across your cheeks.
Blue is playful, yet serious.
It's friendly, yet lonely.
It's joyful, yet gloomy.
Blue is the sympathetic eyes of an infant waiting for a hug.
It's like the endless summer evenings,
Like the days that never end.

Tessa Peoples, Grade 6
Southern Lehigh Middle School

Do You Ever Wonder?

Do you ever wonder what life can be when you do nothing but watch TV?
Do you ever wonder what life can be?
The life that Dr. King never got a chance to see.
Do you ever wonder what life can be if segregation was still what it used to be?
Do you ever wonder why life is like it is today?
People getting killed almost every day.
Well, I do wonder all of those things.
But I wonder how life really is going to be,
In the next year or three.
How life will change you and me.

Petrina-Kenya McFarlane, Grade 4
The Laboratory Charter School of Communication and Languages

Chat Mode

I just got the download now I'm on chat mode.
Thank God it's free I can't pay the fee.
Receives and sends chatting with my friends.
I typed so many messages my fingers were on fire.
Sizzle sizzle sizzle I'm burning up my wire.
Faces in the AOL spaces
Happy, kissing, cool, mad, money mouth, embarrassed, and sad.
Oh no it froze please don't doze.
A day without IM is like a wingless plane or a legless Great Dane.
Hey it's back up now I can get a hookup.
Whose on, is it guitar geek or boomboomcazoom?
Now I've got to sign off got to take off.

Ty Crowley, Grade 6
Mount Nittany Middle School

Christmas

Presents under the tree
Family and friends knock on your door and say "Merry Christmas"
The fresh baked cookies smell glides across your nose
The delightful taste of my grandmother's chicken noodle soup
Having lots of fun
Christmas

Brett Cox, Grade 5
Claysville Elementary School

Shamrock Day
As I woke up in the morn,
It was St. Patrick's Day.
Outside there was a rainbow,
I went out to follow it.
I went through the forest and some trees.
Do you know what I see?
A leprechaun with a pot of gold.
I came up very close,
very quiet like a mouse.
It spotted me!
And the rainbow began to fade.
The leprechaun disappeared.
Next time I'll get the gold.
Happy Shamrock Day!

Rhianna Dupla, Grade 4
Easterly Parkway Elementary School

Summer
Summer, summer warm and hot, going swimming.
Summer, summer having fun, playing, riding bikes
In the summer, summer.

Mary Maule, Grade 4
Avon Grove Intermediate School

Ballet
B eautiful, beloved, breathtaking, is what I think of ballet
A n art of which I have great passion for
L ong hours of pain that in the end really pays off
L ove is the only thing I have for this art
E verything, ballet is everything to me
T ough, ballet isn't all beauty it's lots of hard work!

Jayme Kerr, Grade 6
West Allegheny Middle School

Disregard/Respect
Disregard
uncomplimentary, indifferent
dishonoring, ignored, undeserving
inconsideration, mediocrity, honor, esteem
trusting, reputed, honor
respective, regarding
Respect

Darren Markewinski, Grade 6
St Sebastian Elementary School

Love
Love is deep, deep, deep, it's dark and always sweet.
Love is better, love is humbling.
Love is not hitting and leaving marks.
Love is red roses that stay alive.
Love is love that stays in your heart.
Love is forever lasting.
That is what you call
Love

Sha'Nae Gee, Grade 6
Independence Charter School

Dessert
Cupcakes, pie, and ice cream too!
All sorts of icing: pink, green, and blue.
Chocolate covered strawberries,
Cookies and cake!
What other treat could anyone make?
Brownies, fudge, and milkshakes with whipped cream,
How can I eat it all without a whole team?
Desserts, desserts, and none to lose,
But one remaining question…
Which will I choose?

Missy Schrott, Grade 5
Boyce Middle School

My Liege
Under Banners of Zamorak we ride towards the dawn,
Hold your steel close to hand,
And say farewell to your motherland,
Into the horizon lines,
Spears so sharp in daylight shines,
Attack the realms unknown,
Hordes of brave men fully grown,
With winds from our north star,
Striking shores oh so far,
Across the sea and land,
In armor proud we stand,

As northern gods we're born,
Beautiful women for us they mourn,
Baptized in fire and ice,
Sworn to face the stranger's lies,
Sailing the ocean black and blue,
We'll show the world what is true,
When the night comes down,
Another land…Another crown,

Striking upon the hillsides battlefields burning in glory,
Chanting spells of grave rites Battlefields burning in glory.

Garrick Treaster, Grade 6
Strodes Mills Middle School

It's a Garden
A flower first started out as a seed
Then it grows by water and food
Next, it comes out as a leaf

Once later, a string of greenness pulls up
As it pushes up to the sky
Then, it goes higher and higher and higher

Leaves start coming
And veins keep growing
Next thing you know, it's a garden!

Roomel Reese, Grade 5
Urban League of Pittsburgh Charter School

Spring

Spring is here,
Spring is warm,
Spring is like a drowsy breeze
that keeps on rocking,
and rocking,
until the next season starts.
So cool,
So dreamful,
So relaxing,
Just like a video game
that plays
on
and
on.

Krystian Borek, Grade 6
Hillcrest Elementary School

Ode to Nature

A goose is white,
white as snow.
Its eyes, they sparkle,
like a river's flow.
A feather as soft,
as baby's skin.
Its nose as orange,
as a bright orange sunset.
Its eyes as blue,
as the bright day's sky.
Its wings so wonderful,
it can fly.
A goose's foot,
so floppy and wet,
It is very shiny,
really,
I bet.

Alainna Moppin, Grade 4
Washington Heights Elementary School

Candy

Candy, candy
Always so sweet and dandy
The different kinds
Oh, no one minds
The delicious smell of candy

The chocolate bar
You can smell from afar
It will melt in your hand
If you lay on the sand

Lollipops, suckers
Jawbreakers too
If you know any more
Please tell me, do!

Rebecca Rapp, Grade 5
William Penn Elementary School

Football

F undamentals are fun
O rdinary games
O h no! The other team scored
T ennessee is not the best team
B unch of people join the NFL
A lot of fun
L ots of injuries
L ittle bit rough

Brandon King, Grade 5
Wharton Elementary School

Turtles and Cheetah

Turtle
Slow, boring
Walking, swimming, long living
Reptile, tortoise, cat, leopard
Spotted, furious, exciting
Muscular, fast
Cheetah

Anthony Mazzarini, Grade 6
Our Lady of Grace Elementary School

Absurd

A n abrupt idea
B eneath your skull, a
S tupid, crazy,
U nbelievable,
R idiculous thought in your mind,
D eal with it yourself!

Sasha Scherlinsky, Grade 6
Park Forest Middle School

Basketball

B all handling
A game
S kills
K nock-out
E veryday fun
T oss
B askets
A pass
L ove playing
L ay-ups

Emily Staub, Grade 5
East Union Intermediate Center

Blue Waves

Blue waves
wash away sand
on the beach where I lie,
fulfilling all of the great dreams
I seek.

Kacy Blevins, Grade 6
Bedford Middle School

A Clock's Heartbeat

The clock's heartbeat,
Is a steady pulse.
Slowly and quietly,
It takes its time,
To tock.
It's a rhythmic sound,
Every tick says a rhyme.
As it takes the day long time.

Jocelynn Ritchey, Grade 6
Smith Middle School

Happiness

Happiness is purple.
It sounds like children playing.
It smells like summer blossoms.
It tastes like sweet honey.
Happiness looks like a bird singing.
Happiness is a warm feeling.

Caitlin Thompson, Grade 6
West Branch School

Me

I
play
and
talk.

I fish.
I joke.
I laugh.
I cry.

I have friends.
I have bikes.
I sometimes
tell a lie.

Christopher Miller, Grade 4
Fishing Creek Elementary School

Sunny Spring

Spring is here,
It's getting near.
Kites are floating in the air,
Kids are dancing here and there.

Bees are buzzing in your ear.
They give me such a fear,
Easter is getting here,
It is very near,

In spring there are flowers,
Rain is wet like showers.
Butterflies are coming around,
They always land on the ground.

Alexandra Poskey, Grade 4
Avonworth Elementary School

Butterflies Mean Love

The first time I saw you my stomach had butterflies,
And the very being of me crumbled by the looks of your eyes.
As I gaze out my window I see your face,
And I wonder if I'll ever be in your embrace.
There's not even a trace
Of something more perfect than you.
What is it that I can do
To make you like me as much as I like you.

Aaron Brown, Grade 6
H Austin Snyder Elementary School

Me

I usually smile and like good weather.
I have lots of friends who like staying together.
I want to become an engineer,
And I know this dream will stay very near.
I also love my video game.
That didn't have a hard level that came.
Except the level when I put the monster in shame.
I think I'm going to need a key
To unlock these secrets again about me.

Eric Snyder, Grade 5
Bushkill Elementary School

People at Christmas

Santa
Jolly, fat
Giving, eating, caring
Elves, St. Nick, Christ, God
Teaching, loving, preaching
Holy, helpful
Jesus

Anthony Solt, Grade 4
Cathedral School of St Catharine of Siena

It's All About Me…

Maeve Victoria
Who likes to laugh with friends
Works hard to achieve her goals
Believes in being loyal to friends
Tries to be nice
Likes to buy clothes
Often uses purses
Is trying to succeed in her dance lessons
Daydreams about meeting Dakota Fanning
Watches good TV shows and movies
Gets annoyed when she has to do something she doesn't want to
Has a bad habit of biting her nails
Wishes she could not hold grudges
Doesn't understand friends sometimes
Refuses to listen sometimes
Someday hopes to be an actress

Maeve Victoria Haney, Grade 6
St Genevieve School

Blue

Blue is diving in a pool on a hot summer day.
Blue is as sweet as cold refreshing water.
Blue is what wakes you up in the morning.
Blue is smelling outside on a wet, rainy, spring day,
with trees dripping water, and foggy skies.
It looks like ocean waves or the sky.
Blue sounds like wind hitting your ear on a chilly day.

Justin Zweig, Grade 5
Peebles Elementary School

Rainy Day

Like diamonds falling from the sky.
The raindrops keep falling.
The sun just won't come out.
The flowers will not rise.
The grass is not green, even though it's raining hard.
The sky is a gloomy, gray color.
Tick, tap, tick, the raindrops keep falling.
It's too dark to let you see the color, and
Too cold to let you smile.
I finally decide I can no longer waste the day.
So I run outside to play.
I dance, jump, and sing.
The feeling of the raindrops on my finger tips
Are cool but lovely.
The taste of the rain is so sweet and pure.
The gentle whisper of the wind tickles my ear.
I now realize that rainy days are just as beautiful as sunny days.

Ann Bredin, Grade 6
Our Lady of Mount Carmel School

Clouds

Clouds are puffy.
Clouds are like a big pillow.
Clouds are the standards of the sky.
Clouds are soft like a baby's skin.
If I could I would reach up and grab one.
Clouds are multiples.
If there was only one cloud that would be enough for me.
That one cloud shines through my day.

Shaqueena Watkins, Grade 5
Urban League of Pittsburgh Charter School

Spoiled

Some kids are spoiled some aren't.
I'm one of those people that are.
I get whatever I want.
Overall I'm the most spoiled one of them all.
Inside my head I see what I want.
Later I tell her.
Let's go shopping, she'll agree.
Every day of my life I get spoiled more and more.
She calls me her diva all the time.
I think she likes to spoil me.

Mia Iorfido, Grade 6
Freedom Area Middle School

No Friends

I'm a friend that's been forgotten,
A friend that's been left behind,
I'm all the stars above you,
But never in your mind,
It seems I've been forgotten
But is it really true?
I didn't think it'd be this hard
To spend one day with you.

Johnie Bauer, Grade 6
Home School

The Bauldelaires

The Bauldelaire orphans,
are very cunning.
They always figure out their problems.
Are always lurking
around Count Olaf.
Sunny the baby likes to bite.
Klaus likes to read a lot,
Violet the oldest orphan
is the inventor of the three orphans.
Count Olaf is sneaky
Mr. Poe doesn't help
the orphans much.
The Bauldelaire orphans
have been through a lot of
mischievous adventures.
Always have problems with Sunny
getting or biting things
that might harm her like gum.
Mr. Poe gets the criminals
arrested for attempted murder.

Michael-Tae Marks, Grade 6
Freedom Area Middle School

Caring

Caring is bright blushing red.
It tastes like Dad's Rice Krispies.
It smells like white daisy petals.
It feels like soft silk clothes.
It sounds like nature on a beautiful day.
Caring is good luck all year round.

Marisa Taormina, Grade 4
Fairview Elementary School

Steelers

The best
In pro football
Will win the Super Bowl
They will beat the Seahawks
And get one for the thumb

Brady Warner, Grade 5
Portage Area Elementary/Middle School

Ella

Ella Fitzgerald
Brave and talented
Working hard
Singing for the world
Winner, talented

Phillip Bonanni, Grade 5
Shafer Elementary School

Snowflakes

White, beautiful
Freezing, sparkling, drifting
Cold, lacy, deep, frozen
Falling, glimmering, rolling
Snowmen, snowball fights
Snowflakes

Max Taylor, Grade 4
Memorial Elementary School

Ducks

Ducks
are
real
cool

They swim.
We swim
In ponds
In pools

Sometimes
we are
both hilarious
on Mondays.

Catie McCoy, Grade 4
Fishing Creek Elementary School

I Love You Mom and Dad

I love you
and it's true.
You are the best,
although you got me
a brother who is a pest.
You are the best,
for what you do
and that is why
I love you!

Anastasiya Lizunova, Grade 4
Easterly Parkway Elementary School

The Pig

There once was a pig
That thought he could dig.
He's really, really big,
And he liked to do the Irish jig.

Corey Pace, Grade 4
Christ the King School

My Dog

I love my dog,
He is really crazy,
He is black and white,
And oh so lazy,
He sleeps on the floor,
Right next to my bed,
Always waking me up,
By licking my head,
Jack is his name,
I love him so much,
So soft and furry,
And gentle to touch.

Tina Boyanowski, Grade 6
Sacred Heart of Jesus School

Baseball

I
Love to play baseball
At Tri-Township
In the morning
Because baseball is my passion

James Twomey, Grade 5
Newtown Elementary School

S Is for Summer

S is for summer
A very nice season
It's so much fun
You just want to run
And that's a very good reason

Jessica Yachwak, Grade 4
Our Lady of Peace School

Haircut

Dad gave me a haircut.
I looked like a nut.
He didn't mean to shave my head.
When I was sleeping in bed.
This has put me in quite a rut.

Evan Clare, Grade 5
East Stroudsburg Elementary School

The Bored Boy

So here I sit down and lay
Useless as a lump of clay
On an uncomfortable bale of hay
Incredibly wondering with whom to play

For nobody likes to be home bound
So I ran invisibly amongst the ground
While uncovering, guess what I found
All my friends running around!

Luke Otto, Grade 5
Edgeworth Elementary School

Sand

I am the sand,
Large, yet small
I see people play volleyball
In me, I hide all sorts of treasures
Big ones, small ones, ones with all kinds of measures
There are two parts of me, one wet and one dry
One touches water and the other touches sky
I always get sat on, walked on, or crushed
Sometimes this is just too much
But I like being me, I really do
Now the question is do you like being you?
I am the sand,
Large, yet small
Mary Ellen Francis, Grade 4
General Nash Elementary School

Spring

Spring is the newfound bird,
Flying in the wind.
A drop of rain on the window,
That's what spring is.
The rain falls down,
The puddles grow,
And shrink that cold snow.
The graceful bird flies on.
On and on.
Beyond the end of the endless sky,
To show all that spring has arrived.
Adam Wenger, Grade 6
Conemaugh Township Area Intermediate School

What a Baby Does

What a baby does is play with their toes,
scratch their diapers,
and pull nasty disgusting things from their nose.
But when you try to put them to sleep,
all they do is sniffle and peep,
until you go for a walk and come back,
you find them asleep across your backpack.
Kahleah Manigault, Grade 6
Independence Charter School

The Largest Mall in the USA

In Bloomington Minnesota, there is a place,
That attracts people from every age.
There you can buy for all your need.
Furniture, clothes and bikes with 10 speeds

But wait, don't forget about the fun.
An amusement park for everyone.
A Ferris wheel, a roller coaster and more.
Below, an aquarium to explore.

All that and more at the MALL OF AMERICA!!!
Jacob Siry, Grade 5
Immaculate Conception School

The Description of a Young Man

My eyes are as brown as chocolate cake.
My hair is as brown as a rotten banana.
I am as skinny as a stick.
I shoot a basketball like a gun shoots bullets.
I ride my bike as fast as a Ferrari.
I remember where the buttons are on an X-Box controller
Like Einstein remembered his math facts.
Tyler Mensch, Grade 4
Stackpole Elementary School

Spring

Spring season's coming around.
You can feel it all through town.
The summer heat will come and go,
But while it's here go play with Joe.

When it's hot you will sweat,
But playing with squirt guns will make you wet.
Flowers will decide to bloom,
'Til winter comes and brings their doom.

Now, you know spring's really fun.
You just got to remember it's just begun.
Erik Boyer, Grade 6
Conemaugh Township Area Intermediate School

Fall Leaves

Each little leaf is a dancer,
Twirling and twisting off trees.
Sometimes blowing down the street,
The dancing leaves spin in the breeze.

They dance during day and at night,
Sliding, turning like a rock star.
Leaves are sometimes quiet when they twirl,
Spinning and jumping, that's who they are.

If you step on them they will crunch,
In fall they might even be red.
They will twist if there is a breeze,
If they don't dance, they will go to bed.
Bobbi Tyler, Grade 5
Bermudian Springs Middle School

Yesterday

Yesterday I got fired.
I will never forget that day I got fired.
I want to apply to the chocolate factory.
Today is the day of employment.
When I applied the company accepted me as the
General of the factory.
Now I am rich!!!
Edwin N. Dennis Jr., Grade 6
Independence Charter School

Dolly

You stand on my shelf full of dust,
your eyes never move.

Your heart is empty, but you remember,
the times I laced your black shoes.

Your white dress has yellowed,
your eyes no longer blue.

Your rosy cheeks have faded,
and so have me and you.

Porcelain skin, curly brown hair,
and your painted smile, no more.

Now dirty, ragged
and dust galore.

I remember when we were young
and how you made me so happy;

Yet you're still standing there,
meaning nothing to me.

Mary Guarnieri, Grade 6
St Hilary of Poitiers School

Art

Art is messy
Art is fun
Art is awesome
Art is cool
Art is wonderful

Angela Weiler, Grade 5
Clay Elementary School

Animals

Who saw the ducks
    Swim in lots of lakes?
I, said the skunk,
    Eating berry flakes.

Who saw the mountain lion
    eating beef?
I, said the squirrel,
    Good grief!

Angie Delgado, Grade 4
Fishing Creek Elementary School

Skeletons

Skeletons are very bony
Skeletons never have any money

Skeletons always eat each other
Uh OH I ate my brother

Nicole Woomer, Grade 4
All Saints Catholic School

No Limitations to Your Dreams

Always keep an open mind. You can soar if you try.
Make sure your heart is kind. Spread your wings and fly.
If you need a fresh start, get a clean slate. You're free,
    Never close your gate. Be anyone you want to be.
    Let the whole world know you don't limit dreams.
    They are just coming true. They are like the sunbeams.
Follow the footsteps your own way. You've got it grasped tight.
Try to be special every day. And remember, you have a light.
    It can go out, so keep it bright. Be true to who you are.
Never wish you could walk another street. Be yourself and you'll go far.
    Walk 'til the end and there will be new challenges to meet.

Megan King, Grade 4
Media Childrens House Montessori

Christmas

C andy in the stockings; filled so high you cannot see into the fireplace.
H ot chocolate, with lots of marshmallows.
R eindeer on the rooftops.
I cicles hanging from the roofs in my neighborhood.
S now falling from the sky, like the clouds are falling down.
T all trees in the houses.
M oms baking cookies in the kitchen.
A lot of presents piled so high it makes a hole in the roof.
S anta on my roof almost falling in.

Ryan Merritt, Grade 4
Bushkill Elementary School

Christmas

C ookies reaching out for me with their sweet smell
H ear the choirs sing millions of carols
R inging bells fill the air like a crowd screaming a chant
I n the window candles glisten like a star in the night sky
S weet smells bloom in the air like a spring flower
T insel hanging everywhere you can't even see the houses
M erry people filled with love and joy like a bird singing its song
A ttitudes bright and holy like a church on Sunday morning
S trong love fills the air so much it's almost stuffy.

Erick Bittenbender, Grade 4
Bushkill Elementary School

Blue

I love the color blue.
Blueberries can look, taste, and even smell blue.
I don't like getting swimming pool water in my mouth, even if it tastes blue.
Some people say, "you look sad," and others go, "you look blue."
Sometimes the moon light looks as blue as the day sky.
The moon light is the day sky.
My pen's ink looks as blue as blueberry juice.
My pen's ink is blueberry juice.
Maybe the wind could blow the blue and black berries away.
Sometimes the moon can look like it is a flashlight with blue paper over the lens.
Blue just makes me feel good.

Zakkary McGuire, Grade 5
Peebles Elementary School

Oratory

O pens up to anyone willing to talk
R ight on the spot.
A lways adding in an opinion on
T he conversation, no matter what the topic.
O ther people's thoughts about her mouth don't
R eally matter in the slightest.
Y et she keeps going on and on.

Kaitlyn Humberston, Grade 6
Freedom Area Middle School

Summer

Summer is the best season ever
You won't have to worry about school or anything else
All you worry about is FUN!!

Jump in the pool,
Make a splash
Or lay out in the sun and relax

Hang out at the mall
Or mow the yard
Or run outside and jump

The trampoline is so much fun
Just run around in your bikini
And live in your own paradise

Candace Chesnutwood, Grade 6
Conemaugh Township Area Intermediate School

Basketball

Basketball is a fun sport
You dribble up and down the court
When you score they cheer real loud
That always makes you very proud

Having a foul isn't bad
But sometimes it can make you mad
Passing the ball as a group
Can always get it in the hoop

The other team is winning now
But then they get called for a foul
Shooting one on one
You make them and the game is done

Now the score is 11-10
Hopefully we won't have to play them again
Everyone was cheering in the stands
When we went to shake their hands

Now we won it all
And got to sign the game ball

Erin Rodgers, Grade 5
Westmont Hilltop Middle School

Sisters

My sister is such a pain,
Sometimes I think she was dropped by a crane.

My sister is also weird,
It kind of looks like she has a beard.

I wish I could fly my sister on a jet,
All the way to Tibet.

I guess my sister's all right,
But believe me we'll still have another fight.

Jamie Sumner, Grade 4
Beaver County Christian School

Dolphins

Dolphins can be blue, pink, or gray,
Seeing one may happen any time of the day.
Many are found within the bay,
What a beautiful sight to see them swish and sway.
Unusual sounds they use to communicate,
When playing, resting, or looking for a mate.
They twist and turn and swim off as if late,
I wish them well as they catch their next bait.

Olivia Wess, Grade 6
Bedford Middle School

School

School is really fun.
Sometimes I want to run.
Your work is never done.
There is not time to relax in the sun.
The only thing we know
Is that knowledge would make your brain grow.
Oh how life shows
That school is where we need to go.

Camisha Brown, Grade 6
Independence Charter School

Don't Let Go

Why is it that you let him push you around?
I know what you're thinking…
You hate the way he never talks to you…
He never even says "hi" or "hey"…
But you can't let him go!
What makes him so special?
How can you love someone so much,
and not be able to answer that question?
He's addicting…
You would wait forever just for him to give you the look,
just that one dance…
Because when you are in his arms,
the whole world spins around both of you,
and nothing else matters…
So you keep hanging on!

Rachel Stauffer, Grade 6
Ephrata Middle School

Brownie...

Brownies are alive!
That's how they melt in your mouth.
They rise in the oven,
Like a human stomach.
They're so good,
Nice and chewy.
I want to eat them up
Like a bowl of chili.

Lexie Challis, Grade 6
Freedom Area Middle School

Max

Max is as dumb as a rock.
Max is as cute as a bunny.
Max is as fast as lightning.
Max is as loud as a dragon.
Max is as annoying as
baby sister or brother crying forever.

Andrew Kraft, Grade 5
Newtown Elementary School

Beach Colors

Blue is the beauty of the ocean
Red the sunburn on your face
Tan sand burns your toes
Yellow is the great big sun
Gray seagulls find your food
Pink are the girls' ruffled swimsuits
White is the seashells on the beach
What colors do you see on the beach

Hannah Schrei, Grade 4
Bushkill Elementary School

Recipe for a Bad Sister

First, add a gallon of annoying.
Mix a pound of hateness.
Put a cup of tears.
Stir until boiling.
Add 20 gallons of laziness and failure.
Mix all together.
Then put it in the oven
for the rest of your life at 500°.

Corey Clark, Grade 4
Avonworth Elementary School

Football

Green and Black football jerseys
In winter
At a football stadium
On a snowy field
With football equipment on
Watching fans cheer on seats
On ESPN
Eating hot-dogs.

Kyle Hamilton, Grade 4
Fishing Creek Elementary School

Before Spring

Winter spirits echo
through the silent woods
surrounded by emotionless
outstretched bony and cracking
branches of trees

A thumbnail of light
peeks near the horizon
as icy whistling winds
slip through the cracks
of my creaking window

Spring light
spreads across the world
like when you pierce a hole
into a clear pond
with a smooth pitch-black pebble

Kanako Fujioka, Grade 4
Lincoln Elementary School

The Color White

White is clouds and snow and cold.
White is the taste of cool whip.
White chocolate and vanilla smell white.
White makes me feel plain.
White is the sound of white noise,
and the tips of waves crashing down.
White is the white house, Alaska
and an igloo.
Sugar is white,
cotton is white
white is cold.

Shelby Clemens, Grade 6
Grasse Elementary School

Remembering My Grandma

Remembering my grandma...
While she was once here!
Now she's in Heaven,
With God by her side.

Remembering my grandma...
She watches me all the time
At school
At home
At work
All the time

Remembering my grandma...
She died before, I was born
So I can't remember,
All about her

Abigail Thrush, Grade 6
Chambersburg Area Middle School

St. Patrick Day Treat

Saint Patrick's Day is for the Irish.
May I have some green
ice cream in my dish
even though I'm only part Irish.

John Suber, Grade 4
Immaculate Conception School

Bunny

Bunny
Furry, lovable
Jumping, hopping, running
Bunnies like eating carrots.
Rabbit

Brandon Hummel, Grade 4
West Branch Area Elementary School

Family

Family is a gift
from above.

Family is a package
that comes with
lots of love.

Whenever you're down
or whenever you're sad,
go to your family they'll
make you laugh.

God gave us family to
love and care. With bunnies
hearts and teddy bears.

Family have colors of
green and yellows, family
are really happy fellows.

Take them to a game
and play some pool.
So love your family
they're really cool!

Karly Lindemuth, Grade 5
Holy Family Academy

It

IT always makes fun of me.
IT never, ever talks to me.
IT is not a monster with scary hairs.
All I know, IT never cares.

How do you think that I feel
When IT kicks me in the heel?
Let me tell you, IT is not a mister.
IT is actually, well, my sister.

Shannon Williams, Grade 5
Our Mother of Perpetual Help School

Coffee

Get out the beans from the cool fridge
Grind up two scoops
Roaring, spinning, chopping, grinding
It's roaring like a lion,
Spinning like a top
Next comes the water
Pour the water in
Gush
Gush
Gush
Now turn it on
Waiting, waiting, waiting
It's almost done
Now it's done — pour it in the cup
Next add some milk
Coffee without milk is like a pond without fish
Drink it all up
My dad likes coffee
So I tried it once
It was gross

Mikala Hursh, Grade 6
Mount Nittany Middle School

About America

My country is the place where I like to stay.
It's a good way to spend the day.

The president gets soldiers for the jobs
to protect our country from lots of mobs.

The country is at war and everyone sobs.

Some people may think our country is bad
but they have to be wrong because that's sad.

Our country is good, that's all I got to say,
so let's be friends so our countries will cheer and say, "Yea!!!"
Dionte Herring, Grade 4
Urban League of Pittsburgh Charter School

Halloween

Jack-o'-lanterns glowing bright,
light the way this special night.

Ghosts and goblins can be seen…
Boo! It's Halloween.

Mummies, zombies, give a fright
to little children in the night.

Tonight is the night when dead leaves fly
like witches on switches all through the sky.

Boo! It's Halloween.
Jessica Marinaro, Grade 5
McQuistion Elementary School

Six Flags

Went on a long car ride
it was so boring
nothin' to do
all the cars were driving faster
finally got to park
got in line for huge roller coaster
sat in front
click click, click click
it was getting annoying
finally it stopped
my ears felt better
put my hands up
flew down
the cold afternoon air rushing through my face
after bought a sugary funnel cake
and ice cold lemonade
felt so energetic
went to big water park to cool off
then went home
again with the boring car ride

Peter Metcalfe, Grade 4
Easterly Parkway Elementary School

Fall

Fall
Crisp, Color
Falling, blowing, changing
Leaf, acorn, flowers, grass
Blooming, flying, growing
Fresh, new
Spring

Sarah Martin, Grade 6
Carson Middle School

Jack

There once was a dog named Jack.
Who always asked for a snack.
He wanted pie,
He said he'd die,
I guess he did, 'cause he never came back.

Rachael G. Berry, Grade 5
Wexford Elementary School

Football

Football is not hard to play,
You can play it different ways.
You better not cheat,
You'll get knocked off your feet.
When the quarterback throws the ball,
You better not fall or the other team will get the ball.
When you go for the winning field goal,
The pressure will test your soul.

Kevin Boggs, Grade 5
East Union Intermediate Center

Grandpa

His name is Grandpa
He's the father of my mama.
My Grandpa is very old
And he's in this rehab place.
You see, he had 2 strokes
But he's always making jokes.
He got his knee replaced
And you see pain in his face.
He is strong and proud
But he never says it aloud.
Every time I visit he
Tells me that he loves me.
I always say the same,
For I know it's not a game.
My mother cries,
While time flies.
He is getting much better.
He'll soon see the spring weather.

Kristina Rosus, Grade 6
West Allegheny Middle School

The Puppy

The playful puppy is so cute
Rambunctious little beaut
She likes to zip across the room
Sometimes causing quite a boom

Zoé Schwoebel, Grade 5
State Street Elementary School

A Full Moon

A full moon is like a sugar cookie,
Big and round, bound to be eaten,
Night by night, bite by bite,
The moon is gone like a balloon let go.

Brianne M. McGrath, Grade 6
Guth Elementary School

Moka

Moka
Speedy, intelligent
Eating, playing, comforting
Is so very cute
Golden Retriever

Caroline Shoemaker, Grade 5
Villa Maria Academy Lower School

Snow

Snow
Fun, fluffy,
White, cold, snowy,
Making your toes freeze
Shivering

Brianna Leone, Grade 4
Moscow Elementary Center

Goku

Goku
Strong, nice
Flies, blasts, transforms
Completely powerful
Dragon.

Rotimi Adesokan, Grade 5
St Cyril of Alexandria School

beach

nice blue-green water
white sand in between my toes
fun times in the sun

Alexis Pope, Grade 4
French Creek Elementary School

The Fat Pig

There was a fat pig
It lived in a pen
He rolled in mud-puddles
He hid in his den.

He oinked at the kid
He oinked at the farmer
He oinked at the hen
And he oinked at the butcher.

He was safe from the kid
He was safe from the farmer
He was safe from the hen
But was he safe from the butcher?

Brandon Sandrow, Grade 6
Haverford Middle School

Think

Think positive not negative
Think you can, not you can't
Think good not bad
Think nice not evil
Think giving not receiving
Think better not worse
Think happy not sad
Think relax not stress
Think content not jealous
Think God not Satan
What do you think?

Albert Nejmeh, Grade 6
Locust Grove Mennonite School

Fruity Rainbow

Fruity
Sour Skittles
I drool when I see them
They taste like a fruity rainbow
Sour

Taylor Ott, Grade 4
Stackpole Elementary School

Sisters and Brothers

Sisters
Cool, adventurous
Exploring, enjoying, exciting
Beautiful, smart, weird, ugly
Annoying, boring, unexciting
Unsmart, unkind,
Brothers

Safiyah Junaid, Grade 5
East Stroudsburg Elementary School

Day and Night

Day
Sunlight, cloudiness
Rising, awakening, setting
Cheery, warm, calm, silent
Darkening, gloaming, frightening
Dark, dusk
Night

Michaela Figueroa, Grade 5
Penn-Kidder Campus

Together Forever

We are together
Forever
With friends
Forever

We are together
Forever
With family
Forever

With our families
We are filled with love and cheer
Together
Forever

We will always be
Together
Forever.

Megan Cartia, Grade 4
Central Elementary School

Butterfly Music

Butterflies have wings and fly
they soar real high in the sky

they have sticky legs
they also lay eggs

and most of all they are very pretty
so look for them around your city

Rachel Lynch, Grade 4
Garnet Valley Elementary School

Preparing for Spring

Snow sadly slips sideways surrendering sweet snow cones.
Rain reigns rapidly on rubber roofs.
Green grass gratefully grows gallantly.
Bashful blooms beautifully blush.
Flowers follow flurries fulfilling the fruitful fields.
Summer silently sits stalking spring's simple steps.

Have a happy spring!
Melissa Ballow, Grade 4
McDonald Elementary School

Fairy Tales

Godmothers with golden wands,
Unicorns grazing at foggy ponds.
Hurry up and kiss your prince!
'Cause he's been a frog ever since!
Knights are powerful and very strong,
So they can slay the dragons all day long.
Fairies dance in the colorful flowers,
Discovering all their magical powers.
Animals like donkeys can talk like people,
In a barn, almost like a steeple.
Every princess is wanting that special kiss,
All fairy tales you just can't miss!
Jayme Rhoads, Grade 5
Easterly Parkway Elementary School

Summertime

Summer is the greatest
It comes the latest.
When it is finally here
It makes me want to cheer.

Summer is when joy is in the air
When kids don't have to care.
Everyone will be there.
It's time for everyone to play
Kids everywhere shouting yay.

It's the perfect time of year
Until fall, winter, and spring near.
I wish time could freeze
I pray my hardest and say please.

Oh no it's about to end
Next fall begins.
Although it's great in the past
It won't always last.

It's always hard to let go
But things come and they go.
Thus is the end to my poem.
Kenny Williams, Grade 6
Conemaugh Township Area Intermediate School

Nonni

Some nights I lie awake
Wondering if you're watching me in heaven
I can't see you, but I can remember
I remember the homemade spaghetti
I remember the cookies you gave us when Dad wasn't looking
I remember the handmade Halloween costumes
I remember how much I loved you
And I still do
But I smile
Because I know you're up there
And one day I will be, too
Cullen Sanchez, Grade 5
Lincoln Elementary School

Addicted to You…

When I wake up in the morning,
I wish I had you here.
But then I realized you're sometimes one big fear…
I'm so scared to be hurt by someone who does not care,
I'm so addicted to you, maybe someday you will see…
You say I need to move on,
But there's no one else for me…
I think about you often although it may not seem,
I'm so addicted to you even in my dreams.
You're just one big drug I can't get enough of…
When I'm around you, I can be myself 100%.
I'm just so addicted…
Every time I think about being with you I cry,
Because I know that it will never be.
You love her, I now can see…
I'm addicted to you believe me!
When I see you and your brown shaggy hair,
Also what you wear.
I'm addicted to you…
Morgan Smith, Grade 6
Strodes Mills Middle School

Here to Stay

As I look to the sky,
I think of all the people who died,
Thinking of where they all went,
Hoping their time on this world was well spent.

I will always remember that fateful day,
That almost took her away,
All those screams just clouded your mind,
What a way to go,
In this terrible bind.

Now two years later my gram is live and well,
She has many wonderful stories to tell,
That heart attack almost took her away,
But she is not going anywhere,
She is here to STAY!
Jessica Marsh, Grade 6
Strodes Mills Middle School

The Flying Squirrel
There was a flying squirrel.
He lived in a nest.
He climbs on trees.
He wasn't on his best.

He picked on bugs.
He picked on bats.
He picked on birds.
And he picked on cats.

He was safe from bugs.
He was safe from bats.
He was safe from birds.
But he wasn't safe from cats.
Brian Howe, Grade 6
Haverford Middle School

Heather
Heather
Friendly, talkative
Joking, serving, dribbling
Happy go lucky
"Heather Feather"
Heather Lauer, Grade 5
St Francis of Assisi School

Spring
Some seasons are good
but spring is the best
not too hot not too cold
this season is like gold.

Wherever you look
all you will see
are birds and squirrels running free.

In the morning you drink tea
maybe hot chocolate or coffee.

No matter what you'll have fun
that's why spring is number one!
Zach Santilli, Grade 4
McDonald Elementary School

Christmas
C hristmas all around
H ow nice it is
R iding my sleigh all day long
I cy ground all around
S tanding near the fire
T his cold winter day
M aking snowmen every day
A lot of snow from the winter sky
S anta bringing presents
Nicholas Mariani, Grade 4
Bushkill Elementary School

Remembering the Children*
A land of thick forests and dried sands,
    where tangled bushes grow freely,
    and vines are widely spread,
    and people sip steamed coffee
    as they awaken from their beds.

You may have been a poor fisherman
    who sails on the ocean blue,
    searching for a small sea crab day after day to survive,
    a skillful lumberer,
    who cuts down an old memory from one hundred years past,
    or a young technician
    who wires the town's circuits, flicking a switch oh so very fast.

I will be so grateful of what I possess and how I am treated,
as I remember you.
Scott Brady, Grade 6
Deibler Elementary School
*In remembrance of the children in Congo

Pink
Pink looks like the smooth pink nail polish painted on your fingertips.
It can be an icy popsicle or a cute hair bow on your head.
Pink is a pretty pink pig playfully playing in a mud puddle.
It feels soft and comforting like a fluffy pillow.
Pink is the way the door creaks whisper to me.
The color pink is relaxing like the way you sit on a Friday afternoon,
knowing that school won't start until Monday.
Pink is the berry you just picked off a bush.
It's the smell you get when you gently sniff in the scent.
Pink is the taste of a bubble gum bubble slowly popping against your lips.
It is the sound of a cool breeze in the early spring.
It blows the wind through your hair.
That is…PINK!
Olivia Bowser, Grade 5
Peebles Elementary School

Great Football

One handed catch
You catch the ball with one hand

Touchdown
You get six points

Field goal
One point

Interception
The defense catches the ball

Fumble
Offense drops the ball

Tackle
Defense drops the ball

Position
Your place on the field

Football
Connor O'Sullivan, Grade 4
Avon Grove Intermediate School

Learn About Me

My sandy blond hair is like the desert.
My eyes are blue like the daytime sky.
I'm as short as a dwarf.
I kick like a rocket takes off.
My tricks in video games are as good as a cheetah runs.
I draw as fast as a leprechaun running away with a pot of gold.

Jack Lynes, Grade 4
Stackpole Elementary School

The Truth Is…

The truth is you're the only one for me,
I know I act as if you're nothing but you're everything to me,
I always dream if we could be more than just good friends,
If I could have just one more chance to show it's not the end,
If I could really show how special you are to me,
I'd tell you all my thoughts of how we're meant to be,
Yes, I was embarrassed, stubborn too,
But please, just see how much my feelings are for you,
Even when we aren't together you're all I think about,
All though you've probably moved on I still have no doubt,
I wish just once that we could be together again,
The truth is, I wish it wasn't the very end.

Emily Tomasello, Grade 6
Strodes Mills Middle School

I Met a Little Alien

I met a little alien on Halloween night.
It was dark and shadowy, so she gave me quite a fright.
She spoke English and said, "My name is Kira."
"I'm from the future era."
She said this will a giggle,
so I said my name was Sniggle.
She had a light pink nose,
along with bright pink toes.
I was looking for my sister,
I guess I must have missed her.
She was wearing a light pink plastic nose
and bright pink plastic toes.
Wait a minute!!!

Emily Hofstetter, Grade 4
Marlborough Elementary School

Something for Show and Tell

I asked my teacher if I could bring a lion for show and tell,
she looked at me and said um…well.

So I asked her if I could bring in my pet cat,
she said some people are allergic no you can't bring in that.

Fine, I said I'll settle for a snake.
She said I could bring it in, as long as it was fake.

I asked her what to bring in, I could not think of any others,
oh I said I'll bring in my wild brothers!

Amanda Lam, Grade 5
James Buchanan Elementary School

A World of Winter Gold Moon

A world of winter gold moon dust of an angel's halo
A moon dimly sinks in the dripping pause
The golden dust one level nearer heaven overhead
A life of the moon was a golden gate
That will give brightness to the world
A wild sea catches that gold of the glistening moon
Between two downpours of that world of winter gold moon
Shatters into pieces of glass

Andrea Misetic, Grade 4
Lincoln Elementary School

Onyx

Onyx is as tough as the world's strongest man.
Onyx is an intense defensive lineman.
Onyx is a fearless faithful fighter.
Onyx is brave and ever fearless.
Onyx sounds like a raging thunderstorm
on a summer afternoon.
Onyx smells like a sirloin steak,
fresh off the grill on a summer night.
Onyx is the sight of a thousand warriors
going into battle at the break of dawn.
Onyx is all this
and so much more.

Lowell Smith III, Grade 5
Peebles Elementary School

Ring in the Spring

The cold gray days have slipped away.
Spring is here it's here to stay.
When the birds sing they sound so sweet,
From up in the trees I hear "tweet tweet."

They fly, they glide, and they swim through the air,
From way over here, to way over there.
Soon there'll be flowers to bloom in the sun,
With the help of some rain I can pick them for fun.

Pink, red, blue, and gold,
All of them are bright and bold.
An emerald carpet covers the ground,
And on most mornings dew can be found.

Beautiful animals wake from their nests,
Along with them come other pests.
Like bees and ants and flies and bugs
Spiders, mosquitoes, gnats, and slugs.

Although I don't like these, each one has a purpose,
We all help each other on earth's great surface.
Since daybreak comes early and sunsets are late,
There's more time to play — isn't spring great!

Ty Gable, Grade 5
East Stroudsburg Elementary School

Spring

S is for a sunny spring
P is for swimming in the pool
R is for gentle springtime rain
I is for ice cream
N is for nature at it's best
G is for gardening with my mom.

I is for insects on the wall
S is for the smell of spring

Y is for yellow flowers
E is for being excited about spring
L is for loving my dad
L is for loving my mom
O is for all of my outstanding family
W is for whatever I want to do!
Lucile Hartman, Grade 4
Daniel J Flood Elementary School

Pizza

Pizza
Cheesy, crunchy
Jumping, seeing, eating
That good, crunchy, tasty, hungry
Awesome
Michael Bezpietka, Grade 4
Penn-Kidder Campus

Summer and Winter

Summer
Warm, hot, steaming, burning
Shining, short sleeves, sandals
Freezing, shivering, snowing
Ice, snow balls, sled riding
Heavy clothes
Winter
Joe Cardone, Grade 5
Our Lady of Grace Elementary School

An Angel to Watch Over You

An angel to watch over you,
I hope you get home soon,
An angel to watch over you,
You and all your friends too,
An angel to watch over you,
And someone else as well,
An angel to watch over you,
And maybe God will tell,
An angel to watch over you,
And all of those who fell,
An angel to watch over you,
And someone else will say,
An angel to watch over you,
"I wish you were home today."
Greg Kramp, Grade 6
James Buchanan Elementary School

Birthdays

Birthdays are fun.
Birthdays have people.
Birthdays have pizza.
Birthdays are fun.
Keenan Eichman, Grade 4
Manoa Elementary School

Dime

Penny, nickel, quarter, dime.
Money has changed over time.
Stones, beans even a bone.
Paper and coins in this time zone.
Penny, nickel, quarter, dime.

I charged a dime
When I sold a lime.
I charged a nickel
When I sold a pickle.
I wonder what to charge next time.

Penny, nickel, quarter, dime.
We work with money all the time.
Two, four, six, eight.
Money puts food on the plate.
Like pickles and limes.
Margaret Rohrs, Grade 5
Lincoln Elementary School

Magic Broom

There once was a magic broom,
Who caused a lot of doom,
One day he got split,
And a dog was bit,
Then the magic broom went vroom.
Tyler Conway, Grade 6
California K-8 School

KoKo

KoKo is my pet dog
She sleeps like a log.

KoKo is small
She's not very tall.

KoKo is black, brown, and white
She is such a pretty sight.

When we go get her a treat
She jumps up on her feet.

KoKo is my best friend
I will love her till the very end.
Jessica Bodack, Grade 5
Cheswick Christian Academy

How I Wish

How I wish I could fly
Up into the clouds

Where the snow always flies
And the cold likes to grow

Or should I swim in the ocean
with its giant waves

Full of colorful fish
And under water caves

May I run in the forest
With evergreen trees

Where the wind hits my face
And gives me such peace

I look out my window
And love what I see

Then I finally realize
All that God has given me
Carah Johnson, Grade 6
Sacred Heart Elementary School

The Bus

There once was a guy named Bettis.
He played for the black and gold.
He could shred you into lettuce,
But now he is very old.
Nicole McCusker, Grade 5
State Street Elementary School

Grandma

G ood to have
R eally fun
A wesome to have you
N eeded always
D o everything together
M e and you always
A wesome everywhere
Sydney Brown, Grade 4
Concord Elementary School

Lonely

When I am feeling lonely
I feel like I was deserted
On a thick sand island
The air I breathe is crusty, crispy
and dusty air
Ready to cry many blue tears
Wanting a friend or company
that's all I would like
Maryana Stern, Grade 4
Avonworth Elementary School

Recess

Throw a ball, catch a pass,
It's so much fun, why can't recess last?

Kick a ball, high in the sky,
Watch it doesn't come down and hit you in the eye,

Batting balls in the baseball field,
Use your glove as a shield,

Running, jumping, passing and throwing,
If you try — you'll keep on going,

Hit the ball out of the park,
I wish we could play until dark,

Now it's time to go inside,
It was fun but our game was tied!

Matthew Majocha, Grade 5
Allegheny-Hyde Park Elementary School

A Special Spring Day

I get up in the morning at the crack of dawn.
I awaken my brother; we put our clothes on.
The spring flowers greet us, smelling so fresh and sweet.
We run through the yard, the morning dew on our feet.

Easter is here — bright sunshine, egg hunts and candy,
Treats for all, big and small, even my dog Sandy.
We search for eggs, yellow purple, green blue and red;
We find them everywhere, even under the bed.

Our family is gathered from near and from far,
A flight from Jacksonville or a trip in the car.
We share stories, talk and play games together.
We have a great feast and then walk in nice weather.

I'm tired; it's late. I need to go to my bed.
With a smile on my face, I can now rest my head.
A special spring day, Easter, is done for this year,
But it's the start of the new year; we're in good cheer.

Matthew Regueiro, Grade 5
Edgeworth Elementary School

The Pianist

The pianist plays an incredible song
Never getting one note wrong
If he plays the song real fast
You'll dance and dance and have a blast
If he plays it really slow
You'll be in a trance, that I know
No matter how the pianist plays
He'll put something extra in all of your days.

Matthew Emanuelson, Grade 5
Vandergrift Elementary School

Cooper — My Super Duper Bird!

Cooper is as loud as a full blasted radio
Cooper is like a fluttering snowflake
Cooper is as cute as a new born puppy
Cooper is like a person who dances funny
Cooper is as sweet as chocolate fudge cake
Cooper is like a glowing moon at night
Cooper is as white as a snow covered hill

Pooja Patel, Grade 5
Newtown Elementary School

A Tale

Once upon a time there was a sleepy, sleepy town.
In the town there was a sleepy, sleepy house.
In the house was a sleepy, sleepy bed.
At the front of the bed was a sleepy, sleepy boy.
Behind the boy was a sleepy, sleepy wall.
Up the wall was a sleepy, sleepy rat.
Across the rat was a sleepy, sleepy flea.
Behind the flea was a sleepy, sleepy dream.
In the dream was a sleepy, sleepy tale.
In the tale was a sleepy, sleepy lie.
And in the lie there was…
A story that should not have been told!

Lena Bioni, Grade 5
Claysville Elementary School

All About Me

Alyssa Daney
Playful, colorful, funny
Wishes to go to China
Dreams of being a rock star
Wants to be rich
Who wonders how the Earth and people were formed
Who fears of going on airplanes
Who likes playing Bratz and Barbie's
Who believes in Santa
Who loves my family
Who plans on riding in a limo one time
I know a lot of stuff about me.

Alyssa Daney, Grade 4
Bushkill Elementary School

Christmas

When I rise in the morn
I go downstairs
There my family and relatives are,
And there is the prickly green Christmas tree
When I walk into the kitchen
There's a new and strong aroma in the air
The pancakes are buttery and fresh when it enters my mouth
They're so flexible and spongy
Everybody is laughing and the barks of my dog are so loud
That they fill the whole room up with silence
Yes, it is Christmas morning!!

Bethany Riley, Grade 5
Southside Elementary School

I'm Different
Strange
Fun, interesting
Changing, sustaining, entertaining
Different, funny, plain, average
Snoring, boring, unrestoring
Same, tame
Ordinary Joe
River Dolfi, Grade 5
William Penn Elementary School

Purple Pony
Plip, plop, plip, plop.
Purple Pony in the pasture
purposely pulling other ponytails.
Pink Pony pulls Purple Pony's tail.
Purple Pony never pulls ponytails again.
Plip, plop, plip, plop.
Carly Kramer, Grade 4
Avon Grove Intermediate School

Colors of My Life
White is the hottest fire
While red burns like our desires
Blue is like the sky
While green Granny Smiths fill my pie
Gray is the color that rules dull
Turquoise is the color of my ball
Daniel Devlin, Grade 5
Cheswick Christian Academy

In the Courtyard
wind is lifting the leaves
like a plane leaving the airport
water in the birdbath
looks like a lake to an ant
leaves are as gold
as the sun
every time I step on the rocks
they sound like crunchy snow
autumn sun feels warm
I'm always safe
no matter what

in the courtyard
Patrick DeSanta, Grade 5
Lower Salford Elementary School

Cats
As scrawny as a squirrel,
As fuzzy as a lion,
As frisky as a bear,
Are my cats that I love so much!
Ryan Graham, Grade 4
St Francis of Assisi School

Winter's Coming
A golden tree catches my eye
Leaves dropping
Look like army men
Dive bombing
Getting stuck in the pine tree
Bunches of leaves
Against cold bricks
Look like an ocean tide
That stopped
A birdbath painted
With brown, gold and green leaves
Kids kicking rocks
Making them scatter like marbles
Freezing wind pushes and moves
My sweatshirt
Away from my body
Winter's coming
Wm. Mitchell Simsick, Grade 5
Lower Salford Elementary School

The Wild Horses
H orses gallop
O ver the hills.
R un all over the place.
S ometimes stopping under the trees.
E ating some leaves
S ee the wild horses?
Jasmine Attaway, Grade 5
Wharton Elementary School

The Dragon
A dragon who developed strep throat,
Took a ride on a tiny row boat,
A wild wind started,
The boat and him parted,
And the dragon never stayed afloat.
Jillian Kravatz, Grade 5
Schuylkill Valley Elementary School

Ice Cream
Ice cream, ice cream
You are such a dream.
I like you with cherries,
But some like you with berries.
Ice cream, ice cream
You are soft and round,
I could eat you by the pound.
Chocolate, vanilla, rocky road,
Birthday cake a la mode.
Strawberry, and cookies and cream,
Adding cherries makes me scream.
Ice cream, ice cream
You're cold as snow,
It's a tastes you won't outgrow.
Takoda Losch, Grade 4
Watsontown Elementary School

The Seashore
I am the seashore
Warm and wet
On me you can see the sun set
Wet sand, salty air
You can find this everywhere
Look at me you can see
People trying to water-ski
As the tide washes away
People come for a brand new day
Seagulls flying in the air
Here, there, everywhere
I am the seashore
Warm and wet
On me you can see the sun set
Nicole Garritt, Grade 4
General Nash Elementary School

Peter Cottontail
Funny, nice
Jumping very high
Hopping down the bunny
Trail
Tyler Carroll, Grade 5
Penn-Kidder Campus

Nature
Roses are red violets are blue
The moon is brighter,
But the sunshine is lighter,
The grass is greener
Than leaves on a tree.
The grapes on a tree are sweeter
Than sweet candy could be.
But what is nature without me?
Kathryn Corbino, Grade 4
Manoa Elementary School

A Spring Day
Soft chirping of little birds,
When mother has food

A warm air breeze,
Making the flowers sway

The fresh scent roses,
Filling the air with happiness

The bright blue sky,
Covered with some clouds

The sweet juicy fruit,
Making my taste buds want more.
Nicole Vitiello, Grade 6
Neil Armstrong Middle School

My Life

Drugs won't get you that special degree.
They won't get you to graduation day,
And drugs won't score the winning basket.
Drugs won't do any good.
They aren't a miracle, they're a disaster.
I want to be able to win a basketball game.
I want to be me,
Drug free.

Sarah Miller, Grade 6
Wingate Elementary School

Night

Night is a time we have to sleep
It is not a time to make a peep.

There is nothing bad about the night
It is actually like a magical flight.

The darkened beauty of the trees
The sweet smelling air and the beautiful breeze.

The crickets sing their lovely song
And you close your eyes thinking nothing can go wrong.

The stars way up there in the sky
and the beautiful light of a firefly.

The dark blue sky and the lavender clouds
And you just stand there and say, "Wow."

The night is magical, but I give you a warning
The magic will end when your mom says, "Good morning."

Christian Price, Grade 5
Cheswick Christian Academy

Halloween

On Halloween it's dark and scary
With goblins and witches that are hairy
Black cats are going around
With witches on their brooms around the town
We trick-or-treat to get some candy
On Hallows Eve it is real dandy
Oh no the night is almost over
Let us find my special dog named Rover
And — head — for — home

Anjali Chacko, Grade 6
St Ann Elementary School

Lucky

There once was a leprechaun named Lucky.
Who played in the mud and got yucky.
He got a shower,
Which lasted an hour.
Now you know the story of Lucky.

Billy Mann, Grade 4
West Branch Area Elementary School

Look What I Found

Look what I found!
It was sitting on the ground.
I wouldn't call it tall.
I wouldn't call it small.
I bet you'll think it's really cool.
It won't even fit through the door at school.
It's completely covered with fuzz.
Don't you wish you knew what it was?

Sean Crawford, Grade 5
Chalutzim Academy

A Marsupial Mouse

I knew an old man named Dan,
Who worked as a trustworthy mailman.

He lived with his spouse named Ann,
Who loved to keep her house spic-and-span.

They lived in an old gray house
With a very fat marsupial mouse
Near the shaggy, broken down boathouse.

The slithering, smooth mouse,
Ran scarcely around the house
Because he was being chased,
By an alley cat named Grace.

The hungry cat
That was as blind as a bat,
Slipped on a broken down plaque
And landed in the old women's hat.

The marsupial mouse,
Ran out of the house
As fast as a flying grouse,
And hid in that old, shaggy boathouse.

Kevin Brumbaugh, Grade 6
Carson Middle School

Spring

I can feel the warm air and bugs on my arms.

I can taste the outdoor picnic food and cold treats
from loving parents and kind friends.

I can hear the birds chirping and the bugs buzzing
and the children laughing and screaming.

I can smell the mildewy smell of rain and morning dew.

I can see all the flowers blooming and the children
playing and the sun shining bright in the bright blue sky.

Esther Rosen, Grade 4
Colonial Elementary School

Light Pink

Light pink is a beautiful sunset and my adorable dog and it is light as a feather.
Light pink is the taste of fresh, cold vanilla ice cream.
A rose and pie fresh out of the oven smell light pink.
Lying on a pillow doing nothing makes me feel light pink.
Light pink is the sound of birds chirping in the cool spring breeze and splashing water.
Light pink is like the beach, my house, and it's like laughing and screaming at an amusement park.
Having a fun time with my family is also light pink.
Light pink is like eating a fresh bowl of sweet, ripe strawberries.

Josie Nitschmann, Grade 5
McMurray Elementary School

9/11 Heaven*

It was an ordinary day at least it started out that way.
She was on the plane to see her dad but wishes that she never had
Everything was going great until I at home felt a little fate.
Instead of good it was really bad and made me feel kind of sad.
She looked around, it looked so strange she looked out farther at the range.
There was some screaming in the front, it sounded kind of bold and blunt.
She took a turn, she was going so fast that surely she would burn.
The towers were close her eyes grew bigger then she heard a sound like someone pulled a trigger.
The plane flew through the Twin Towers with so much force and power
The flames were big and horrible and the pain wasn't even tolerable.
I was on that plane that day but I made it through all the way.
But as for my friend it was the end for she just had to die.
She's the one I told you about and I hold her in my heart no doubt.
It was September 11 it was a really scary day I wish she had never died that way.
Because someone hated the United States my sister had to die with the greatest pain.
They didn't just take my sister's life over 3,000 families felt the same strife.
I didn't write this poem based on a true story but to give the victims a little glory.

Kirstin Evancho, Grade 6
Holy Family Academy
*In loving memory of all the victims of Sept. 11

Ode to My Hailey

How it looks.
Tannish/White — It's as tannish/white as a blind.
White tail — It wags as fast as a tail.
Square chin — It's as square as a picture frame.
Big belly — The biggest belly I ever saw.
What it likes.
Marshmallows — She likes marshmallows more than treats.
Ice cubes — When she's eating them she looks like people on ice skates.
Shoe strings — She loves dangly ones.
3 ft toy flower — It's as big as me (almost).
Appealing Meals
Graham crackers — She likes graham crackers more than dog food.
Cat food — She eats cat food and she's a dog.
Treats — Treats are like toys to her.
Yogurt — It is one of her favorite.
Little Appealing Peculiarities
Relative cats — She wants to make friends with her but the cat thinks she wants to kill her.
Beats up bigger dogs than her — She likes to beat them up when they walk by when she's outside.
Lays behind a toilet — She does that more than any animal I know.
When hair is long — She looks like a mop when you spin her around.

Benjamin Colosimo, Grade 6
St Sebastian Elementary School

Summer Camp

Summer camp

       Having a good time.

Jump rope

       Jumping high, touching the sky.

Kickball

       Fun game.

Gimp

       Make a lot of stuff.

Playing

       Sweat a lot.

Time to go

       Sadness comes.

But remember

       You get to go again tomorrow.

Grace Andrejev, Grade 4
Avon Grove Intermediate School

Beginning of Spring

I hear the birds singing in the trees,
as I feel the thick breeze.
I see flowers, so beautiful and fragrant that are about to bloom,
Spring will be here soon.
Pine begins opening, and bows in the breeze,
which causes me to sneeze.
I feel the energy in spring that fills me with joy,
I'm allowed to play outside, Oh Boy!
I see flowers that are blooming in the evening sun,
Spring is sure a lot of fun.
Breeze starts to mumble,
it causes me to tremble.
When it rains it drips down my face,
it makes my heart pace.
The feeling of the warm water calms me, jus so you know,
it makes it easier to feel the wind blow.

Samantha O'Neill, Grade 5
St Ambrose School

Lunch

Lunch has bad food every day,
sometimes it even tastes like hay.

Lunch is supposed to be the best part of the day,
but it's not when the food can be used like clay.

Though I have always thought lunch tasted bad,
it sometimes makes me feel so sad.

When I eat it does not taste sweet,
it is more like eating a baseball cleat.

Sometimes I just want to throw it away,
but I can't because I'm so hungry today.

Jessica Scalise, Grade 6
Neil Armstrong Middle School

Grandma

I remember my Grandma.
I remember how happy she always looked.
I remember how she would wrap her arms around me
    when I walked in the room.
I remember the twinkle in her eyes when
    I would talk to her.
I remember when I was over to her home
    she acted like I was the only thing that existed.
I remember when she would make me tea.
I remember how we would sit on the swing
    and talk for hours.
I remember the day she died and how I
    did not know how to act.
I remember my Grandma.

Natalie Hamilton, Grade 5
Claysville Elementary School

Crying

I see everyone crying around me
I see my mom starting to cry too
My dad rushes in the hospital
My mom running behind
I go into the room where my grandma lies
I see myself crying too
I can't even look at her
the sparkle in her eyes are gone
I try to look but I can't
I can't hear anything around me
feels like I'm going to die
I feel my heart beating and it won't stop
my mom is crying on the floor
and she won't stop
in my head I'm screaming
but I have to be strong
but all I know is she's with God
I know we'll meet again

NaDajiah Moon, Grade 5
East Stroudsburg Elementary School

Flowers

Flowers coming up through the ground,
Can't you see them all around?

Pansies, violets, and daffodils, too,
I'll pick a flower and give it to you.

They need rain, soil, and sun to grow,
But first you must have a seed to sow.

Make sure you water them every night,
Then your beautiful flowers will grow just right!

But then when your flowers disappear,
Don't worry, they'll be back for spring next year.

Sarah Brown, Grade 6
Moravian Academy Middle School

The Candy Store

The candy counter carries
many kinds of chocolate.

The sweet smell starts
on the sidewalk outside of the store.

Even the massive money machine
smells much like milk chocolate.

The rainbow rows of ravishing racks
of tasty terrific treats tempted us.

The lovely ladies lunged
for a lemon-lime lollipop.

Sarah Brown, Grade 6
Neil Armstrong Middle School

New York City

Big lights
City sights
Time Square
It's like a fair
Funny smells
Christmas bells
Lots and lots and lots of shops
Those are places I will stop
Broadway
It's a play
I will go there any day
Oh! How I love New York City

Caroline Bondi, Grade 6
St Ann Elementary School

Clouds

Clouds
White, fluffy
Dancing, floating, crashing
Soft like a pillow
Cumulus

Miguel Martinez, Grade 5
Penn-Kidder Campus

Lulu

Lazy Lulu
Lazy, boring, sluggish, slow
Why is she so lazy?
I don't know

Hunter Pierson, Grade 5
Newtown Elementary School

The Forest

Forest filled with trees
For the squirrels and the bees
There is mighty peace

Stephen Hemmerle, Grade 4
Center Elementary School

A Greek Philosopher

There once was a man named Democritus. He was born in the city of Thrace.
He developed an Atomic Theory that put a smile on his face.
He went to his teacher Leucippus, to discuss this amazing theory,
Democritus is also known to always be very cheery.
This theory was about the atom,
And how it created color, such as the color of macadam.
This theory was also about how the atom caused things to taste the way they do.
But it did not have to do with why things smell, such as the smell of a shoe.
A sweet taste is due to an atom that is round and small.
But any other taste may be due to an atom that is not small at all.
Democritus said quotes such as, "constant delay means work undone."
Which means don't put work off to the last minute even if you're doing something fun.
Many of his quotes had very thoughtful meanings.
Some may even have been tips for cleaning.
Democritus helped us learn about atoms today.
Because when he was working he would never fool around or play.
Democritus definitely did not invent the lever.
But people always say he was very, very clever.

Abigail Lynch, Grade 6
Cathedral School of St Catharine of Siena

Dreams

Dreams
A story that comes in your sleep.
Dreams can be wonderful,
like a child receiving a puppy on his birthday.
Dreams can be frightening,
like when a bare branch brushes your window on a black night.

Dreams
They can make you cry and call your mom,
like when a baby cries at night and her mother goes to comfort her.
They can be frustrating like when you wake up in your dream
and you can't fall back to sleep.
They can be disappointing like when you earn something
in your sleep and then you wake up it's all gone.

Dreams
They are a thought in your head waiting for sleep,
like a rain cloud waiting to burst out.
There is a dream for every person to be had,
they are a thought in your head that can be happy or sad.
All in all, dreams are just dreams.

David Williams, Grade 6
Mount Nittany Middle School

Winter Blessings

Let the snow embrace your travels.
Let the wind control everything light for a little more than a second.
Let the cold give you a good feeling and still shiver.
And let yourself travel safely through your bitter journey.
Let it snow!

Kyle Esposito, Grade 6
Deibler Elementary School

Gibson

Curled up into a small ball
Lying, sleeping, curled up
Belly rubs and ear scratching
Cuddling up, warm soft hair against my face
Victoria Vitale, Grade 5
East Stroudsburg Elementary School

When Jesus Was Born

The wind whistled softly in a dark night,
And the whole world saw a marvelous light,
He lay in a manger, a baby asleep.
People came to watch Him: shepherds, goats, and sheep.
The three kings set down their beautiful gifts.
Thinking of this night, my poor spirit lifts!
The kings knelt quietly and praised the precious gem.
The little baby boy born in Bethlehem!
The stars twinkled down on the little baby.
Next to Him was a man and a lady.
The cold snow drifted down to chill the whole night.
It was cold, dark; but Jesus was the true light.
Helen Karabin, Grade 5
Verna Montessori School

Sea

I'm sailing on a sailboat
to see what I can see.
Sharks, starfish, seahorses, seaweed, and sun
stop to stare at me.

The scary sharks are swimming
looking for their prey.
The sandy starfish stay still
preparing for their slumber.

The silky sea horses
swim in the water.
The slippery seaweed
drifts silently throughout the sea.

The shining sun is so bright
it blinds every sight.
This is what I see
in the sea.

Kristen Elliott, Grade 6
Neil Armstrong Middle School

Basketball

When they dribble me on the court.
My head gets pounded on the ground.
I love when people play with me.
I like to hear the buzzer go off.
They shoot me and make me in the hoop.
And when the buzzer goes off
We won the game.
Derek Fajtak, Grade 6
Freedom Area Middle School

Summer

Summer is my favorite season
of the year.

Football, kickball, basketball, softball, and release,
Great games we play with relief.

Hanging all day every week sweet people
all over the street.

Swimming and tanning is always great!
Parties with friends and family Wahoo!

While I sit here thinking summer is near.
I can't wait fore summer to get here!
Rebecca Will, Grade 6
West Allegheny Middle School

Spring

Birds chirping in a tree
To welcome the morning
Pine tree scent in the air
To scare winter away
For those of you who do not know
I LOVE SPRING!!
Madeleine Thurston, Grade 6
West Allegheny Middle School

The Champions

We made it to the championship game,
My team was feeling great.
We were happy to see
The other team was very, very late.

Finally we started playing,
I had the ball —
Then took a shot
It didn't go in at all.

We took our time out —
We needed to regroup.
Focus on what we were doing
Keep our eyes on the hoop.

Finally it was fourth quarter,
There were eighteen seconds on the clock.
We were dominating the game
And weren't about to stop.

I was proud of myself and my team
Competing at such a high level.
We were victorious in the end
And all received a gold medal.
Mikey Santiago, Grade 5
Hamilton Elementary School

Moon

The moon, like a wheel
Tumbles month to month.
Starting clear going behind a wall of sky
Moving at speeds you can dream
Yet slow enough to see.
Stars are merely obstacles in the way.
Sitting up in the sky looking down on us,
Seems weightless, just hovering.
Alex Hawk, Grade 6
Freedom Area Middle School

I Like Lots of Things

I like soccer and football.
I like basketball and movies.
But I do not like chapped lips.
I like candy and pets.
I like swimming and Heelys.
But I love my family and an iPod.
Robert Zimmerman, Grade 4
Maureen M Welch Elementary School

Snowball Fights

Intense, crazy
Running, throwing, hiding
Fun, painful, freezing, tiring
Ducking, pounding, packing
Hard, compact
Winter action
Draven McFadden, Grade 4
Memorial Elementary School

Snow

The snow is bright
It's like a white light
It lies on the ground
Without any sound
It looks very fine
And sparkles with shine
It makes good forts
Of all sorts
It gives you fun
Without the sun
Bryant Weller, Grade 5
Southside Elementary School

Babe Ruth's Bat

I'm Babe Ruth's bat,
The ball is my enemy,
I quiver and shake when I hit the ball,
I help him hit home runs,
Once and awhile I crack,
That hurts a lot,
I will go down in history,
I'm Babe Ruth's bat.
Dan Waldrop, Grade 6
Freedom Area Middle School

The Mall

When I go to the mall
I want it all.
I buy clothes, jewelry, and a softball.
When I buy my stuff I have to call
My friends and my family,
I always bounce off the wall!
Alexia Recchia, Grade 4
Christ the King School

Elvis Presley

I know a famous person
Who people love and I know why.
He sang many songs on stage
"Elvis!" was the people's cry.

He used a ukulele
And he strummed on his guitar.
He had concerts very often
It's no wonder he's a star.

He had lots of well known songs
That he sang with his good voice.
With the great career he chose
He had made an awesome choice.

He sang about a hound dog
And a cuddly teddy bear
A jailhouse rock, suspicious minds
And a blue suede shoe pair.

The dreaded day came to the world
The day that Elvis died.
But his music is with us every day
And he fills our hearts with pride.
Mary Snyder, Grade 5
Villa Maria Academy Lower School

Late

My name is Kate,
I was late for my date,
It was down the block,
From the grand station clock.

We went to a diner,
That couldn't be much finer,
We didn't each much,
But I love their breakfast brunch.

After that night,
Inside me there isn't that fright,
To go on a date,
To be so utterly late.
Caitlin McNamara, Grade 6
Our Lady of Grace Elementary School

Family

Loving and caring
With sweet tender hearts
If you're feeling bad
Their smile will make you glad
It's great to be around them
Clare Hanrahan, Grade 4
Sol Feinstone Elementary School

Sports

S pring into action
P laying
O utside
R unning
T urning and falling
S preading summer fun!
Mary Trax, Grade 6
West Allegheny Middle School

Seasons

The bright sun shines on,
Trees above the great land,
A wonderful sight!
Snowflakes around us,
Goes swish and swoop a lot,
As they make their way toward land.
Jessica Nace, Grade 6
St Maria Goretti School

Roses

Roses
can be bright red
with sharp thorns on the stem,
and the petals so delicate
and soft.
Kayla Whitfield, Grade 6
Bedford Middle School

Sun and Moon

Sun
Independent radiant
Glowing, shining, glistening
Clouds, daytime, nighttime, stars
Reflecting, gleaming, shimmering
Mysterious astonishing
Moon
Kadie Clancy, Grade 6
California K-8 School

Summer

Oh summer it is so warm
And driving bikes
And trees are blooming
And going for a walk
And going on hikes
Evan Albertini, Grade 4
Panther Valley Elementary School

Baseball Is My Life

I have always wanted to hit a homerun
If I did it would be a stun.

You always need your bat
But don't forget your hat.

You need your cleats
To go to practice meets.

When you catch a fly ball
You feel like you have done it all.

And always bring your glove
When you go out to play the game you love.

Nicholas Casner, Grade 6
Strodes Mills Middle School

Bitter-Sweet

There's no one to hold you,
No one to love you
No one to be by your side
No one to make you smile or laugh

You feel left out,
You feel all weird
Nobody there
Year after year

Then one day you receive a book
With dreams and wonders that cannot be told
It says you're going, leaving sometime soon
Someplace far and wide with magic too

It says you'll always have someone to hold on tight
You'll always have someone to love all night
You'll always have someone to be at your side
You'll have someone to make you smile and laugh

This is my story,
that was my past.
It's a new beginning,
And I'm having a blast!

Catie Riccelli, Grade 6
Sacred Heart Elementary School

Homework

Homework stinks, phew
We have it every night
The smell is rotten it's not sweet
When I get home I wash my bag and the things inside
Not only once, but twelve times you see
That smell thing is finally clean

Elizabeth McCutcheon, Grade 6
H Austin Snyder Elementary School

Chrissy and Smokey

These cats are loud, they pounce and play
they wake me up at night.
They hiss, they scratch, they purr of course
but I love them just the same.
They eat their food but always want to play!
At night they settle down a little
but they still pounce and play!

Morgan Reiss, Grade 4
Christ the King School

Sick

I'm sick! This is not fair!
Oh, I'm sick! Does anyone care?
My mom leaves the room and closes the door.
Oh, I can't take it anymore!

Jillian Gratz, Grade 4
Our Lady of Peace School

America

This great land was found in 1492
"When Christopher Columbus sailed the ocean blue."
Pilgrims came here from England for religious ideals
They met natives here
And shared meals together
But then took their land
From the grasp of their hands.

1776 is when our land became a nation.
Led by a great leader, George Washington,
Who beat the British and
Supported the Declaration of Independence.

We fought many more wars,
And even a civil one.
Changed our flags many times
Had many great leaders,
America has an amazing history
And in 100 years,
People will be saying that
about our time.

Joshua Greenberg, Grade 6
United Hebrew Institute

Friendliness Is...

Friendliness is when you're loving, truthful
    kind, and helpful,
When you put someone before yourself.
Friendliness is a firefighter, doctor, a policeman too.
It's when you put something in to consideration
    that's not all about you.
Friendliness is God,
He's the most friendly of all,
This is a lesson we all most know,
Be friendly and kind wherever you go.

Emily Havranek, Grade 4
Beaver County Christian School

Springtime Is in the Air!

Springtime is in the air,
Birdies chirping everywhere.
Flowers flowers growing right now,
Look at the pretty pansies WOW!

I can see a deer who yawned,
He is now drinking from my pond.
I hear the pretty horsies neigh,
Tons of flowers bloom in May!

Me and my friends roll around,
On the green and grassy ground.
The sky will soon turn the color red,
When everyone's snug in their bed.

Jessica Keast, Grade 4
Avonworth Elementary School

Me

I am Me
I am who I want to be
I am what God made me
I have to be like this to be me
This is who I am
I am like no one else
Don't try to change me
Just accept me
This is who I am
I am Me

LaShana James, Grade 6
Independence Charter School

Spring Come Back

Spring come back
So much snow
I wish it will soon go
Cannot wait for spring
And hear the birds sing
See the flowers blooming
Snow go away
Want another sunny day
Spring come back

Sara Anne Geisler, Grade 6
Curwensville Area Elementary School

Samuel McCay

If you were Samuel McCay,
You'd play baseball every day.
If he swung and if he struck,
He would have such great luck.

Today's the day, Samuel McCay,
Will get put in the Hall of Fame.
He is as good as he can be,
He'll be talked about in history.

Amanda Martin, Grade 5
East Union Intermediate Center

Boredom

Boredom is boring like a swimming pool on a cold winter day;
Boredom is not fun when you have nothing to play;

Happiness is happy, and excitement makes you run;
Boredom is like a hot dog without mustard or a bun;

Boredom is like nothing except for being bored;
It is like listening to your dad snore;

I wish boredom was like a sandwich with some spices and some flounder;
But that would be like putting legs on a snake and not calling it a salamander;

Boredom is like a broken playground;
With boredom you have nothing to do.

Joseph Cortese, Grade 6
Neil Armstrong Middle School

What I Love About Books

The excitement of wondering, "What comes next?"
The amazing stories, sucking you in, so you can't put the book down
The fresh smell of a brand new book
Sneaking them into your pocket, to read when things get boring
The pictures on the cover
Are reasons why I love books.

Philip Feibusch, Grade 5
Newtown Elementary School

That Black Dog

Once I had a dog named Jess, I love the times we played chess.
If he got stuck I would help him so, like the times we made fun of Pinocchio.
Or if we would run beside the creek or race along the golden trees.
But when Jess knew it was time to go, he barked his last words that I only know.
The words he barked said Jack, my boy, meet me at the beautiful shore.
And so I did I ran and ran and there he was running in the sand.

Jack Martus, Grade 4
Avonworth Elementary School

The Mysterious Chair

The mysterious rocking chair will sit on the back porch
Of the house of never return
The rocking chair draws you closer
With a creaking sound of a wooden floor board screaming for help
When you walk to the rocking chair
It rocks with the wind
With that sound
You walk even slower like a lion sneaking up on its prey
You see the rocking chair waiting there glancing at you as it inspires you closer with
Its hollow wooden arms
Pulling and pulling
But as you fall on the rocking chair
It takes you back and forth
And back and forth
And rocking and rocking you away to a place
Where your bed will take you

Chase Coleman, Grade 6
Hillcrest Elementary School

I Can't Write a Poem!

I can't write a poem
It's just too hard
What will I do to get out of this homework?
Should I fail or should I try my best?
I don't know anything about poems
I asked myself, how can I try my best?
I asked my teacher "how do I write a poem?"
She said, "it's easy, you'll see!"
I went home and told my mom
"I need to write a poem!"
She said "oh really, that's so easy."
I started my poem, but all I had down is my name!
I need help with writing a poem and a lot of it, too!

Elena Becirovic, Grade 4
Washington Heights Elementary School

I Feel

I feel nervous when it's my first day in a new class.
I don't know anybody and nobody knows me.
I just feel like staying close to somebody I know well.
I don't know where things are.
I feel afraid that I will get lost.
I don't like being a new girl.

Kanzy Mourad, Grade 4
Avonworth Elementary School

Summer Fun

S occer is fun when played with friends.
U nless you live up north summer is hot.
M alls are always open.
M osquitoes are on the prowl every night.
E veryone is frolicking in the sun.
R ivers and streams are cool to swim in.

Jusdan Griffith, Grade 6
Conemaugh Township Area Intermediate School

By Myself*

I'm a soccer player scoring the winning goal.
I'm a dancer on Broadway.
I'm a football player scoring a touchdown.
I'm a cheerleader cheering everyone on.
I'm a famous Irish dancer dancing in Ireland.
I'm a basketball player winning the game.
I'm a flute player in musicals.
I'm a gymnast that wins many gold medals.
I'm a poet writing many poems.
I'm a doctor helping people.
I'm a kite flying high in the sky.
I'm a kid having fun.
I'm whatever I want to be
An anything I care to be
What I care to be
Is me!

Sara Tait, Grade 5
East Stroudsburg Elementary School
*Inspired by Eloise Greenfield.

When a Cloudy Day Is Near

When a cloudy day is near,
Put on a smile and spread good cheer.
Even though the sky is blue,
I'm always going to love you.
Put a smile on your face and don't be blue,
Friends and family are near to you.
So next time you look outside,
Think about what's inside.
How many times do you think it has lied?
Your heart will always be your guide.
Each and every day you'll see,
The special person you have come to be.
So when a cloudy day is here,
Think of people far and near.
Pass a smile on to your family and friends,
This kind of cheer never ends.

Lindsey Lenhart, Grade 6
Saegertown Elementary School

Friends

It's ok to be sad,
It can be turned into glad.
just remember your friends when you're feeling that bad.
At anytime at all,
Just give them a call.
Your friends are the key, to unlocking the door.
The door of friendship throughout the world!

Maggi Secrest, Grade 6
Bedford Middle School

Weird Fall Day

Today is a weird kind of day
honey locust tree
looks like it's sweeping the air
plants in whiskey barrels
look like they are sad
leaves twirling in every direction
the stillness of the wind is very odd
my hair is blowing in my face
feels more like feathers in my hair
honey locust tree leaves look like
they've been caught in the pine's branches
and put in jail
the darkness of the clouds
makes me feel like
I'm in a haunted mansion
pine tree is clinging to the courtyard floor
so it wouldn't fly away
tree branches are scattered about
looking hopeless

That's what I call a weird day

Brianna Williams, Grade 5
Lower Salford Elementary School

Snowy Day
It's snowing the children say.
It snowed 5 inches or more.
That means no school today.
Getting out the sled and more,
We had to clean the floor.
Outside cold and gray.
It's a snowy day.
Samantha Edwards, Grade 6
Grasse Elementary School

Friends
Friends are always caring
Friends are always sharing
Sometimes friends are happy
Sometimes friends are sad
Sometimes friends will fight
Sometimes friends are mad
My mom, dad and sister
Are the best friends I've ever had
Marisa Dever, Grade 4
Sacred Heart School

The Wind Is a Breath
The wind is a breath
Breathing fast and deep
After running.
It breathes soft and quietly
When hiding.
Sometimes whistling,
Sometimes howling.
It likes to pretend
It's many things.
But still as I recall
It is a breath forevermore.
Jacob Niedergall, Grade 6
Freedom Area Middle School

Garbage
Broken toys, scraps, and more
maybe a rotten apple core
an old left shoe, a headless bear
a dented can, a rotten pear
chicken bones from someone's meal
a crumpled paper, an orange peel
a popped balloon, a tattered shirt
an old tin can filled with dirt
a half eaten hamburger covered in mold
a glass of hot chocolate that's really cold
a wilted flower covered in mustard
the soggy remains of someone's custard
a muddy glove, a rusty pin
all are in the garbage bin
Meghan Shea, Grade 5
Pocopson Elementary School

The Beach
The beach is welcoming,
The beach is great,
Football, baseball, or soccer,
Swim or surf,
Fly a kite,
Or just relax,
Warm sand under me,
Waves crash on top of me,
Picnicking people everywhere,
Seagulls overhead,
Seashells and crabs,
There is fun to be had,
On the beach.
Ryan Payerle, Grade 5
Rolling Hills Elementary School

Fly
Most days I wish I can fly
Up up up and touch the sky
Oh wouldn't it be fun to go and soar
Because every other day is a bore

I would fly like a bird in the sky
And leave all my worries behind
In the valley over the meadow
I would have feathers soft as a pillow

In and out, side to side
Up and down with all my pride
Quickly, slowly, all around
I just want my feet to leave the ground
Mary Clair, Grade 6
St Rosalia Academy

Thanksgiving
T aking as much food as you can
H aving fun playing football
A sking if you can stay longer
N ew football games being played
K illing turkeys
S tarting to get hungry
G etting a lot of food
I ndividual plates
V ery hungry
I nside watching football
N ever ending hunger
G reat food
Steven Urkuski, Grade 5
Robeson Elementary School

Lightning and Rain
flying in the sky
lightning and rain from above
in the dark cloud
Yana Kostyuk, Grade 4
Center Elementary School

John Deere Tractor
I am a John Deere tractor
I plow and disk the fields
I have a big diesel engine
And I am four wheeled.

When I am bailing
They're either round or square
Then you have to wrap them
And sometimes it will tear.
Timmy Warne, Grade 5
McMurray Elementary School

C-h-e-e-r-l-e-a-d-i-n-g
Yells and cheers is all you hear.
Yelling and spelling B-O-L-D.
Ughing and wowing when doing lifts,
Oops, when someone's hand slips.
Doing a cradle landing and ahhing
when four hands catch you.
Owing when pulling a muscle.
Wowing when doing a thrustle.
Ahhing when doing flips.
Laughing when being joyful.
Cheerleading is enjoyable.
Caroline Bandurska, Grade 6
MMI Preparatory School

The Cat
Snowy
Wild and playful
Purring, loving, sleeping
Sleeps on my bed every night
Cat
Marie Dillner, Grade 5
East Union Intermediate Center

Springtime
Springtime is fun
You play in the sun
Springtime is cool
You play in the pool
Springtime is warm
But be careful of the bee swarm!!!
Marissa Torbert, Grade 4
Central Elementary School

War
War
Crazy, scary
Exciting, frightening, crying
It is very dangerous
Battle
Devon Stone, Grade 5
Penn-Kidder Campus

The Reasons Why

The sky, the earth, the clouds up high,
The moonlit dinners all the time,
The sun, the snow, the ocean blue,
The reasons why I fell in love with you.
The singers' voices, the bands that played,
The times we've shared to have and to save.
The lasting sentence that we all heard,
The time you said the magic word.
Oh the reasons why, every time I try,
To sleep at night, to hold you tight,
Oh the reasons why, the reasons why.
2006, the time we kissed,
2005, the time we cried.
The reasons why, nobody knows the reasons why,
The reasons why.

Carrie Hill, Grade 4
Bushkill Elementary School

Stars in the Sky

My stars.
Stars in the sky make me want to cry.
Shine brightly, pretty, and unique.
After they shine, they sleep.
Sleep, sleep, then they wake up and shine.
My stars.

My stars.
I depend on,
let my dream shoot through the sky like a shooting star.
Bright, lightly, and all mine.
All mine, outside of my window and all mine.
Now show me the way, light my way.
My stars.

My stars.
Wait until tonight, it'll be quite a delight.
Small, big, and medium.
Whose stars, what stars, where are those stars.
Wait until tonight, is when you will see…
My stars.

Chelcie Rojas, Grade 6
Independence Charter School

What Is a Rainbow

R ed is like a big plump cherry
O range is like a feather from a parrot
Y ellow is like a shock of lightning
G reen is like the shell of a watermelon
B lue is like the warm water of the Caribbean
I ndigo is like the bottom of an ocean
V iolet is like the wild lilies that grow in a field
And well, a rainbow is considered all of these things

Meghan Mae Burgdolt, Grade 5
Claysville Elementary School

Going Somewhere, Going Somewhere

I'm going somewhere, going somewhere
where it's peaceful and sometimes quiet
where the birds sing and fly free
I'm going somewhere, going somewhere
where cars drive near
where no one can see
I'm going somewhere, going somewhere
where I can relax
where no one minds if I garden
I'm going somewhere, going somewhere
where tons of trees grow
where my friends and I tried to make a fence
I'm going somewhere, going somewhere
where we hide
I'm going somewhere, going somewhere
I'm going to the miniature jungle…want to come along.

Ayana Cattell, Grade 4
Easterly Parkway Elementary School

Summer Is

Summer is yellow
It sounds like birds chirping
It smells like sunscreen
It tastes like ice cream
It looks like a big swimming pool
Summer is a sun shining bright in the sky

Georgia Renner, Grade 6
Guth Elementary School

Spring

Spring is one of my favorite seasons
I look forward to it every year.
Although I wait long for spring,
Waiting has never been a fear.

The temperature is just right!
The flowers smell so wonderful and refreshing.
The bees are flying everywhere,
Even if one stings me, I don't care.

I like to be outside in spring,
Climbing in the trees.
It's fun to roll down hills,
I love playing in the breeze.

Spring is such a nice season,
With the birds chirping loudly.
Even if it rains a lot,
My favorite part is when it's hot.

Sitting in the treetops,
Looking straight ahead,
Thinking of all the things of spring
I have inside my head.

Elizabeth Depew, Grade 4
Brecknock Elementary School

Soft Snow

Snow falls gently
Snow is so white
Snow falls so softly
Snow is very cold
Snow falls peacefully
Snow is fun to play in
Snow falls just so nicely
Snow is all right

Cristian Magliocca, Grade 6
Freedom Area Middle School

TV

TV is so funny
You could watch Bugs Bunny,
I used to watch Animal Planet
Sometimes even Billy the Bandit.

Nnamdi Ihejirika, Grade 4
Sacred Heart School

Winter

Is winter here already?
Yes my friend it is.
It's so freezing cold.
Snow is starting to fall.

It is so white and pleasing.
I love winter.
Let's go sled riding.
It's late let's go get some hot cocoa.

Colton Costello, Grade 6
Freedom Area Middle School

Seashore

Swimming at the seashore
Suntan lotion and the salty sea
Searching for seashells as the sun sets

Alison Keil, Grade 5
Schnecksville School

I Am Myself

I am myself and no one else,
No matter what people say.
I am unique and different,
I love myself in every way.

I am nice and very fun,
I am very smart too.
Sometimes I'm like a newborn calf,
Who doesn't know what to do.

Whatever I am
I know this much is true.
I will never stop being myself.
And you should always be you.

Courtney Bogansky, Grade 6
MMI Preparatory School

The School Desk

I am a beaten up school desk,
Sitting there while kids write on me.
I am made to put books in.
Yet I only find trash,
I am a beaten up school desk.

Emily Slingluff, Grade 6
Freedom Area Middle School

Bunny

Bunny
Furry, cuddly
Eating, jumping, drinking
The bunny likes carrots.
Rabbit

Kimberly Ward, Grade 4
West Branch Area Elementary School

Forest

Birds live in nice nests,
The Squirrels live in tall tree trunks
The Deer eat berries

Chipmunks eat small nuts,
Eagles fly over tall trees
Frogs hop here and there.

Skunks spray a stink smell,
Bunnies live in small burrows
The Fox hunts at night.

Michael Taylor, Grade 4
Sacred Heart School

Summer

Here comes summer
with sun
with rain
Here comes summer
with fun
with games
Bye-Bye summer
I had a blast
I can't believe
you flew so fast!

Paige Sheeler, Grade 4
Easterly Parkway Elementary School

Wolf Dreams

There was a wolf by the mountain.
The red wolf was by the fountain.
The wolf saw a jump.
That wolf was a lump.
So the gray wolf left the mountain.

Patricia McFee, Grade 4
Penn-Kidder Campus

Clouds

Big white balls of fluff
billowing in the big sky
just don't rain on me.

Anna Zerkle, Grade 5
McMurray Elementary School

Music

Music
Guitars, drums
Playing it and strumming it
I like to play guitars and drums
ROCK ON!

Gregory Pantuso, Grade 4
South Park Elementary Center

Winter Geese

Hear them calling in the distance
See a V-shape in the air
No one knows why they do it
To one could only wonder where

Wonder what they're saying
Saying as they fly
See them overhead
As they pass, so quickly by

Winter comes and winter goes
Soon they've all flow south
But we've Robins to look forward to
With wiggling worms in their mouth

Meghan Walsh, Grade 5
Our Mother of Perpetual Help School

Alone

I am loneliness,
Loneliness is me.
We live together,
In perfect harmony.
I am alone,
With no one around.
Just the sky above,
and below the ground.
I don't complain,
Just stay on my own.
I don't really mind,
Staying alone.
But then I dream,
Of getting to play,
With somebody else,
On a beautiful day.
But I know,
This will never come true.
I'll stay alone,
That's all that I do.

Molly Coates, Grade 5
Pocopson Elementary School

Munchy Crunchy Popcorn Fair

Come to the popcorn fair if you have the munchies.
Popcorn's full of butter, salt and crunchies.
It's a puffy cloud of butter.
It makes my heart go flutter.
It makes my hands so greasy,
But it never makes me queasy.
When I make it, it makes a loud pop.
When I eat it, I can't stop.
I could eat one hundred liters.
While I'm in the movie theaters.

Morgan Hoover, Grade 4
Watsontown Elementary School

Friends Forever

We're getting older, though not wanting to admit it
Dreaming of future events
Boyfriends and dates
Though never forgetting the simple things

Things like little girls in make-up and too big shoes
Lying on sleeping bags
Life was so different
So simple, so care free

Still sharing movies on lazy days
Between school and boys
Laughing at silly jokes
Phone calls and letters when we're just minutes away
Just wanting to stay in touch

We're older now, though it's tough to say
We are all growing older every day
Through thick and thin
From big hats to big sunglasses
Friends are Forever

Lauren Mayer, Grade 6
Bridle Path Elementary School

Autumn Cherry Tree

The autumn cherry tree sparkles
in the sunlight like hot pink.
In the autumn,
the autumn cherry tree grows
shiny pink that shines from the top.
The sap runs down the trunk like rubies falling on a cloud.

James Dierkes, Grade 4
Souderton Charter School Collaborative

A Dead Boy

There is a boy who is dead.
When he was born he was dropped on his head.
It did him no good
In his short childhood.
And of course he was a redhead.

Robert Tramontina, Grade 4
South Park Elementary Center

Recess

Recess is fun,
especially in the sun.

Recess is time away from your studies,
so you can go outside and play with your buddies.

Proctors watching us part of the day,
giving us time away to play.

Many kids love to play four-square,
which forces them to learn how to share.

There's always someone who tends to fall down,
bumping their head, cracking their crown.

Krista Fiedler, Grade 6
Neil Armstrong Middle School

Summer Sun

As the rumbling moved away,
The sun was up and on its way.
In the distance, the sun peeks through,
Looking down at me and you,

Clouds cleared, the sun's light shone bright
Looking up it's such a delight.
The sun's glow spread throughout the sky,
Friendly like a butterfly.

Summer Knaub, Grade 5
Bermudian Springs Middle School

Dreams

Follow your dreams most tame or wild
Whether you're an elder, adult, or child
Follow your dreams for they do come true
If you believe, believe that they do
A big job, a little job, a college or high school
If you think it's interesting or down right cool
Dreams will happen if you follow your heart
Just believe, believe from the start

Dara Bernstein, Grade 4
Lower Gwynedd Elementary School

Basketball

Basketball is my favorite sport,
I love the way I dribble up and down the court.
Shoot and score, you got two more,
Cool call, get the ball.
Don't forget to pass it off.
Now Bethel's back in the game,
And when you shoot don't forget to aim.
Ten more seconds left to play,
Shoot one more and you've won the game!!!

McKenzie Michalski, Grade 6
Neil Armstrong Middle School

My Cat Onyx

I loved my cat.
Why did he go?
For I loved him so,
In my heart remains that cat.

He loved me like a sister.
We had so much fun.
He didn't like the sun.
He didn't survive last winter.

In my heart he will stay.
Black like night,
Loved by first sight.
In hearts of my family he will stay.
Alexis Broadwater, Grade 4
Panther Valley Elementary School

Bahamas

Bahamas are so cool,
that you would be a fool,
to never see the sight,
of Bahamas at night.

You would have no clue,
of the color of the blue,
that it might be a fright,
to never see the sight.

To see all the fish,
you could only wish,
to see the sight,
with such delight.

The sands so white,
and looks so bright,
even at night,
it might be a fright,
to never see the sight.
Logan Goodhart, Grade 6
Chambersburg Area Middle School

Missing Pop

Sad, unhappy,
Angry, crying, screaming.
Praying that he will come back.
Everybody talking about their pop.
Emily Mountjoy, Grade 4
Bushkill Elementary School

Friends

You can trust your friends
They can trust you and they help you
They do you a favor and you do one too
They will stay with you 'till the end.
Christie Lodge, Grade 4
Manoa Elementary School

Army Green

Army green tastes like ice cream on a hot day,
putting white cold snow in your mouth,
and eating a ripe green pear picked off a tree.

Army green smells like chlorine from a big pool,
hot chocolate on a VERY cold day,
and a piece of mint candy melting in your mouth.

Army green sounds like hail hitting the roof of your house,
a person who got a bee sting,
and thunder BOOMING outside your window.

Army green feels like a rough piece of snakeskin on the ground,
melting ice cream dripping on your shoe,
and shuffling your fingers in your hair over and over again.

Army green looks like the dull blue sky,
someone very gloomy on a rainy day,
and the stillness of a leaf floating in the air.
Ryan Eisenacher, Grade 4
Indian Lane Elementary School

The Ocean

The ocean has unending entertainment.
From fishing to building a sand castle fit for a king.
It's like a vast prairie that goes on forever.
As the waves crash, they sound like an echo in the distance.
Relax.
As the wind blows I can taste the saltwater upon my lips.
The ocean is as beautiful as a butterfly.
With striped colors of blue, green, and purple across it.
As each wave breaks they sparkle like the stars in the sky.
It is so calming, but can be dangerous and destructive.
The sea is mysterious to me.
The ocean breeze is like the sweet aroma coming from a flower.
The sea is a miraculous place to be.
For me there is only one word to describe the ocean.
Amazing.
Christopher Szekely, Grade 6
Our Lady of Mount Carmel School

The Chaos Beast

Cute and cuddly he appears.
When he is huge you should fear.
For he made dragons emerge as little bears.
This creature is made of water.
He can drown you when you're reaching for a quarter.
Or even worse while attempting to pick up your own daughter.
Chaos is so strong that he may cause you to freeze.
Or even worse he may put a spell on you that causes you to continuously sneeze.
When you see chaos coming your way, you should immediately run.
Do not bother stopping at the store to purchase a bun.
I am trying to tell you he is a fearsome beast,
WATCH OUT! His water tornadoes will make you a dragon's feast!
Tyreek Elam, Grade 5
Russell Conwell Middle School

I Made a Mistake

I went to the bathroom to brush my teeth,
I made a mistake…and brushed my feet.
I went to my room to get a pair of shorts,
I made a mistake…and got some warts.
I went to the kitchen to fix the sink,
I made a mistake…and I winked.
I went outside to have some fun,
I made a mistake…and I won.
I went bungy jumping to get some air,
I made a mistake…and ripped my hair.
I went sky diving with my friend,
I made a mistake…and brought a hen.
I went home to go to bed,
I made a mistake and…fell a sleep on The End.

Alec Hofberg, Grade 5
Newtown Elementary School

Christmas Eve Is on Its Way

We went to get our Christmas tree on this snowy afternoon,
As my family knows Santa will arrive very soon.
My brother and I decorated the tree all afternoon long,
While our parents taught us some new Christmas songs.
My dad hung the final decorations onto our home,
As I cut snowmen out of shiny white foam.
I then wrapped gifts with colorful ribbons and tags;
Some were with wrapping paper and others in bags.
Our entire family went outside to build angels out of snow;
It soon became cold because the wind began to blow.
We went inside and ate our evening meal;
And there were cards with envelopes to be sealed.
We watched some movies and drank hot tea,
And looked at the drawing my brother wanted us to see.
It was a picture he'd drawn all by himself.
It was done of Santa, Mrs. Claus, and three little elves.
My family brushed their teeth and combed their hair,
And went to bed because Santa soon would be there.

Spencer Noble, Grade 6
Connoquenessing Elementary School

To Be Sixteen

To be sixteen and on my own
Riding in my car with my hair wind blown.
Blasting my music for all the world to hear
I might wear makeup now, but I won't drink beer.
My curfew's been extended, I have more time to play
So driving with my friends is not a waste of my day.
I can talk on my cell phone and go where I want
I'll lead the boys chasing me on quite the hunt.
Because now I'm old enough to hold hands and date
But I'll still go out with my friends and never be late.
To be sixteen is the greatest thing ever
I won't get stuck without a ride, no not again, never.

Eileen Barker, Grade 6
Locust Grove Mennonite School

The Little Cartoon

One day I drew a cartoon on a page.
It came to life in this way:

It danced, it sang, it jumped and it yelled.
It scared me and I jumped too!

The cartoon was sad!
It needed a friend,
so I drew an old duck.
They quacked and played together.

I hung the picture on my wall and,
Every night I look at it and laugh!

Chelsea Lyn Dividock, Grade 5
Portage Area Elementary/Middle School

It's My Turn

Standing in the wings
thinking my thoughts through
my heart beating to the music in my mind
as I tap my foot in time with the tune.
The rehearsals were hard.
Where they worth it?
I close my eyes.
The song before me ends,
I take a breath,
when I open my eyes,
I hear my melody calling me…
it's my turn!

Cassidy Giordano, Grade 5
Annunciation B V M School

Ode to Backpacking

I am very bored as we have been in the car for 10 hours,
"Are we there yet?" I say.
We make a left onto a smooth road,
Black like coal,
After about a mile or so a wooden building comes in sight,
"Is that where we are going?" asked my brother.
"Yes, that is where we get our canoe," said my dad.
It was only the tree of us,
Finally we are renting our green canoe,
I see my dad take our canoe and supplies to a boat,
We all got on the boat called the water taxi,
A man who tied up the canoe and drove followed us on,
Finally we were off,
Wind was blowing like a tornado by the speed of the boat,
We pulled up into an alcove where there was land,
Excitingly, we all got off of the boat,
We unloaded our supplies before the boat left,
There was a path that was smooth, secluded, and sunny,
We put our packs on,
Paddles of the canoe in both hands,
We were off for my first ever backpacking trip.

Matt Junkin, Grade 6
Hershey Middle School

Adam

Adam
Nice, active
Bowling, loves baseball
Keeper of secrets, inventor
Smart
Christopher Mundy, Grade 4
Hereford Elementary School

Spring

The sun is shining
It tells the flowers to sing
Today is spring
Olga Vilovchik, Grade 5
Rhawnhurst School

A Wonderful Dog

R eign was rough but sweet.
E xcellent at going potty outside.
I ndependent and free.
G one to Heaven but.
N ever will she be forgotten.
Katie Fishman, Grade 6
H Austin Snyder Elementary School

Rain

When rain patters down,
against my exposed dry skin,
pouring down like ice.
Lauren Davoli, Grade 6
Allison Park Elementary School

What I Feel

When I look at the sun,
I think of it as a bright orange.

When I look at the clouds,
I think of them as crunched up tissues.

When I look at the sky,
I think of it as a bright blue ocean.

When I look at you,
My heart goes in motion.
Samantha Chumura, Grade 5
State Street Elementary School

Snow

Snow
White, cold,
Sparkling, shining, piling
Snow day is the best of all
Snowflake
Molly O'Brien, Grade 5
Villa Maria Academy Lower School

Ice Skating

Glide, spin
Flying, soaring, jumping
Graceful, hopping, sliding, falling
Floating, sailing, skimming
Turn, dance
Ice skating
Ann Shetler, Grade 4
Memorial Elementary School

New Life

Think of just hatching
You wouldn't know what to do
But then your mother and father come
To love and care about you
Alex Hatton, Grade 5
Robeson Elementary School

Comet

Comet
Soft, warm
Hopping, chewing, kissing
Kisses me a lot.
Rabbit
Samantha Heintzelman, Grade 4
Christ the King School

Books

Books are fun
Books are cool
Books help you study
To get good grades in school.

Some books are adventures
Some books are sad
Some books are meaningless
They can get you mad.

Some books are about dogs
Some books are about cats
Some books are about dinosaurs
Maybe dirty rats.

Most books have words
They make a good story
Even the Bible.
They bring God lots of glory.
Sean Dunleavy, Grade 6
St Ann Elementary School

My Family

I love my family
They're so nice, they make me scream.
They love me for me.
I love them for who they are.
Saeda Bretz, Grade 4
Fishing Creek Elementary School

If Animals Could Talk

If animals could talk
What would they say?
Would they tell you
To stay to play?
If you met a snake
While walking along,
Would it sound like
It was singing a song?
If your pet dog
Wanted to run away
He could just tell you
He was going to play.
If a monkey was sad
He could whine, just a tad.
If your cat was rather skittish
He could tell you in British
That the bird had flown out of his cage.
If animals could talk
What would they say?
And would you like
To keep it that way?
Lily Hunt, Grade 5
Central Elementary School

Why Should I?

Why should I share,
The brush for my hair?
Why should I look.
At the school handbook?
Why should I read,
About the apostles creed?
Why should I know,
How ants grow?
Why should I clean.
The room of the teen?
Why should I live in the state,
That I hate?
Why should I knit mittens,
For kittens?
Well I'm always outsmarted,
For I've already started.
And now I'm not able to stop!
Molly Ann Flannery, Grade 5
Hatfield Elementary School

Football

QB goes into shotgun.
Calls hut.
QB sees a guy open in the backfield.
A few seconds left,
Throws it.
The WR catches it for the touchdown.
Nicholas Talerico, Grade 6
Freedom Area Middle School

I Dreamed of Loving You

Every night I'm dreaming of you
Wishing I'd be with you
Staring at you every day
But I just can't say hey
We hung out as friends
Hoping eventually you would become my boyfriend
You saying that you love me
Why can't you see that we were meant to be
I've always dreamed of loving you
And I wish you do too

Athena Knight, Grade 6
Smith Middle School

Fall

Leaves are falling
Trees are shedding
Fall is coming
The wind is blowing
School is here
Get 100's every year
It's almost Halloween
Lots of candy in your bag
A scary costume seen
Happy Halloween!

Ryan Haninchick, Grade 6
St Ann Elementary School

I Am Me

I am a person all my own.
You can't change me my destiny is sewn.
I don't want to be just like you.
I am strong and I am true.
I will be free because I am strong.
You can't tell me what's right and what's wrong.
You can't tell me how to act.
It's my life and that's a fact.
I am a person who is free.
I am the best person I can be.

Stephanie Lesher, Grade 6
Assumption BVM School

September 11th

On September 11, 2001
People were not having any fun.
Two planes crashed into the Twin Towers
They were very stressful hours.
People sacrificed their lives for others
Including men, friends, and mothers.
That day the sky was very clear
Everyone shed at least a tear.
People throughout the USA
Couldn't believe what happened that day!
That horrible day in September
Is a day we will always remember

Nicole Krzywicki, Grade 6
St Boniface School

Flying Fish

Flying fish fly faster than
flipping felines in a barrel filled with fruit,
and a family of fire ants on top of
a Ferrari going 55 MPH
on the first of February.

Ryan Steere, Grade 6
Allison Park Elementary School

Math Homework

I don't know what I've been told,
Math homework is getting old.
I don't know what has been said,
All those numbers are getting to my head.
I don't know but I would bet,
Next week's homework is already set.
I don't know but I do hear,
We've had too much math homework this year.

Meghan Minton, Grade 6
Neil Armstrong Middle School

Red

Red is fire station and burning.
Red is the taste of fruit punch.
Fire and firecrackers smell Red.
Being mad makes me feel Red.
Red is the sound of alarm bells and fire.
Red is fire station, mobile home, and brick house.
Chasing bulls are Red.
Getting mad is also Red.
Red is hot.

Marko Elmer Brigich, Grade 6
Allison Park Elementary School

Guardian Angel

Nanny
I wish you were still here with me
I wish you were home at Ma's house
I wish you were home where you belong
You were always there for me
But now you're gone
And I don't know what to do without you.
I love you and miss you
Nanny.
Hopefully we will meet again in Heaven
Where I can see your face and hear your voice again.
Look over me while I am here on Earth
And help me to make the right choices.
Nanny
Be my Guardian Angel!
Nanny,
I love you and miss you
More than you can ever imagine.

Kylie Tobasco, Grade 6
Elizabeth Forward Middle School

An Owl at Night

In the woods one November night,
A hooting owl cause such a fright.
Flying through the flashing lightning,
Never saw a scene so frightening.

Then we sprinted quickly ahead,
We fell on some leaves like a bed.
Then we quickly sprang up in the night,
To see the owl soaring like a kite.

Josh Kleckner, Grade 5
Bermudian Springs Middle School

Spring

I love spring.
It's always fun.
It's my favorite thing.
I wish I had the sun.

Phillip Michael Hopkins, Grade 5
State Street Elementary School

Books

Books
Adventurous, fantasy
Interesting, boring, exciting
Different genres are fun
Reading

Meeghan Rossi, Grade 5
Penn-Kidder Campus

Easter Break

E aster bunny fat and round
A ppetizing Easter dinner
S urprising gifts
T reats for miles
E lectrifying with fun
R emember the holiday

Nolan Glisan, Grade 5
Wharton Elementary School

Spring

Spring is my favorite time of year.
Birds are singing in my ear.

Flowers are blooming all around.
All the animals make a sound.

The green grass begins to grow.
There will be no more snow.

The rabbits are running all about.
It's a season that makes you shout.

Soon there will be no more school.
And I can swim all day in my pool.

Adam Stoerrle, Grade 6
Moravian Academy Middle School

A Recipe for Evil

First, put in 1/2 cup of hatred
Next, add a gallon of name-calling
Afterwards, pour 20 lb. of bullying
Now, smother it in jealousy
Then, put in 75 oz. of a bad attitude
After that, mix until it turns black
Finally, bake at 1° for a minute
Now, eat!

Austin Harvey, Grade 4
Avonworth Elementary School

Snowflakes

Ballerinas
Twirling around
Dancing down on a winter's day
With pretty designs
On their dresses
Dancing in a winter's play
They cover the hard cold ground
And
When the warm sun comes out
They quietly dance away

Haley Kramer, Grade 4
Avon Grove Intermediate School

Seasons

Snow falls from the sky,
There is hundreds of snowflakes
It falls silently.

Flowers bloom in spring
With some petals on the top
They are beautiful.

The sun is real hot
Blazing all over my skin
I'd like to go swim.

The leaves fall from trees
They fall onto the rooftops
They fall on the ground.

Alyssa Sniechoski, Grade 4
Sacred Heart School

Soldier

S aving lives
O ld and young
L oving hearts
D oing their job
I ntelligent
E tiquette (social code, formalities)
R escuers

Colton Miller, Grade 6
Our Lady of Grace Elementary School

Snow

Slowly falling down
Melting on the ground.

Trudging through the cold wet snow
Leaving footprints as I go.

Accumulations overnight
It's making everything so bright.

Karina Alkhasyan, Grade 6
Moss Side Middle School

I Want a Pet!

Every day I ask my mom
May I please have a pet?
She always says I'll think about it,
But she always forgets.
The one day I asked her,
And she said YES!
She asked me what pet I wanted
I took a minute to think
Then I responded a little bit later
I said "I want an alligator."

Aimee Rosenberger, Grade 5
James Buchanan Elementary School

Beaver

Beaver resting
Hibernation is now here
Quietly sleeping

Maelan Towler, Grade 5
Pocopson Elementary School

Billy Bob, a Barracuda, and Jessica Simpson

Billy Bob
Bounced badly
To order
The bananas
In the
Big bouncy bog
On his
Blue bicycle.
But on
His way
Back he
Met a barracuda
Then he met
Jessica Simpson
And they lived
Happily
Ever
After.
The
End.

Andrew Ward, Grade 4
Conway Elementary School

Love Is…

Love is…
   A big hug from your mom and dad.

Love is…
   Getting to eat ice cream for no special occasion.

Love is…
   Playing with your little brother even when you don't want to.

Love is…
   Enjoying your summer vacation with friends.

Love is…
   Unconditional, like the love you get from a little puppy.

Love is…
   The willingness to make new friends and keep the old.

Love is…
   Playing fun games and laughing with your family.

Love is…
   God!

Rachel Hutchison, Grade 4
Beaver County Christian School

I Wish

I wish elephants could fly
Chocolate could grow off trees
I wish school lasted two days a week
It could rain chocolate chip cookies
I wish I could be a kid forever
There were brooms instead of cars
I wish there was a tenth planet
There was no subject like English
I wish that you could spell a word anyway you want
There were only ten grades of school
I wish you could be anything you want when you grow up
That boys were kinder
I wish the Earth was a shape of a triangle
That Earth had three moons
I wish that I was the richest kid in the world
That all the planets looked like Earth

Jacquelyn Creitz, Grade 5
Schnecksville School

Mom

There is a handicapped spot
In the Wal-mart parking lot
Filled by someone who doesn't need it
Who doesn't have the right permit
My handicapped mom says, "Thanks a lot!"

Nick Poole, Grade 5
Claysville Elementary School

Spring

Oh, how happy, the sun is bright,
Kids are playing and enjoying the sight.

Everyone is happy and playing together,
Because they just love this wonderful weather.

We are so happy the sun is out,
So all the boys and girls will shout.

It's Spring! It's Spring! There is no doubt!
Let's go outside! Come on and come out!

The bees are buzzing and the crows are crowing
You must cut your grass, it is rapidly growing!

Ah, yes, it is spring, we are filled with pride!
Now come on already, let's go outside

Jeremy Cravener, Grade 6
Sacred Heart Elementary School

Red

If there was no other color but red,
You would wake every morning in your big red bed.
Red shirts, red pants, and more red hats,
And what would walk by your feet would be your fluffy red cat.
Your house, the grass, and even the sky,
Would be red with no doubt why.
Your school, your teacher, your principal, too,
Would all be red and so would you!
Everyone's else's skin and hair,
Would also be red along with their chair.
It's not good to live in just one color,
I'm so glad that we have others.

Rachel Hammersley, Grade 5
Robeson Elementary School

Tears of Love

These are my tears of love,
And they shall not be wiped away.
They shall remain to heal my broken heart,
And give me the hope I once had before.

Evan Brandes, Grade 6
Linglestown Middle School

About Dolphins

The dolphins like to swim around,
Splishing and splashing making sounds.
In and out of the waves they swim,
Racing each other like in a gym.

The dolphins dive deep into the dark,
And swim around with the great white shark.
Up and down the ocean they go,
Where they go next, you will never know.

Brittany Lauver, Grade 5
Bermudian Springs Middle School

Sewing Machine
I am a sewing machine
I can fix your clothes
Beware of my needle
I can nip your nose.

I sew really fast
You can use different fabric
So many things you can make
It is like magic.
Amanda Sherwin, Grade 5
McMurray Elementary School

Warm
As the sun
seriously scorches my skin,
I think about
the cold winter
and it's snow
that looks like a bundle of white flowers.
Don't forget about
sledding down the biggest hill
in the neighborhood
and making snow angels that really fly
and look over us
but for now
I'm stuck in summer
what a bummer.
Caitlin Dininni-Parker, Grade 6
Mount Nittany Middle School

Evolution
I'm going through evolution,
A microscopic revolution,
My ears appear atop my head,
My mind is filling up with dread,
My light blue hair into a brown,
My normal smile into a frown,
No longer human you can see,
Fur growing uncontrollably,
A tail sprouts out from my behind,
Transforming warps my fragile mind,
My five feet tall into a three,
It's made a monkey out of me.
Joshua Martin Corrales, Grade 6
Independence Charter School

Disrespect/Respect
Disrespect
Mean, hurtful
Bullying, hatred, shivering
Dislike, horror, disgust, insufferable
Admired, honored, regarded
Behavior, attitude
Respect
Nick Masci, Grade 6
St Sebastian Elementary School

The Cafeteria at Lunch Time
The cafeteria at lunch time is like a stampede of horses.
Each person trying to get to the best courses.
People trying to get to the snacks,
Everyone loves that!
When the lunch ladies put out the cake,
There's none left for me to take.
Sitting down's the hardest part;
It's like trying to find a parking place at the food mart.
You chat and chat with your friends like you haven't seen them in ages!
People are as loud as monkeys trying to get out of their cages.
When it's finally time to go the teacher comes and we are stunned.
Because we know that the second half of the day has just begun.
Chelsea Rush, Grade 6
Guth Elementary School

Red
Red is like the fierce bright color in a warrior's eye.
Crispy, autumn leaves,
In December, a Christmas decoration swaying on a tree,
The color of a fire truck racing to the rescue,
Or an elegant ladybug protecting a farmers plants.
Dylan Nagle's Hair,
Beautiful,
Fierce,
Loving,
Tasty, juicy apples,
Bright,
The sight of Gettysburg after many hardships of blood stained battle.
Hyper little foxes running about,
Sweet smelling strawberries on a breezy summer morning.
Blood, love, fierce, bright, that, is the color red.
Tyler Edmond, Grade 6
Southern Lehigh Middle School

Light Blue
Light blue tastes like soft, fluffy cotton candy at Fantasy Island,
sweet crusty blueberry pie straight from the oven,
and an icy cold slushy melting in my mouth.

Light blue smells like grandma's blueberry pie waiting for me in the oven,
a blueberry dry erase marker,
and a sweet blueberry Jolly Rancher.

Light blue sounds like the crashing of waves on the beach,
rippling water on a quiet pond,
and the crunch of snow under my boots.

Light blue feels like a slushy melting in a cold cup,
a warm quilt covering my bed,
and sadness in a shy world.

Light blue looks like a beautiful budding flower,
a fragile snowflake falling from the heavens,
and the bountiful sky filled with clouds.
Emma Miller, Grade 4
Indian Lane Elementary School

Relaxed Is…

Relaxed is the color light blue
It sounds like waves crashing at the beach
It smells like fresh air
It tastes like cold ice cream
It looks like the white clouds floating in the sky
It feels like a big comfy bed

Bored is the color white
It sounds like opera
It smells like broccoli
It tastes like old rotten spinach
It looks like paint drying
It feels like the feeling you get when you're alone

Joe Sulat, Grade 6
Guth Elementary School

Teddy Bear

Teddy is the color of sweet pink
Teddy feels like a smooth furry friend
Teddy tastes like cuddly sweetness
Teddy smells like chocolate
Teddy looks like flowers blooming
Teddy sounds like clouds floating in the sky.

Sajida Uddin, Grade 5
Rhawnhurst School

The Beach

Eagerly waiting to arrive at the peaceful shore
Turquoise waves rippling and crashing,
While tan children avoid a splashing
Pink and white shells scattered
Grainy white sand that covers the land
Breathe in the salty air
Smelling, relaxing, energizing

Kaitlin Brody, Grade 6
Bridle Path Elementary School

One Must Remember

One must remember
    that His love is not based on only actions
    for He loves the sinners, though their ways are hurtful.
One must remember
    that He does not love only the faithful,
    for His love reaches not only those who seek Him,
    but also those who are trapped in darkness.
One must remember
    that His love is not based upon appearance.
    He loves those with black and white, yellow and red skins,
    He loves them all.
One must remember
    that His love comes from remarkable passion for the poor,
    the rich, the young and the old.
He came to Earth on Christmas,
    so that His love may shine in every heart.

Leah Daigle, Grade 6
Verna Montessori School

Kitten in the Tornado

When they saw the tornado was gone,
They realized it had torn up their lawn.
When they found their belongings on the ground,
They took one last look around.
And there in a pile, in the dirt,
Was a small kitten who wasn't even hurt.
They brushed her off, gave her to Cindy,
From that point on, we decided to call her "Windy."

Ashley Thompson, Grade 6
Freedom Area Middle School

Childhood Home

As you sit there all alone,
Thinking of you childhood home,
Town so sweet, nothing wrong,
'Till Hitler came and made you not-so-strong,
You wish you could have done something,
As you sit there all alone,
Thinking of your childhood home.

MacKayla Menges, Grade 6
Chambersburg Area Middle School

Christmas

C olorful lights on houses like a rainbow
H ouses decorated with gleaming lights
R oaring wind blowing through the air
I always get presents
S inging songs of the season
T hrowing snowballs at my friends
M others making cakes and cookies
A round the neighborhood houses decorated nicely
S now-covered fields and trees.

Nick Fischer, Grade 4
Bushkill Elementary School

My Dream

My dream is to fly away into the sun
Where everything comes true
My dream is to finally have peace
So that not only my dream can come true,
But so that other people's dreams can come true
My dream is to write my heart out
And have one perfect poem
And have that one perfect poem
Be free for the whole world to read
And maybe that one perfect poem
Can make a difference
For the whole world
My dream is set,
And if I really work hard at it
Then maybe just maybe
My dream will come true

Tori Hartmann, Grade 6
Sol Feinstone Elementary School

Sound

Did you ever wonder about all the different sounds?
Like the drip, drip, dripping of the sink.
Or the tap, tap, tapping of someone's shoes.
The clink, clink, clinking of metal.
The zap, zap, zapping of the electric line.
Even the snore, snore, snoring of your brother sleeping at night.
Sounds are everywhere, even when you want to find a place with no sounds at all,
Sound will still find you.

Sorcha Smith, Grade 5
Robeson Elementary School

Moonlit Path

Outside on the moonlit path, a pure noise rang out, a silky laugh,
Swiftly glide out and move about, under the velvet sky,
A single red rose laid gently on the ground,
dew drops sprinkled it, so earthbound to the ground,
pick it up and move so swift, for into the night music shall lift
Carefully keep to the music and dance to the beat, after a moment the music
stopped, break up the dream, before you are seen,
Turn around, walk back to your home, but before you go in, listen for a moan,
Silence, so quiet bring out a candle and light it. No one laughed, hence turn back,
and as you closed the door, you heard a single silky laugh, tingle the air.

Leah Houser, Grade 6
Our Mother of Perpetual Help School

Chicago

Chicago is a big city, where there are many things to explore.
There are museums, zoos, and aquariums, and many different stores.
Come visit the Field Museum, where you can see bones of dinosaurs.
Jane, the T-Rex is there as well, and believe me this place gets high scores.
The Shedd Aquarium holds many adventures, there are sharks and a beluga whale.
Don't forget the Caribbean Reef Dive, I'll be sure to add this to my trail.
The Sears Tower is interesting too, 110 stories, 1,450 feet tall.
Skydeck with a beautiful view, the Sears Tower truly has it all.
The Brookfield Zoo is really neat, it's open every day.
A painting pig, a baby dolphin, I can't wait to be on my way.
As you can clearly see, Chicago is cool.
From zoos to museums, it's like learning in school.

Mackenzie Schuler, Grade 5
Immaculate Conception School

Lost My Clothes

It seems everyone knows, 'bout how I lost my clothes.
Me and Julia share a gym locker. And Min and I always mock her.
In gym we played Mat Ball. Then me Elizabeth slam and fall.
Bloody lip and a scarred arm.
To the nurse, was our curse.
I came back with an ice pack. But Julia had my jeans in her gym sack.
I searched for Julia all around school. Many people stared at me thinking that I was so uncool.
Then I saw Kevin in the hall. I called to him, "Where's Julia? At the mall?"
Kevin yelled into the classroom door,
"Hey Julia, Haley wants her clothes back!" And Julia scurried out the door with her gym sack.
As I changed in the bathroom, I thought, "My reputation is doomed!"
We went back into the classroom, Julia and me, and we whispered to each other ever so softly,
"What a crazy day in P. E.!"

Haley Lawler, Grade 6
Arcola Intermediate School

Tutor

I am not good in math you see,
So the school got a tutor just for me,

My tutor is sitting here I think teaching me how to borrow,
While I am daydreaming and thinking about tomorrow,

I really am not enjoying this,
I want to go have some Swiss-Miss,

I am wondering when this will end,
So I can go to the mall and buy the latest trends,

She finally says we're done,
So I went out and had lots of fun!

Jennifer Nastold, Grade 6
Neil Armstrong Middle School

Touchdown

I saw a touchdown pass thrown
I saw a touchdown pass thrown

The football soaring through the air
Landing gracefully in the receiver's hands

The extra point is good
The extra point is good

Ryan Fitzgerald, Grade 6
St Hilary of Poitiers School

Shopping

S tores filled with people
H urrying to find cool clothes
O pening and shutting dressing room doors
P eeking to see if anyone is in there then
P opping their bodies in the air and
I don't even want to get started on those slow cashiers
N ever giving the right amount of money all I can think now is
G ood I'm out of that store

Dana Salanik, Grade 6
St Maria Goretti School

The Flower Cycle

A simple seed is worth so much.
Feeling a daisy is smooth on the touch.
All the colors glisten so bright,
In the rain but not out of sight,
When the gardener carefully waters the flower,
The water floats out of the can like a gently cool shower.
The gardener knows what's best for the plant.
After all, she is my favorite aunt.
Choosing the right vase is usually rough.
But gardening in general is never rather tough.

Mira Taylor, Grade 6
Moravian Academy Middle School

Gold

What is the color gold?
Gold's touch is like being out on the beach
on a scorching hot day.
It tastes almost like pitzelle cookies
because they're so rich and flaky in their flavor.
Gold sounds like money floating in the air,
like snowflakes on a cold, dusky, winter day.
The color gold is an appreciative thing.
Gold is being in heaven.
Its smell is milk chocolate
screaming my name to come and taste it.
Gold is gracious, grazing animals in wide open fields.
That is the color gold.

Madeline Pope, Grade 6
Peebles Elementary School

Super Bowl Yellow

Yellow tastes like…
Pain for Seattle
Victory for Pittsburgh
Fire bursting off the sun
Yellow smells like…
Victory in the hands of Big Ben
The Vince Lombardi trophy in Bus's hand.
A banana pie smashed in Matt Hasselback's face
Yellow sounds like…
The yellow terrible towels flying
Pain because of fire
A wet sponge
Yellow looks like…
The yellow hair on the Steelers fans
The Steelers' seats squeaking at Heinz Field
Bananas
Yellow feels like…
Ben Roethlisberger
Jerome Bettis
Joey Porter

Tyler Butz, Grade 4
Indian Lane Elementary School

Light

As I walk through an alley
I see light out of nowhere
Shining like a thousand suns
I look towards the high heavens
and see Alpha and Omega looking
down on me chanting something in
a language I cannot understand
I feel safe as the light warms me
and I look above me once more
I say a mighty prayer
and continue on in the darkness feeling unreal
Watching the gray sky stretch
forever across the world

Anna Wadhwani, Grade 4
Lincoln Elementary School

Dogs

Dogs they eat like hogs,
'Cause they are dogs,
They chew on stuff,
'Cause they are ruff,
Even though they are cute and cuddly,
They might not even be your buddy,
Even though dogs are not always good,
Those dogs gotta have food!

Jordan Witmer, Grade 6
Strodes Mills Middle School

Happiness

Loving
seems blue like the ocean.
Happiness
is like all people living
in harmony forever.
Loving and caring for each other.
Happiness
is priceless like love.

Nathan Orr, Grade 4
South Park Elementary Center

The Footprint

While walking I found,
Something patted in the ground.
Could it be? What I see?
My own or someone else's
I take off my shoes
And go to the lake
And think of what I will make…
I wade in the water and get my feet wet
Now I wonder what will be next.
So now I'm through.
I will run to my shoes
When I reach the tree where I left them
I look to see the view behind me
Then I see it was ME that did it.
I run with my shoes
To tell my mother the news.
She said that was my own tracks.
She said that was my own…
FOOTPRINT

Cailee Gordinier, Grade 4
Lionville Elementary School

Birthdays

Birthdays
Turning older
Having more grown-up things
It's happening so fast it's weird
Awesome!

Alexis Young, Grade 4
Penn-Kidder Campus

The City

People
    running
        speeding
            just to get across town.

RUSH HOUR!
    The smell of gas and fast food.

People
    screaming
        yelling at each other.

THE NIGHT!
    Friends and family
        go to the movie
This town is never sleeping!

Traffic
    speeding.
I hear sirens
    when I drive by people playing sports

and people screaming GO GO GO!

Olivia Danylko, Grade 6
St George Catholic School

What a Day

On the merry-go-round
in a late summer day
eating old corn chips
what a day

I have a huge test tomorrow
to my dismay
I hate school
what a day

Jesse Lauman, Grade 6
Grasse Elementary School

Katrina

a vulnerable city
a big wave that came
the people in need
of prayers
heartfelt good wishes
our sympathy
the caring needs to be shown
they cry out for help
but few people hear
the help is still needed
though the waters receded long ago
Katrina
the big wave that came

Allison E. Quilty, Grade 6
Southern Lehigh Middle School

White

White is a new start,
An empty mind.
White is what I see in new places.
In white I see the light,
Of new beginnings.
Friends with bright faces,
Sad or happy eyes.
White is what I love so much.
White is what I see in any kind of end.
White is the paradise above,
The land I love.

Tyler Corbley, Grade 5
Rolling Hills Elementary School

Softball

I like softball, yes I do
I like softball, how about you?
I play softball in the fall
But I can't play softball in the mall.
I pitch, I bat, I wear a hat
The coach will yell if we chat.
If I make my coach really proud
He will cheer super loud.
Softball is so fun to play
Hitting a homer can make my day
Have you ever played? You really should
I'd be on your team if I could.
See you later, got to go
My softball team needs me, you know!

Theresa Gibson, Grade 5
Vandergrift Elementary School

Redwood Forest

Redwood Forest
The godly trees grow
They are majestic and rare
It's incredible

Garrett Rizzo, Grade 5
Penn-Kidder Campus

Love

Love sparkles like pink roses
After a light spring rain.
Love cradles white clouds
In its arms.
Love tastes like a soft
Hershey's chocolate bar.
Love sounds like a flute
Playing outside on a brisk
Spring morning.
Love smells like a fruity perfume
Sprinkled on a bride.

Melissa Smith, Grade 4
South Park Elementary Center

L.O.V.E.
Love is like a rose petal floating down a stream
Love is that feeling with someone you see
Love is the bond with a person you meet
Love is that feeling when you speak
Love is an emotion
An emotion that lives so deep
Love is a heart beat
The shadow from the deep
The angel you see
And
The love you keep.

Gervon D. Williams, Grade 6
Chambersburg Area Middle School

Last Second Shot
My team is in the championship
With only five seconds to go
We are only down two points
But who will take the shot nobody really knows
My coach calls timeout
And we get in a huddle
"You" he did shout
"Take the last shot"
We walk on the floor hoping to win
Get in our spots
And he throws the ball in
With only seconds to go
I start to dribble
Take a glance at the clock
One more step and I shoot the ball
Up and up it began to fall
With a "swish" it went in that's what I saw
My team had won the game
And everybody started yelling my name
I was in a dream I really had thought
And this is the story of the last second shot

Nicholas Stonesifer, Grade 6
Chambersburg Area Middle School

School Mornings
Waking up at 6 o'clock,
It's a trouble now and then to put on a sock.

Getting up early there's no wonder why,
For an hour or two I'm as blind as a fly.

Always I think that this is a mock,
No wonder I'm afraid to look at the clock.

I wish we had school at nine,
Then that extra sleep would be all mine.

The afternoons are okay,
Because it's not the morning it's the day.

Michael Konopelski, Grade 6
Neil Armstrong Middle School

Lily Pad
A lily pad is like a frog's throne
Or playground
Or resting place.
A lily pad is a home.

Home to creatures above.
A roof for the ones underneath.
A place we know frogs love.
It's hard to believe it's only a simple little leaf!

Each one a different shade,
Dark, light but still all green.
On a day full of gloom and gray
That can really brighten the scene.

Until you really think about it
A lily pad doesn't seem like much.
But its soft and fuzzy surface makes it comforting
And the split down the side really adds a nice touch.

Erin Barth, Grade 6
Our Lady of Mount Carmel School

That Is Love
Love is powerful and strong,
With pure love, nothing can go wrong,
When you get that warm and fuzzy feeling inside,
That is love.
Being there when I sweat, fail, or cry.
I want someone who is always there for me,
Someone who loves me for who I am and want to be.
Always encouraging me to reach for a star,
Telling me to be the best that you are.
Flipping blond hair and a twinkling blue eye,
And a smile that makes me just want to fly.
He's my knight in shining armor, as some may say,
Lifting me off my feet in that very special way,
Or making me laugh 'till the end of the day.
That is love.
If this is all that he would do,
Then I'll always return it true.
That is love!

Kelsey King, Grade 6
Southern Lehigh Middle School

Beta
Eddie
Mixed colors
Moves through castles in water
"Fighting fish"
Big for a beta fish
Goes through phases like when he doesn't eat
Then, the next time, he eats

Lucas Sanders, Grade 4
Urban League of Pittsburgh Charter School

Goodnight Snow Lake

Shivering in the frigid cold breeze
Feeling the snow on my hat and coat
Spying the lake, about to freeze
Watching ducks still swimming afloat

Sitting in a tree, up so high
The rosy cardinal perches like a king
The majestic eagle ready to fly
Young eagles nested into a ring

Sunbeams falling atop the trees
The lake is shining with bright light
The wind is blowing with great ease
The earth is sighing its goodnight

Tori Andrewson, Grade 5
Edgeworth Elementary School

Best Friends

B rilliant
E ntertaining
S porty
T alkative

F ashion freaks
R eally cool
I nseparable
E njoyable
N ights at the movies
D aring
S hop-a-holics

Taylor Patterson, Grade 6
Our Lady of Grace Elementary School

Nature

The sky is bright blue
When the sun shines through

The birds whirl and fly
while the moths flitter by

The sun warms my head
And releases my dread
The bees hum and drone
As I sit on a stone

Glittering fish in the lake
Make me forget my mistake

Here in this place
My heart is at rest

All sin and sorrow are now released
And everything is at peace

Philip DiGregorio, Grade 6
Sacred Heart Elementary School

The Mountains

The mountains hovering high above
The fluffy white snow shaped like a dove
The snow hung as the blizzard blew by
And we said a sorrowful goodbye

The huge vast mountains passing us over
On our travels we brought Dover
Leaving the mountains made me feel ill
As I watched I leaned on the windowsill

The weightless powder swirling around
The road guiding us over a mound
The pavement seemed to never end
As we glided around the bend

Kelsey Kirby, Grade 5
Edgeworth Elementary School

Baseball

B atting, concentration, focus and desire
A team sport
S portsmanship
E verybody's included
B oys playing together
A chievement
L ove of the game
L eagues for young and old

Jon Tomaro, Grade 5
Rolling Hills Elementary School

Spring

Flowers flow into sight
Longer days, peaceful nights.
Gentle winds blow their way
Spring has arrived here today

Clouds are portraits
Of what is yet to come
They are friends of the birds and trees
And stars and the sun

The green grass is like a velvet carpet
Lying beneath our feet
We hear people laughing
And the birds chirp "tweet."

Emma Modrak, Grade 6
St Valentine Elementary School

Stars

Stars
shining, glittering
sparkling, beautiful light
jewels high above us

Emma Doerfler, Grade 4
St Sebastian Elementary School

Baseball

Baseball
Screaming fans
Hitting, running, fielding
"Nice hit," "Great pitch!"
Baseball

Softball
Underhand pitch
Popup, grounder, chest pass
Fast pitch, slow pitch
Softball

Hitting
Heavy bat
Ready to run
Strike 3, ball 1
Hitting

Pitching
Speed pitch
Target catcher's glove
Strike, don't walk batter
Pitching

Lauren Angelina, Grade 4
Indian Lane Elementary School

Me and My Mom

Thirza
always loving
having fun and helping
always say she loves Thirzita
Mommy

Thirzita Buell, Grade 4
Penn-Kidder Campus

The Sun

The sun
goes down over the mountains
but then the bright moon comes
like a lantern
shining.

Darian Fetters, Grade 6
Bedford Middle School

Spring

Blooming flowers everywhere,
Spring clothes, not a tear
Sun so bright,
What a sight!
Soon we can go to the pool,
How nice, that will rule!
Pretty flowers, beautiful sight,
Barely can see them in the night

Ashley Gochenaur, Grade 4
Hans Herr Elementary School

9/11

On this day there was devastation all across the nation.
When the Twin Towers came down everyone had a frown.
On this one day of the year we're all filled with fear.
On this day no child wants to play.
This day is 9/11.

Adam Hoffman, Grade 5
Concord Elementary School

Waiting Is…

Waiting for school to end,
Waiting for a chatterbox to get the chickenpox,
Waiting for your mother to come home from work,
Waiting for traffic to move,
Lingering for your food to get done,
Waiting for the show to start,
Remaining in line for your favorite ride,
Waiting for fun to come.

Calen Smith, Grade 4
Beaver County Christian School

My Sister

M y big sister
E yes watching over me
L oves animals
I nfluence on me
S he is very loving and caring
S he always tries her best to make me happy
A lways there when I need her

Tiffany Pronti, Grade 6
H Austin Snyder Elementary School

The Shore

The shore is a place where the water is as
The sky on a sunny day.
The sand is hot and very pale.
The rocks are piled high to form jewels.
The shore is a wonderful place to relax and get a sun tan.
The hot blazing sun beams right at you.
What a summery bright sight having a blast of delight.
Beautiful seas, Caribbean rocks, with flowers blooming brightly.
Going to the shore seeing the blue waters
What a spectacular sight.

Simona Levchenko, Grade 5
Rolling Hills Elementary School

Dirty Dishes

This is my wish
I wish I did not have to wash one single dish,
Grubby and green and greasy and all.
That is the worst thing I ever saw.
I better get out the soap,
Maybe it won't be so gross, I hope.

Tiffany Bowes, Grade 6
Luther Memorial Learning Center

Just Us Girls

Just us girls are under pressure,
Looking at the world, we feel we just don't measure.

Just us girls always follow the latest fad,
Because you get made fun of if you wear flowers or plaid.

Just us girls can laugh all night long,
Simply because a friend sang a song.

Just us girls are on the road to success.
You'll know us in the future because, we did our best!

Emily Heathcote, Grade 5
McQuistion Elementary School

No More

Wars on Earth throughout the ages,
Buy a World War II book — many pages.

Now we're in another war,
Loved ones lost, seen no more.

What a devastation to this very land we live in,
And yet we strive, to stay alive, and have a new beginin'.

We have stayed together as a nation,
To stop most kinds of segregation.

A greater war we fight, now this is true,
Is against ourselves and what we do.

Rachael Wigton, Grade 4
McQuistion Elementary School

Video Games

I like to play video games when school is done for the day.
Even though my mom will say,
"Please pick up your toys and put them away,
Before you start to play for the day."
When my day is done and night has come,
I go to my room to have more fun.
Playing games that make my mind run,
And trying to win to be number one.
If I don't succeed to be the top seed,
I will try once again and not pretend,
To play my games when a new day begins.

Kaleb Guy, Grade 4
Philipsburg Elementary School

Alaska

A fter the snowstorm we had an avalanche
L asting thirty seconds
A fter it ended we all started to dig
S hovels, ice picks, and jackhammers were used
K indly donated by hardware stores
A nd we finally found some survivors

Tyler Williams, Grade 6
H Austin Snyder Elementary School

Fear

Fear is black.
It sounds like screams.
It smells like a dead animal.
It tastes like saltwater.
It looks like a shadow in the night.
Fear feels like the cold hand of nothing.

Josh Drezner, Grade 5
West Branch School

Butterfly

Butterfly
Quiet, gentle
Fluttering, skimming, gliding
Winged creation
Graceful song

Cameron Foxhall, Grade 5
Wexford Elementary School

Football

Football is an aggressive sport to play,
It takes a lot of hard work.
You have to practice every day,
It gets tiring, along the way.
But, you have to keep up,
In order to play.

Austin Brent, Grade 5
East Union Intermediate Center

The World's Love!

Love is magic
Cherish it all the way
You're lucky if you have it
Let it sway through your way

People need it most
Hopefully it will come upon you
So don't let it coast
This should be something on cue

Just like a boomerang
May all the love you give
Come right back to you!

Kristen Helene Pentz, Grade 6
Curwensville Area Elementary School

Dragon

Roaring beast with sharp green claws
An orange flame surrounds its paws.
He searches for someone to fight
Though, it's usually a knight.
And as you hear a loud scream,
It disappears without a team.

Anastasiya Yezhova, Grade 4
Easterly Parkway Elementary School

The Hare and Turtle

The turtle and hare had a race
And ran at a very good pace
Although the hare was tricky
So his feet got sticky
So the turtle won by reaching home base

Christine Reid, Grade 4
Moscow Elementary Center

April Afternoon

I stood in the park
  Rough with grass and countryside
One single boy stood out
  From the curve on the slide

There were no other people
  That could have seen the boy I saw —
I stood and watched the boy
  As he ran into the wall!!

Tiphereth Brennan-Wells, Grade 6
Haverford Middle School

Football

Football
running, catching
punting, kicking, throwing
screaming, surprise, winning, jumping
Touchdown!

Khaaliq Lynch, Grade 4
Penn-Kidder Campus

The Moon

The moon
gleams with the stars
astonished, I look up
into the beautiful night sky
such peace.

Cary Shoemaker, Grade 6
Bedford Middle School

New Jersey Shop Rite

I got an apple.
Not a banana.
Not an orange.
Not a lemon.
Not a lime.

I heard Cesar Rosas, Conrad Lozano,
Louie Perez, David Hidalgo,
Steve Berlin and Victor Bisseti.
The security guard said "no dancing!"
I met those guys.

I was day dreaming.

Dominic Passante-Contaldi, Grade 6
Independence Charter School

Sadness

Sadness is like a gray fog,
enveloping you,
closing you off like a velvet curtain.
Sometimes bringing tears,
flowing down your face,
like a winding river.
Sometimes bringing fear,
that your heart will shatter,
into a thousand tiny pieces,
like a broken mirror.
Sometimes bringing comfort,
that calms the soul,
easing the pain,
bringing peace.

Nicholas Poe, Grade 6
Neil Armstrong Middle School

Springtime!

Spring's almost here —
  what a cheer.
The shining sun,
  the warmth of the air.
Twirling leaves are flowing by
  in the sky.
My hair blows
  freely all around,
    now it looks
    like a twister
that just tore up the under ground.
Spring's almost here!
  I tell you now.

Taylor McGlone, Grade 5
St Ambrose School

I Hear a Thump

I hear a thump
While I sit on my stump
While I read a book
And then I look then I see a bear
That bear was covered in hair

Abbey Jordan, Grade 4
West Bradford Elementary School

The Picnic Ant

I'm just a happy ant,
  sitting on the ground.
These people give me scrumptious food,
  with plastic all around.
  It all looks so yummy,
  and I really want that!
But I don't think I'll get that far,
  because they have a…SPLAT!

Andrew Yoho, Grade 6
Freedom Area Middle School

Jan

There once was a very fat man.
He couldn't even fit in a van.
So he went to the gym,
And got very slim.
And that is how he met Jan.

Ericka Thomas, Grade 4
Avonworth Elementary School

Index